THE AFRICAN-AMERICAN
MOSAIC

D1235290

LIBRARY
OF CONGRESS
RESOURCE
GUIDE

AFRO-AMERICAN MONUMENT.

THE AFRICAN-AMERICAN MOSAIC

A LIBRARY OF CONGRESS

RESOURCE GUIDE

FOR THE STUDY OF

BLACK HISTORY AND CULTURE

edited by

DEBRA NEWMAN HAM

with contributions by

Beverly Brannan, prints and photographs

Dena J. Epstein, music

Ronald Grim, maps and atlases

Debra Newman Ham, manuscripts

Ardie S. Myers, general collections

David L. Parker, motion pictures

Rosemary Fry Plakas, rare books

Brian Taves, motion pictures

LIBRARY OF CONGRESS   Washington   1993

⊗ *The paper in this publication meets the requirements for permanence established by the American National Standard* ANSI/NISO Z39.48–1992, *Permanence of Paper for Publications and Documents in Libraries and Archives.*

Library of Congress Cataloging-in-Publication Data
Library of Congress.

    The African-American mosaic: a Library of Congress resource guide for the study of Black history and culture / edited by Debra Newman Ham; with contributions by Beverly Brannan . . . [et al.].

       p.   cm.

    Includes bibliographical references and index.

    ISBN 0-8444-0800-x (alk. paper)

   —— —— *Copy 3 Z663.A74   1993*

    1. Afro-Americans—History—Sources—Bibliography—Catalogs. 2. Library of Congress—Catalogs. I. Ham, Debra Newman, 1948– II. Brannan, Beverly W., 1946– .   III. Title.

Z1361.N39L47   1993

[E184.6]

016.973'0496073—dc20

                                      93-21605

                                         CIP

Designed by Adrianne Onderdonk Dudden

For sale by the Superintendent of Documents U.S. Government Printing Office Washington, D.C. 20402

FRONTISPIECE: *"Afro-American Monument," a chromolithograph showing the history of African-Americans from 1619 to 1897, published for the Tennessee Centennial Exposition in Nashville in 1897. (PP PGA LC-USZ62–2239; LC-USZC4–2329 [color])*

CONTENTS

PART ONE: AFRICAN-AMERICANS IN THE ANTEBELLUM PERIOD

CHAPTER ONE

CHAPTER TWO

CHAPTER THREE

PART TWO: FOREVER FREE—EMANCIPATION AND BEYOND

CHAPTER FOUR

CHAPTER FIVE

FOREWORD

The Library of Congress, the oldest national cultural institution in the United States, is also the world's largest repository of recorded knowledge. The holdings are universal and diverse, reflecting the vision of the Library's founder, Thomas Jefferson, whose collections formed the Library's original core. The formats which store this knowledge are also varied—books, periodicals, manuscripts, prints, photographs, motion pictures, sound recordings, films, microform, microfiche, CD-ROM. The list goes on.

As the United States has grown more conscious of its diverse heritage, the extensive collections on African-American history and culture held by the national library have drawn more interest. Yet the size, variety, and value of these great collections are not sufficiently known. Moreover, serious researchers have had to become extremely sophisticated sleuths in order to uncover the *full* range of relevant materials. This has been unavoidable because the collections are housed in three different buildings on Capitol Hill and at distant secondary storage facilities, and because books and other materials are served to readers from many reading rooms within the institution.

Publication of *The African-American Mosaic* should ease the researcher's task. Here in a single volume, the Library of Congress has presented a broad survey of its holdings in the history and culture of black Americans in the United States. Many items are unique. Even readers who are unable to make the trip to Washington, D.C., will profit from the publication's information on general reference works. Eventually the Library hopes to make much of this unique material available electronically to readers everywhere.

This volume is the second in a series of topical guides. The first, published in 1992, was *Keys to the Encounter: A Library of Congress Resource Guide for the Study of the Age of Discovery*, by Louis De Vorsey, Jr. Subsequent volumes will deal with native American studies and World War II.

We will be pleased if this publication eases the work of researchers everywhere and induces readers to come in person to explore the collections. As Americans become more aware of the many strands that constitute the national culture, we hope this volume will also make a modest contribution to greater knowledge and understanding among our citizens.

James H. Billington
The Librarian of Congress

ARREST IN BOSTON.

THE ESCAPE ON SHIPBOARD.

DEPARTURE FROM BOSTON.

THE SALE.

THE ADDRESS.

AUCTION

THE PRISON.

Anthony Burns

DRAWN BY BARRY FROM A DAGUERREOTYPE BY WHIPPLE & BLACK.   JOHN ANDREW SC.

ENTERED ACCORDING TO ACT OF CONGRESS, IN THE YEAR 1855, BY ANTHONY BURNS
IN THE CLERK'S OFFICE OF THE DISTRICT COURT OF MASSACHUSETTS.

R. M. EDWARDS, PRINTER,
189 CONGRESS STREET, BOSTON.

PREFACE

In weaving together the work of eight contributors to this guide, I have tried to highlight for researchers a variety of the sources relating to African-American history and culture that the Library of Congress holds in its general and special collections. Because the resources relating to black Americans are vast, it is impossible to list every pertinent item. This guide does not pretend to serve as an item-level index or even a collection-level survey of Library holdings. The authors hope, however, that these pages will alert users to the richness of our collections and encourage increased use of little-known materials.

For over a century the Library of Congress has systematically collected black history resources, but even before this systematic effort began, resources relating to African-Americans were amassed as part of the Library's commitment to the larger study of American history. Originally established for the United States Congress in 1800, the Library—located in the U.S. Capitol—was burned by the British during the War of 1812. After the war the Congress purchased former president Thomas Jefferson's personal library, which included books with information relating to African-Americans, particularly the slave trade, domestic slavery, and abolition.

As Library holdings grew, additional titles relating to African-American history and culture were added. When the copyright law passed in 1870, however, requiring two copies of each work to be submitted with the copyright application, the number of materials relating to African-Americans in the Library increased dramatically. Books, plays, newspapers and other periodicals, sheet music, prints, photographs nostalgic of the Old South, caricatures of freed slaves, population maps, and countless items in "Negro dialect" flooded the Library, along with serious works by and about blacks.

By 1897 when a separate Library of Congress building was occupied, African-American librarian Daniel Alexander Payne Murray, who worked at the Library for over fifty years, had already initiated an acquisition policy to bring to the Library published materials by and about blacks. As technological progress led to new inventions, sound recordings and films, also protected by copyright laws, consequently became a part of the Library's holdings. Many of these had a bearing on black history and culture. Manuscript collections that included information about everything from slaves and slaveholders to free blacks and African-American professionals and politicians also found their way into the Library's holdings.

This guide provides titles of bibliographies, other guides, finding aids, and individual items relating to black history and culture in the Library, many of which yield far more information than we could include here. The result is a rich mosaic of African-American life that depicts scorn and admiration, defeat and triumph, tears and laughter.

Debra Newman Ham
Specialist in
Afro-American History and Culture
Manuscript Division

"Anthony Burns," a wood engraving with letterpress (Boston: R.M. Edwards, 1855), shows the fugitive slave whose arrest touched off protests in Boston in 1854. (PP Reilly 1855–7. LC-USZ62–90750)

◆ NOTE TO RESEARCHERS

Please call or write to Library staff:

> Library of Congress
> Washington, D.C. 20540
>   202 707-5522

before coming to the Library:

- ◆ to learn about the hours in various reading rooms,

- ◆ to find out whether appointments are necessary,

- ◆ to determine whether the use or reproduction of any of the materials described herein is restricted,

- ◆ to ascertain whether books or microfilm are available through interlibrary loan,

- ◆ and to get information about duplication policies and costs.

This guide, which is arranged chronologically, discusses Library of Congress collections that relate to African-American history and culture. PART 1 of the guide includes materials about the antebellum period. PART 2 begins with the Civil War, moves into the Reconstruction era—which includes materials dating to about 1880—and ends with what we call the Booker T. Washington era, which spans the years from 1880 to about 1915. PART 3 discusses twentieth-century materials in the Library's collections.

Related materials found in various divisions of the Library are described together within the appropriate period. Materials about the American Colonization Society, for example, can be found in the Library's general collections, the Manuscript Division (MSS), the Prints and Photographs Division (PP), the Rare Book and Special Collections Division (Rare Bk), and the Geography and Map Division (GM). All of these resources are discussed in chapter 2.

To help identify printed materials in the general and special collections, the authors have provided call numbers and publication information for all titles mentioned. Descriptions of manuscripts include name and date span for each of the collections. Materials from the Prints and Photographs Division are identified by lot number, reproduction number (the prefix LC-USZ indicates that a black-and-white negative exists and LC-USZ C2 or C4 identifies a color transparency), and collection title. Motion pictures are identified by title and date, sound recordings by recording company and issue number, and microform by microform number.

Below is a key to help the user identify the citations in this guide. It uses several brief references for materials relating to Duke Ellington that are described in several places in the guide to illustrate the various citations. (For a complete list of pages referring to Ellington materials, see the index.)

The great jazz composer Duke Ellington entitled his autobiography, *Music Is My Mistress* (Garden City, N.Y.: Doubleday, 1973; ML410.E14A3). **1**

Files relating to Ellington's selection as the 1959 recipient of the coveted Spingarn medal are among the papers of the National Association for the Advancement of Colored People (MSS, records 1909–82). **2**

One particularly interesting series of photographs, taken by Gordon Parks, documents the Ellington Orchestra playing at the Hurricane Club in Manhattan. A full-length image shows Ellington seated at the piano with two band members in the background (PP lot 819, repro. no. LC-USW3-23953). **3**

---

1   Publication information and a Library of Congress call number appear after each book mentioned. For periodicals, call numbers only are supplied. Newspapers have no call numbers because the Library arranges and retrieves them alphabetically by title.

2   Citations for collections in the Manuscript Division include information about the type of material and the date span of the documents.

3   Prints and Photographs Division materials are often divided into related groupings called *lots*. Materials are cataloged in lots to preserve a unity of creator, subject, source, or format. Each grouping is assigned a shelf location in the form of a lot number, which is simply the next available number for lots. The division assigns a reproduction number when an item is reproduced for the first time and the photographic negative becomes part of the collections from which further reproductions can be made.

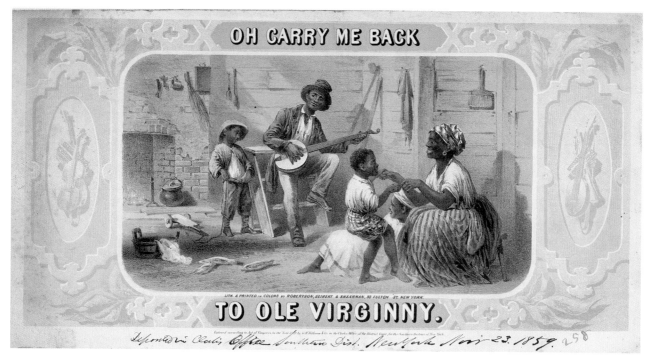

"Oh Carry Me Back to Ole Virginny," a tobacco label deposited for copyright in New York in November 1859. (Lithograph, PP lot 10618–61. LC-USZC4–2356)

ABBREVIATIONS

AP		American Periodical Series
GM		Geography and Map Division
LHG Ref		Local History and Genealogy Reference Collection
LL		Law Library
	LL RBR	LL Rare Book Room
M/B/RS		Motion Picture, Broadcasting, and Recorded Sound Division
MicRR		Microform Reading Room
MRR		Main Reading Room
	MRR Ref	Main Reading Room Reference Collection
MSS		Manuscript Division
	MSS Ref	Manuscript Division Reference Collection
n.d.		no date
n.p.		no place
n.p.		no publisher
PP		Prints and Photographs Division
	ADE	Architecture, Design, and Engineering Filing Series
	FP	Fine Print Filing Series
	HABS	Historic American Buildings Survey
	PGA	Popular and Applied Graphic Art Filing Series
	PH	Photograph Filing Series
	POS	Poster Filing Series
	PP Ref	PP Reference Collection
	SSF	Specific Subject File
	SSI	Specific Subject Index
	Stereo	Stereograph Filing Series
Rare Bk		Rare Book and Special Collections Division
	Am Imp Coll	American Imprints Collection
	Anthony Coll	Susan B. Anthony Collection
	CSA Coll	Confederate States of America Collection

Juv Spl Coll	Juvenile Supplement Collection
Mur Coll	Daniel Murray Collection
Mur Pam Coll	Daniel Murray Pamphlet Collection
Stn Coll	Alfred Whital Stern Collection
Ton Coll	Joseph M. Toner Collection
Reilly	Bernard Reilly, *American Political Prints, 1766–1876: A Catalog of the Collections in the Library of Congress* (Boston: G. K. Hall, 1991; E183.3.R45 1991)
RR	reproduction restricted

"Effects of the Fugitive-Slave-Law," signed Th. Kaufmann, New York, 1850. The lithograph condemns the Fugitive Slave Act passed by Congress in September of that year. (PP Reilly, 1850-5. LC-USZ62–1286)

ACKNOWLEDGMENTS

Those of us who have worked on this guide would like to thank our supervisors for allowing us to pursue this project, which took longer than any of us anticipated—three years instead of one—but which has proved to be worthwhile in many ways. We are grateful to the Publishing Office for deciding to encourage a team of Library employees to conceptualize and execute this work. Evelyn Sinclair, our Publishing Office liaison and textual editor, was always gracious and encouraging. Her professional expertise and calm demeanor helped us over difficult spots in the guide and assisted us in its successful completion. Her editorial artistry transformed many of our mundane sentences.

Several other Library staff members have carefully read drafts of this manuscript in its entirety and made insightful suggestions and comments. We would particularly like to thank Wayne Shirley, specialist in the Music Division, who regularly offered words of encouragement, wrote interlinear comments, made suggestions and corrections, and prepared a memorandum with helpful information relating to each chapter. John J. McDonough, nineteenth century specialist in the Manuscript Division, read and commented on most of the chapters in this volume, and made useful recommendations. Leonard Hodges, a retired member of the Order Division, read the manuscript and assisted us with mechanics for references to resources in various Library reading rooms.

Members of the Manuscript Division staff read individual chapters and offered aid. Of particular note is Oliver Orr, retired Civil War specialist, who tactfully suggested means by which the editor could skirt historical controversies in the Civil War chapter. Brian McGuire, a Manuscript Division archivist, provided background information for some of the motion picture descriptions. Manuscript Division clerk-typist Nelson Holston facilitated circulation of numerous drafts to the guide team. Marita Harper of the Order Division, David Turner of the Congressional Research Service, and Allene Hayes, Office of the Deputy Librarian of Congress, presented valuable support in the initial stages of the preparation of the guide. Thanks go also to Larry Boyer, team leader of the History and Political Science Team, Betty Culpepper, team leader of the Social Sciences Team, and the reference librarians in the Humanities and Social Sciences Division who checked dozens of book citations for accuracy: Mary Catherine Ammen, Elizabeth Jenkins-Joffe, David Kelly, Lynn Pedigo, Kathy Woodrell, and Sheridan Harvey. Robin Bullard and Carlin René Sayles in the Geography and Map Division provided valuable assistance.

Additions and corrections were submitted by Samuel Brylawski of the Recorded Sound Reference Center; Joseph Hickerson, Judith Gray, and Gerald Parsons of the American Folklife Center; and Gary Greenfield, Natalie Gawdiak, Keith Ann Stiverson, Susan Watkins, and T. Daniel Burney of the Law Library. Madeline Matz of the Motion Picture, Broadcasting, and Recorded Sound Division offered assistance with the description of motion pictures, as did Eric Kulberg, David Sawyer, and Melvin Stephens. Walter Zvonchenko of the Performing Arts Library Section provided bibliographic assistance, as did Gail Austin of Collections Services.

We thank the following Prints and Photographs Division staff members for reading various drafts of the guide: Chief Stephen E. Ostrow, Assistant Chief Elisabeth Parker, reading room head Mary Ison, Processing Section head Helena Zinkham, and, especially, Curatorial Section head Bernard Reilly. Other staff who commented on the text, supplied information, rehoused collections, or suggested illustrations are: Jennifer Brathovde, Cristina Carbone, Karen Chittenden, Verna Curtis, Sam Daniel, Jennifer Frank, Janice Grenci, George Hobart, Marilyn Ibach, Tabatha Irving, Carol Johnson, Harry Katz, Maja Keech, Megan Keister, Jeanne Korda, Jacqueline Manapsal, Gregory Marcangelo, Tracy Meehleib, Philip Michel, Elena Millie, Anne Mitchell, Mary Mundy, Barbara Orbach Natanson, C. Ford Peatross, Pamela Posz, Carol Pulin, Sarah Rouse, Marcy Silver, Diane Tepfer, and Jane Van Nimmen. Special thanks go to Shira Nichaman, academic intern from The George Washington University in the spring of 1990, who prepared the initial inventory of the Prints and Photographs Division's African-American holdings and produced an itemized list of blacks in the Civil War collection. John Vlach, a professor of American Studies at The George Washington University, shared the findings of his survey of the Historic Americans Buildings Survey collection and read early drafts of the antebellum chapters. Russ Karel, an independent researcher, provided helpful information about images of African-Americans between the world wars.

CONTRIBUTORS

BEVERLY BRANNAN, curator of photography in the Prints and Photographs Division since 1974, has two master's degrees, one in library science from the University of Maryland and another in American Studies from The George Washington University. She is coeditor of *A Kentucky Album: Farm Security Photographs, 1935–1943* (Lexington: University Press of Kentucky, 1986; F456.K35 1986) and *Documenting America, 1935–1943* (Berkeley: University of California Press in association with the Library of Congress, 1988; E806.D616 1988) and has written several articles on the Library's photography collections.

DENA J. EPSTEIN, now retired, received her library degrees from the University of Illinois. Formerly a music librarian at the Joseph Regenstein Library of the University of Chicago, she served as president of the Music Library Association from 1977 to 1979. Among her many works is *Sinful Tunes and Spirituals: Black Folk Music to the Civil War* (Urbana: University of Illinois Press, 1977; ML 3556.E8), winner of the Chicago Folklore Prize and the Francis Butler Simkins Award from the Southern Historical Association. Epstein is the only contributor to this volume who is not currently a member of the Library staff.

RONALD GRIM, who has worked at the Library of Congress since 1982, is currently the head of the Reference and Bibliography Section of the Geography and Map Division. Previously, he worked for ten years in the Cartographic and Architectural Branch of the National Archives and Records Administration, where he was also in charge of reference activities. He holds a doctorate in historical geography from the University of Maryland, where his research focused on settlement patterns in colonial Virginia. He is the author of *Historical Geography of the United States: A Guide to Information Sources* (Detroit: Gale Research Co., 1982; Z1247.G74 1982).

DEBRA NEWMAN HAM, specialist in Afro-American history and culture in the Manuscript Division, earned a doctorate in African history from Howard University. She is the author of a number of articles and finding aids and received the C. F. W. Coker Prize from the Society of American Archivists for her publication *Black History: A Guide to Civilian Records in the National Archives* (Washington: National Archives, 1984; Z1361.N39N576 1984). Before coming to the Library in 1986, Ham was African-American history specialist at the National Archives and Records Administration.

ARDIE S. MYERS, who holds a master's degree in library science from Columbia University and one in American studies with a concentration in African-American studies from The George Washington University, is a reference specialist and recommending officer in African-American studies for the Humanities and Social Sciences Division. Myers has written on the Harlem Renaissance and is the author of bibliographies about Martin Luther King, Jr., and the March on Washington, both of which were published in the *Library of Congress Information Bulletin* (December 23, 1985, and August 29, 1988). She also prepared the reference aid "Afro-Americana in the Microfilm Reading Room" (General Reading Rooms Division, December 1983).

DAVID L. PARKER, assistant head of the Curatorial Section of the Motion Picture, Broadcasting, and Recorded Sound Division, did doctoral work in film at Ohio State University. In addition to doing work as a filmmaker, Parker is coauthor of many articles, including several in *Close-Up: The Hollywood Director* (Metuchen, N.J.: Scarecrow Press, 1976; PN1998.A2C55), edited by Jon Tuska. He is the coauthor of *Guide to Dance in Film* (Detroit, Mich.: Gale Research Co., 1978; GV1779.P37) and is writing a biography of director Lewis Milestone, whose forty films include *All Quiet on the Western Front* (1930) and *Of Mice and Men* (1939).

ROSEMARY FRY PLAKAS, American history specialist in the Rare Book and Special Collections Division, holds a master's degree in American studies from the University of Wyoming and has done doctoral work at The George Washington University. In addition to serving as an editor of *Letters of Delegates to Congress, 1774–1789* (Washington: Library of Congress, 1976; JK1033.L47) and compiling bibliographies related to the American Revolutionary era, Plakas has written guides and lectures relating to early Americana and to Columbian and Hispanic sources and has produced an exhibit about the Library's Daniel A. P. Murray collection of Afro-Americana.

BRIAN TAVES, of the Motion Picture, Broadcasting, and Recorded Sound Division, earned his doctorate in cinema studies from the University of Southern California. He is the author of numerous articles and books, such as *Robert Florey, the French Expressionist* (Metuchen, N.J.: Scarecrow Press, 1987; PN1998A3F5548), *The Romance of Adventure: The Genre of Historical Adventure Movies* (Jackson: University Press of Mississippi, 1993) and *The Jules Verne Encyclopedia* (Metuchen, N.J.: Scarecrow Press, forthcoming), which includes a history of the Library's Verne collection.

PART ONE

AFRICAN-AMERICANS IN THE ANTEBELLUM PERIOD

"The Parting," collector's card no. 4 from "Stephens' Album Varieties: The Slave in 1863," copyright 1864. (PP lot 5174. LC-USZC4–2525; LC-USZ62–41838)

During the years of its existence, slavery became so intertwined in the fabric of American life that virtually every facet of society was touched by it. Library of Congress holdings reflect the pervasiveness of the American slave culture as it affected the nation's economic, social, and political life. The Library's book, manuscript, print and photograph, microform, newspaper, law, music, and map collections chronicle African-American life in the antebellum period. The materials cover topics such as the African and domestic slave trade, the plantation economy, slave life, slavery and popular culture, abolition and antislavery efforts, the rise of sectionalism, and the status of free blacks before the Civil War.

CHAPTER ONE

SLAVERY — THE PECULIAR INSTITUTION

Peculiar institution, an expression for slavery that came into popular use during the early nineteenth century, referred to the distinctive nature of chattel slavery in the American South. Although slavery had previously existed in many places and forms throughout the world, Library of Congress holdings demonstrate that the peculiar institution that arose in tandem with the Southern plantation economy was unique in many ways. Involuntary immigrants from Africa and their heirs were rarely as industrious as their owners wanted them to be, yet their labor was coveted and used for over two hundred years. In addition to enjoying the proceeds from the crops that slaves produced, many people, both North and South, profited greatly from the African slave trade and from the sale of manufactured products to plantations.

Survey plat dated 1796 of Notley Young's plantations on the Potomac River shows landholdings of one of the original proprietors of the site that became the city of Washington. Slave quarters are drawn in black. By surveyor Nicholas King. (GM G3851.G46 1796.K58 Vault)

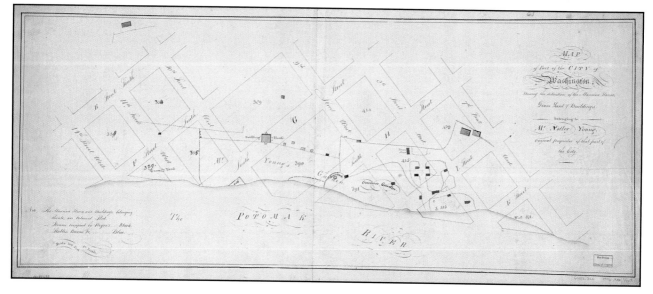

THE AFRICAN SLAVE TRADE

As of January 1, 1808, the United States Congress outlawed the African slave trade, but domestic trading was lawful and illegal commerce in Africans continued until the Civil War. The Library of Congress computerized catalog lists over seven hundred titles relating to the slave trade, including an array of demographic, economic, and biographical studies.

Some bibliographies which serve as guides to the numerous publications on the African slave trade are located in the Library's Main Reading Room collection. Among them are Peter C. Hogg's *The African Slave Trade and Its Suppression: A Classified and Annotated Bibliography of Books, Pamphlets, and Periodical Articles* (London: Frank Cass, 1973; Z7164.S6H63 1973) and two by Joseph Calder Miller, *Slavery, a Comparative Teaching Bibliography* (Honolulu: Crossroads Press, 1977; Z7164.S6 M54) and *Slavery: A Worldwide Bibliography, 1900–1982* (White Plains, N.Y.: Kraus International, 1985; Z7164.S6.M543 1985), which is unannotated but comprehensive. The Miller bibliographies include the slave trade as only one of many subjects relating to the peculiar institution.

Materials in the book collection relating to the slave trade range from a collection of first-person accounts edited by Philip Curtin, *Africa Remembered: Narratives by West Africans from the Era of the Slave Trade* (Madison: University of Wisconsin Press, 1967; DT471.C8), to ship logs, slave auction account books, and other items providing documentary evidence of the slavery experience such as those in the multivolume work *Documents Illustrative of the History of the Slave Trade to America*, edited by Elizabeth Donnan (Washington: Carnegie Institution of America, 1930–35; 4 vols. E441.D68). This compilation includes documents from a wide range of sources and includes some directly relating to the African slave trade, such as records from

"The Africans of the Slave Bark 'Wildfire,'" a wood engraving made from a daguerreotype, which shows slaves taken into Key West on April 30, 1860. Harper's Weekly, June 2, 1860. *(PP. LC-USZ62–19607)*

the Royal African Company, the Spanish Archives, and private records of African voyagers and traders. Many documents also relate to the domestic slave trade.

Records relating to the slave trade are also found in *Extracts from the Records of the African Companies* (Washington: Association for the Study of Negro Life and History, ca. 1930; HT1322.F5), collected by Ruth Anna Fisher, one of the first African-American professional employees of the Manuscript Division of the Library of Congress. Fisher worked primarily in Great Britain, gathering information about United States history in British archives for the Library's Foreign Copying Program. The African companies referred to in Fisher's title are the British trading companies that dealt in slaves. Among selections from the records are entries from the 1703 "Memorandum Book Kept at the West African Cape Coast Castle," where slaves were held before the Atlantic passage, and abstracts of letters received by the Royal African Company from agents on the African coast. The documents reflect the political climate in West Africa and the complex negotiations between African and European slave dealers. Fisher, who compiled *Extracts* from records at the British Treasury and Colonial Offices, first published the material in a 1928 article in the *Journal of Negro History* (vol. 13, 1928, pp. 286–394; E185.J86).

Another guide to materials on the slave trade, *The African Slave Trade from the Fifteenth to the Nineteenth Century: Reports and Papers of the Meeting of Experts*, published by the United Nations Educational, Scientific, and Cultural Organization (Paris: UNESCO, 1979; HT985.A33), summarizes twentieth-century research trends up to the late 1970s and reports the findings that were presented at a meeting held at Port-au-Prince, Haiti, in 1978. Papers cover the "Slave Trade in the Indian Ocean," "The Slave Atlantic Economies 1451–1870," and "The Slave Trade

in the Caribbean and Latin America." One paper estimates that between fifteen and thirty million slaves were taken from Africa. Another, "Negro Resistance to Slavery and the Atlantic Slave Trade from Africa to Black America," by Oruno D. Lara, describes the violence of the trade, stating that "the whole history of the slave trade is a sequence of revolts" (p. 103). The participating scholars agreed upon guidelines for estimates of statistics relating to the slave trade.

William E. B. DuBois's Harvard doctoral dissertation, *The Suppression of the African Slave-Trade to the United States of America, 1638–1870* (New York: Longmans, Green, and Co., 1896; E441.D81) is one of the earliest scholarly treatments of the trade. In a study published a half century later, *The Atlantic Slave Trade: A Census* (Madison: University of Wisconsin Press, 1969; HT975.C8), Africanist Philip Curtin argues that only about ten million Africans were taken from the African continent during the four centuries of the Atlantic Ocean trade. His study includes a detailed chapter on statistics entitled "The Slave Trade and the Numbers Game: A Review of the Literature," in which he discusses the range of estimates about the number of Africans brought to the West, which go as high as forty million. *The Atlantic Slave Trade: Effects on Economies, Societies, and Peoples in Africa, the Americas, and Europe* (Durham: Duke University Press, 1992; HT855.A85 1992), edited by Joseph E. Inikori and Stanley L. Engerman is a collection of papers originating from the conference "The Atlantic Slave Trade: Who Gained and Who Lost," held October 1988 at the University of Rochester. Papers deal with the social costs of forced migration, Atlantic slavery, and the rise of the western world, including "The Numbers, Origins, and Destinations of Slaves in the Eighteenth Century Angolan Slave Trade," by Joseph C. Miller; "The Slave Trade: The Formal Demography of a Global System," by Patrick

Manning; Johannes Postma's "The Dispersal of African Slaves in the West by Dutch Slave Traders, 1630–1803"; and Seymour Drescher's "The Ending of the Slave Trade and the Evolution of European Scientific Racism."

One of the earliest personal accounts of the African slave trade and slavery, housed in the Library's Rare Book and Special Collections Division, is an autobiography entitled *The Interesting Narrative of the Life of Olaudah Equiano, or Gus-* *tavus Vassa, the African* (Norwich: The Author, 1794; HT869.E6A3 1794 Rare Bk). This personal narrative, which was quite popular when it was published in 1789, recounts the author's childhood in Africa and his life on board British merchantmen from 1758 to 1788—first as a slave and later for hire. It includes descriptions of his travels to England, Turkey, the West Indies, and the Atlantic seacoast. An engraved portrait of Equiano is the frontispiece of the volume. A

The Interesting Narrative of the Life of Olaudah Equiano, or Gustavus Vassa, the African *(Norwich: The Author, 1794; HT869.E6A3 1794 Rare Bk). (LC-USZ62–54026)*

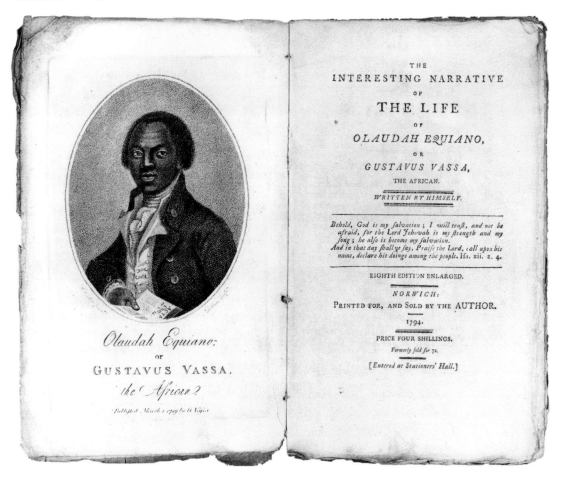

Russian translation of Vassa's biography is in the Rare Book and Special Collections Division's Gennadii Vasil'evich Yudin Collection (n.p., n.d; HT869.E6A38 1794 Rare Bk).

The Rare Book and Special Collections Division broadside holdings include a depiction of the placement of nearly five hundred slaves in the stowage of the British slave ship *Brookes* (Portfolio 282:43 oversize, Rare Bk), Royal African Company broadsides relating to the slave trade (Portfolio 326:1–30, Rare Bk), and original advertisements for slave sales (Portfolio 1:33, 186:27, Rare Bk). Another broadside, entitled "The Negro Woman's Appeal to Her White Sisters" (Portfolio 65:8, Rare Bk), portrays a kneeling black woman clutching a Bible with broken chains nearby. The appeal, a poem, includes these lines:

> Ye wives and ye mothers, your influence
>   extend—
> Ye sisters, ye daughters, the helpless defend—
> These strong ties are severed for one crime
>   alone,
> Possessing a colour less fair than your own.
> Ah! why must the tints of complexion be made
> A plea for the wrongs which poor Afric
>   invade?
>
> . . . .
>
> "Do justly," I hear is the sacred command—
> Then why steal the poor negro [sic] from his
>   native land?

Although there is no comprehensive subject access to the broadsides, a four-volume *Catalog of Broadsides in the Rare Book Division* (Boston: G.K. Hall, 1972; Z1231.B7A5 MRR Ref, Rare Bk Ref) provides author, title, chronological, and geographic access to nearly thirty thousand items. Materials in the Geography and Map Division of the Library provide information relating to the geographical components of the trade between North American, West African, and West Indian ports. This "triangular trade" is portrayed graphically in the National Geo-

graphic Society's *Historical Atlas of the United States* (Washington: National Geographic Society, 1988; G1201.S1N3 1988), which also shows the African origins and New World destinations of black captives; the distribution of the slave population, primarily in the southeastern United States in 1790, 1810, and 1830; and the internal migrations of the slave population within the United States.

The legal aspects of the slave trade are discussed in a variety of Library holdings. Paul Finkelman has compiled *The African Slave Trade and American Courts: The Pamphlet Literature* (New York: Garland Publishing Co., 1988; 2 vols. KF4545.S5A5 1988 ser. 5) to bring together a collection of pamphlets relating to the trade and the American legal system. Finkelman's *Slave Trade and Migration: Domestic and Foreign* (New York: Garland Publishing Co., 1989; E441.S58 1989) consists of articles about the movement of the black population from Africa to North America and the migration patterns of African-Americans within in the territorial United States. The deliberations of American colonial governments relating to African-Americans including matters relating to the slave trade and slavery can be located in the microfilm edition of *Published Colonial Records of the American Colonies* (New Haven: Research Publications, 1970; 85/10009 ⟨LL⟩), which is located in the Law Library.

Early official documents relating to the American slave trade can also be found by using the printed *Journals of the Continental Congress, 1774–1789* (Washington: U.S. Government Printing Office, 1904–37; 34 vols. J10.A5), edited by Worthington Chauncey Ford and Gaillard Hunt. A useful index to these volumes is Peter M. Bergman's *The Negro in the Continental Congress* (New York: Bergman, 1969; E185.B47); his index to the records of the early Republic published in *The Negro in the Congressional Record, 1789–1801* (New York: Bergman, 1969; E185.B467) is also helpful. (The latter volume does not index the serial officially entitled the *Congressional Record* (KF35), which did not exist before 1873.)

In each of the individual indexes to the volumes of *Letters of Delegates to Congress, 1774–1789* (Washington: Library of Congress, 1976–; JK1033.L47), edited by Paul H. Smith with other historians in the Library's Manuscript Division, are numerous references to slavery and the slave trade. Additional primary documents by the founding fathers relating to African-Americans are published in *The Records of the Federal Convention of 1787* (New Haven: Yale University Press, 1966; 4 vols. KF4510.U547 1966), edited by Max Farrand. James H. Hutson, chief of the Library's Manuscript Division, prepared a *Supplement to Max Farrand's The Records of the Federal Convention of 1787* (New Haven: Yale University Press, 1987; KF4510.U547. 1966 Suppl.) with a cumulative index to the Farrand volumes. The supplement contains the subject categories such as slavery, the slave trade, fugitive slaves, slave representation, and Negroes. The Hutson volume includes a petition to the convention from the Pennsylvania Society for the Abolition of Slavery about "dooming of our African Brethren to perpetual Slavery and Misery," which states in part:

By all the Attributes, therefore, of the Deity which are offended by this inhuman traffic . . . , the Society implores the present Convention to make the Suppression of the African trade in the United States, a part of their deliberations. (pp. 44–45, June 2, 1787)

The Law Library holds both printed and microfilm copies of proceedings of Congress (LL-KF35, Microfilm LL-089), including the *Journals*, 1789 to the present, the *Annals of Congress*, 1789–1824, the *Register of Debates*, 1824–33, the *Congressional Globe*, 1833–73, and the *Congressional Record*, 1873 to the present. Indexes provide access to information relating to the slave trade. Also available in the Law Library is

United States Statutes at Large (New York: Little, Brown, 1845–78, vols. 1–17, and Washington: U.S. Government Printing Office, vol. 18–; KF54.U5). Volume 1 includes a March 22, 1794, House of Representatives "Act to Prohibit the Carrying of the Slave Trade from the United States to any Foreign Place or Country," stating, in part, "no person . . . shall prepare a ship or vessel . . . for the purpose of carrying on any trade or traffic in slaves to any foreign country" (p. 347).

Various aspects of the African slave trade are documented in eighteenth- and nineteenth-century holdings located in the Manuscript Division. A useful finding aid for Africa-related materials in the division is Aloha South's *Guide to Non-Federal Archives and Manuscripts in the United States Relating to Africa* (New York: Hans Zell Publishers, 1989; 2 vols. CD3002.S68 1989), which indicates fifteen Manuscript Division collections that have information relating to the African slave trade and cites collections with material relating to interaction between black Americans and Africans in the antebellum period.

Another finding aid for manuscript materials relating to European aspects of the African slave trade is *Manuscript Sources in the Library of Congress for Research on the American Revolution* (Washington: Library of Congress, 1975; Z1238.U57 1975), a comprehensive guide prepared by John R. Sellers and other Manuscript Division historians. Beginning in 1905 the Library initiated a Foreign Copying Program to reproduce materials relating to United States history in foreign archives. Archival collections in France, Spain, Germany, and England containing documents relating to the trade are described in *Manuscript Sources*. A typical document, a tabular account from the John Rylands Library in Manchester, England (no. 1297), consists of a list of forty-three slaving voyages, 1744 to 1774, designating ship names and where and when slaves were captured and sold, and giving their value, total numbers, deaths, and the average price per slave. The cargoes were sold mainly in the West Indies, but five ships went to Maryland and the Carolinas. The records of the British secretary of state (no. 1428) include lists of ships cleared from Senegal, with ports of origin and destination, 1767 to 1777. Other British records concern importation of Africans, legislation relating to blacks, and the slave population in the West Indies.

"To be sold . . . a cargo of 170 prime young likely healthy Guinea Slaves," Savannah, July 25, 1774. Photograph of a broadside. (PP SSF—Slavery in the U.S. LC-USZ62–16876)

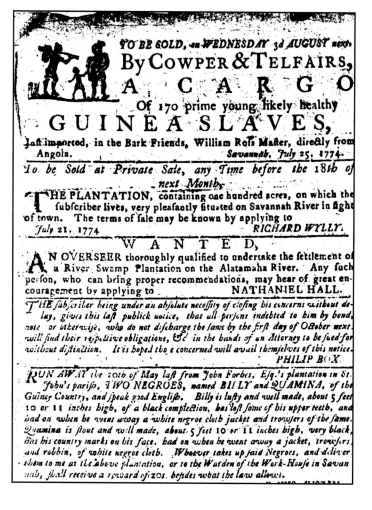

THE DOMESTIC SLAVE TRADE

Both the *Guide to Non-Federal Archives and Manuscripts* and *Manuscript Sources* provide information about Manuscript Division holdings relating to American aspects of the domestic and foreign slave trade, including collections of several individuals who were directly engaged in the trade. For example, the records of Levinus Clarkson (MSS, records 1772–93) indicate that his interest in entering the African slave trade was heightened after he received invitations from "several guineamen" to engage in it. A resident of Charleston, South Carolina, Clarkson kept correspondence and business records relating to economic conditions involving the trade. Some of the business records of Dutilh and Wachsmuth of Philadelphia (MSS, records 1781–1800), most of which are in French, relate to the shipment of slaves from the Gold Coast and Angola.

The papers of Oliver Pollock (MSS, papers 1737–1823, a part of the Peter Force Collection) contain some items relating to Pollock's commercial dealings in the slave trade with merchants in Natchez, Pensacola, Philadelphia, and Richmond. The Black History Miscellany (MSS, papers 1706–1944) collection contains materials relating to slave ships such as the *Wanderer*, a yacht charged with bringing Africans to Georgia in 1858, and other documents relating to the slave trade, including insurance documents.

Some collections in the Manuscript Division relate to mutinies of African captives aboard slavers. The New Hampshire Records, Miscellaneous (MSS, records 1652–1792, Force Collection) include William Priest's testimony of March 1765 regarding a slave revolt aboard the brigantine *Hope* of New London, which occurred while the vessel was traveling from West Africa to the West Indies with about forty-five slaves. Priest reported that "the slaves rose and killed the carpenter" and wounded two others before they were suppressed.

Probably the best known mutiny occurred in 1839 when the Africans aboard the *Amistad* revolted and killed most of the white crew, keeping only a few seamen to direct them back to Africa. The white seamen deceived the Africans, however, by guiding the vessel toward Africa during the day but steering toward the United States at night. When the *Amistad* mutineers were captured off the coast of New York, abolitionists came to their defense, arguing that they should be free men.

The Lewis Tappan collection (MSS, papers 1812–72) contains information about efforts to secure the freedom of the Africans, including the manuscript brief of former president John Quincy Adams's successful defense of the *Amistad* Africans before the Supreme Court of the United States. The Adams diaries (MSS, microfilm 1639–1889, Adams Family Papers) provide information relating to the *Amistad* incident. The papers of President Martin Van Buren (MSS, microfilm 1781–1868), who was in office at the time of the trials, also contain some information about the affair. Because the *Amistad* mutiny has generated a great deal of research, the Library holds approximately fifty full-length books on the subject. There are also documents relating to the mutiny in the Papers of the British and Foreign Anti-Slavery Society, London (MSS, microfilm 1839–1868). These papers were selected from documents at the Rhodes House, Oxford, England, and include other materials about American slavery, the slave trade, and colonization.

Perhaps the earliest published likeness of the leader of the *Amistad* captives is a lithographed portrait published in 1839. Entitled "Joseph Cinquez, the brave Congolese chief . . . who now lies in jail in arms at New Haven, Conn. awaiting his trial for daring for freedom," the lithograph is among the holdings of the Prints

"*Joseph Cinquez,*" a lithograph drawn by James or Isaac Sheffield, 1839, and published in the New York Sun. Cinquez led a revolt of African slaves aboard the Amistad en route to Cuba in June 1839. (PP PGA A Beach. LC-USZ62–12960)

and Photographs Division. Cinquez's words to his fellow Africans after the mutiny provide the text for the image: "Brothers, we have done that which we proposed. . . . I am resolved it is better to die than be a white man's slave" (PP PGA-A Beach, repro. no. LC-USZ62-12960).

Some Manuscript Division collections relate to efforts to suppress the African slave trade. Much of the early correspondence between the managers of the American Colonization Society (MSS, microfilm 1792–1964), its agents, and black settlers in Liberia yields information about attempts to eliminate the slave trade along the Liberian coast. Among the papers of U.S. naval officer Andrew Hull Foote (MSS, papers 1822–90), who commanded the U.S.S. *Perry* on the African coast from 1849 to 1851, are copies of letters relating to the use of the United States flag on vessels engaged in the trade and the efforts of British naval officers to suppress the illegal trade by boarding and searching American ships. Foote's letters in 1851 cover subjects such as the waning of the slave trade and the attempt to use colonization as a means of ending the trade. Other Manuscript Division collections that include scattered materials relating to the African slave trade are Great Britain, Naval Logbooks (MSS, logbooks 1808–40) and the Naval Historical Foundation collection (MSS, various dates). An indexed aid is *Naval Historical Foundation Manuscript Collection: A Catalog* (Washington: Library of Congress, 1974; Z663.N37 MSS Ref), which includes references under Africa and slave trade.

The journals of Benjamin Moran (MSS, journals 1851–75), kept while he was a diplomat in London, discuss the right of the British to board vessels flying the American flag to search for slaves. The letterbook of Richard Traill Spence (MSS, papers 1822–23) was maintained by Spence while he was serving as commander of the U.S.S. *Cyane* during a tour of West Africa to prevent the transport of slaves and to protect the settlement in Liberia. The Manuscript Division also holds a few papers of English philanthropist William Wilberforce (MSS, papers 1780–1833) some of which relate to his efforts to abolish the British slave trade.

As the African slave trade declined in importance in the United States, domestic slave traders flourished throughout the South. The papers of the Cornelius Chase family (MSS, papers 1815–1947) contain correspondence, business records, canceled checks, account books, receipts, and legal papers relating to the slave trade for the period from 1853 to 1864. Chase corresponded with slave traders such as E.C. Moore, Smith and Maddox, Browning, Moore and Company, Dickerson, Hill and Company, and E.H. Stokes. Alabama judge Turner Reav-

is's (MSS, records 1842–90) account book includes information about the purchase of food supplies and slaves. The Sterritt family papers (MSS, papers 1798–1859) contain bills of sales for slaves, and the Black History Miscellany collection (MSS, papers 1706–1944) has information about several slave trading vessels, slave deeds which document the legal aspects of the sale of human beings, and court records detailing disputes over the ownership of slaves. Slavery records among the materials in the Carter G. Woodson collection (MSS, microfilm 1796–1933) consist of correspondence with former slaves, bills of sale, copies of broadsides relating to slavery, certificates of freedom, and an 1822 insurance policy on a cargo of slaves. References relating to the practice of owners hiring out their slaves are found in the records of Huie, Reid, & Company (MSS, records 1784–95) of Dumfries, Virginia. Many other collections not mentioned here also contain materials that shed light on various aspects of the slave trade.

Book and magazine illustrations and prints in the Library's collections relating to the slave trade can be located through the Graphics File in the Prints and Photographs Division, which provides subject access. These illustrations show African slave markets and slave ships, images of the Middle Passage, and importation of Africans into the United States. The illustrated periodicals card catalog, an index prepared by Library staff, provides subject access to illustrations in nineteenth-century newspapers such as *Harper's Weekly, London Illustrated News,* and *Frank Leslie's Weekly Illustrated Newspaper.* Among the items listed in the catalog are images of the brig *Vigilante,* described as "a vessel employed in the slave trade," a crowded slave ship, a Brazilian slaver, and slave auctions in Charleston and New Orleans.

In addition to materials relating to the African slave trade, *Documents Illustrative of the History of the Slave Trade to America* (Washington: Carnegie Institution of America, 1930–35; 4 vols. E441.D68), edited by Elizabeth Donnan, includes records from a wide range of sources. Relating to the domestic slave trade are such documents as John Rolfe's 1619 letter to Sir Edwin Sandys informing him that blacks had arrived in Virginia, legal documents relating to slavery, auction records, transcripts of African-American oral traditions, excerpts from Thomas Jefferson's *Notes on the State of Virginia* (originally published in Paris in 1784–85), and a variety of other items pertaining to black Americans.

Another collection of printed primary sources is Willie Lee Rose's *Documentary History of Slavery in North America* (New York: Oxford University Press, 1976; E441.D64) which contains a chapter called "Slaves on the Block." The documents selected describe slave auctions in Alexandria, Richmond, Natchez, and New Orleans. An October 8, 1852, letter in the *Documentary History* details a personal aspect of slavery. It is from a slave woman in Charlottesville, Virginia, named Maria Perkins, to her husband Richard:

Dear Husband I write you a letter to let you know my distress my master has sold albert to a trader on Monday. . . . Myself and other child is for sale also and I want you to let [me] hear from you very soon. . . . I don't want you to wait till Christmas. . . . (p. 151)

Other subjects covered are slavery in the Revolutionary era, slave revolts and plots, slavery laws, slave protests, slave work, slave masters, the slave family, and slave beliefs and amusements.

Emma Langdon Roche's *Historic Sketches of the South* (New York: Knickerbocker Press, 1914; E447.R67), Frederic Bancroft's *Slave-Trading in the Old South* (Baltimore, Md.: J. H. Furst Company, 1931; E442.B21), and Wendell Holmes Stephenson's *Isaac Franklin, Slave Trader and Planter of the Old South* (Gloucester, Mass.: Peter Smith, 1968; F213.F73 1968) provide information

about the operation of the domestic slave trade.

Broadside materials in the Library relating to the trade include one entitled "Slave Market of America" (Portfolio 118:26 double oversize, Rare Bk) produced by the American Anti-Slavery Society in 1836, with vignettes depicting a scene of free blacks in Washington, D.C., being sold because of their failure to pay jail fees; a view of the Alexandria harbor with ships receiving a cargo of slaves; and a line of slaves with a J. W. Neal & Company overseer holding a whip. Notices of rewards for the return of runaway slaves are also found in the collection (Portfolio 1:12, Rare Bk).

PLANTATION LIFE AND ECONOMY

One particularly useful historical atlas for the spatial distribution of slaves is Sam B. Hilliard's *Atlas of Antebellum Southern Agriculture* (Baton Rouge: Louisiana State University Press, 1984; G1281.J1H5 1984), located in the Geography and Map Division. Most of the 111 maps are useful for understanding the relationship between slave population and agricultural production in the southeastern United States from 1790 to 1860. Not only do these maps show the distribution of slave population and slaves as a percentage of the total population for each decade, but they record the size of slave holdings and the amount of acreage in improved land and individual farms. Over half of the maps focus on the spatial distribution of various types of livestock and major crops like wheat, corn, or cotton as well as selected crops of localized importance such as rice, tobacco, and hemp.

Two works which provide primary source material about plantation life are *American Negro Slavery: A Documentary History* (Columbia: University of South Carolina Press, 1976; E441.A577 1976) edited by Michael Mullin and *Slavery and the Southern Economy* (New York: Harcourt,

Brace & World, 1966; E441.W876), a collection of articles edited by Harold D. Woodman. The latter includes statistical information about the slave population in selected southern states, lists slaves and slaveholders by state, and provides cotton production prices and other economic indicators.

Records, account books, and journals of many southern plantations are found in the collections in the Manuscript Division. Many of the founding fathers—George Washington (MSS, microfilm 1697–1799), Thomas Jefferson (MSS, microfilm 1763–1959), James Madison (MSS, microfilm 1723–1859), and James Monroe (MSS, microfilm 1650–1842) as well as later presidents— were themselves slaveholders and their papers contain information about the management of their plantations and their views toward the institution of slavery. An 1809 bill of sale in the Carter G. Woodson collection (MSS, microfilm 1796–1933) conveys a slave or indentured servant from former President Thomas Jefferson to President Madison:

I hereby assign & convey to James Madison President [Uni]ted States, the within named servant, John . . . for the remaining term of his service . . . for the consideration of two hundred and thirty one dollars 21 cents. . . .

Woodson acquired the bill of sale from a descendant of the servant. Thomas Jefferson maintained a "Farm Book" in which he recorded many details relating to his estates, including information about the labor and management of his slaves. *Thomas Jefferson's Farm Book, with Commentary and Relevant Extracts from Other Writings* (Princeton: Published for the American Philosophical Society by Princeton University Press, 1953; S451.V8J4), edited by Edwin Morris Betts, includes a photographic reproduction of the original manuscript.

President Andrew Jackson (MSS, microfilm 1770–1860) was also a slaveholder, as were a number of leading government officials such as Supreme Court Chief Justice Roger Brooke Taney (MSS, microfilm 1815–59), James Henry Hammond (MSS, microfilm 1774–1875), governor of South Carolina and a U.S. senator and representative before the Civil War, and Alexander Hamilton Stephens (MSS, microfilm 1784–1891), a congressman who later became vice president of the Confederate States of America and governor of Georgia. Stephens's papers include correspondence with his ex-slaves after the Civil War.

President James Knox Polk's papers (MSS, microfilm 1775–1891) contain information about slavery and plantation matters. In the correspondence of his wife, Sarah C. Polk, included among the president's papers, are letters exchanged with her plantation overseer, many of which are published in John Spencer Bassett's book *The Southern Plantation Overseer as Revealed in His Letters* (Northampton, Mass.: Smith College, 1925; E443.B25).

Among the small collection of papers in the Manuscript Division relating to Virginia soldier and statesman William Byrd III (MSS, papers 1757) is a 1757 "List Book of . . . Lands, Negroes, Stocks, etc." In addition to listing clothing, shoes, supplies and their costs, he lists male and female slaves on his estates at Roanoke River, Westover, and The Falls of James River. The list indicates the occupations of some of the slaves: overseer, foreman, coachman, gardener, butcher, ferryman, carpenter, cooper, miller, blacksmith, shoemaker, carter, tender, housekeeper, houseservant, and postilion. The list also shows the price of slaves and indicates that several were hired out but that others were either too young or old to work.

Byrd's father, William Byrd II, kept detailed shorthand diaries of his life in Virginia including information about his interactions with his slaves. Two published accounts are *The Secret Diary of William Byrd of Westover, 1709–1712*, edited by Louis B. Wright and Marion Tinling (Richmond, Va.: Dietz Press, 1941; reprint, New York: Arno Press, 1972; F229.B9715 1972) and *Another Secret Diary of William Byrd of Westover, 1739–1741*, edited by Maude H. Woodfin (Richmond, Va.: Dietz Press, 1942; F229.B9717).

Although President John Adams (MSS, microfilm 1639–1889, Adams Family Papers) was not a slaveholder, his diaries, located in the Massachusetts Historical Society, include information about Africa, slavery, the slave trade, and several of his black household servants. The diaries of his son, President John Quincy Adams (MSS, microfilm 1639–1889, Adams Family Papers), include much information about Africa, slavery, the slave trade, the rise of abolition sentiment, free blacks, colonization, fugitive slaves, slave revolts and mutinies, black seamen, the Missouri Compromise, kidnapping and smuggling of blacks, and international negotiations about the slave trade. The papers of both presidents are available on microfilm in the Manuscript Division. They have also been published and are indexed.

During the colonial period and until the American Revolution, slavery was legal in the northern states. Letters of Heinrich Urban Cleve (MSS, papers 1777–78, Force Collection), a Hessian army officer, yield information about life and customs in New England including his impressions of slavery in that region.

There are numerous plantation records in the Manuscript Division for Georgia, South Carolina, Virginia, and other southern states which contain correspondence, account books, work schedules, production records, and vital statistics relating to slaves. Other records provide varying perspectives on slavery. For example, the Daniel Turner (MSS, papers 1792–1808) collection contains letters from Turner to his family about his medical practice in St. Mary's, Georgia. He discusses his views on slavery, local agriculture and cotton growing, and medical treat-

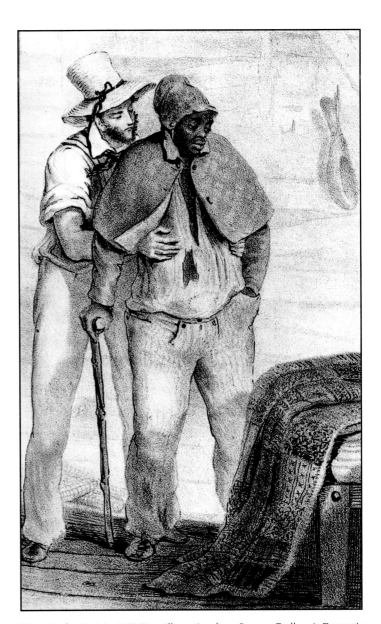

"Live Stock, Virginia 1830," an illustration from Frances Trollope's Domestic Manners of the Americans *(London: Printed for Whittaker, Treacher & Co., 1832; E165.T84 Rare Bk). (LC-USZ62–30864)*

The family in front of the Stirrup Branch Plantation for Capt. James Rembert's birthday, June 8, 1857. (Tintype, PP. LC-USZ62–46605)

The slaves assembled in back of the Stirrup Branch Plantation to be photographed for Capt. James Rembert's birthday, June 8, 1857. (Tintype, PP. LC-USZ62–46606)

ment of African-Americans. The Thomas Pinck-ney papers (MSS, papers 1751–1847) include a list of slaves on his South Carolina estate, stating their age, sex, trade, and place of residence. The papers of Virginia overseer Anthony Mullins (MSS, papers 1772–88), relate to crops, livestock, and the care of slaves on the Willis Creek plantation, which was owned by Archibald Cary.

Among the papers of English traveler John Benwell (MSS, papers 1846–52) is a manuscript entitled "On the Moral and Physical Condition of the Slave in North America," describing Benwell's travels through the South in 1840 and his subsequent observations on slavery, railroads, and the writings of Harriet Beecher Stowe. Papers of Felix Limongi (MSS, papers 1832–80) relate to various legal problems arising from the institution of slavery.

An 1860 letter from northerner William A. Galbraith (MSS, papers 1860–65) to his wife describes a slave auction in Charleston, South Carolina:

Yesterday . . . I attended a sale of some slaves at the Auction Mart. It is an everyday occurrence here but was new to me. . . . There were four boys and an old man . . . some twenty bidders and speculators made up the balance of the group.

Galbraith attributes the evident desire for freedom on the part of one mulatto slave to "the white blood that was in him" rebelling against "the humiliation to which he was subjected."

Most photographic portraits of slaves and slaveholders in the Prints and Photographs Division's collection show well-dressed house servants, especially elderly nursemaids. One particularly interesting group photograph copied from 1857 tintypes shows three generations of the James Rembert family, a family of South Carolina slave owners, standing in front of the Stirrup Branch Plantation house while in a com-panion portrait their slaves are posed behind the house according to rank (PP repro. no. LC-USZ62-46605). The photograph caption, describing the group of about thirty slaves, reads, "Four uniformed house servants are on porch; foreman named Nero is at left of field hand group; second yard boy middle front; first yard boy middle forefront; cook right forefront" (PP lot 11334; repro. no. LC-USZ62-46606).

SOCIETY, LAW, AND THE PECULIAR INSTITUTION

Both proponents and opponents of slavery are represented in *Slavery Tracts and Pamphlets from the West India Committee* (MicRR 83/425, Guide no. 69), a microfilm publication available in the Microfilm Reading Room. The collection of 375 publications is located in the Institute of Commonwealth Studies in London and consists of early nineteenth-century source materials from Great Britain and the West Indies. It yields information about parliamentary deliberations relating to Britain and its North American colonies.

Slavery (Sanford, N.C.: Microfilming Corporation of America, 1982; MicRR Microfiche 1021) is a microfiche collection of printed primary source materials relating to various aspects of slavery. Sources were selected from the Library of Congress and six other research institutions with large collections on slavery. Scholars who worked on the document selection board included John Hope Franklin, Kenneth Stampp, Stanley Engerman, Robert W. Fogel, Eugene D. Genovese, Winthrop D. Jordan, Herbert S. Klein, and Franklin W. Knight. Complete copies of pamphlets, books, and periodicals pertaining to slavery are available in this collection. A separate guide, *Slavery, a Bibliography and Union List of the Microform Collection* (Sanford, N.C.:

Microfilming Corporation of America, 1982; Z7164.S6.M53 1980, MicRR) edited by Henry Barnard, facilitates use of these materials. In the guide each title has a code letter which indicates that it relates to a particular aspect of slavery, such as the trade, revolts, legal and economic matters, church policies, proslavery and antislavery debates, colonization, and other topics.

Edited by Kenneth M. Stampp, *Records of Antebellum Southern Plantations from the Revolution through the Civil War* (MSS, microfilm 1658–1955; Frederick, Md.: University Publications of America, 1985–89), available in the Manuscript Division, reproduces on microfilm materials drawn from major manuscript repositories throughout the South that give information about sugar, rice, and cotton plantations; daily lives of owners, slaves, and overseers and their families; correspondence and business records; and journals and diaries. Library of Congress materials selected for inclusion in this microfilm series include the papers of Virginia planters William B. Randolph, Hill Carter, and James Bruce and those of two South Carolina attorneys, Edward Frost and Franklin Elmore. Frost, a slaveholder himself, represented other slaveholders in court, and Elmore, also a slave owner, was concerned about the use of slaves in various capacities, including as workers in antebellum industrial firms such as iron foundries.

The American Culture Series, 1793–1875 (Ann Arbor: University Microfilms International, 1979; MicRR 02191, guide Z1215.A583) is a reproduction of early American books and pamphlets about American life for almost four centuries. The controversy and discussion prompted by the question of slavery from the nation's beginnings are reflected in the writings in this series, for example, Anthony Benezet's "Observations on the Inslaving, Importing and Purchasing of Negroes," a sixteen-page tract printed by Christopher Sower in 1760. Proslavery and antislavery tracts, treatises on slavery, and slave narra-

tives, as well as anthologies and miscellaneous writings relating to slavery, are included in the series. The complete 908-page book edited by E. N. Elliott entitled *Cotton Is King and Pro-Slavery Arguments* (Augusta, Ga.: Pritchard, Abbott & Loomis, 1860; E449.E48) is part of the series, also. Elliott's work includes the writings of proslavery advocates such as William Harper and James Henry Hammond.

Slave codes for individual states, available in the Law Library, have been collected in volumes such as Theodore Brantner Wilson's *The Black Codes of the South* (University: University of Alabama Press, 1965; KF4757.W54), *A Sketch of the Laws Relating to Slavery in the Several States of the United States of America*, by George M. Stroud (Philadelphia: Kimber and Sharpless, 1827; KF4545.S5S8 1827; Law Office Americana 7 "Stroud" [LL RBR]), and *The Slavery Code of the District of Columbia with Notes and Judicial Decisions Explanatory of the Same* (Washington: L. Towers & Co., Printers, 1862; KF4545.S5A3 1862 [LL RBR]). The author of this volume is identified only as "a member of the Washington Bar."

The *Black Code of the District of Columbia, in Force September 1st, 1848*, by Worthington G. Snethen (New York: A. & F. Anti-Slavery Society, 1848; Law Office Americana 7 "Snethen" [LL RBR]) includes subjects such as "baptism no title to freedom," "slaves guilty of pilfering and stealing—how punished," "punishment for slaves striking white persons," and "penalty against masters of vessels for concealing slaves on board." A bound manuscript in the Law Library, "Slave Code of the District of Columbia, 1860" (Law Library, D.C. 2 1860), states in part:

A slave is a human being, who is by law deprived of his or her liberty for life, and is the property of another. A slave has no political rights and generally has no civil rights.

A multivolume work on blacks and the judicial system is Helen Honor Tunnicliff Catterall's

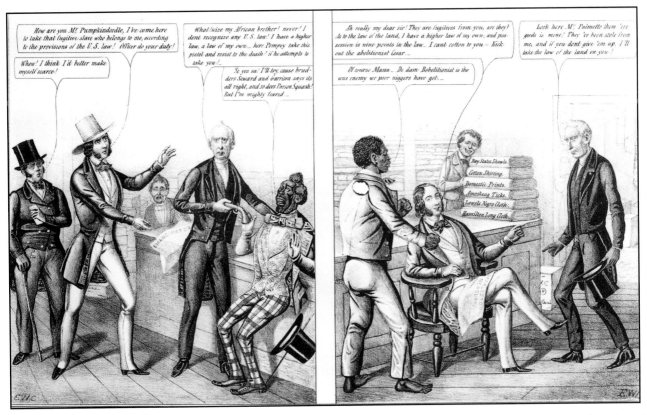

"What's Sauce for the Goose Is Sauce for the Gander," a lithograph by Edward Williams Clay (New York, 1851), presents a prosouthern view of northern opposition to enforcement of the Fugitive Slave Act. (PP Reilly 1851–5. LC-USZ62–89722)

Judicial Cases Concerning American Slavery and the Negro (Washington: Carnegie Institution of Washington, 1926–37; 5 vols. KF4545.S5C3 1926). It includes cases relating to slavery in Great Britain, Jamaica, and Canada, as well as in the United States.

Slavery in the Courtroom: An Annotated Bibliography of American Cases (Washington: Library of Congress, 1985; KF4545.S5A123 1985) is a compilation by Paul Finkelman concerning some one hundred cases from materials in the Law Library's Rare Book Room and other Library collections. Chapters address the African slave trade, slave revolts, abolitionists, fugitive slaves, and slaves living in free jurisdictions.

Finkelman is also the editor of *Slavery, Revolutionary America, and the New Nation* (New York: Garland Publishing Co., 1989; E269.N3 S58 1989). The microfiche collection *State Slavery Statutes* (Frederick, Md.: University Publications of America, 1989; LL 90/10000) is edited with introductory notes by Paul Finkelman. *Essays in the Constitutional History of the United States in the Formative Period, 1775–1789* edited by J. Franklin Jameson and first published in 1889 (Freeport, N.Y.: Books for Libraries Press, 1970; KF4541.A2J3 1970b) is also located in the Law Library. The volume includes Jeffrey Brackett's essay, "The Status of the Slave, 1775–1789."

An account of early missionary efforts among African-Americans by Francis Brokesby entitled *Some Proposals Towards Propagating of the Gospel in Our American Plantations* (London: G. Sawbridge, 1708; BV2783.B83 1708 Rare Bk), which outlines strategies for evangelizing both Indians and blacks, can be found in the Rare Book and Special Collections Division. In his *Letters from the Rev. Samuel Davies, &c. Shewing the State of Religion (Particularly Among the Negroes) in Virginia* (London: n.p., 1757; BV2783.D3 Rare Bk), Davies reports his success in Hanover, Virginia, in baptizing hundreds of slaves and distributing books sent from England to encourage reading and religious instruction among them.

Antebellum cartographic records in the Library's Geography and Map Division depict, either directly or indirectly, African-American settlement patterns. Landownership maps show the location of plantations and farms within a county, indicating the boundaries and contents of individual plantations or landholdings. Although these maps do not normally show the detail of slave population patterns, they do document the broader settlement pattern of the slave owners and their agricultural enterprises. The earliest comprehensive landownership mapping for a single state was Robert Mills's survey during the 1820s called *Atlas of the State of South Carolina* (Columbia? S.C.: n.p., 1825; G1305.M5 1825 vault). Published in an atlas format, these maps made up the first state atlas to include single maps of individual counties. They show rural settlements, the road network, schools, churches, mills, landings, and towns and give the names of landowners.

At about the same time that Mills's maps were being produced, John Wood and Herman Böye were preparing a similar set of maps of Virginia counties. Never published either as single maps or in atlas format, these county maps were used to prepare a comprehensive map of the state. Original manuscript copies of some of Wood's maps survive in the Virginia State Library and the National Archives, and the Library of Congress holds photostatic copies of those in the Virginia State Library. An excellent reference tool for plantation settlement patterns, these maps show individual farms, mills, and roads in several counties throughout Virginia and what is now West Virginia. These and other landownership maps for slave states can be located by using Richard W. Stephenson's *Land Ownership Maps: A Checklist of Nineteenth Century United States County Maps in the Library of Congress* (Washington: Library of Congress, 1967; Z6027.U5U54). The maps are available in the Geography and Map Division as negative photostats and on microfiche.

Closely related to county landownership maps are cadastral maps of individual estates or landholdings. Most are manuscript drawings (and not very common in the Library's holdings). Some of the best examples are the several maps and plats that George Washington prepared for his various landholdings. In 1793 Washington prepared a survey entitled, when it was published, *A Map of General Washington's Farm of Mount Vernon* (London: W. J. and J. Richardson, 1801; G3882.M7 1793.W4 Vault). It shows Washington's home plantation, Mount Vernon, and four adjoining plantations, taking up a total of eight thousand acres. Although the map shows the mansion house, outbuildings, fields, and wooded areas, there is no indication of slave quarters. In 1766 Washington had surveyed a parcel of land adjacent to Mount Vernon called River Farm. The manuscript plat, entitled "A Plan of my Farm on Little Huntg. Creek & Potomk. R." (G3882.M7 1766.W3 Vault), shows a group of small buildings that scholars have identified as slave quarters.

The living quarters and work sites of slaves have been extensively documented in the Historic American Buildings Survey records held in the Prints and Photographs Division. First compiled in the 1930s, records devoted to recording plantation houses sometimes include plans, elevations, photographs, and research notes about outbuildings such as slave quarters, barns, well houses, smokehouses, kitchens, dairies, and various sheds. More than seven hundred images from over three hundred locations in the southern United States have been identified in the subject indexes to the survey. The inclusion of exact dimensions and detailed descriptions of building materials and layouts of plantation buildings and the distances between them makes it possible to reconstruct the plantation layout. One of the most unusual buildings documented is a "slave keep" in an Alabama bank where slaves were deposited and held as collateral when their owners defaulted on loan payments (PP HABS ALA, 45–HUVI, 3A-1). Some of the records indicate which buildings were constructed with slave labor. For example, fif-

teen photographs of the General William Floyd House at Mastic Beach, Suffolk County, New York, probably built in the 1720s, include captions stating that most of the construction was done by slaves (PP HABS NY, 52-MAST, 1-). More than two hundred HABS photographs and drawings of slave quarters along with the testimonies of some former slaves appear in *Back of the Big House: The Architecture of Plantation Slavery*, by John Michael Vlach (Chapel Hill: University of North Carolina Press, 1993; E443.V58 1993).

Slave quarters and artifacts related to slavery were documented when photographers attached to Union troops moved into the South with their regiments and took pictures of the people they were fighting to free. In the Mathew Brady Collection in the Prints and Photographs Division is a photograph made at Smith's Plantation in the Beaufort area of South Carolina, showing former slave women sitting

Slave quarters on The Oaks plantation, Leiton, Colbert County, Alabama, documented by the Historic American Buildings Survey, 1935. (PP HABS ALA-362 ALA-17–Leit.V 1A-1)

on a pile of cotton, while men sit or stand nearby. The view includes benches, barrels, and other furniture needed in the work yard, as well as sheds and wagons (PP repro. no. LC-B811–159). Other images made at Beaufort show the town, plantation houses, and former slaves in partial Union uniforms serving as waiters at the officers' mess. Port Royal Island images, attributed to photographer Sam A. Cooley, an army photographer not connected with Brady's enterprise, show slaves near their quarters (PP lot 4205, Civ War).

Ruins of slave cabins at Kingsley Plantation and overgrown graves of slaves in Fort George Island, Florida, were photographed between 1883 and 1892 by Niagara Falls landscape photographer George Barker (PP lot 3282–1). A slave market in Saint Augustine (PP lot 3282–2), a slave cabin, and a quilt made by slaves (PP lot 3282–3) are shown in other photographs.

At the turn of the century the Detroit Publishing Company produced stereos—two identical images viewed through a binocular-type viewer called a stereoscope producing a three-dimensional image—for home entertainment and study photographs for mass distribution. Among them are three photos of the abandoned slave quarters at The Hermitage in Savannah, Georgia (PP lot 9085). Detroit Publishing Company views of Saint Augustine, Florida, include blacks posed at the slave market, the Battery of Fort Marion, the Old City Gate, and outdoor views of landmarks (PP lot 9082). The "slave pen" in Alexandria, Virginia, where slaves were held until they were auctioned, is shown in a photograph now in the Herman Haupt Collection (PP lot 11486, repro. no. LC-USZ62-27657).

THE SLAVE'S PERSPECTIVE

There are a few collections in the Manuscript Division that discuss slavery from the vantage point of the slave. African-American diplomat, orator, author, and abolitionist Frederick Douglass (MSS, papers 1841–1967) wrote and updated his autobiography several times during his life. These manuscripts are among his papers in the Manuscript Division. Michael Shiner (MSS, diary 1813–65), a slave who was hired out as a worker in the Washington Navy Yard, kept a diary about his own life and important events in Washington, D.C. He also discusses the kidnapping and sale of his wife and his successful journey to rescue her. In his handwritten autobiography Houston Hartsfield Holloway (n.d.) discusses his lot as a slave in Georgia. Although he describes a relatively mild life under benign masters, he writes that his response was "Amen, amen, amen" when his master announced that his slaves had been emancipated. Holloway recorded that his master said that he too was glad slavery had ended and felt as if he also had been freed. Holloway's memoir continues the record of his life through the turn of the century. John Washington's handwritten autobiography (MSS, microfilm n.d.), entitled "Memorys of the Past," provides information about his life as a slave, his education, and his emancipation. He explains that his mother "taught him to spell" when he was between the ages of four and eight.

Jupiter Hammon, who wrote poetry before 1800, was a New York slave for his entire life. Oscar Wegelin hails Hammon as America's first black poet in *Jupiter Hammon, American Negro Poet: Selections from His Writings and a Bibliography* (New York: C. F. Heartman, 1915; PS767. H15Z8 Rare Bk). In *Address to the Negroes in the State of New-York* (New York: Samuel Wood, 1806; E185.7.H3 1806 Rare Bk) Hammon recommends respectful behavior of slaves to masters and urges his brothers to seek freedom through religion.

Certainly the most extensive collection relating to the slave's view of the world in the

Manuscript Division is the United States Works Projects Administration (WPA) (MSS, papers 1627–1940) Slave Narrative collection. These materials, collected in the 1930s, give accounts of the institution of slavery by hundreds of individuals who had been held in bondage in the southern states. Besides the original narratives in the Manuscript Division, a microfilm edition of the *Slave Narratives: A Folk History of Slavery in the United States from Interviews with Former Slaves* is available in the Microform Reading Room (MicRR no. 974). A guide to the microfilm edition by Martia G. Goodson is entitled "An Introductory Essay and Subject Index to Selected Interviews from the Slave Narrative Collection" (MicRR Guide no. 53, University Microfilm International order no. 78–128).

Index to the American Slave, edited by Donald M. Jacobs (Westport, Conn.: Greenwood Press, 1981; E444.A45 Supplement 3) provides access to the series *The American Slave: A Composite Autobiography* (Westport, Conn.: Greenwood Press, 1977, 1979; Supplements 1, 12 vols., and 2, 10 vols., E444.A45), a compilation of the slave narratives edited by George Rawick. Volumes in Rawick's series contain not only WPA narratives but also narratives independently collected by researchers at Texas and Fisk Universities.

A few sound recordings made by former slaves are found in the Library's Archive of Folk Culture. "Recordings of Slave Narratives and Related Materials in the Archive of Folk Culture: Reference Tapes," a finding aid, lists titles such as, "Monolog on the Emancipation, Sung and Spoken by Wallace Quarterman," recorded at Frederica, Georgia, by Alan Lomax, Zora Neale Hurston, and Mary Elizabeth Barnicle in 1935; "Monolog on White Marsters, Spoken by Joe McDonald," recorded at Livingston, Alabama, by John A. and Ruby T. Lomax; and "Interview with Mrs. Laura Smalley; Discusses Slavery Days, Whipping Slaves . . . ," recorded in 1941 in Hempstead, Texas, by John Henry Faulk.

Many separately published slave autobiographies and biographies also exist. One of the earliest works of African-American authorship is the slave narrative of Briton Hammon published in 1760 with the lengthy title *A Narrative of the Uncommon Sufferings, and Surprizing* [sic] *Deliverance of Briton Hammon, A Negro Man . . . Servant to General Winslow, of Marshfield* (Boston: Green & Russell, 1760; F314.H22 American Imprints Coll. Rare Bk). Charles Ball, in *Slavery in the United States* (Lewistown, Pa.: J. W. Shugert, 1836; E444.B18 Rare Bk), recounts fifty years as a slave in Maryland, South Carolina, and Georgia, his eventual escape as a stowaway, and his naval service during the War of 1812. The authenticity of this narrative has been questioned, since it was transcribed and edited by abolitionists who supported its publication. In contrast, Henry Bibb's *Narrative of the Life and Adventures of Henry Bibb, an American Slave* (New York: The Author, 1849; E444.B58 Rare Bk) is considered one of the best of the genre. Bibb was born into slavery in Kentucky in 1815. He recounts his

"The Sabbath among Slaves," from Henry Bibb's Narrative of the Life and Adventures of Henry Bibb, an American Slave *(New York: The Author, 1849; E444.B58 Rare Bk). (LC-USZ62–107750)*

sufferings, escapes, recaptures, and unsuccessful attempts to free his family. Bibb lectured for the Liberty party in Ohio and Michigan during the 1840s and fled to Canada after the Fugitive Slave Act of 1850. His narrative includes illustrations depicting the celebration of the Sabbath among the slaves and a slave sale.

In *Life and Sufferings of Leonard Black, a Fugitive from Slavery* (Providence, R.I.: L. Black, 1847; E450.B58A3 1847 Rare Bk), Black tells of his childhood experiences as a slave in Baltimore, and of his life with a black pastor in Portland, Maine, and Boston. He published with the hope of earning enough money for additional ministerial training. Another narrative, the *Memoirs of Elleanor Eldridge* (Providence, R.I.: B.T. Albro, 1838; E185.97.E37 Rare Bk), was so popular when it was published that it was reissued at least four times in seven years.

The Slave's Narrative (New York: Oxford University Press, 1985; E444.S575 1985), a critical anthology edited by Charles T. Davis and Henry Louis Gates, Jr., contains a selected bibliography of narratives for the period 1760 to 1865. Pertinent information describing the advantages and limitations of the narratives may be found in William L. Andrews's *To Tell a Free Story: The First Century of Afro-American Autobiography, 1760–1865* (Urbana: University of Illinois Press, 1986; E185.96.A57 1986), and Paul D. Escott's *Slavery Remembered: A Record of Twentieth-Century Slave Narratives* (Chapel Hill: University of North Carolina Press, 1979; E443.E82). Andrews includes two essays, one concerning autobiographies of African-Americans from 1760 to 1865 and the other about biographies for the same period. *Great Slave Narratives* (Boston: Beacon Press, 1969; E444.B67), compiled by Arna Bontemps, includes an informative introduction.

John W. Blassingame compiled a variety of slave documents in *Slave Testimony: Two Centuries of Letters, Speeches, Interviews, and Autobiographies* (Baton Rouge: Louisiana State University Press, 1977; E444.S57). In a forty-page introduction, he explains the intricate task of determining the validity of slave documents, observing that the testimony of both slaves and their masters requires careful scrutiny.

An extensive compilation of slave letters can be found in Carter G. Woodson's *The Mind of the Negro as Reflected in Letters Written during the Crisis, 1800–1860* (Washington: Association for the Study of Negro Life and History, 1926; E185.W8877). In this collection Woodson reprints letters from antislavery journals and newspapers. Woodson also edited a collection of biographical writings entitled *Negro Orators and Their Orations* (Washington: Associated Publishers, 1925; PS663.N4W6). *Blacks in Bondage: Letters of American Slaves* (New York: M. Wiener Publishing, 1988; E444.B62 1988), edited by Robert Starobin, includes correspondence of literate slaves such as drivers, house servants, and artisans.

The narratives document the various ways that African-Americans resisted slavery, many by running away and becoming fugitives and others by shirking their responsibilities or by diversionary activities. Although there is printed evidence to document some conspiracies and insurrections, the actual number of slave revolts is uncertain. Herbert Aptheker's *American Negro Slave Revolts* (New York: Columbia University Press, 1944; H31.C7 no. 501a) states that there were 250 slave insurrections and conspiracies, whereas Winthrop Jordan's *White Over Black: American Attitudes toward the Negro, 1550–1812* (Chapel Hill: University of North Carolina Press, 1968; E185.J69) claims 12 at most. The authors give divergent definitions of the type of activity that could be called a revolt.

William F. Cheek's *Black Resistance before the Civil War* (Beverly Hills, Calif.: Glencoe Press, 1970; E447.C47) provides a general introduction to the subject of slave resistance. It also contains

SLAVERY—THE PECULIAR INSTITUTION · 23

a selected bibliography for the general reader, and explains how slave narratives may be used to document slave resistance, citing the slave narratives of Anthony Burns and Charles Ball as examples.

In 1739 the most serious revolt during the colonial period—known as the Stono rebellion—took place in Stono, South Carolina, an area southwest of Charleston, and resulted in the deaths of sixty-five blacks and whites. Peter H. Wood's *Black Majority: Negroes in Colonial South Carolina from 1670 through the Stono Rebellion* (New York: Knopf, 1974; E445.S7W66) discusses the causes and effects of the violence. Another serious slave revolt was led by a literate, enslaved preacher named Nat Turner in 1831. During the revolt in Southampton County, Virginia, Turner and the slaves who were with him killed over fifty whites. A discussion of the reasons for the Turner insurrection appears in a November 19, 1831, letter from the governor of Virginia, John Floyd (MSS, papers 1823–67), to James Hamilton, the governor of South Carolina. Floyd writes that the "spirit of insubordination" among Virginia slaves had been fired by Yankee peddlers teaching about the Revolutionary War, encouraged by pious female slave owners who wanted blacks to learn how to read the Bible, and inflamed by black preachers teaching equality before God. Floyd also blames incendiary publications written by men such as black militant David Walker and white radical abolitionist William Lloyd Garrison (MSS, papers 1835–75, Massachusetts Historical Society microfilm 1833–82), the outspoken editor of the *Liberator*, an antislavery newspaper published from 1831 to 1866. *David Walker's Appeal in Four Articles, Together with a Preamble, to the Coloured Citizens of the World, But in Particular, and Very Expressly, to Those of the United States of America* (New York: Hill and Wang, 1965; E446.W178), edited and with an introduction by Charles M.

"But I did not want to go . . . ," an engraving illustrating Jesse Torrey's American Slave Trade; or, An Account of the Manner in Which the Slave Dealers Take Free People from Some of the United States of America, and Carry Them Away, and Sell Them as Slaves in Other of the States *(London: J.M. Cobbett, 1822; E446.T694 Rare Bk). (LC-USZ62–30836)*

$200 Reward.

RANAWAY from the subscriber, on the night of Thursday, the 30th of September,

FIVE NEGRO SLAVES,

To-wit: one Negro man, his wife, and three children.

The man is a black negro, full height, very erect, his face a little thin. He is about forty years of age, and calls himself *Washington Reed*, and is known by the name of Washington. He is probably well dressed, possibly takes with him an ivory headed cane, and is of good address. Several of his teeth are gone.

Mary, his wife, is about thirty years of age, a bright mulatto woman, and quite stout and strong.

The oldest of the children is a boy, of the name of FIELDING, twelve years of age, a dark mulatto, with heavy eyelids. He probably wore a new cloth cap.

MATILDA, the second child, is a girl, six years of age, rather a dark mulatto, but a bright and smart looking child.

MALCOLM, the youngest, is a boy, four years old, a lighter mulatto than the last, and about equally as bright. He probably also wore a cloth cap. If examined, he will be found to have a swelling at the navel.

Washington and Mary have lived at or near St. Louis, with the subscriber, for about 15 years.

It is supposed that they are making their way to Chicago, and that a white man accompanies them, that they will travel chiefly at night, and most probably in a covered wagon.

A reward of **$150** will be paid for their apprehension, so that I can get them, if taken within one hundred miles of St. Louis, and **$200** if taken beyond that, and secured so that I can get them, and other reasonable additional charges, if delivered to the subscriber, or to THOMAS ALLEN, Esq., at St. Louis, Mo. The above negroes, for the last few years, have been in possession of Thomas Allen, Esq., of St. Louis.

WM. RUSSELL.

ST. LOUIS, Oct. 1, 1847.

"$200 Reward. Ranaway from the subscriber . . . Five Negro Slaves," Saint Louis, 1 October 1847. (Broadside Collection, Port 86:2, Rare Bk. LC-USZ62–62797)

Wiltse, was originally published in September 1829. Walker, a free black, wrote in his *Appeal* that blacks should strike out for freedom:

The man who would not fight under our Lord and Master Jesus Christ, in the glorious and heavenly cause of freedom and of God—to be delivered from the most wretched, abject and servile slavery, that ever a people was afflicted with since the foundation of the world, to the present day—ought to be kept with all of his children or family, in slavery, or in chains, to be butchered by his *cruel enemies.* (P. 12)

Less than one year after the appearance of the *Appeal*, which was banned in states throughout the country, Walker was found dead of unknown causes in front of his used-clothing shop in Boston, Massachusetts.

Among the published works devoted to particular rebellions are *The Confessions of Nat Turner, the Leader of the Late Insurrection in Southampton, Virginia* (Richmond: T.R. Gray, 1832; F232.S7T9 Rare Bk) and *The Nat Turner Rebellion:*

The Historical Event and the Modern Controversy (New York: Harper & Row, 1971; F232.S7D8), edited by John B. Duff and Peter M. Mitchell. *The Trial Record of Denmark Vesey*, with an introduction by John Oliver Killens (Boston: Beacon, 1970; KF223.V4K4 1970), is a reprint of an 1822 publication by Vesey entitled *An Official Report of the Trials of Sundry Negroes, Charged with an Attempt to Raise an Insurrection in the State of South Carolina* (Charleston: James R. Schenck, 1822; KF223.V4V47 1822).

General works concerning slave rebellions include Joseph Cephas Carroll's *Slave Insurrections in the United States, 1800–1865* (Boston: Chapman & Grimes, 1938; E447.C27); *Slave Insurrections: Selected Documents*, by Joshua Coffin and others (Westport, Conn.: Negro Universities Press, 1970; E447.S57 1970); and William S. Drewry's *Slave Insurrections in Virginia, 1830–1865* (Washington: The Neale Co., 1900; F232.S7D6).

Information on runaway slaves is generally found in newspapers, broadsides, and periodical articles. In four volumes Lathan A. Windley compiled *Runaway Slave Advertisements: A Documentary History from the 1730s to 1790* (Westport, Conn.: Greenwood Press, 1983; E446.W73 1983) for Virginia, North Carolina, Georgia, Maryland, and South Carolina. The entries can be used to locate more extensive articles relating to runaways in the newspapers cited and in other sources. Advertisements relating to runaways and sales of slaves can be found in the Library's extensive antebellum newspaper collection for both northern and southern states. Advertisements for slaves usually noted skills or other abilities slaves possessed. Also about runaways, *Blacks Who Stole Themselves: Advertisements for Runaways in the Pennsylvania Gazette, 1728–90* (Philadelphia: University of Pennsylvania Press, 1989; E443.B525 1989) was edited by Billy G. Smith and Richard Wijtowicz. Broadsides also advertised runaways and sales of slaves. An extensive collection is in the Rare Book and Special Collections Division. Paul Finkelman edited *Rebellions, Resistance, and Runaways within the Slave South* (New York: Garland, 1989; E447.R43 1989) and *Fugitive Slaves* (New York: Garland, 1989; E450.F955 1989), both part of the multivolume series Articles on American Slavery.

Illustrations and political cartoons from both British and American publications dating from about 1720 to 1864 (see PP Graphics File lot 4422-A) are some of the earliest images relating to slavery in the Prints and Photographs Division. Advertisements for slave sales and auctions, newspaper notices about runaway slaves, and illustrations relating to fugitive slave laws, corporal punishment and kidnapping, or slave life are among the early graphic sources.

Many runaways were assisted by individuals who secretly sheltered or transported them on their way to free states or Canada in the system of escape known as the underground railroad. The Frederick Douglass (MSS, microfilm 1841–1967) papers in the Manuscript Division include information about fugitive slaves and the work of abolitionists and conductors on the underground railroad, as do the American Missionary Association records (MSS, Amistad Research Center microfilm 1846–82). One classic volume is William Still's *The Underground Rail Road: A Record of Facts, Authentic Narratives, Letters, &c., Narrating the Hardships, Hairbreadth Escapes, and Death Struggles of the Slaves in Their Efforts for Freedom as Related by Themselves and Others* (Philadelphia: Porter & Coates, 1872; E450.S85 Rare Bk). Over 120 other titles in the general collection relate to the underground railroad.

"The Oberlin Rescuers at Cuyahoga Co. Jail, April 1859." Albumen silver print; T. J. Rice, photographer. (PP SSF—Negro Slavery–Underground Railroad. LC-USZ62–73349)

Routes to freedom are diagrammed in *The American Heritage Pictorial Atlas of United States History*, edited by Hilde Heun Kagan (New York: American Heritage Publishing Company, 1966; G1201.S1A4 1966) and the *Historical Atlas of the United States* (Washington: National Geographic Society, 1988; G1201.S1N3 1988), both of which are available in the Geography and Map Division.

Portraits of "Oberlin [Ohio] Rescuers" show twenty individuals who assisted fugitive slaves in their flight to freedom (PP SSF-Negro Slavery—Abolition Movement; repro. no. LC-USZ62-73349). Photographs taken in the 1940s show sites where New York state underground railroad conductors hid runaways (PP SSF–Negro Slavery—Underground Railroad). Other images depict underground railroad sites in the Washington, D.C., area (PP SSI indexes "Negro Slavery—Underground Railroad"). Station sites in the District of Columbia area include a burial vault at Mt. Zion Church in Georgetown, the Israel African Methodist Episcopal Church (now Metropolitan A.M.E.), and the wharf in Alexandria, Virginia, where several boat owners assisted runaways.

AFRICAN-AMERICANS AND POPULAR CULTURE

Although they were not originally intended to document slave life, cityscapes occasionally include images of slaves. Blacks appear as figures in the foreground of these scenes as observers, or in service occupations such as cooks, nursemaids, and groomsmen. These scenes were published in newspapers such as *Harper's Magazine* (New York, 1850–1900; 101 vols. AP2.H3), *Frank Leslie's Weekly* (New York, 1855–91, 73 vols., MicRR 02282), and *Ballou's Pictorial Drawing-Room Companion* (Boston: F. Gleason, 1851–[59]; 17 vols. MicRR 05422 no. 250–52 AP). *Cur-rier & Ives: A Catalogue Raisonné* (Detroit: Gale Research Company, 1983; NE2312.C8A4 1983a), a comprehensive illustrated catalog with an introduction by Bernard F. Reilly, Jr., lists their lithographs, which often feature African-Americans as incidental figures.

Nineteenth-century advertisers depicted blacks as servants on consumer goods to cause white purchasers to associate the product with a luxurious plantation lifestyle. Advertisements for stoves, food, coffee, banjos, harmonicas, guitars, tobacco, liquor, toiletries, stove black, paint, shoe polish, bleach and many other consumer items include images—many of them caricatures—of blacks. In the tobacco labels collection we find a label dated 1859 for "Southern Rights Segars," showing a prosperous-looking black couple in front of fields where slaves are working. Other labels show a banjo player and a black family in a sentimental domestic scene (an image based on an Eastman Johnson painting). Many of these images can be found among the ephemera holdings of the Prints and Photographs Division (PP lot 10618-61).

Before 1863 currency in the United States was issued by hundreds of state and local banks rather than by the federal government. Many southern banks issued bank notes illustrated with southern products and themes such as riverboats, cotton plants, and slaves. Engraving proofs for vignettes on bank notes copyrighted during the 1850s show blacks as the foundation of southern capital. The designs on these notes registered by the New York engraving firm Bald, Cousland & Company and now among the copyright deposits in the Library's collections show black men as field hands, grooms, stable hands, and teamsters and women as mothers and field hands (PP lots 12593, 11344). Vignettes of slaves working, 1859–60, appear among engravings from the American Bank Note Company collection (PP lot 12595). Northern engravers produced these designs for the southern market.

Barroom Dancing, *by John Lewis Krimmel, 1820. Watercolor and pencil. (PP DRWG 1–Krimmel no. 1, A size. LC-USZ62–94848; LC-USZC4–1388 [color])*

Starting in the 1830s after black-face comedian Dan Rice became popular for his stage routine about blacks, caricatures of African-Americans often appeared on sheet music covers. A lithograph dated 1845 for the title "The Fugitive's Song," held in the Prints and Photographs Division, shows the youthful Frederick Douglass as a runaway slave (PP lot 10615–59; repro. no. LC-USZ62-7823). Done in Boston, a seedbed of abolitionism, the portrait of Douglass is a faithful likeness, but the lithograph also shows horsemen and their dogs on the southern shore of a river with the barefoot Douglass, on the northern shore, heading in the direction of a signpost pointing toward New England. The truth is that Douglass escaped on a regular passenger train with borrowed freedom documents from a black seaman.

Music produced by African-Americans during the slavery era has been acclaimed worldwide and is documented in materials in the Music Division. The earliest references to black music appear in travel accounts, missionary reports, and legal documents. Several reference books identify materials relating to this music. These include a work by Dena J. Epstein, *Sinful Tunes and Spirituals: Black Folk Music to the Civil War* (Urbana: University of Illinois Press, 1977;

ML3556.E8), another by Eileen Southern and Josephine Wright, *African-American Traditions in Song, Sermon, Tale, and Dance, 1600s-1920: An Annotated Bibliography of Literature, Collections, and Artworks* (New York: Greenwood Press, 1990; Z5956.A47S68 1990), and an index by Arthur R. LaBrew, *Black Musicians of the Colonial Period, 1700–1800: A Preliminary Index of Names Compiled from Various Sources* (Detroit: LaBrew, 1977; ML 3556.L22).

The earliest works related to African-American music published separately and available in the Music Division are pseudo-African songs from the English stage imported to the colonies, such as "The Suffering Negro" (London: G. Goulding, 1790; M1621.S) and two by Charles Dibdin, "Negro Philosophy . . . [from] *The General Election*," (New York: J. Hewitt, 1797? M1.A1H Case) and "The Negro and His Banjer . . . [from] *The Wags*" (London: The Author, 1790? M1507.D54 Case). James Fisin's "An African Love Song" (New York: G. Gilfert, 1799?; M1.A11 vol. 3, no. 10 Case), is another example.

At the same time as black music was gaining popularity, pseudo-African-American songs were laying the groundwork for the minstrel theater. How much these songs owed to anonymous black musicians is still a matter of dispute. The caricature they presented of black performers gained wide popularity with white audiences, preparing the way for blacks to enter the professional theater after the Civil War. Examples of these early songs housed in the Music Division include "Jim Crow" (Boston: Oliver Ditson, n.d. M1622.J Case), "Jenny Get Your Hoe Cake Done, the Celebrated Banjo Song" (New York: Firth & Hall, 1840; M1.A12 V4), and "Ginger Blue" (n.p.: 1841; M1.A12V vol. 6).

A history of the minstrel theater, the most popular American entertainment of the nineteenth century, can be found in Robert C. Toll's *Blacking Up: The Minstrel Show in Nineteenth Century America* (New York: Oxford University

Press, 1974; ML1711.T64). The numerous collections of minstrel music found today in the Music Division attest to its popularity. Examples include John C. Scherpf's "African Quadrilles, Selected from the Most Admired Negro Melodies" (New York: F. Riley, 1844–47; M1.A12I vol. 13); "Music of the Ethiopian Serenaders" (Philadelphia: E. Ferrett & Co. [1845?]; M1.A13E Case), and *Christy's Plantation Melodies* (Philadelphia: Fisher & Brothers, 1851–53; M1628.C55P5). A further source of antebellum minstrel music is the set of four *Ethiopian Glee Books* (Boston: Elias Howe and Oliver Ditson, 1848–50; 4 vols. M1670.C43). These books, with their oblong format and their settings in four-part chorus, parodied the Glee Books popular in America in the 1840s. The versions they print are sometimes so corrupted that they cannot be sung. One song bears the note "If dese words will not go wid dis music, probably some other will." Nevertheless, they document the mix of styles in the antebellum minstrel show.

Several pieces demonstrate the existence of black Creole music during the first half of the nineteenth century. Composed sometime in 1844, "Danse Nègre Creole: Black Creole Dance Set by French Violinist Henri Vieuxtemps," a manuscript in private hands, was published for the first time in John H. Baron's article "Vieuxtemps (and Ole Bull) in New Orleans," *American Music* 8 (Summer 1990: 210–26; ML1.A497). The first identified use of African-American folk thematic material in a public concert was performed by its composer Louis Moreau Gottschalk in Paris in 1849. Gottschalk, born in New Orleans in 1829, was beginning his concert career in the 1840s after training in France. Drawing on his memories of the black music he had heard as a child in Louisiana, he introduced his own compositions, "Bamboula" and "La Savane," written between 1846 and 1849. "Le Bananier, Chanson Nègre," composed somewhat later, also became extremely popular in Europe

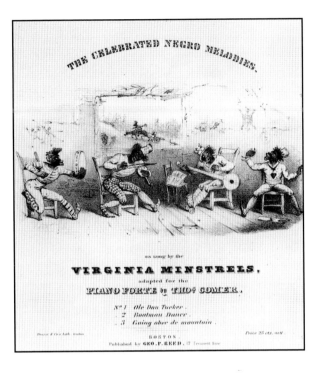

"The Celebrated Negro Melodies, as Sung by the Virginia Minstrels," music cover (Boston: Geo. P. Reed, "entered according to act of Congress in the year 1843"). (PP lot 10615–62. LC-USZ62–42353)

"Jenny Get Your Hoe Cake Done," the celebrated banjo song (New York: Firth & Hall, 1840; M1.A12.V4). (LC-USZ62–107763)

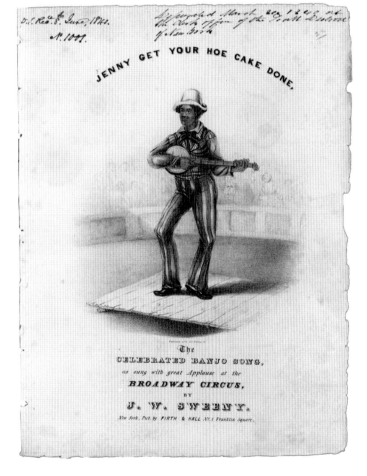

and beginning in 1853, in the United States, when Gottschalk made an American tour. "Bamboula (Danse de Nègres)" (M30.G), "Le Bananier: Chanson Nègre" (M25.G), and "The Banjo, an American Sketch" (M25.G) are represented in the Music Division by editions from a much later date than 1853. Gwendolyn Brooks wrote a poem about Gottschalk entitled *Gottschalk and the Grande Tarantelle* (Chicago: David Co., 1988; PS3503.R7244G68 1988).

Even as slaves, blacks were able to make an impact on American culture by creativity in music and other endeavors. From the seventeenth century on, slave owners began to emancipate slaves for various reasons and other blacks bought their own freedom or ran away. Thus, in every region free black communities began to draw from the cultures of Africa and Europe to produce a new and different heritage.

CHAPTER TWO

FREE BLACKS IN THE ANTEBELLUM PERIOD

From the seventeenth century on there was a small free black population in the country. These African-Americans were usually emancipated by reason of diligent work, good conduct, familial connections, or commendable service. The methods for manumission included court actions, instructions in owners' wills, purchase of one's own or family members' freedom with money earned when hired out, or governmental decrees such as emancipation laws or rewards for military service. Throughout the South the law declared that children followed the condition of the mother. Thus when children were born to a free mother, they were free also.

REVOLUTIONARY WAR ERA

In 1776 during the Revolutionary War Lord Dunmore of Virginia declared all blacks free who would join the British forces. Although Dunmore was slow to act on this promise, thousands of black families eventually fled to freedom behind British lines. A comprehensive and helpful work, *Revolutionary America, 1763–1789: A Bibliography* (Washington: Library of Congress, 1984; 2 vols. Z1238.G3), by Ronald M. Gephart, a Manuscript Division historian, includes information about sources which discuss slavery as a war issue and blacks as participants in the war, beneficiaries of the war, and members of the labor force.

One of the books Gephart cites, Benjamin Quarles's *The Negro in the American Revolution* (Chapel Hill: University of North Carolina Press, 1961; E269.N3Q3), which has a useful bibliography, discusses the reluctance of white Americans to allow blacks to bear arms and reviews the military and naval service of African-Americans in both American and British forces as cooks, artisans, guides, spies, sailors, and soldiers. Another study cited, by William C. Nell, entitled *The Colored Patriots of the American*

Revolution, which was originally published in 1855 (New York: Arno Press, 1968; E269.N3N4 1968), provides information about the contributions of blacks in the revolutionary era as soldiers, community leaders, and intellectuals. George Livermore's work *An Historical Research Respecting the Opinions of the Founders of the Republic on Negroes as Slaves, as Citizens, and as Soldiers* (Boston: A. Williams, 1863; 4th ed. E185.L79 1968; MicRR 70072) explains opinions

In "The Bloody Massacre Perpetrated in King Street, Boston, on March 5, 1770" by the British 29th Regiment, the black seaman Crispus Attucks was among the five men shot and killed. Paul Revere's hand-colored etching of the Boston Massacre was effective propaganda for the patriots. (PP FP XVIII R 45Z no. 1, A size. LC-USZ62–35522; LC-USZC4–110 [color])

on the use of blacks as soldiers by both American and British forces during the war and presents discussions about the institution of slavery during debates relating to the Declaration of Independence, the Articles of Confederation, the Constitution, and state conventions ratifying the Constitution.

Two other useful studies (also cited in Gephart) are George H. Moore, *Historical Notes on the Employment of Negroes in the American Army of the Revolution* (New York: C.T. Evans, 1862; E269.N3M8), which yields information about the type of services African-Americans performed during the war, and Sidney Kaplan and Emma Nogrady Kaplan, *The Black Presence in the Era of the American Revolution* (revised edition, Amherst: University of Massachusetts Press, 1989; E269.N3K36 1989). The latter was originally published in 1973 as an exhibit catalog for the Smithsonian Institution's National Portrait Gallery. The amply illustrated text centers around the African-American pursuit of freedom in the revolutionary era through petitions, circular letters, court action, British and American military service, religious activism, and literary expression.

Black Laws of Virginia: A Summary of the Legislative Acts of Virginia Concerning Negroes from Earliest Times to the Present (Richmond: Whittet & Shepperson, 1936; E185.93.V8G9), by June Purcell Guild, presents the texts of several private laws relating to Virginia blacks who served in the American Revolution. In the chapter "War and the Negro," a 1783 law is cited:

During the Revolutionary War, many slaves were enlisted by their owners as substitutes for free persons, and were represented to the recruiting officers as free, and afterward the owners, contrary to the principles of justice have attempted to force the slaves to return to servitude. Because such slaves have contributed toward American liberty and independence, they are all deemed free and may sue, in forma pauperis, and may recover damages if detained.

Black Laws of Virginia also has information about an 1812 pension that was awarded to a Virginia black man named Aaron Weaver who served in the navy during the Revolutionary War, receiving "two dangerous wounds in an engagement at the mouth of the York River." Another pension was given by the Virginia legislature to Richard Nicken, "a man of color," who had enlisted for three years during the Revolutionary War.

In *Manuscript Sources in the Library of Congress for Research on the American Revolution* (Washington: Library of Congress, 1975; Z1238.U57 1957), John R. Sellers and his coauthors provide useful information about African-Americans who served with the patriots or the crown and about black refugees. In 1770 a black seaman, Crispus Attucks, was killed by British soldiers in Boston along with four others. American patriots used annual commemorations of this event—called the Boston Massacre—as a means of stirring revolutionary fervor and anti-British sentiment. Both the John Adams papers (MSS, microfilm 1639–1889, Adams Family Papers) and the Jabez Fitch diary (MSS, diary 1775–76) contain descriptions of anniversaries of the Boston Massacre. Paul Revere made probably the best known image from the revolutionary period when he did the etching known as "The Bloody Massacre perpetrated in King Street Boston on March 5th, 1770." Revere's etching, in the Prints and Photographs Division, shows British soldiers firing into a crowd that includes Attucks (PP FP XVIII R45Z, no. 1-A; repro. no. LC-USZ62-35522 or LC-USZC4-110).

Lord Dunmore's announcement promising freedom to all black men who would join him caused a great deal of consternation among the patriots. Manuscript Division holdings such as the papers of George Johnston in the William Johnston family collection (MSS, papers 1775–1866), the Edgehill-Randolph collection (MSS, microfilm of originals at the Massachusetts Institute of Technology, 1775–1827), and the Garrett Minor papers (MSS, papers 1765–98) have information about Dunmore's policies and the colonists' reaction to them. The Samuel Adams papers (MSS, photostats of originals at the New York Public Library, 1635–1826) include a few letters that discuss the role of blacks in revolutionary America. The George Washington collection (MSS, papers and microfilm 1697–1799) also includes comment on the debate about using blacks as soldiers. Papers of Continental Congress delegate Henry Laurens (MSS, papers 1724–92, microfilm 1747–96) include letters relating to his son John's plan for raising a regiment of slaves for the Continental Army. In addition to these papers, the Library holds reproductions of original Laurens materials at the South Carolina Historical Society in Charleston. The 1777 minutes of the Schenectady, New York, Committee of Correspondence, Safety, and Protection (MSS, Force Collection, 1777–78) contain orders relating to the control of Loyalists, Indians, and blacks.

Two orderly books called Great Britain, Army (MSS, journals 1781), have information about blacks who were assigned to work for British regiments. At Yorktown, where there were over one thousand African-American laborers and refugees, many blacks suffered from smallpox. A September 15, 1781, entry records that "Great abuses have been committed in victualling the Negroes, the Dep Qr Mr Genl has directions to receive the returns of the different departments, and to appoint a person to attend to the issuing of their provisions."

There was much controversy after the war about the slaves who were liberated by the British and others and subsequently taken to the West Indies, Canada, and England. Americans demanded their return or payment for their value. Great Britain Board of Commissioners for Superintending Embarkation of the British Army from New York (MSS, Force Papers microfilm

1783) papers state that the Americans attempted to prevent the "destruction, or carrying away of Negroes, or other property, of the American inhabitants," during the British evacuation.

The British side of this story can be followed in *Documents of the American Revolution, 1770–1783* (Dublin: Irish University Press, 1972–81; 21 vols. E203.G68 1972), edited by K. G. Davies, and the *Report on American Manuscripts in the Royal Institution of Great Britain* (Boston: Gregg Press, 1972; reprint, 4 vols. E267.G782), originally published by the Historical Manuscripts Commission of Great Britain in 1907. The complete microfilm collections from which these works are drawn are also available in Great Britain, Public Record Office, Colonial Office, Series 5 (MSS, microfilm 1739–1805) and Public Record Office, Carleton Papers (MSS, microfilm, 1747–83, PRO 30/55).

Images relating to the treatment and condition of slaves, the work of black servants such as groomsmen, or the incidental inclusion of African-Americans in group scenes at military or political gatherings can be located by consulting Donald Cresswell's *The American Revolution in Drawings and Prints* (Washington: Library of Congress, 1975; E209.U54 1975 or Z663.A835 MRR alcove), a comprehensive annotated guide to graphics in the Library's prints and photographs collections pertaining to the Revolutionary era, dating from 1765 to 1790. The volume indexes "Negroes" and "Africa" but also contains images in which blacks appear as part of crowd scenes, as in a German etching where a black man is present at the rear of a crowd protesting the Stamp Act in 1765.

Map holdings help show the location and distribution of the African-American population during the Revolutionary period. John R. Sellers and Patricia Molen Van Ee edited *Maps and Charts of North America and the West Indies, 1750–1789* (Washington: Library of Congress, 1981; Z6027.N68U54 1981), a guide to holdings

"Horrid Massacre in Virginia," 1831, pictures the Nat Turner rebellion. Woodcut from an antiabolitionist tract entitled Authentic and Impartial Narrative . . ., *by Samuel Warner ([New York]: Warner & West, 1831; F232.S7W2 Rare Bk). (LC-USZ62–38902)*

of revolutionary era maps with several entries under "Negroes." *The Atlas of Early American History: The Revolutionary Era, 1760–1790*, edited by Lester J. Cappon, Barbara Bartz Petchenik, and John H. Long (Princeton: Princeton University Press, 1976; G1201.S3A8 1976) shows locations of Revolutionary War battles, reconstructs the distribution of the slave population for 1775 and 1790, and displays the free black population in 1790.

FREE BLACKS IN A SLAVE SOCIETY

County landownership maps can be useful for locating rural residences of free blacks. During the 1850s cartographer Simon Martenet prepared such maps for a number of Maryland counties. Published immediately before the Civil War, they give detailed information about the rural and urban landscape of the southern states in the antebellum period (GM). Although the emphasis of these maps is white landownership, the Montgomery County, Maryland, map, for example, shows some of the free black homesteads that developed around the Quaker settlement of Sandy Spring.

Interestingly, one of the principals involved in the initial surveying of the District of Columbia was Benjamin Banneker, a black mathematician who worked as a surveyor. No maps bear Banneker's name, but Andrew Ellicott's 1794 map of the Territory of Columbia is based on the 1791–92 survey of the boundaries of the ten-mile square district in which Banneker played a role. Another useful set of maps associated with the early surveys establishing the federal district is a series of landownership surveys prepared by the city surveyor Nicholas King. These maps were primarily intended to show the relationship of existing buildings to proposed streets in the new capital city. Some of them, such as the plat for Notley Young's land, show not only the mansion house and associated outbuildings but also the slave quarters.

The daily lives of free blacks can be glimpsed in such manuscripts as the Roberts Family papers (MSS, papers 1734–1944), which include documents that African-Americans were required to carry and display upon demand in order to verify their free status as well as an 1832 contract for the construction of the first African Methodist Episcopal Church in Indiana. The papers of white educator Myrtilla Miner (MSS, microfilm 1825–1950) primarily concern her School for Free Colored Girls in Washington, D.C., in the 1850s, and contain essays and drawings by her students. The papers reflect the stiff opposition she encountered in this endeavor and include materials on topics such as slavery, feminism, and the Civil War. One of Miner's correspondents was Harriet Beecher Stowe.

Hiram Revels, born free in 1827, was the first black United States senator. In an autobiographical sketch, now in the Carter G. Woodson collection (MSS, papers 1796–1933), Revels stresses that during his early years the social climate for free blacks in North Carolina was relatively temperate:

Prior to the Nat Turner insurrection, in the state of Virginia, the state of North Carolina was noted for its mildness toward its free colored people, whom they allowed to vote, discuss political questions, hold religious meetings, preach the gospel together with some educational advantages. But after that insurrection they changed their policy in regard to free Negroes. For at the first meeting of their legislature, laws were passed depriving them of all political, religious, and educational privileges.

All of the other slaveholding states which did not have laws forbidding the education of slaves passed similar laws after the Turner rebellion.

The first page of a fourteen-page autobiographical statement in the hand of Hiram Revels, senator from Mississippi and the first of his race to serve in either house of Congress. (Carter G. Woodson collection, MSS)

A memoir by Daniel Russell (MSS, journal n.d.), who was born in Rappahannock County, Virginia, to a free mother and a slave father, includes some information about his early life. Writing about the difficulties that enslavement placed on his family, he says, "As my father was a slave he was deprived of the time he otherwise should have had. After he had completed his masters work, . . . he would return by twilight to the bosom of his family." About his mother, he writes, "She impressed in our minds the great beneficial results that pure honest characters and industrious habits would produce."

Free blacks were not generally accorded the same privileges as white citizens, as can be seen in Franklin Johnson's *The Development of State Legislation Concerning the Free Negro* (Westport, Conn.: Greenwood Press, 1979; KF4757.Z95 J63 1979, MicRR 37714), originally published in 1919. In several states blacks could vote and have free access to public places, but in others they could not. States changed their rulings regarding the rights and privileges of free blacks depending on the political climate. Pennsylvania had no racial prohibition and some blacks did exercise the right to vote until 1838, when voting in the state was restricted to white males. Blacks were not allowed to vote again until after the passage of the Fifteenth Amendment. The papers of James G. Birney (MSS, papers 1830–90) include a journal with research notes, probably compiled by William Birney in the 1890s, with entries relating to publications, laws, and printed speeches and articles affecting the status of African-Americans in the eighteenth and nineteenth centuries.

Also reviewing the social and legal status of free blacks in the North and South are Lorenzo Greene's 1942 study *The Negro in Colonial New England* (reprint, New York: Atheneum, 1968; E445.N5 G7 1968), *North of Slavery: The Negro in the Free States, 1790–1860* (Chicago: University of Chicago Press, 1961; E185.9.L5) by Leon Litwack, and Ira Berlin's *Slaves without Masters: The Free Negro in the Antebellum South* (New York: Pantheon Books, 1975; E185.18.B47 1975).

An extensive bibliographical essay about free blacks is found in volume 2 of Philip Sheldon Foner's *History of Black Americans* (Westport, Conn.: Greenwood Press, 1975–; E185.F5915). Foner's essay includes sections on restriction on freedom, self-purchase, economic status, education, churches, civic organizations, segregation, riots, voting, the black press, and black professionals. A collection of articles entitled *Free Blacks in America, 1800–1860* (Belmont, Calif.: Wadsworth Publishing Company, 1971; E185.B812), edited by John H. Bracey, Jr., August Meier, and Elliott Rudwick, yields information about the lives of free blacks in the states of Mississippi, North Carolina, New York, and California, and the cities of Charleston, New Orleans, Cincinnati, and Providence.

Volumes 1 and 2 of the series *Black Communities and Urban Development in America, 1720–1990* (New York: Garland Publishing, 1991; 10 vols. E185.5.B515 1991), edited by Kenneth L. Kusmer, are titled *The Colonial and Early National Period* and *Antebellum America*. The second includes articles by various authors about black communities in Charleston, Baton Rouge, New Orleans, Richmond, Memphis, Cincinnati, Washington, Philadelphia, New York, Buffalo, and Boston.

A full-length study of African-Americans in one local area, *Philadelphia's Black Elite: Activism, Accommodation, and the Struggle for Autonomy, 1787–1848* (Philadelphia: Temple University Press, 1988; F158.9.N4W56 1988), by Julie Winch, demonstrates the types of struggles that free blacks faced after the passage of the gradual abolition act of Pennsylvania in 1780. W. E. B. DuBois's earlier study, *The Philadelphia Negro* (Philadelphia: Published for the University, 1899; F158.9.N3D8) discusses the social and economic conditions of blacks in the city and traces the legislative history of race relations there.

A satirical series of broadsides about free blacks in Philadelphia in 1828 by cartoonist Edward W. Clay, entitled *Life in Philadelphia* (PP PGA-A Clay), shows small etchings of fictionalized, stereotyped "dandies," most of whom are black. Cartoons such as the series called the Bobalition of Slavery (Portfolio 52-no. 13a [LC-USZ62-40669], 53-no. 11 and no. 28, Rare Bk) ridicule celebrations by free blacks in Boston commemorating the abolition of the African slave trade.

By 1820 African-American musicians had formed bands in Philadelphia that achieved more than local popularity. Francis Johnson, the most eminent black band leader, composed marches and dance music which were published in arrangements, including his "Recognition March on the Independence of Hayti," for the piano and flute (Philadelphia: G. Willig, [182?]; M1.A13J Case). The manuscript of his "General Cadwalader's March" (ML96.J742 Case) is another surviving example of his work. In 1837–38 Johnson's band toured France and England, the first American musical ensemble to do so.

Other black Philadelphia bandmasters are James Hemmenway, who composed "The Philadelphia Hop Waltz" (Philadelphia: G. Willig [18??]; M1.A13 H Case) and Isaac Hazzard, who wrote the "Miss Lucy Neal Quadrille" (Philadelphia: G. Willig, 1844; M1.A12I9). Justin Holland was a highly skilled performer on the guitar whose tutor for that instrument, *Holland's Comprehensive Method for the Guitar* (Boston: Oliver Ditson Co., 1875; MT382.H73), was widely accepted.

In New Orleans a group of well-trained free black musicians nurtured by the free black community was able to support itself playing for dances and parades. Some of their composi-

"Have you any flesh coloured silk stockings, young man?," an etching by Edward W. Clay from Life in Philadelphia (plate 11), published by W. Simpson, May 1829. (PP PGA–Clay, Edward W.–Life in Philadelphia, A size. LC-USZC4–2441)

tions were published locally, but eventually the members of this group emigrated to France in search of better opportunities. Such names as Richard Lambert, Lucien Lambert, Edmund Dédé, and Samuel Snaër are described with portraits, lists of compositions, and reference bibliography in Lucius R. Wyatt's "Six Composers of Nineteenth-Century New Orleans" in the *Black Music Research Newsletter* (Spring 1987: 4–9; ML3556.B583).

Free blacks expressed their political views in a number of ways. One was through regular meetings—called conventions—for the purpose of taking concerted action to promote the political, social, and economic uplift of the race.

The Library's general collection includes a number of books, articles, and proceedings relating to these conventions. A general introduction to the convention movement is provided in John W. Cromwell's article on "The Early Negro Convention Movements" (*American Negro Academy Occasional Paper,* no. 9; MicRR 22541).

Howard Bell was among the first to write scholarly accounts of the conventions, including his Northwestern University doctoral dissertation, *A Survey of the Negro Convention Movement, 1830–1864* (New York: Arno Press, 1969; E185.B38 1969). He edited *Minutes of the Proceedings of the National Negro Conventions 1830–64* (New York: Arno Press and the New York Times, 1969; E185.5.B44 1969). Philip S. Foner and George E. Walker edited published materials from twelve conventions in *Proceedings of the Black State Conventions, 1840–1865* (Philadelphia: Temple University Press, 1979–; E184.5.P75).

One of the national organizations advocating emancipation and equal opportunities for blacks from 1794 to 1829, a period during which twenty-four conventions were held, was the American Convention for Promoting the Abolition of Slavery and Improving the Condition of the African Race. The convention, which attempted to protect and improve conditions for free blacks, published and circulated antislavery tracts, petitioned Congress and state legislatures for abolition, advocated civil rights for all people regardless of color, prepared guidelines for local conventions, collated information about state slavery laws, and performed other tasks designed to hasten the abolition of slavery. With the establishment of the American Antislavery Society in 1831, however, interest in the convention waned. No conventions were held between 1830 and 1837, and in 1838 delegations from Pennsylvania, New York, and Delaware met and officially dissolved the American Convention.

Because no library owns a complete set of the original convention proceedings, Peter Bergman Publishers made a special effort to acquire a comprehensive collection. The publisher borrowed scattered copies from the libraries and reprinted them in a three-volume series entitled *The American Convention for Promoting the Abolition of Slavery and Improving the Condition of the African Race* (New York: Bergman Publishers, 1969; 3 vols. E446.A513). Unabridged, the series includes minutes, resolutions, reports, and tracts and is available in the Library's general collections. Some of the original convention publications are in the Rare Book and Special Collections Division.

AFRICAN-AMERICAN WRITERS

Concurrent with the political movements, the free black community and some slave masters nurtured literary endeavors. African-Americans expressed themselves in poetry before they wrote short stories, plays, novels, or other literary forms. Most celebrated of African-American poets of the eighteenth century is Phillis Wheatley, who published *Poems on Various Subjects: Religious and Moral* (London: A. Bell, 1773; PS866.W55 1773 Rare Bk) just before the Revolutionary War. Enslaved in Africa when she was about eight, Wheatley was purchased by John Wheatley of Boston and educated by her master. Proving herself to be a precocious student, Phillis began writing poetry at thirteen. *Poems* was published in London in 1773, where Wheatley was sent by her owners to recuperate from ill health. The volume includes Wheatley's poem "To the Right Honourable William, Earl of Dartmouth":

> Should you, my lord, while you peruse my song,
> Wonder from whence my love of *Freedom* sprung,

Whence flow these wishes for the common
   good,
By feeling hearts alone best understood,
I, young in life, by seeming cruel fate
Was snatch'd from *Afric's* fancy'd happy seat:
What pangs excruciating must molest,
What sorrows labour in my parent's breast?
Steel'd was that soul and by no misery mov'd
That from a father seiz'd his babe belov'd:
Such, such my case. And can I then but pray
Others may never feel tyrannic sway?

Wheatley was freed as an adult. An extensive bibliography of works relates to her poetry, and several biographies have been written, including three by William Henry Robinson: *Phillis Wheatley: A Bio-Bibliography* (Boston: G.K. Hall, 1981; Z8969.285.R62); *Phillis Wheatley and Her Writings* (New York: Garland, 1984; PS866.W5Z688 1984), and *Phillis Wheatley in the Black American Beginnings* (Detroit: Broadside Press, 1975; PS866.W5Z69).

An extensive study of nineteenth-century African-American poetry is Joan Sherman's *Invisible Poets* (Urbana: University of Illinois Press, 1989; PS153.N5S48 1989), which identifies unknown and unheralded black poets, noting that in the nineteenth century there were at least 130 blacks who published poetry, five of whom were born in slavery. Much of the early black poetry appeared in periodicals of the day. Another of Sherman's works is *African-American Poetry of the Nineteenth Century* (Urbana: University of Illinois Press, 1992; PS591.N4A35 1992).

A historical and critical discussion of black poets and their literature is found in J. Saunders Redding's *To Make a Poet Black* (Ithaca: Cornell University Press, 1988; PS153.N5R4 1988). Two indexes by Dorothy Hilton Chapman identify poetry: *Index to Black Poetry* (Boston: G.K. Hall, 1974; PS153.N5C45) and *Index to Poetry by Black American Women* (New York: Greenwood Press, 1986; Z1229.N39C45 1986). An important anthology is Langston Hughes's and Arna Bontemps's *The Poetry of the Negro, 1746–1970* (Gar-

den City, N.Y.: Doubleday, 1949; PN6109.7.H8). Blyden Jackson and Louis D. Rubin's *Black Poetry in America: Two Essays in Historical Interpretation* lists reference sources relating to black poetry by chronological period. Biographical information on the major authors may be obtained from *Afro-American Writers before the Harlem Renaissance* (Detroit: Gale, 1986; PS153.N5A393 1986).

Other sources for early poetry are Dorothy Porter Wesley's *North American Negro Poets, a Bibliographical Checklist of Their Writings, 1760–1944* (Hattiesburg, Miss.: The Book Farm, 1945; Z1361.N39P6 Rare Bk), and William Henry Robinson's *Early Black American Poets* (Dubuque, Iowa: W. C. Brown, 1969; PS591.N4R6).

Black poets like Frances E. W. Harper and George Whitfield used poetry and other literary forms to protest against the institution of slavery and to argue for equal treatment of all regardless of race. Whitfield's *Remarks on the Injustice and Immorality of Slavery in Eight Letters* (London: J. Stephens, 1830; MicRR 82/534 H) is such a protest. Harper published several collections of verse that exhorted slaves to action and elicited the sympathy of whites for the plight of slaves. Her volume *Poems on Miscellaneous Subjects* (Boston: J.B. Yerrington, 1854; PS1799.H7P7 1854) includes "The Slave Auction," whose first two stanzas evoke compassion:

The sale began—young girls were there,
   Defenceless in their wretchedness,
Whole stifled sobs of deep despair
   Revealed their anguish and distress.

And mothers stood with streaming eyes,
   And saw their dearest children sold;
Unheeded rose their bitter cries,
   While tyrants bartered them for gold.

Various forms of antebellum African-American literature are treated in *The Negro Author: His Development in America to 1900* (New York: Columbia University Press, 1931;

PS153.N5L65), by Vernon Loggins, who discusses poetry, fiction, and nonfiction writers. Benjamin Brawley compiled selections of black authors' work and provided a historical and critical context for them in *Early Negro American Writers* (Chapel Hill: University of North Carolina Press, 1935; PS508.N3B7). The work of black poets such as Phillis Wheatley, Lucy Terry, and George Moses Horton, early prose writers such as David Walker, Lemuel Haynes, and Frederick Douglass, and early African-American journalists is treated in *The Long Beginning, 1746–1895* (Baton Rouge: Louisiana State University Press, 1989; PS153.N5J33 1989) by Blyden Jackson, the first volume of the two-volume series entitled A History of Afro-American Literature.

The New Cavalcade: African American Writing from 1760 to the Present (Washington: Howard University Press, 1991; PS508.N3N48 1991), edited by Arthur P. Davis, J. Saunders Redding, and Joyce Ann Joyce, provides an anthology of "the best prose and poetry" written by blacks. Dorothy Porter Wesley's "Early American Negro Writings: A Bibliographical Study," in the *Papers of the Bibliographical Society of America* 39 (May 1945; Z1008.B51P) reviews sources with information about the life and work of early writers. Little-known black writing that appeared in such early periodicals as the *Weekly Anglo-African* (New York: Arno Press, 1968; E185.A582), the first black literary magazine, published from 1859 to 1865, can be found in *Black Literature, 1827–1940* (Alexandria, Va.: Chadwyck-Healey, Inc., 1987; MicRR, microfiche 90/7069). Trudier Harris's and Thadious Davis's *Afro-American Writers before the Harlem Renaissance* (Detroit: Gale, 1986; PS153.B5A393 1986) and Bernard W. Bell's *The Afro-American Novel and Its Tradition* (Amherst: University of Massachusetts Press, 1987; PS153.N5B43 1987) review the work of antebellum African-American writers.

Lucy Terry's "Bars Fight" (1746), now recognized as the first known poem by an African-American woman, is reprinted in Ann Shockley's *Afro-American Women Writers: An Anthology and Critical Guide* (Boston: G.K. Hall, 1988; PS508.N3A36 1988), a history and critical introduction to early black women's writings. Jean Fagan Yellin and Cynthia D. Bond provide another useful source of information about women in *The Pen Is Ours: A Listing of Writings by and about African-American Women before 1910* (New York: Oxford University Press, 1991; Z1229.N39Y44 1991).

The Library holds many editions of the works of black writers. Only one year after Harriet Beecher Stowe's *Uncle Tom's Cabin* (Boston: J. P. Jewett, 1852; 2 vols. PS2954.U5 1852d) captured national attention, William Wells Brown published *Clotel: or, The President's Daughter* (1853; reprint, New York: Collier Books, 1970; PZ23.B8199), believed to be the earliest novel written by an African-American. Tracing the misfortunes of three generations of slave women, Brown depicted the injustices of slavery and the peculiar institution's assaults upon the black family. Brown, who had escaped from his Kentucky slave master in his youth, was active on the antislavery lecture circuit and served as a delegate to the World Peace Congress in Paris in 1849. Other black literary "firsts" for Brown include *The Escape* (reprint, Philadelphia: Rhistoric Publications, 1969; PS1139.B9E8 1969), the first play by an African-American, and *Three Years in Europe* (London: C. Gilpin, 1852; MicRR 79267), the first travel account. Publisher, journalist, and abolitionist James Redpath issued the campfire edition of Brown's popular *Clotelle: A Tale of the Southern States* (Boston: J. Redpath, 1864; PZ3.B8199 Rare Bk) to "relieve the monotony" of camp life of the Union soldiers and "kindle their zeal in the cause of universal emancipation."

The first novel known to be written by a

black woman in the United States is Harriet E. Wilson's *Our Nig* (Boston: Rand & Avery, 1859; Juv Spl Coll, Rare Bk). Martin R. Delany's *Blake: or, The Huts of America, a Novel* (Boston: Beacon Press, 1970; PZ3.D3737 B13) was initially serialized in the *Weekly Anglo-African* (New York: Arno Press, 1968; E185.A582) during 1861 and 1862. Delany was also the author of several nonfiction works, including *The Condition, Elevation, Emigration, and Destiny of the Colored People of the United States; Politically Considered* (Philadelphia: Author, 1852; MicRR 32736 E, formerly E185.D33).

Two finding guides identify dramatic works written by blacks: William French's *Afro-American Poetry and Drama, 1760–1975* (Detroit: Gale Research Co., 1979; Z1229.N39A37) and *Nineteenth Century American Drama: A Finding Guide* by Don L. Hixon and Don A. Hennessee (Metuchen, N.J.: Scarecrow, 1977; PS632.H57). Hixon and Hennessee's guide *Three Centuries of Drama: American and English, 1500–1800* (New York: Readex Microprint Corp., 1956–; MicRR Microopaque 84/2) lists minstrel plays—comedies with white actors in blackface or with black actors—and plays that had blacks in their casts.

Other reference works on African-American drama are James V. Hatch's *Black Image on the American Stage: A Bibliography of Plays and Musicals, 1776–1970* (New York: Drama Book Store Publications, 1970; Z5784.N4H35) and Bernard Peterson's *Early Black American Playwrights and Dramatic Writers: A Biographical Directory and Catalog of Plays, Films, and Broadcasting Scripts* (New York: Greenwood Press, 1990; PS153.N5 P44 1990).

Black dramatists from the earliest period can be found in James V. Hatch's *Black Playwrights, 1823–1977: An Annotated Bibliography of Plays* (New York: Bowker, 1977; Z1231.D7H37) and its sequel, *More Black American Playwrights: A Bibliography* (Metuchen, N.J.: Scarecrow, 1978; Z1229.N39A73). *Black American Playwrights,*

1800 to the Present: A Bibliography (Metuchen, N.J.: Scarecrow, 1976; Z1229.N39A7) by Esther Spring Arata and Nicholas J. Rotati provides the names of plays, indicates whether the play or actors won awards, and reviews the critical appraisal of the works.

Rhonnie Lynn Washington's *Dissertations Concerning Black Theatre* (Albany, N.Y.: State University of New York, 1988; Z5781.W35 1988) indexes theses such as Fannin S. Belcher's "The Place of the Negro in the Evolution of the American Theater, 1767 to 1940" (MicRR 69–176658) and Jeanne-Marie Anderson's "Dramas by Black American Playwrights Produced on the New York Professional Stage" (MicRR DDJ 78–05440). Also useful are Sterling Brown's *Negro Poetry and Drama* (Washington: Associates in Negro Folk Education, 1937; PS153.N5B68) and the symposium addresses in "The American Theatre: A Cultural Process," in *The American Theatre: A Sum of Its Parts* (New York: Samuel French, Inc., 1969; PN2220.S9 1969). The two-volume work edited by Errol Hill, *The Theatre of Black America: A Collection of Critical Essays* (New York: Applause, 1987; PN2270.A35T48 1987), offers critical discussion.

Black plays can be found in James V. Hatch's *Black Theater USA: Forty-Five Plays by Black Americans, 1847–1974* (New York: The Free Press, 1974; PS628.N4H3) and *Roots of African American Drama: An Anthology of Early Plays, 1858–1938*, edited by Leo Hamalian and James V. Hatch (Detroit: Wayne State University Press, 1991; PS628.N4R66 1991), which includes William Wells Brown's *Escape, or, A Leap for Freedom* (1858) and Pauline Hopkins's *Peculiar Sam, or The Underground Railroad* (1879).

Works by black antebellum writers as well as materials by whites about blacks are reproduced in the *Early American Imprint* microform series, 1639–1800 and 1801–19 (New York: Redex Microprint Co., 1964–1984+; MicRR 85/431), including some of the earliest writing of social, cultural, historical, or literary importance. Examples are two poems entitled "Slavery" by white poet Hannah More (nos. 21269, 21270), and Benjamin Banneker's almanacs (no. 23148—1792; nos. 24071, 24072—1793; no. 25140—1794; no. 26608–13—1795; no. 28231—1796; no. 30019–20—1797), published from 1792 to 1797 by Goddard and Angell in Baltimore, Maryland. Banneker's 1791 letter to Secretary of State Thomas Jefferson on racial prejudice and slavery is also reproduced (no. 24073).

THE BLACK PRESS

We wish to plead our own cause. Too long have others spoken for us. Too long has the publick been deceived by misrepresentations, in things which concern us dearly. . . .

With these words in its editorial, the first issue of the first black-controlled newspaper in America appeared on March 12, 1827. The founders of *Freedom's Journal* (MicRR 22992.E), John B. Russwurm and Samuel Cornish, chose a masthead that stated that the paper was "devoted to the improvement of the colored population." Although published in the format of a newspaper, the contents of the journal were similar to the features of a magazine. Samuel Cornish resigned shortly after the paper's first issue, and Russwurm edited the work alone until 1829, when Cornish again resumed the editorship and changed its name to *Rights for All*. Issues of both papers are available in the Newspaper and Current Periodical Reading Room.

Specific information on black newspapers is available in "The Black Press Held by the Library of Congress," compiled by John Pluge, Jr., October 1977, for the Newspaper and Current Periodical Reading Room and Armistead Pride's *Negro Newspapers on Microfilm: A Selected List* (Washington: Library of Congress Photo-

Frederick Douglass (ca. 1817–1895) was born a slave in Tuckahoe, Maryland, but escaped in 1838. Despite the difficult work and travel schedules he kept as an abolitionist, journalist, diplomat, and civil servant, Douglass and his wife Anna brought up five children. (PP. LC-USZ62–24165)

duplication Service, 1953; Z6944.N39P7). Pluge's list is arranged in two parts: by state and local area and alphabetically by name of newspaper.

In *The Negro Press in the United States* (c1922; reprint, College Park, Md.: McGrath Publishing Co., 1968; PN4888.N4D4 1968), Frederick Detweiler states that there were twenty-four black periodicals published before the Civil War. In *Before the Mayflower: A History of Black America* (5th ed., Chicago: Johnson Publishing Co., 1982; E185.B4 1982), however, Lerone Bennett notes that forty black newspapers were published before the war. Armistead Pride's *The Black Press: A Bibliography* (Jefferson City, Mo.: n.p., 1968; Z6944.N39P68), Irvine Garland Penn's *The Afro-American Press and Its Editors* (Springfield, Mass.: Willey & Co., 1891; PN4888.N4P4 Rare Bk; New York: Arno Press, 1969; PN4888.N4P4 1969), and Roland Wolseley's *The Black Press, U.S.A.* (reprint, Ames, Iowa: Iowa State University Press, 1990; PN4888.N4W6) give general information on black newspapers.

One of the best known and most articulate free black spokesmen during the antebellum years, Frederick Douglass published the newspaper *North Star* from 1847 to 1851, later calling it the *Frederick Douglass Paper.* It included articles and opinion pieces advocating the abolition of slavery, as did the *Douglass' Monthly* (MicRR 5062). Douglass's speeches and writings and comment on them are found in *The Frederick Douglass Papers* (New Haven: Yale University Press, 1979–; E449.D733), edited by John Blassingame and others. The volumes include "I Have Come to Tell You Something about Slavery" (1841), "The Horrors of Slavery and England's Duty to Free the Bondsman" (1846), "Is the Constitution Pro-Slavery? A Debate between Frederick Douglass, Charles C. Burleigh, Gerrit Smith, Parker Pillsbury, Samuel Ringgold Ward, and Stephen S. Foster" (1850), and "The Dred Scott Decision" (1857).

Anna Murray Douglass (ca. 1813–1882) was born free on Maryland's Eastern Shore, moving to Baltimore to find work at age seventeen. She met and fell in love with a slave named Frederick Bailey and helped him escape to the North, where she married him. He changed his name to Frederick Douglass. (Photolithograph, Frederick Douglass Papers, MSS. LC-MS–18879–3)

THE BLACK CHURCH

After being pulled from the pews in 1787 while worshipping with an integrated congregation in Philadelphia, a group of black believers, led by Richard Allen and Absalom Jones, formed the Free African Society for worship and mutual aid among black Philadelphians. Two formal groups subsequently grew out of this organization: the African Methodist Episcopal denomination, led by Allen, and the Episcopal Church of Saint Thomas, led by Jones. The *Early American Imprint* microform series, 1609–1800 and 1801–19 (New York: Readex Microprint Co., 1964–84 + ; MicRR 85/431) includes a twenty-one-page publication *Articles of Association of the African Methodist Episcopal Church* (no. 36095), originally published in 1799. The A.M.E. Church also published a newspaper entitled the *Christian Recorder* (MicRR 51537).

The humanitarian contributions of Richard Allen and the members of the A.M.E. Church during a yellow fever epidemic in Philadelphia are recorded in *A Narrative of the Proceedings of the Black People, During the Late Awful Calamity in Philadelphia, in the Year 1793* (Philadelphia: William W. Woodward, 1794; Am Imp Coll 1794, Rare Bk). African-American minister Noah Calwell Cannon, a leader in the A.M.E. Church in Zanesville, Ohio, advocated brotherly love as a remedy to race prejudice among men. His *Rock of Wisdom: An Explanation of the Sacred Scriptures* (n.p., 1833; BS511.C2 Rare Bk) is considered one of the earliest theological works by a black person.

Images relating to the A.M.E. Church include an 1844 lithographic portrait of Juliann Jane Tillman, a preacher in the A.M.E. Church in Philadelphia, done by A. Hoffy (PP PGA-A Hoffy; LC-USZ62-54596) and a portrait of Rev. R. T. Breckenridge in Bethel Church receiving a gold snuff box from Rev. Daniel Stokes on De-

"Mrs. Juliann Jane Tillman, Preacher of the A.M.E. Church," Philadelphia. Lithograph from life by A. Hoffy, printed by P.S. Duval, 1844. (PP. LC-USZ62– 54596)

cember 18, 1845, as a gift of gratitude from the colored people of Baltimore (PP PGA-B Presentation; LC-USZ62-22957). Photographs of the Bethel A.M.E. Church in Richmond, Wayne County, Indiana, built in 1854 (PP HABS IND, 89-RICH, 8–), document architectural settings. Other denominations are represented in the collections as well, by, for instance, a portrait of Rev. Christopher Rush, second superintendent of the Methodist Episcopal Zion Church in America (PP PGA-A–Currier, N., repro. no. LC-USZ62–15339).

The records of the Presbyterian Church in the U.S.A., Presbytery of Washington City (MSS, records 1823–1936) include periodic reports noting the size and condition of denominational African-American Sunday schools and churches in the region. An 1825 report states that "There are several very encouraging Sunday Schools for people of colour, some of whom, through missionary labours & other means, manifest a pleasing change of deportment & give evidence of piety" (vol. 1, p. 33).

Beginning in the early nineteenth century, independent African-American churches began to issue appropriate hymnals for their own use. The first of these, Bishop Richard Allen's *A Collection of Spiritual Songs and Hymns* (Philadelphia: John Ormrod, 1801) was compiled for use in the A.M.E. church. A copy can be found in the Microform Reading Room in the *Early American Imprints,* 2d series, edited by Ralph R. Shaw and Richard H. Shoemaker (New York: Readex Microprint Co., 1964–82; MicRR no. 2 [1801–20]; nos. 38, 39). Like most early hymnals it contains words but no music. For a history of the hymnody of a prominent black church, see Jon Michael Spencer's "The Hymnody of the African Methodist Episcopal Church" in *American Music* (8 [Fall 1990]:274–93; ML1.A497).

A comprehensive bibliography of African-American religion, *The Howard University Bibli-ography of African and Afro-American Religious Studies* (Wilmington, Del.: Scholarly Resources, 1977; Z1361.N39W555), was compiled by Ethel L. Williams and Clifton F. Brown. It begins with references to the African background, including publications relating to ancient Egypt and Kush and works about missionary activities in Africa, and then provides citations to sources on slavery in the United States and its manifestations in church settings and on the impact of the African background on black denominations.

Another bibliography, *Directory of African American Religious Bodies: A Compendium by the Howard University School of Divinity,* edited by Wardell J. Payne (Washington: Howard University Press, 1991; BR563.N4D57 1991), not only serves as a directory but contains encyclopedic entries on the history of black denominations, providing, for example, date founded, membership, and regularly scheduled meetings.

Carter G. Woodson's *The History of the Negro Church* (Washington: Associated Publishers, 1921; BR563.N4W6) was the first general history of the black church. In it, Woodson explains the motivation of blacks for establishing their own churches, recounts the role of the missionaries in their development, discusses pioneering black preachers, and traces the rise of early black denominations and sects. He also relates how the church became for blacks an agency of pride and self-respect.

The impact of slavery on Africans arriving in America included loss of African languages and ethnic ties. In *The Negro Church in America* (New York: Schocken Books, c1963; BR563.N4F7), E. Franklin Frazier begins with enslavement and then relates how free blacks, wishing to establish their own churches, founded the Free African Society in Philadelphia. Frazier gives biographical accounts of prominent early black churchmen Absalom Jones, Richard Allen, and Peter Williams.

A general history, *The Black Church in the African American Experience* (Durham: Duke University Press, 1990; BR563.N4L55 1990), presents, according to authors C. Eric Lincoln and Lawrence A. Mamiya, a wide-ranging study of churches and clergy of the seven major black denominations.

Essays and histories of prominent preachers, institutions, and doctrines of the black church are found in David W. Wills and Richard Newman's *Black Apostles at Home and Abroad: Afro-Americans and the Christian Mission from the Revolution to Reconstruction* (Boston: G. K. Hall, 1982; BR563.N4B564 1982) and *African American Religious Studies: An Interdisciplinary Anthology* (Durham: Duke University Press, 1989; BR563.N4A36 1989), edited by Gayraud Wilmore. *Black Apostles* provides "a collective portrait of some of the leading figures in Afro-American religious life in the period between the Revolution and Reconstruction," including Lemuel Haynes and his Vermont ministry, Rebecca Cox Jackson, and Henry Highland Garnet. Essays in *African American Religious Studies* express the defining qualities of black religion, showing how elements of black religion differ from other religions. Particularly relevant to the slavery experience is C. Eric Lincoln's introductory essay on the development of black religion and Joseph Washington's essay on folk religion.

AFRICAN COLONIZATION

Colonization of freed blacks in Africa as an alternative to their emancipation in the United States appealed to a small percentage of blacks and whites. In 1787 England established the colony of Sierra Leone on the west coast of Africa to resettle blacks from the West Indies, Canada, and England who had been emancipated by their masters or rewarded for service in the Revolutionary War. The William Thornton papers (MSS, papers 1741–1858) include a few letters relating to the colonization of African-Americans in Sierra Leone.

Paul Cuffe (sometimes spelled Cuffee) (MSS, microfilm of originals in the New Bedford Public Library 1742–1963), a Quaker shipmaster from Massachusetts of mixed black and native American ancestry, attempted to win funds from Congress to settle black Americans in Sierra Leone. Hampered in this endeavor by the War of 1812, Cuffe decided to take thirty-eight blacks to Sierra Leone at his own expense in 1815. Before he was able to fully develop his colonization experiment, he died, but not before he was able to make a presentation about his plans before a group that would name itself the American Society for Colonizing the Free People of Color in the United States.

Cuffe, who became prosperous after the Revolution, published his *Memoir of Captain Paul Cuffee, a Man of Color* (York, Eng.: W. Alexander, 1812; E185.97.C96 Rare Bk) telling of his successful 1780 petition to the state to grant him, his brother, and other free blacks the right to vote and other privileges of citizenship accorded to taxpayers. A biographical sketch by his great grandson Horatio Howard, *A Self-Made Man, Capt. Paul Cuffee* (New York? 1913?; E185.97.C96H68 Mur Coll, Rare Bk), includes photographs of a ceremony placing a monument at Cuffe's grave.

Although some of the founders of the American Colonization Society (ACS) (MSS, microfilm 1792–1964) simply wanted to rid the United States of free blacks, there were others who favored the end of slavery but did not believe that blacks and whites could or should live together as equals in America. With this view the founders evolved the idea of removing willing blacks from the United States and returning them to Africa where they could enjoy freedom without daily competition with whites. Evangelical members of the society hoped that the freed blacks would be effective agents of the gospel in Africa. The records in this collection give information about the establishment of Liberia as the settlement for black colonists, efforts to manage and defend the colony, fund-raising for the society, the recruitment of willing settlers, and opportunities for blacks to lead in the development and government of the new African nation.

The diary of Christian Wiltberger (MSS, microfilm 1820–21), an American Colonization Society agent, records his journey aboard the schooner *Nautilus* to West Africa as part of the society's efforts to found an African colony, and includes his comments on various internal problems within the society, difficulties encountered in obtaining land in Sierra Leone, and events leading to the choice of the Liberian settlement. Daniel Coker (MSS, microfilm 1821, Force Collection), a black settler in the initial ACS settlement in Sierra Leone, was a Methodist minister who kept a journal recording daily events of settlers and society agents, including illnesses, deaths, weather, and political conditions. Because of difficulties in Sierra Leone, in 1822 settlers with the aid of Lt. Robert Stockton, captain of the United States Schooner *Nautilus*, traveled a short distance south on the African coast to purchase land at Cape Mesurado to found a settlement that would later be named Monrovia (after President James Monroe), and would eventually become the capital of the Liberian Republic. Both the Colonization Society records and the Joseph Jenkins Roberts Family papers (MSS, papers 1809–1977) document aspects of that freeborn Virginia black's ascendancy to the presidency of Liberia in 1847 and yield information about the development of the Liberian nation. The papers of James G. Birney (MSS, papers 1830–90), detail his work with colonization and abolition efforts.

The Colonization Society's periodical, the *African Repository and Colonial Journal* (MicRR 19711, 01104 no. 49), was first published in 1825 and continued to be issued each month until the last decade of that century. This periodical, which provides a vast amount of information about Liberia including passenger lists of black Americans who settled there, is available on microfilm and in the Rare Book and Special Collections Division along with the ACS annual reports and publications, as well as dozens of volumes on the history of the colonization movement. Svend Holsoe's *Bibliography on Liberia* (Newark: Department of Anthropology, University of Delaware, 1971–; Z3821.H6) lists books and articles about Liberia and publications relating to colonization. Numerous books and reports have been prepared by state historical societies. Two interesting scholarly works about Liberia are *Dear Master: Letters of a Slave Family* (Athens: University of Georgia Press, 1990; E444.D42), edited by Randall Miller, and *Slaves No More: Letters from Liberia, 1833–1869* (Lexington: University Press of Kentucky, 1980; DT633.2), edited by Bell I. Wiley, both of which include correspondence between black settlers in Liberia and their former owners, relatives, or friends in the United States. Several useful histories of the colonization movement are Charles Henry Huberich's *Political and Legislative History of Liberia: A Documentary History of the Constitutions, Laws, and Treaties* (New York: Central Book Co., 1947; 2 vols. DT632.H8), P. J. Staudenraus's *The African Colonization Movement, 1816–65* (New York: Columbia University Press, 1961; E448.S78), and Tom Wing Shick's *Behold the Promised Land: A History of Afro-American Settler Society in Nineteenth Century Liberia* (Baltimore: Johns Hopkins University Press, 1980; DT633.S47).

Approximately 550 photographs in the Prints and Photographs Division depict founders and promoters of the American Colonization Soci-

An unidentified woman, possibly Mrs. Urias McGill. Daguerreotype by Augustus Washington, ca. 1850s. (PP DAG Coll no. 1029)

ety, nineteenth-century Liberian officials and their activities, and, principally, the life of the indigenous West African peoples. The collection, arranged by subject, is described in the divisional catalog. Of special interest is the group of twenty-nine daguerreotype and four tintype portraits (PP lot 8554-DAG), which includes portraits of the first president of the Liberian Republic, Joseph Jenkins Roberts, and his wife Jane, both of whom were American-born mulattoes (PP lot 8554–DAG 1000, 1001; repro. no. LC-USZ62-41178, -41177).

The ACS images include several daguerreotype portraits by a free black photographer named Augustus Washington. He is the earliest black photographer in America whose work is known to have survived. Born in the early 1820s, Washington began practicing daguerreotypy in Hanover, New Hampshire, about 1843 while attending Dartmouth College. In 1844 he moved to Hartford, Connecticut, where he operated a daguerrean studio from about 1847 until 1853. In 1854 he moved to Liberia, operating a studio there for a year. He worked as an itinerant photographer in Sierra Leone and Liberia but no examples of this work are known to have survived. Included in the ACS collection are Washington's portraits of Liberian President Stephen Allen Benson (PP lot 8554–DAG 1022; LC-USZ62-41188), two individuals, possibly Mr. and Mrs. Urias McGill (PP lot 8554–DAG 1028, 1029), and two unidentified individuals (PP lot 8554–DAG 1013, 1017; LC-USZ62-41179, -41183).

Twenty-two maps accessioned with ACS records show early settlements in Liberia, indigenous political subdivisions, and some of the lots that were assigned to the settlers (GM). Also in the Geography and Map Division collections are several maps of nineteenth-century Liberia, one of which is a map that ACS agent Jehudi Ashmun prepared for his book *History of the American Colony in Liberia, from December 1821 to 1823* (Washington: Way and Gideon, 1826; MicRR 58315 DT). Another shows the dates that certain areas of Liberia were ceded to the society by indigenous chiefs. A detailed map of Liberia (1879) by Benjamin Anderson, probably the same black American explorer who wrote the *Narrative of a Journey to Musardu* (New York: W. Green, 1870; DT625.A54), reflects his travels to the Liberian interior.

Colonization schemes were launched by other organizations as well. A letterbook of James Redpath (MSS, microfilm 1861), a journalist, abolitionist, and educator who emigrated from Scotland to the United States and worked for the Haitian government, contains correspondence relating to his duties as general agent of emigration to Haiti and commercial agent for Haiti at Philadelphia. Most of his work involved recruiting free blacks, chiefly from New York, Boston, Philadelphia, Washington, D.C., and Canada. His correspondents include William H. Seward, Charles Sumner, and various Haitian officials.

A facsimile of a minstrel song about the Haitian emigration, "Ching a Ring Chaw" (originally entitled "Sambo's Dress to he' Bred'rin") is available in the Music Division in *Series of Old American Songs* (Providence: Brown University Library, 1936; M1629.B89S4 Case). The hopes of the emigrants are in the lyrics:

Dar too we are sure to make our darters de
fine lad-e,
An wen dey husbans take, dey bove the
common grad-e
An den perhaps our son, he rise in glorious
splender,
An be like Washington, he contry's defender.

Free blacks and many whites were not content that only a small percentage of the black population was free. From the earliest days of slavery, concerned Americans waged efforts to abolish slavery.

Joseph Jenkins Roberts, born in Virginia to free parents, migrated to Liberia in 1829, was appointed governor by the American Colonization Society in 1842, and became Liberia's first president when it proclaimed independence in July 1847. Daguerreotype by Rufus Anson, ca. 1848. (PP DAG Coll no. 1000. LC-USZ62–44732)

CHAPTER THREE

ABOLITIONISTS, ANTISLAVERY MOVEMENTS, AND THE RISE OF THE SECTIONAL CONTROVERSY

Protests against the African slave trade began as soon as it became obvious that the peculiar institution was going to find a place in American life. Before and during the Revolutionary War many colonists discussed the contradiction that arose when they demanded freedom from England for themselves while some of them held African-Americans in bondage. Debates during the Constitutional Convention proved that slavery was a volatile national issue that could be handled only by compromise. The compromises reached, however, were unsatisfactory to northerners and southerners alike, and the debates between slave and free states and between abolitionists and slaveholders became increasingly acrimonious after the turn of the nineteenth century as new states requested admission to the Union.

ANTISLAVERY LITERATURE

Many abolitionists published their protests or aired them in public forums with published proceedings, resulting in the development of a vast array of antislavery literature. Eighteenth-century sermons and orations by Quakers and others against the evils and injustices of the slave trade, including Anthony Benezet's *Observations on the Inslaving, Importing, and Purchasing of Negroes* (Germantown, Pa.: Christopher Sower, 1760; Am Imp Coll 1760, Rare Bk), James Swan's *Dissuasion to Great-Britain and the Colonies, from the Slave Trade to Africa, Shewing the Injustice Thereof, &c* (Boston: E. Russell, 1772; Am Imp Coll 1772, Rare Bk), and Jonathan Edwards's 1791 sermon on *Injustice and Impolicy of the Slave Trade and of the Slavery of Africans* (New Haven: T. & S. Green, 1791; Am Imp Coll 1791, Rare Bk) are in the Library's rare book collections.

In the general collections, Louis Filler's *Crusade against Slavery* (Algonac, Mich.: Reference

Publications, 1986; E449.F493 1986), which contains a twenty-five-page bibliographical essay, provides an introduction to antislavery publications produced by organizations and individuals, and describes other types of abolition sources. Arthur Zilversmit's *The First Emancipation: The Abolition of Slavery in the North* (Chicago: University of Chicago Press, 1967; E446. Z5) cites general sources for research on abolition in the North, such as state legislative proceedings, antislavery publications, and other printed sources relating to the activities of abo-

An inscription from William H. Topp to Lydia Mott, 1853, is followed by one from Mott to Susan B. Anthony, 1874. A note about Topp ("a colored man in Albany, New York") appears to have been written by Anthony in 1902, on the half title page of a volume of Uncle Tom's Cabin *(1853; PS2954.U5 1853 Rare Bk).*

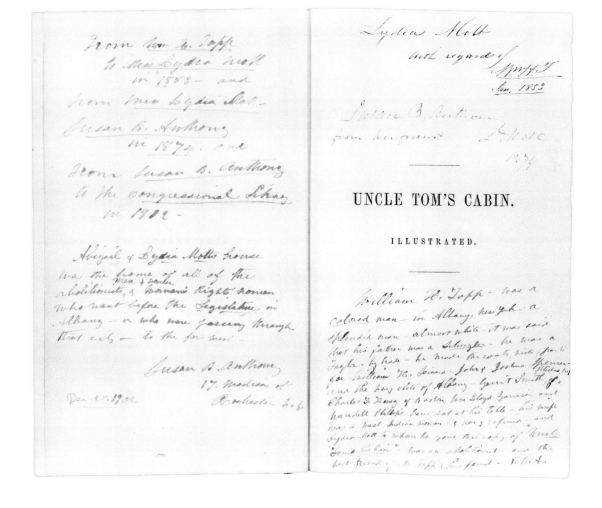

litionists. An unannotated *Bibliography of Anti-Slavery in America* (Westport, Conn.: Greenwood Press, 1981; Z1249.S6D8) by Dwight Dumond contains the most extensive listing of antislavery publications available, and *The Neglected Period of Anti-Slavery in America (1808–1831)* (Boston: Ginn and Company, 1908; E446. A21) by Alice Dana Adams lists the cities in which abolitionists organized antislavery societies.

Access to proslavery and antislavery reports and documents of the United States Congress is provided by the *CIS U.S. Serial Set Index, 1789–1969* (Washington: Congressional Information Service, 1979; 36 vols. Z1223.Z9C65). *Index* headings relating to the antislavery effort are "abolition," "slavers," "slavery," "suppression," "fugitives," "Friends [Quakers]," and others. Printed records of the state legislatures for the colonial and national periods such as the *Proceedings and Debates of the General Assembly of Pennsylvania* (4 vols.) (Philadelphia, 1787–88) are available in the Rare Book Reading Room (J87.P4 1787c Rare Bk). State documents relating to abolition can be located using microform *Records of the States of the United States of America* (Washington: Library of Congress, 1949; MicRR 1550, 1551, Guide Z663.96.G8 and Z1223.5. A1U47), a compilation of colonial, state, and territorial archival materials. The six main classes of materials are statutory laws and legislative, constitutional, administrative, executive, and court records. The supplement also includes information about African-Americans in county and city records, records of American Indian nations, and colonial census reports. In almost every state the Quakers took the lead in abolitionist causes but others also participated.

The *Abolitionist Periodicals Collection* (MicRR 01278–01288, 01384–01396, Guide 35-G) is an assemblage of antislavery literature preserved by the Library. The subjects of the articles range from the emancipation of individual slaves and the abolition of the institution of slavery to Christian beliefs about human bondage. Among the titles represented are the *American Jubilee*, a weekly published in New York during the years 1854 and 1855, the *Anti-Slavery Bugle* from Salem, Ohio, for June 1845 and the years 1851 to 1861, and the Boston *Cradle of Liberty*, with various issues for the years 1839 and 1840. Other abolition titles are contained in the *American Periodical Series* (Ann Arbor: University Microfilms International, 1942–75; III ser., MicRR 01103, 01104, 05422), the largest collection of American periodicals on microfilm.

The *Anti-Slavery Collection, 18th-19th Centuries* (London: World Microfilms, 1978; MicRR 82/434) microfilm publication was reproduced from originals at the Society of Friends Library in London. Its contents include miscellaneous tracts, pamphlets, periodicals, conference proceedings, petitions, committee reports, and other materials, such as a typed copy of Thomas Clarkson's "Chronological Bibliography of Anti-Slavery Tracts." Clarkson's bibliography is derived from sources he used in writing his 1808 *History of the Rise, Progress, and Accomplishment of the Abolition of the Slave Trade* (Philadelphia: J.P. Parke, 1808; HT1162.C6 1808a). Antislavery tracts in this collection include J. Philmore's *Two Dialogues on the Man-Trade* (1760), J. Ady's *Case of . . . the Oppressed Africans* (1783), and *Thoughts . . . on the Slavery and Commerce of the Human Species* (1787), by Ottobah Cugoano.

An annotated index to correspondence in the multivolume *Antislavery Newspapers and Periodicals* edited by John W. Blassingame, Mae G. Henderson, and Jessica M. Dunn (Boston: G. K. Hall, 1980; 5 vols. Z1249.S6A57) for the period from 1817 to 1871 is available in the Main Reading Room and the Newspaper and Current Periodical Reading Room. The volumes index the letters found in the first antislavery newspaper, the *Philanthropist*, as well as the *Emancipator: The Genius of Universal Emancipation*, the *Observer*, the *African Observer*, the *Abolition Intelligencer*, the *National Antislavery Standard*, the *Liberator, Human Rights*, the *Emancipator*, the *Anti-Slavery Record*, the *Friend of Man, Pennsylvania Freeman, Advocate of Freedom*, and the *American and Foreign Anti-Slavery Reporter*.

A similar index, available for black newspapers, is Donald M. Jacobs's *Antebellum Black Newspapers* (Westport, Conn.: Greenwood Press, 1976; E185.5J33) which gives subject access to *Freedom's Journal*, 1827–29, the *Rights of All*, 1829, the *Weekly Advocate*, 1827, and the *Colored American*, 1837–41. The Library holds copies of newspapers published by Frederick Douglass, including the *North Star*, 1847–51, and various issues of the *Frederick Douglass Paper*, 1851–60. All of these newspapers regularly attacked the institution of slavery and advocated equal rights for all, regardless of color.

Nineteen antislavery scrapbooks compiled by George Thompson and F. W. Chesson preserve news clippings and some transcribed letters relating to both local and national antislavery activities dating from 1835 to 1886 (E449.S43 Rare Bk). A broadside of John Greenleaf Whittier's abolitionist poem "Our Countrymen in Chains" is graphically illustrated by a large woodcut of a shackled black man asking, "Am I not a man and a brother?" (Portfolio 118:32a Rare Bk).

The personal library of women's rights activist Susan Brownell Anthony reflects her leadership in the women's suffrage movement and contains significant antislavery material. Before sending her books to the Library of Congress in 1903, Anthony inscribed many of the volumes. In the 1878 edition of the Olive Gilbert's *Narrative of Sojourner Truth, a Northern Slave* (Battle Creek: The Author, 1878; E185.97.T875 Anthony Coll, Rare Bk), Anthony wrote that Truth was a "wonderful woman, . . . had she been educated, no woman could have matched her." On her copy of Sarah Bradford's Tubman biography, *Harriet, the Moses of Her People* (New York: J. J. Little & Co., 1901; E444.T893 Anthony Coll, Rare Bk), Anthony remarked in 1903, "This most wonderful woman is still alive, I saw her but the other day" at a gathering of former abolitionists. Tubman, who escaped slavery in 1849, was responsible for the freedom of over three hundred slaves—including her parents—during at least nineteen underground railroad expeditions.

Susan B. Anthony's copies of the *Monthly Offering*, edited by John Collins, 1840–42, were a gift to her from Lydia Mott of Albany. Anthony collected antislavery speeches of such leading abolitionists as James Birney, Lydia Child, Frederick Douglass, William Lloyd Garrison, Wendell Phillips, and Parker Pillsbury, proceedings of conventions such as a Colored National Convention in 1853 and that of the American Anti-Slavery Society in 1860, and journals like Garrison's *Liberator* (35 vols., 1831–65) and *National Anti-Slavery Standard* (34 vols., 1840–72).

Anthony's inscriptions explain that her copy of Harriet Beecher Stowe's *Uncle Tom's Cabin* (Boston: J.P. Jewett, 1853; PS2954.U5 1853 Rare Bk) was originally given to Lydia Mott by her black friend William Topp, and subsequently given by Mott to Anthony. In 1903 Anthony admonishes "generations to come" to "be thankful that the crime of slavery is done away with although we are still far from just to the negro" [*sic*].

The Susan Brownell Anthony papers (MSS, microfilm 1846–1934) relate to the American Anti-Slavery Society and document Anthony's efforts to ensure that blacks had the right to vote. Included in her papers are "Make the Slave's Case Our Own," ca. 1859, and "The No Union with Slave-holders Campaign," "What Is American Slavery?," and "Judge Taney," all articles dated 1861. Anthony's correspondence is found also in other collections in the Manuscript Division.

The American Anti-Slavery Almanac, for 1843 *(New York: American Anti-Slavery Society, 184–; E449.A509 1843 Rare Bk).*

ANTISLAVERY ORGANIZATIONS

Conference proceedings of antislavery organizations such as the American Convention for Promoting the Abolition of Slavery (1794–1829, 1837; E446.A51 Rare Bk) and the Anti-Slavery Convention of American Women (Philadelphia: Anti-Slavery Convention, 1837–39; E449.A6235 Rare Bk) are in the Library's rare book collections, as is a copy of the *Proceedings* of the Illinois Anti-Slavery Convention, which founded the Illinois Anti-Slavery Society in 1837 in Upper Alton, Illinois (Alton: Parks and Breath, 1838; E449.I29 Rare Bk).

Approximately one thousand titles relating to antislavery societies—including state, local, and foreign organizations—can be located in the Library's general collections by consulting the name of the organization in the printed and computerized catalogs. For example, proceedings published by the societies are available for the Ohio Antislavery Convention, meeting in Putnam in 1835 (E449.O36); the Rhode Island State Anti-Slavery Convention, Providence, 1836 (E449.R47); and the Massachusetts Abolition Society's Boston meeting in 1839 (E449.M411). Foreign antislavery society materials may also be found in the general collections and in the Microform Reading Room.

Various reports of antislavery organizations, among them the *Annual Reports of the Philadelphia Female Anti-Slavery Society* (Philadelphia: Philadelphia Female Anti-Slavery Society, 1840–69; E449.P54) and annual reports of the American Anti-Slavery Society (1834–39, 1855–61; E449.A517 Ton Coll, Rare Bk), shed light on the operations of these organizations. Publications such as issues of the *Liberty Bell* (15 vols. E449.L69 Rare Bk), the journal of the Massachusetts Anti-Slavery Society edited by Maria Chapman, 1839–58, and the American Anti-Slavery *Almanac* for the years 1836 to 1847 (Boston: Webster and Southard; E449.A509 Rare Bk) are in the Rare Book Collection. Foreign antislavery society materials, including the pamphlet *Society for the Amelioration and Final Abolition of Slavery* (Liverpool: James Smith, Printer, [1814?]; E302.M192 1783, vol. 1, no. 5. Madison Pam Coll, Rare Bk) are in the rare book, general, and Microform Reading Room collections.

Organizational reports sometimes relate specific incidents pertaining to abolition efforts. For example, a *Report of a Delegate to the 1838 Convention Including an Account of the Riot* (Boston: I. Knapp, 1838; E449.A62344 Rare Bk) discusses a disturbance in Philadelphia during a meeting of female abolitionists. An incensed white crowd burned down a hall in which black and white women abolitionists were meeting:

Our conversation was interrupted before 9 o'clock by the cry of "Fire." Pennsylvania Hall was in flames! The mob had accomplished the work by breaking in the doors, and deliberately kindling a fire in the house—in view of the city of Philadelphia! (p. 19)

Quakers, the earliest advocates of abolition in the United States, worked in behalf of both slaves and free blacks. The papers of the Pennsylvania Abolition Society (MSS microfilm, 1774–1916), reproduced from originals at the Historical Society of Pennsylvania, and the records of the Friends Association for Advocating the Cause of Slaves (MSS, records 1837–41) document their work. Other collections relating to abolition organizations vary in volume from one item to thousands of items. Some of these are the Cummington Massachusetts Anti-Slavery Society (MSS, records 1835), the Anti-Slavery Society of London (MSS, photostats 1823–40), the Western Anti-Slavery Society (MSS, microfilm 1834–58), the American and Foreign Anti-Slavery Society (MSS, records 1850), and the American Anti-Slavery Society (MSS, records 1833–40).

The intensification of the slavery debate between northern and southern churches, particularly in the decade before the Civil War, is reflected in the records of the American Home Missionary Society (MSS, microfilm of the originals at the Amistad Research Center 1816–94). The American Missionary Association (MSS, Amistad microfilm 1846–82) was active in the abolition movement and in providing aid and education to fugitive slaves in the North and in Canada. This association favored antislavery political action and any other antislavery activity considered consistent with Christian principles, including assisting slaves to escape by hiding them in the series of locations known as the underground railroad. Published indexes are available for both the American Home Missionary Society and the American Missionary Association records.

ABOLITIONISM AS A POPULAR MOVEMENT

From June 1851 to April 1852 Harriet Beecher Stowe published in serial form a story entitled "Uncle Tom's Cabin; or, Life among the Lowly," in the Washington, D.C., *National Era*. When *Uncle Tom's Cabin* appeared as a book in March 1852 (Boston: J. P. Jewett, 1852; 2 vols. PS2954. U5 1852d), it sold three hundred thousand copies in one year. Before 1860 over one million copies had sold in the United States and over two million copies abroad, principally in England. Stowe's novel, inspired by the Fugitive Slave Act of 1850, and appearing in its wake, added measurably to the polarization of abolitionist and anti-abolitionist sentiment. Carl Sandburg reports in *Abraham Lincoln: The War Years* (New York: Harcourt, Brace & Co., 1939; 4 vols. E457.4.S36) that during a White House visit President Lincoln greeted Stowe with out-

stretched hands, saying, "So you're the little woman who wrote the book that made this great war" (vol. 2, p. 201).

Approximately one hundred and fifty books in the Library's collections concern *Uncle Tom's Cabin*, including American and foreign editions, children's books, and rare and special editions available only in the Rare Book Room. Some studies examine the book's impact on American life and others critique its literary value. It is generally conceded that *Uncle Tom's Cabin* is based on a number of sources with which Stowe was familiar, such as Theodore Dwight Weld's *American Slavery As It Is* (New York: American Anti-Slavery Society, 1839; E449.W442 1839) as well as on her personal knowledge of the lives of slaves.

An ex-slave, Josiah Henson, claimed that he was the model for Uncle Tom, although some circumstances in his life differ greatly from those of Stowe's lead character. He entitled his autobiography *The Life of Josiah Henson, Formerly a Slave, Now an Inhabitant of Canada* (Boston: A. D. Phelps, 1849; E444.H52). Another edition of his autobiography, *Uncle Tom's Story of His Life: An Autobiography of the Rev. Josiah Henson, 1789–1876* (2d ed., London: Frank Cass & Co., 1971; E444.H5244 1971), with a preface by Harriet Beecher Stowe and introductory notes by George Sturge, S. Morley, and C. Duncan Rice, discusses the origin of Stowe's famous work.

A sketch of Henson, "the original of the 'Uncle Tom,'" from the pen of Julia McKinley, "who knew Josiah Henson personally," is in the Carter G. Woodson collection (MSS, papers 1796–1933). McKinley states:

It was while on a mission in New England for the cause of bettering conditions of his race, a brief story of his life was published. This fell into the hands of Mrs. Beecher Stowe, and stirred her soul with profound compassion. She invited him to visit her, and in 1849 at Andover, Mass., she heard

"A Dream Caused by the Perusal of Mrs. H. Beecher Stowe's Popular Work Uncle Tom's Cabin," a lithograph by C. R. Milne, Louisville, Kentucky, 1853. In the background, demons throw copies of Uncle Tom's Cabin, which had appeared serially in 1851 and in book form in 1852, into a fire. The author, Quakers, and abolitionism are satirized. (PP Reilly 1853–1. LC-USZ62–15058)

OPPOSITE PAGE: "Uncle Tom's Cabin," poster with woodcut by Alfred S. Seer, New York, 1879. (PP POS Theater 1882 U5.1, D size. LC-USZ61–824)

from his own lips the details of his life and sufferings, and gave to the world the famous book . . . Uncle Tom's Cabin.

Stowe herself later wrote a *Key to Uncle Tom's Cabin* (Boston: J. P. Jewett, 1853; E449.S8959) in which she explained some of the incidents in the story and her motivations for writing them.

Stowe's book was often produced as a play, so that many who did not read it had the opportunity to see it dramatized. Beginning in 1852 these plays provided an entrance onto the stage for many black performers. Although the major roles were played by whites, music frequently was performed by black choirs. George C. Howard's song for Topsy, "Oh, I'se So Wicked" (New York: Horace Waters, 1854; M1.A13H), which provided an opportunity for a black singer, can be found in the Music Division. As the years went by, spirituals sung by black choirs became an increasingly popular feature of productions of *Uncle Tom's Cabin*.

The popular literature of abolitionism goes far beyond *Uncle Tom's Cabin*. Stowe herself did not address the subject in fiction after *Dred: A Tale of the Great Dismal Swamp* (Boston: Phillips, Sampson and Co., 1856; PZ3.S89D), a fictional consideration of the complicity of the northern churches with southern slaveholding. The whole history of antebellum New England literature is intertwined with the history of abolitionism. Ralph Waldo Emerson, who tried to avoid being labeled as an abolitionist, aired his antislavery views in poems such as "Ode, Inscribed to W. H. Channing," in *Poems* (4th ed., Boston: James Munroe and Co., 1847; PS1624.A1 1847d). *A Sermon of Slavery, Delivered Jan. 31, 1841* (Boston: Thurston and Tory, 1843; E449.P25) by Boston Unitarian clergyman Theodore Parker is but one example of his fiery antislavery messages. The first edition of Henry Wadsworth Longfellow's *Poems on Slavery* (Cambridge, Mass.: J. Owen, 1842; PS2265.A1 1842 Rare Bk) is in the Rare Book Collection.

The poetical works of New Englander John Greenleaf Whittier include "Ichabod,' his response to Daniel Webster's vote in favor of the Fugitive Slave Law, and "Massachusetts to Virginia," with the lines "No fetters in the Bay State—no slave upon our land!" These may be found in many editions, including *Poems* (New York: Crowell, 1902; PS3250.P02). The abolitionist poems of James Russell Lowell, such as "The Present Crisis (1844)" with the lines "Once to every man and nation comes the moment to decide . . ." may be found in Lowell's *Complete Poetical Works* (Boston and New York: Houghton Mifflin, 1900; PS2305.A1 1900). Another New Englander, whose work reached from the abolitionist movement to the civil rights period, is Henry David Thoreau. His essay "On Civil Disobedience" was first published under the title "Resistance to Civil Government" and appears in *Aesthetic Papers* (Boston: Elizabeth P. Peabody, 1849; AP2.A27 Rare Bk).

Many methods were used to raise money for the abolition effort, including fairs and bazaars. Advertisements for some of these events are in the broadside collection in the Rare Book and Special Collections Division. The Twenty-Fourth Annual Boston Antislavery Bazaar, sponsored by thirty-two women including Maria Chapman, Lydia Maria Child, and Lydia Parker, was held in December 1858. The broadside advertising it (Portfolio 63:26 Rare Bk) calls for contributions of money and salable goods to support the bazaar.

Early in the 1840s antislavery organizations began to use songs to build enthusiasm at their meetings. These songs served much the same purpose as freedom songs in the civil rights movement of the 1960s. Ten antislavery hymns from the New England Anti-Slavery Convention in 1859 (Portfolio 64:23 Rare Bk) are included in the broadside collection. *Antislavery Hymns* (Hopedale, Mass.: Community Press, 1844), a pamphlet of thirty-six pages which was to be sold to aid the cause of human rights, is reproduced in the *American Culture Series* (Ann Arbor: University Microfilms International, 1979; MicRR 02191 no. 549.021), available in the Microform Reading Room. An antislavery agent and orator, William Wells Brown compiled *The Anti-Slavery Harp* (Boston: Bela Marsh, 1849; M1664.A35B8 and E449.B883), and the music publisher Horace Waters issued *The Harp of Freedom* (New York: Horace Waters, 1862; M1639. H32 Case). Both publications are available in the Music Division.

Popular entertainers like the Hutchinson family lent their talents to the movement. Music covers such as the ones for songs like "Get Off the Track" (1844), which begins, "Ho, the car Emancipation Rides majestic through the Nation" and ends with the rousing chorus "Roll It Along Through the Nation, Freedom's car, Emancipation" (PP lot 10615–59; repro. no. LC-USZ62-68922) demonstrate this support. The *Western Bell: A Collection of Glees, Quartets, and Choruses* (Boston: Oliver Ditson, 1857; M1578. P45W3), by Edward A. Perkins and Frederick H. Pease, is a choral collection with several songs protesting inequities for white laborers who resided in slave states and urging Freesoilers to emigrate to the West. It was popular enough to be reissued in 1885, long after the Civil War.

Even maps and atlases in the Geography and Map Division record the growing sectionalism that was developing before the Civil War. A group of ten miscellaneous maps, filed under the heading "United States—Slavery" in the division's uncataloged Titled Collection, depict the conflict between the free and slave states in the antebellum years. These political maps are of a fairly general nature, either showing the extent of slavery in the period from 1775 to 1865 or indicating which states and territories were categorized as slave or free in the years immediately preceding the Civil War. Two of these

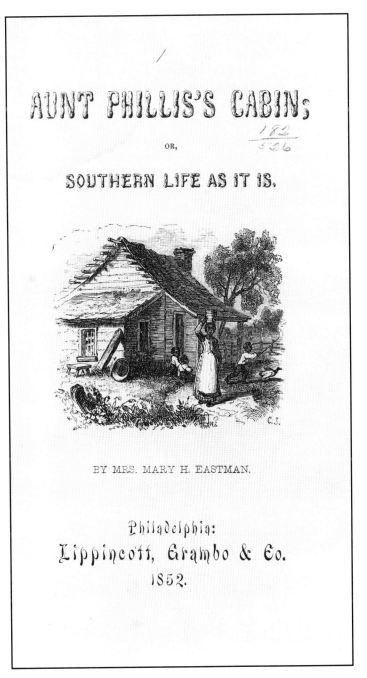

Aunt Phillis's Cabin; or, Southern Life as It Is, by Mary H. Eastman (Philadelphia: Lippincott, Grambo & Co., 1852; PZ3.E138A Rare Bk). Title page illustrated by wood engraving. (LC-USZ62–107753)

maps are of particular note. One, "Reynolds's Political Map of the United States, designed to exhibit the comparative area of the Free and Slave States" (1865), includes tables giving statistics from each of the states from the 1850 census, the 1852 presidential election results, congressional representation by state, and the number of slaves held by owners, as well as reproducing portraits of John C. Fremont and William L. Dayton, the 1856 Republican presidential and vice presidential candidates. The other map, entitled "Historical Geography," by John F. Smith (1888) superimposes stylized trees over the northern and southern states,

calling the northern tree "God's Blessing Liberty" and labeling the southern one "God's Curse Slavery." It compares North and South to good and evil as symbolized in the Garden of Eden.

Historical atlases sometimes include maps depicting the growing division within the nation. A classic, *Atlas of the Historical Geography of the United States*, compiled by Charles O. Paullin and John K. Wright (New York: American Geographical Society; Washington: Carnegie Institution, 1932; G1201.S1P3 1932), records not only the distribution of slaves as a percentage of the total population for each ten-year period from

"The Resurrection of Henry Box Brown at Philadelphia." Lithograph, 1850. (PP Reilly 1850–4. LC-USZ62–1283)

1790 to 1860 but also includes a series of maps showing states which abolished slavery in the years 1800, 1820, 1854, 1863, and 1865.

The American Heritage Pictorial Atlas of United States History, edited by Hilde Heun Kagan (New York: American Heritage Publishing Co., 1966; G1201.S1A4 1966) covers, in a chapter entitled "The Nation Divided," political sectionalism, slave versus free states, the Missouri Compromise, the Compromise of 1850, the Kansas-Nebraska Act of 1854, the slave trade, abolition, slave population, the underground railroad, and the vote by county for the South's secession. The *Historical Atlas of the United States* (Washington: National Geographic Society, 1988; G1201.S1N3 1988) shows the distribution of slaves and free blacks.

Political satires and other prints relating to the rising sectional controversy can be located by using *American Political Prints, 1766–1876: A Catalog of the Collections in the Library of Congress* (Boston, G.K. Hall, 1991; E183.3.R45 1991) by Bernard Reilly, Jr. Indexed in the catalog—which is organized by year—under "slavery—as a campaign issue" and "abolitionists and abolitionism," are numerous prints relating to the antislavery movement from the 1830s through the 1850s found in the Library's collections. Portraits of some of the more celebrated fugitive slaves and other African-Americans who gained prominence through the antislavery cause include Henry "Box" Brown, Anthony Burns, Joseph Cinquez, and Dred Scott.

ABOLITIONISTS

Portraits of white leaders of both the abolition and proslavery movements are available in the Prints and Photographs Division Biographical File, which is arranged in alphabetical order by surname. Distinguished figures in these categories include individuals such as Charles Sum-

ner, William Lloyd Garrison, Sarah and Angelina Grimke, Cassius Clay, and Henry Clay.

The Black Abolitionist Papers (MSS, microfilm 1830–65; and printed volumes, Chapel Hill: University of North Carolina Press, 1985–92, 5 vols.; E449.B624 1985) include correspondence, speeches, essays, petitions, and editorials of individuals such as Alexander Crummell, Charles Purvis, Sarah Remond, Charles Lenox Remond, Frederick Douglass, William Craft, Mary Ann Shadd Cary, Henry Highland Garnet, John Russwurm, James Forten, and many others. The papers, collected from various repositories, document black abolitionists' activities in Canada, the British Isles, and the United States. An extensive printed index to the microfilm is available and several published volumes, edited by C. Peter Ripley and others, contain selected materials from the microfilm, including documents such as the 1843 "Annual Report of the Colored Vigilant Committee of Detroit," "Resolutions of a Meeting of Boston Blacks, Convened at the First Independent Baptist Church" in 1844, and "Speech by James Forten, Jr., Delivered before the Philadelphia Female Anti-Slavery Society" in 1836.

Antislavery efforts of African-Americans are described by Benjamin Quarles in *Black Abolitionists* (New York: Oxford University Press, 1969; E449.Q17) and *Blacks in the Abolition Movement* (Belmont, Calif.: Wadsworth Publishing Co., 1971; E449.B794), a collection of articles edited by John H. Bracey, Jr., August Meier, and Elliott Rudwick.

A small collection of materials relating to black abolitionist Sojourner Truth (MSS, papers 1853–83) and materials relating to one of the best known white abolitionists, William Lloyd Garrison (MSS, papers 1835–75, microfilm 1805–75), who was both an outspoken writer and editor of the *Liberator* and an able organizer, are held in the Manuscript Division. Originals of the Library's microfilmed reproductions of the

Garrison papers are located at the Massachusetts Historical Society. In the first issue of the *Liberator*, Garrison stated his position on abolition: "I am in earnest—I will not equivocate—I will not excuse—I will not retreat a single inch AND I WILL BE HEARD."

Secretary of the Treasury Salmon Portland Chase (MSS, microfilm 1755–1898) was involved in many antislavery activities and corresponded regularly with other abolitionists such as Cassius Marcellus Clay (MSS, papers 1817–77) and Joshua Leavitt (MSS, papers 1812–1901). A portion of the papers of Anna Elizabeth Dickinson (MSS, papers 1859–1951) concern her activities on behalf of abolition. Her correspondents include Frederick Douglass and William Lloyd Garrison. Carolyn Wells Dall's papers (MSS, microfilm 1811–1917), reproduced from originals in the Massachusetts Historical Society, yield information about her work with various antislavery groups. The Library holds a few originals of the papers of Lydia Maria Child (MSS, papers 1856–76, microfiche 1817–80) and a large microfiche collection reproduced from originals in various libraries. Some of the many other abolitionists represented in Manuscript Division collections are:

John Albion Andrew (MSS, Massachusetts Historical Society microfilm 1772–1895),
James G. Birney (MSS, papers 1830–90),
Joshua Reed Giddings (MSS, papers 1839–99),
Sarah Moore Grimke (MSS, papers 1844–71),
Theodore Dwight Weld (MSS, papers 1836–88),
and Gideon Welles (MSS, microfilm 1777–1911).

A small collection of Harriet Beecher Stowe papers (MSS, papers 1866–85) is in the Manuscript Division, as well as correspondence and other materials relating to her activities in the John Benwell (MSS, journal 1840), Myrtilla Miner (MSS, microfilm 1825–1950), Edwin McMasters Stanton (MSS, microfilm 1831–70), John Curtiss Underwood (MSS, papers 1856–73), and Isabella Beecher Hooker (MSS, microfiche 1834–1902) collections. Originals of the Hooker papers are at the Hartford Stowe-Day Memorial Library.

ABOLITION AND PUBLIC OFFICIALS

The papers of various statesmen and presidents reflect the rise of the controversy between northern and southern states as new states were added to the Union. Southerners became increasingly adamant about their right to hold slaves while abolitionists displayed more and more fervor in denouncing chattel slavery's expansion into new territories. Congress was so deluged with petitions demanding the abolition of slavery that southern sympathizers were able to have a "gag rule" passed, which from 1836 to 1844 provided that all antislavery petitions be tabled without consideration by Congress. John Quincy Adams (MSS, microfilm 1639–1889, Adams Family Papers), who was a representative from Massachusetts at the time that the gag rule was in effect, fought tirelessly against it. His diaries document aspects of the growing sectional controversy over abolition and the possible secession of the Southern states. The original diaries are in the Massachusetts Historical Society. The papers of Daniel Webster (MSS, Dartmouth microfilm 1800–1900, papers and transcripts 1800–1900) also include information about slavery, abolition, and the Fugitive Slave Law of 1850. The papers of Caleb Cushing (MSS, papers 1785–1906), who served as attorney general under President Franklin Pierce, include a folder of antislavery petitions and other materials relating to the abolition question and the Dred Scott case.

Although no nineteenth-century antebellum president was able to avoid the slavery ques-

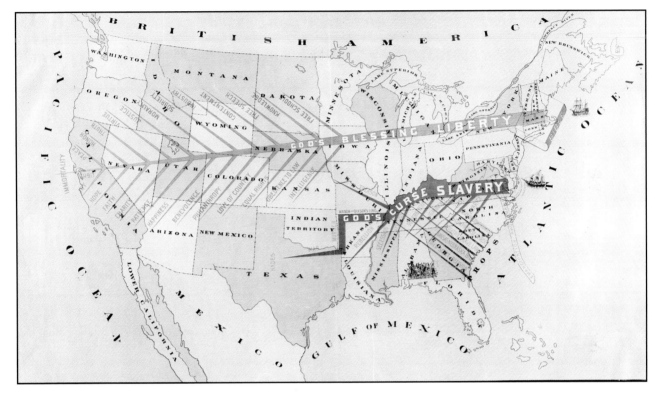

A northern view of slavery in the United States. Orcutt Lithographing Company, Chicago, 1888. (GM negative 713)

tion, James Buchanan, who became president just before the 1857 Supreme Court Dred Scott decision, left papers (MSS, papers 1829–87, microfilm, 1775–1868) that are especially helpful in documenting the growing antagonism between the North and the South. The Library's microfilm edition of Buchanan papers is reproduced from originals at the Historical Society of Pennsylvania. The Manuscript Division holds some papers of Roger Brooke Taney (MSS, papers 1815–59), the chief justice during the Scott case who wrote the decision that declared that blacks "were beings of an inferior order, and altogether unfit to associate with the white race either in social or political relations; and so far inferior that they had no rights which the white man was bound to respect." The Carl Brent Swisher papers (MSS, papers 1836–1962) consist chiefly of reproductions of correspondence, reports, records, and newspapers gathered by Swisher from various sources for a history of Roger B. Taney's tenure as chief justice of the Supreme Court, 1836–64. Among the topics covered in the collection are slavery, the slave

"The Rail Candidate," an 1860 lithograph, shows candidate Abraham Lincoln riding the antislavery plank from the 1860 Republican platform, supported by a black man and Horace Greeley, abolitionist editor of the New York Tribune. (PP Reilly 1860–31. LC-USZ62–10393)

trade, and emancipation. The Benjamin Robbins Curtis collection (MSS, papers 1831–79) contains a few papers concerning the Dred Scott case including some Taney correspondence.

During the Buchanan administration, in 1859, John Brown and his followers attacked the Harpers Ferry arsenal. A few John Brown documents (MSS, papers 1839–61) provide information about him, as do the papers of President Millard Fillmore (MSS, papers and microfilm of originals at the Buffalo and Erie County Historical Society 1809–1925), Henry Alexander Wise (MSS, microfilm 1836–1928), Jeremiah Sullivan Black (MSS, microfilm 1813–1904), Calvin Cutter (MSS, undated transcript), and a letter by Eliza Lee Cabot Follen (MSS, 1859). A Currier & Ives print shows John Brown on his way to be executed (PP PGA–A Currier & Ives—John Brown—The Martyr; repro. no. LC-USZ62-2890).

Thomas Featherstonhaugh compiled a collection of articles related to John Brown (E451.B84 Rare Bk) and a scrapbook with newspaper clippings from 1899 to 1905, some of which he wrote and others about his efforts to have posthumous honors given to the members of the Harpers Ferry raid. He was involved in having the corpses of seven of the raiders, one of whom was a black man named Dangerfield Newby, removed from their Harpers Ferry burial place and reinterred on Brown's farm in North Elba, New York (E451.B842 Rare Bk, MicRR 49374). A medical doctor, Featherstonhaugh worked with black leaders such as Frederick Douglass, Blanche K. Bruce, Francis J. Grimke, and John R. Lynch to have a monument erected to Brown and his raiders in Harp-

ers Ferry. Characterizing Brown's efforts, the committee wrote:

John Brown is . . . lifted above self, family, friend or race. It was not Caucasian for Caucasian, nor white man for white man, not rich man for rich man; but it was Caucasian for Ethiopian, rich man for poor man, white man for black man; the man admitted and respected dying for the man despised and rejected.

In 1860 abolitionist James Redpath published two books, the *Public Life of Capt. John Brown* (Boston: Thayer and Eldridge, 1860; E451.R32 Stn Coll, Rare Bk) and *Echoes of Harper's Ferry* (Boston: Thayer and Eldridge, 1860; E451.R31 Ton Coll, Rare Bk), a collection of antislavery papers and letters sent to John Brown in prison. *Echoes* contains the first publication of Henry David Thoreau's lecture "A Plea for Captain John Brown," in which he states, "I hear many condemn these men because they were so few. When were the good and the brave ever in a majority? I shall not be forward to think him mistaken in his method who quickest succeeds to liberate the slave."

Toward the end of the Buchanan administration, in December 1860, Kentucky senator John Jordan Crittenden (MSS, microfilm 1782–1888) proposed a constitutional amendment that would allow slavery to exist in all U.S. territories south of latitude thirty-six degrees thirty minutes, but President-elect Abraham Lincoln would not hear of any extension of slavery in the territories. The compromise got nowhere; the nation was not ready for compromise. Southerners were calling for secession and northerners for war.

PART TWO

FOREVER FREE — EMANCIPATION AND BEYOND

"Free!," collector's card no. 8 in "Stephens' Album Varieties: The Slave in 1863," copyright 1864. (PP lot 5174. LC-USZC4–2521; LC-USZ62–41836)

The question of slavery had been avoided, argued, and compromised upon from the time of the Constitutional Convention. By the Civil War, the issue could no longer be ignored. As Union soldiers moved into the South, slaves flocked to their camps. During the war, blacks in rebel states were emancipated and afterward the Thirteenth Amendment freed all slaves and declared them to be citizens of the United States. It was difficult for former owners to see their "property" as equals or difficult even for some abolitionists to encourage African-Americans in their pursuit of happiness. Blacks faced the difficulty of surviving as a free people. One freedman, Houston Hartsfield Holloway, wrote, "For we colored people did not know how to be free and the white people did not know how to have a free colored person about them." The following chapters on the Civil War, Reconstruction and its aftermath, and the Booker T. Washington era discuss Library holdings relating to the progress of African-Americans to the eve of World War I.

CHAPTER FOUR

THE CIVIL WAR

During the course of the Civil War, blacks served as support workers, spies, scouts, and soldiers. Thousands of African-Americans would lose their lives in their pursuit of freedom. Some would return home as heroes, basking in the praises of their officers, wearing congressional Medals of Honor and other badges of courage, and celebrating a new day of freedom. Yet, in the early years of the war, Union as well as Confederate leaders vacillated about the use of blacks in the military and pondered the postwar status of African-Americans.

POLICIES REGARDING BLACKS

Although President Abraham Lincoln envisioned paying masters to free their slaves and providing freed people with an education or a colonization plan, few abolitionists offered practical suggestions about the future status of a free black population. In the opening months of the war, no clear policy evolved. Free blacks who offered themselves for military service were turned away. President Lincoln remained as reluctant to allow black men to enlist as soldiers as he was to declare the slaves free, and blacks were allowed only a limited role in the war effort for the first three years. Nevertheless, in the earliest successful southern campaigns, slaves from miles around left their owners and sought refuge behind Union lines, and free black men independently began to practice military drills.

In 1861 Gen. Benjamin F. Butler (MSS, papers 1831–96) refused to return several slaves who had sought refuge at Fort Monroe in Virginia, declaring them to be "contraband of war." Subsequently, Union leaders vacillated between sometimes allowing "contrabands" to travel and camp with Union troops as support workers and at other times returning them to their owners. Papers of U.S. Secretary of War Edwin McMasters Stanton (MSS, microfilm and papers 1831–70) and James Morrison MacKaye (MSS, papers 1824–1953) discuss the treatment of contrabands and the use of free blacks and runaway slaves as soldiers. A diary probably kept by A. P. Smith of the New York State Volunteers—16th Regiment (MSS, diary 1861–62) yields information about the reaction of Union soldiers to orders to return runaway slaves. Subsequently, a prolonged debate ensued among Union leaders over the formal use of armed black men in combat.

The papers of Abraham Lincoln (MSS, papers and microfilm 1774–1948) in the Manuscript Division include the Library's own holdings along with microfilm reproductions of materials in the Huntington and the New York Public Libraries. These materials and those in the Alfred Whital Stern Collection of Lincolniana in the Rare Book Room address the abolition controversy, the secession crisis, and the prosecution of the Civil War as well as the debate about emancipation and the use of black soldiers and workers. Other items in the Stern Collection relating to African-American history and culture can be located by using the *Catalog of the Alfred Whital Stern Collection of Lincolniana* (Washington: Library of Congress, 1960; Z8505.U47).

Civil War Manuscripts: A Guide to Collections in the Manuscript Division of the Library of Congress (Washington: Library of Congress, 1986; Z1242.L48 1986), by John R. Sellers, gives a detailed account of sources in the Manuscript Division relating to African-American military service and matters such as the housing, health, medical treatment, diet, emancipation, and the education of blacks. It also identifies collections that show the effect of slavery, the war, and emancipation on the American population.

As the war progressed, Confederate leaders began to show an increased dependence on slave labor to help in erecting fortifications, dig-

Christian A. Fleetwood, sergeant major of the 5th Colored Troops, 3d Division, 18th Army Corps, received the Congressional Medal of Honor on September 29, 1864, for action at Chaffin's Farm near Richmond. (MSS. LC-USZ62–44731)

ging trenches, acting as teamsters, and performing all sorts of manual work. The George Washington Campbell collection (MSS, papers 1793–1886) contains four letters from Gen. Robert E. Lee and his assistant adjutant general to Gen. Richard S. Ewell concerning military organization, desertions in the Confederate Army, the defense of Richmond, and the use of blacks in the army. The papers of Douglas J. and Rufus W. Cater (MSS, papers 1859–65) of the 19th Louisiana Volunteers also contain discussions about the use of blacks as soldiers in the Confederate Army, as do materials in the John S. Jackman collection (MSS, papers 1861–1908) relating to impressment of blacks by the Confederates. President Lincoln realized that striking a decisive blow against slavery and thus denying the South its main labor force could prove an effective method of breaking Confederate military resistance.

Another impetus for emancipation was that abolitionists both at home and abroad were urging Lincoln to free the slaves. Not all slaves states had joined the Confederacy, however, and the president was loathe to lose their support. Lincoln believed that the preservation of the Union should be the most important motivation for the conflict, but by the summer of 1862 his deliberations over the state of the war and the slavery issue led him to his decision to emancipate slaves in the rebel states. After Lincoln drafted several early versions of the document, the Emancipation Proclamation became law on the first day of the new year in 1863. It stated, in part, that "all persons held as slaves within any State, or any designated part of a State, the people whereof shall then be in rebellion against the United States, shall be then, thence forward, and forever free. . . ."

The diaries of Union corporal Joseph Bloomfield Osborn (MSS, papers 1857–65) and Pvt. Charles H. Woodwell (MSS, diary 1862–63) de-

scribe some reactions to its issuance. Woodwell, who was with the 5th Massachusetts Volunteers, wrote on January 1, 1863:

In the evening the colored people of Newbern assembled in the churches, where they were addressed by Agents of the government, who informed them that they were now free, and that all slaves in North Carolina who could escape from their masters would be free also. There was a tumult of rejoicing among the blacks, and the meetings were prolonged to a late hour.

Lincoln's first draft of the proclamation, dated July 22, 1862, is in his papers in the Manuscript Division; the New York State Library holds Lincoln's draft of the Preliminary Proclamation of September 22. Lincoln's handwritten manuscript of the final proclamation was sold for the benefit of the soldiers, and it subsequently burned in the Chicago fire of 1871. Reproductions of it are in the Lincoln papers in the Manuscript Division and in the National Archives. The Stern Collection includes a copy of the first separate printing of the Preliminary Proclamation of September 22, 1862, as well as copies of two variant printings of the proclamation that were dispatched as general orders to the Union Army and Navy and a copy of the first separate printing of the final proclamation. Facsimile editions of the National Archives official engrossed Emancipation Proclamation are in the Rare Book Collection (E453. L75 Rare Bk). A discussion of the various manuscript drafts and printed editions by Charles Eberstadt, "Lincoln's Emancipation Proclamation," is found in the *New Colophon* (1950; 312–56; Z1007.C72). John Hope Franklin's book *The Emancipation Proclamation* (Garden City, N.Y.: Doubleday, 1963; E453.F8 Stn Coll, Rare Bk) is one of over fifty titles about the history of the proclamation available in the Library.

Ehrgott and Forbriger, a Cincinnati lithography firm, published an 1863 calendar with a drawing titled "President Lincoln Writing the Proclamation of Freedom," based on David Gilmore Blythe's painting of the same subject. In this calendar, drawings are visual symbols suggesting the historical, political, and philosophical precedents for the Emancipation Proclamation. Lincoln is portrayed working on the document in his shirtsleeves and slippers in a cluttered study, near an open window. His left hand rests on a Bible, which in turn rests on a copy of the Constitution in his lap (PP-B Ehrgott, Forbriger; repro. nos. LC-USZ62-2069, LC-USZC4-1425). On another page of the calendar, entitled "1862," two black children work while another wears chains and a white child watches idly. In the companion drawing called "1863," the roles are reversed to show the white child at work while the three black children stand idle (PP repro. no. LC-USZ62–90749).

After the proclamation was issued, many were pleased that the president had finally taken a firm stand against slavery. Some young white men facing the draft, however, were displeased that they would be fighting to free slaves who would then compete with them for employment. Poor whites were also perturbed that wealthy men who could afford to pay a fee for a substitute could be freed from service but the poor had no alternatives. When white laborers in New York City, already in competition with blacks, were drafted in the spring of 1863, some reacted violently. Though blacks were not the only objects of wrath, some were assaulted mercilessly. Beginning in late July, a weeklong riot engulfed the city and many black people were killed, beaten, or left homeless. Information relating to the New York draft riots appears in Manuscript Division papers of Union general Joseph Warren Keifer (MSS, papers 1861–65) and New York businessman Richard Lathers (MSS, papers 1826–1901) and in the diary of Helen Varnum Hill McCalla (MSS, diary 1863, 1865).

The papers of another New York City businessman, Charles Butler, (MSS, papers 1819–1905) include a letter from Butler to his daughter, dated July 18, 1863, describing the antidraft riots in New York City. He writes:

Monday the thirteenth instant I found the city in a high state of excitement (at least the upper part of it) and learned that a riot had commenced on 46th Street and 3rd Avenue in which a very large number of persons were engaged and that they had already set fire to a block of buildings and had assaulted several peaceable citizens and were committing acts of violence upon every thing and every body. In the afternoon at 3 o'clock I witnessed the progress of the riot down 5th Avenue at the corner of 37th St. They had just set the colored orphan asylum on fire.

Publications describing the conditions that led to the draft riots include Iver Bernstein's *The New York City Draft Riots: Their Significance for American Society and Politics in the Age of the Civil War* (New York: Oxford University Press, 1990; F128.44.B47 1990); James McCague's *The Second Rebellion: The Story of the New York Draft Riots of 1863* (New York: Dial, 1968; F128. 44.M3); and *The Bloody Week: Riot, Murder, and Arson* (New York n.p., n.d.; F128.44.B63 Rare Bk), a thirty-two-page pamphlet compiled from records of the official investigation of the riot.

After the riots ended, some New York businessmen organized to help the needy riot victims. This group later published a pamphlet entitled *Report of the Committee of Merchants for the Relief of Colored People, Suffering from the Late Riots in the City of New York* (New York: George A. Whitehorne, 1863; F128.44.N646), which contains excerpts from newspaper accounts about incidents occurring during the riot and brief biographical accounts of the victims. Drafting and recruiting during the Civil War are the subjects of prints showing black New York City recruits and the draft riots (PP Graphics File lot 4420-O).

"View of Transparency" pictures an enormous illuminated transparency displayed on the front of the federal recruiting office for black troops in Philadelphia on November 1, 1864, to celebrate the emancipation of slaves in Maryland. Wood engraving, printed in colors, with letterpress. (PP Reilly 1864–44. LC-USZ62–40720)

AFRICAN-AMERICANS IN THE MILITARY

Although some black workers had been used in the Union Army in 1862, blacks were not actively recruited until it became apparent the war would be long and costly. Faced with a shortage of men among the rank and file, the War Department in 1863 finally established a policy encouraging the use of black men and, subsequently, thousands were actively recruited. By the end of the war, over 186,000 black men had enlisted, resulting in a ratio of one black soldier to every eight white soldiers. Most units of black soldiers were led by white commissioned officers and both black and white noncommissioned officers. *Civil War Manuscripts* (Sellers) includes information about the U.S. Colored Cavalry, U.S. Colored Infantry, the 1st and 3d South Carolina Infantries of African Descent, the Zouaves de Afrique, and others. Beginning in 1863 black men fought in most military campaigns, resulting in the loss of over 38,000 black soldiers by the end of the war.

The recruitment, training, and performance of black troops, as well as their treatment as prisoners of war, can be investigated in the papers of Frederick Douglass (MSS, microfilm 1841–1967) and John Mercer Langston (MSS, microfilm 1853–98), both of whom helped raise black regiments. (The originals of the Langston papers are at Fisk University.) A letter from the War Department to Douglass, dated August 13, 1863, directs him "to proceed to Vicksburg, Mississippi, to assist in recruiting colored troops." Douglass's papers include detailed letters from his son Charles during his war service. Charles wrote to his father from Washington, D.C., on October 18, 1865, when most battles had come to an end, saying, "colored soldiers are pouring in here very fast and are to garrison the city. The colored people here are rejoicing over it."

One of the first people to urge blacks to become soldiers was Alfred M. Green, a noted lecturer, teacher, and member of the black convention movement. His pamphlet *Letters and Discussions on the Formation of Colored Regiments* (Philadelphia: Ringwalt & Brown, Steam Power Printers, 1862; E540.N3G9 1969) admonishes blacks to consider whether they want to participate fully as American citizens, saying:

It is a foolish idea for us to still be nursing our past grievances to our own detriment, when we should as one man grasp the sword—grasp the most favorable opportunity of becoming inured to that service that must burst the fetters of the enslaved and enfranchise the nominally free of the North.

Green's essays previously appeared in the *Anglo-African* magazine (reprint, New York: Arno Press, 1968; E185.A582) and other publications.

The 102-page *Diary of James T. Ayers, Civil War Recruiter* (Springfield: Illinois State, 1947; E601.A9 Stn Coll, Rare Bk), edited by John Hope Franklin, is located in the Rare Book Collection. Ayers, a "lay preacher who served in Sherman's army," recounts the policies and procedures used in the recruitment of black soldiers, such as compensating loyal owners $300 per month for each recruit. Ayers gave free blacks two reasons to enlist: the "moral obligation to fight slavery" and the "munificent" salary of $10 per month along with "free issue of food and clothing."

John H. Taggart's twelve-page pamphlet *Free Military School for Applicants for Commands of Colored Troops* (Philadelphia: 1863; E540.N3P5 1863) discusses the board that the U.S. government established to determine the qualifications of those who wanted to become officers of black units. White officer candidates were sent to military schools where they learned infantry tactics, army regulations, and general information. This pamphlet sets forth the physical and academic requirements for officers.

The cover for no. 3 in a series of collector's cards known as "Stephens' Album Varieties" announces the subject: "The Slave in 1863." These chromolithographs, "in oil colors, from original designs by Henry L. Stephens [1824–1882]," were deposited for copyright January 14, 1864, by William A. Stephens, proprietor. (PP lot 5174. LC-USZC4–2529)

An individual's account of participation in the conflict is found in the diaries of Christian Abraham Fleetwood (MSS, microfilm 1797–1945), a sergeant major in the 4th U.S. Colored Infantry and a recipient of the Congressional Medal of Honor. The diaries concern campaigns in Virginia and North Carolina and provide information about skirmishes on Virginia's lower peninsula, the siege of Petersburg, Gen. Benjamin F. Butler's Fort Fisher expedition, camp life, disease, and President Lincoln's visit to the front lines in June 1864. Other materials in Fleetwood's Civil War papers are orders, awards, passes, his discharge, a list of officers in the 4th, 5th, 6th, 36th, 38th, and 39th Colored Regiments and the 54th Massachusetts Infantry, the names and service records of fifteen black officers, and photographs of black recipients of the Congressional Medal of Honor. Fleetwood's medal was for bravery in battle at Chapin's farm, Virginia, where, on September 29, 1864, after two color sergeants had been shot down, he seized the colors and carried them throughout the rest of the fight. A photograph in the Manuscript Division shows Christian Fleetwood in dress uniform (PP repro. no. LC-USZ62–44731). Fleetwood correspondence can also be found in the Mary Church Terrell (MSS, microfilm 1851–1962) and Carter G. Woodson (MSS, microfilm 1796–1933) collections. Fleetwood wrote *The Negro as a Soldier; Written by Christian A. Fleetwood, Late Sergeant-Major 4th U. S. Colored Troops, for the Negro Congress, at the Cotton States and International Exposition Atlanta, Ga., November 11 to November 23, 1895* (Washington: Howard University, 1895; E185.63.F59 Mur Pam Coll, Rare Bk).

A thirty-five page autobiography by Lieutenant F. W. Browne entitled "My Service in the 1st U.S. Colored Cavalry," in the Black History Miscellany collection (MSS, papers 1706–1944), discusses the cavalry:

The first colored cavalry regiment had in its ranks a rather better class of men than the infantry regiment had, some being from the North and some being outlaw Negroes who in slavery days had been able to maintain their liberty in the swamps of Eastern Virginia and North Carolina.

The Miscellany collection also includes lists of officers and men in the 2d U.S. Colored Infantry and a report by Col. Thomas J. Morgan on the service of the 14th U.S. Colored Infantry, October 31, 1864, Decatur, Georgia.

The Roberts Family papers (MSS, papers 1734–1944) include eight letters from Pvt. Junius B. Roberts, 28th U.S. Colored Infantry, to his family concerning his service as an orderly in a military hospital in Alexandria, Virginia. They provide some information on deaths, disease, and hospital care. He wrote to his father on May 8, 1864, as follows:

we got to Washington last nite about nine oh clock and we staid in town at headquarters until nine oh clock this morning then we marched out to camp. It is seven miles from the city. . . . There is about three Ridgements of colerd in camp here. . . . our camp is on gineral lees farm, write on the battle ground we drill writs on the graves.

"Memorys of the Past," a memoir written by former slave John Washington (MSS, undated microfilm), describes his life for the period from 1838 to 1862, when he lived in several locations in Virginia, especially the Fredericksburg region. The 119-page document includes information about the capture of Fredericksburg by Union troops, Washington's own emancipation from slavery, and his work as an aide to Gen. Rufus King.

The "Historic Record, 51st U.S. Col'd Infantry," in the papers of white Union chaplain George North Carruthers (MSS, papers 1864–69), cover the period from May 1863 to April 1866. In ninety-five pages the record gives a detailed account of the organization and initial combat service of the unit, monthly reports, and vital statistics of 181 African-American couples married by Carruthers. It outlines the performance of the 51st on labor and combat missions in Louisiana, Mississippi, Alabama, and Florida. The record also describes some of the peonage, fraud, and forced conscription blacks encountered.

The John Aldrich Stephenson Collection of the Papers of the Hand, Fiske, and Aldrich Families (MSS, papers 1745–1966) includes correspondence from Asa Fiske relating to his 1863 assignment to serve as assistant superintendent of contrabands for the Department of West Tennessee under superintendent Col. John Eaton. Fiske directed the care of several thousand former slaves, which involved procuring food, clothing, bedding, and medical supplies for them. He also was concerned about their moral and spiritual lives and on one occasion performed marriage ceremonies for 119 contraband couples simultaneously. Fiske wrote in a letter of reminiscences to his granddaughter—"You Little Villuines"—in May 1914, "This great Wedding day produced most remarkable results on the good order and morality of the entire camp" and remarked that the "sacredness of the Marital compact was . . . rigidly observed." He also took a speaking tour to raise money to help contrabands and was a strong proponent for the establishment of the Freedmen's Bureau.

The John Curtiss Underwood collection (MSS, papers 1856–73) includes documents discussing Underwood's recruitment and organization of a black company, and the papers of Edward W. Kinsley (MSS, papers 1863–65), a captain of the 54th Massachusetts Volunteers, concern pay for black troops and morale and casualties in the 54th and 55th Massachusetts regiments.

HISTORICAL ACCOUNTS OF AFRICAN-AMERICAN PARTICIPATION

One writer noted in *The Civil War Digest* (new and enlarged edition: New York, Grosset and Dunlap, 1960; E468.N44) that by 1960, a century after the war's commencement, over forty thousand books had been written about it. The Library of Congress collections include about fourteen thousand books on the war. Prominent among the general histories of blacks in the Civil War are those by Benjamin Quarles, *The Negro in the Civil War* (Boston: Little, Brown & Co., 1969; E540.N3Q3 1969), Dudley Cornish, *The Sable Arm: Negro Troops in the Union Army, 1861–1865* (New York: Norton, 1966; E540.N3C77), and Hondon B. Hargrove, *Black Union Soldiers in the Civil War* (Jefferson, N.C.: McFarland, 1988; E540.N3H35 1988). James M. McPherson's *The Negro's Civil War* (New York: Pantheon Books, 1965; E540.N3M25) includes documents that show the efforts blacks made to obtain their freedom. In addition, a collection of articles which first appeared in the *Civil War Times* (Gettysburg, Pa.: Historical Times, Inc.; 3 vols. E461.C56) are collected in the anthology *The Negro in the Civil War* (Philadelphia: Eastern Acorn Press, 1988; E540.N3N43 1988) and provide a good introduction to the roles of blacks.

Two volumes of *Freedom, a Documentary History of Emancipation, 1861–1867*, edited by Ira Berlin (New York: Cambridge University Press, 1982–90; 3 vols. E185.2F88), offer both the scholar and the general reader an introduction to the subject. *The Destruction of Slavery* (vol. 1) and *The Black Military Experience* (vol. 2) both contain informative introductions and useful documentary materials. Another general history is *Negro Americans in the Civil War: From Slavery to Citizenship* by Charles H. Wesley and

Patricia W. Romero (New York: Publishers Co., 1967–68; E540.N3W4 1968), which is part of the International Library of Negro Life and History series.

An important reference source, *The Civil War Digest* has an introduction by historian Allan Nevins and a bibliographic section, "A Basic Civil War Library," which lists "essential titles necessary to give an individual a sound foundation" on the Civil War. Thomas Livermore's *Numbers and Losses in the Civil War in America, 1861–1865* (Bloomington, Ind.: Indiana University Press, 1957; E491.L77 1957) and *Blacks in the*

Military: Essential Documents (Wilmington, Del.: Scholarly Resources, 1981; UB418.A47B55 1981), edited by Bernard C. Nalty and Morris J. MacGregor, both provide primary sources about African-American participation in the war.

The Photographic History of the Civil War (New York: The Review of Reviews, 1911–57; 11 vols. E468.7.M67; PP Ref), a visual documentary edited by Francis Trevelyn Miller, often depicts blacks in a disparaging manner but reveals how black soldiers and freedmen were perceived by some. At one point, so many blacks followed the Union troops that they impeded military

"Band of the 107th U.S. Colored Infantry, Arlington, Va., November 1865," members carrying their music and over-the-shoulder instruments, photographed by William M. Smith. Albumen silver print. (Civil War File, PP. LC-B8171–7861)

operations. It is reported here that General Sherman told one old black man, "If the Negroes continued to swarm after the Army it would fail in its purpose and they would not get their freedom." Photographs have captions such as "The Guns that Sherman Took Along" and "Negroes Flocking in the Army's Path." Other images from a section called "The Lighter Side" include derisive captions such as "Sambo's Right to Be Kilt," accompanied by a poem of that title supposedly written by "Private Miles O'Reilly," and "I'll Let Sambo Be Murthered Instead of Myself," showing the "Colored Infantry" at Fort Lincoln, 1862.

Image of War, 1861–1865 (Garden City, N.Y.: Doubleday, 1981–84; 6 vols. E470.E52, PP Ref), another pictorial documentary, in a chapter entitled "Slaves No More" (vol. 3), portrays black families, troops, and laborers. An important work, *Winslow Homer's Images of Blacks: The Civil War and Reconstruction Years* (Austin: University of Texas Press, 1988; ND237.H7A4 1988a, PP Ref) by Peter H. Wood and Karen C. C. Dalton also provides visual sources. The Time-Life series on the Civil War, composed of twenty-seven separately titled volumes, has a *Master Index* (Alexandria, Va.: Time-Life Books, 1987; E468.7.T57, PP Ref) with numerous references to blacks.

The *Rebellion Record* (New York: G.P. Putnam, 1861–63; and D. Van Nostrand, 1864–68; 11 vols. E468.R29), is divided into a diary of events, documents, and poetry. This comprehensive compilation is particularly useful because it includes a chronology and a collection of narratives, illustrative incidents, and articles from both white and black newspapers and magazines. The *Record* reflects the editor's attempt to produce a "compact history of the war that distinguishes fact from rumor, but also demonstrates the period's picturesque and poetic aspects." Entries include an article from May 9–11, 1861, *Memphis Bulletin* stating that

"Make Way for Liberty!," collector's card no. 10 in "Stephens' Album Varieties: The Slave in 1863," copyright 1864. (PP lot 5174. LC-USZC4–2519; LC-USZ62–53190)

the Confederates made the first attempt to arm blacks. An item from the *Charleston Evening News* of May 1, 1861, in the "Rumors and Incidents" section concerns the Cockade Black Diamond, a unit of black soldiers. Another entry relates that in Petersburg, Virginia, 120 free blacks wearing red shirts and dark pants, and bearing a Confederate flag, marched through the city on the way to Norfolk to work on harbor fortifications there. The *Record* lists laws and regulations relating to blacks, including an act passed by the U.S. Congress on July 17, 1862, permitting blacks to perform military labor such as constructing entrenchments and other camp services. Other entries relate anecdotes about black troops and provide the lyrics for songs and poems about contrabands.

The Confederate States of America Collection includes publications relating to laws, statutes, and journals of state legislatures. Of special interest are the *General Emancipation Ballad* (n.p., 1863? E484.C74 CSA Coll, Rare Bk), *An Ordinance Organizing and Establishing Patrols for the Police of Slaves in the Parish of St. Landry* (Opelousas, La.: Opelousas Patriot, 1863; E445.L8S2 CSA Coll, Rare Bk; MicRR 83/5315-E), Ebenezer Warren's *Nellie Norton, a Vindication of Southern Slavery from the Old and New Testament* (Macon: Burke, Boykin & Co., 1864; E453.W28 CSA Coll, Rare Bk), and a *Speech of Hon. Thos. S. Gholson, of Virginia, on the Policy of Employing Negro Troops* (Richmond: G.P. Evans & Co., 1865; E585.N3G4 CSA Coll, Rare Bk). The comprehensive bibliographies *Era of the Civil War, 1820–1876* (Carlisle Barracks, Pa.: U.S. Army Military History Institute, 1982; Z1242.U588 1982) and *The U.S. Army and the Negro* (Carlisle Barracks, Pa.: U.S. Army Military History Research Collection, 1975; 2 vols. Z1361.N39U39 1975 and supplement), by John Slonaker, are available.

Lenwood G. Davis and George Hill's unannotated bibliography *Blacks in the American Armed Forces, 1776–1983* (Westport, Conn.: Greenwood Press, 1985; Z1249.M5D38 1985) includes "Blacks in the Civil War," a chapter which cites over two hundred books and articles on the African-American military experience. Charles E. Dornbusch's *Military Bibliography of the Civil War* (New York: New York Public Library and Arno Press, 1972; 3 vols. Z1242.D612) was originally published in 1961–62 by the New York Public Library as *Regimental Publications and Personal Narratives of the Civil War: Northern States in Seven Parts.* Under "Col-

ored Troops," volume 2 lists publications pertaining to black regiments. Some entries indicate locations in the Library of Congress, but others may also be held by the Library as well. Volume 3 includes annotated references under "Negroes" to materials about blacks in books, articles, and speeches.

The official published compilation by the U.S. War Department, *The War of the Rebellion: A Compilation of the Official Records of the Union and Confederate Armies* (Washington: Government Printing Office, 1901; 128 vols. E454), lists U.S. Colored Troops and regiments, regiment numbers, and previous names in its cumulative index and separate volume indexes. Records pertaining to black soldiers appear in several volumes under the headings "Colored Troops" and "Negroes." The battalion lists and statistics about black troops also yield summaries of important events. Special reports include the "Military Treatment of Captured and Fugitive Slaves." The *Official Records* reveal the evolving political posture toward slaves, black soldiers, contrabands, and African-Americans in general. In them, it is possible to find such specific information as the date the House of Representatives determined that it was no longer necessary to return fugitive slaves to disloyal masters.

A companion series, *Official Records of the Union and Confederate Navies in the War of the Rebellion* (Washington: Government Printing Office, 1894–1922; 30 vols. E591.U58), compiled by the U.S. Naval War Records Office, also provides information about blacks. Frederick H. Dyer's *Compendium of the War of the Rebellion* (New York: T. Yoseloff, 1959; 3 vols. E491.D99 1959) is particularly useful for its regimental histories but also includes statistics and lists of campaigns and battles. The U.S. Adjutant-General's Office *Official Army Register of the Volunteer Forces of the Army for 1861, '62, '63, '64, '65* (Washington: Government Printing Office, 1865?; 8 vols. E494.U538 LHG Ref) contains a roster of officers by regiment in the U.S. Colored Troops. The volumes give the dates regiments were organized and mustered in and out of service. Notable battles in which black soldiers participated, such as the Bermuda Hundred, Petersburg, and Chapin's Farm, are listed and losses recorded.

Other official documents important for the study of the Civil War include the *Congressional Globe* (Washington: Government Printing Office, 1833–73; KF35), found in the Law Library and Microform Reading Rooms, which records the debates and actions of Congress. Members of the Thirty-sixth through the Thirty-eighth Congress, many of whose papers are in the Manuscript Division collections, discussed such issues as the abolition of slavery, the slave trade, the Fort Pillow incident, repeal of the Fugitive Slave Act, and freedmen's affairs. Annual and cumulative indexes provide subject access. *Members of Congress: A Checklist of Their Papers in the Manuscript Division, Library of Congress* (Washington: Library of Congress, 1980; Z1236.U613 1979) by John J. McDonough facilitates access to the Library's congressional materials for this period.

Besides the *Congressional Globe*, the U.S. Congress also published hearings, documents, and reports on the legislation it considered. Prominent is *House Report 65* by the Committee on the Conduct of the War on the Fort Pillow Massacre (Serial set no. 1206, 38th Cong., 1st sess.), which states that the Fort Pillow massacre represented "a scene of cruelty and murder without a parallel in civilized warfare." At Fort Pillow in Tennessee approximately half the defeated Union soldiers were African-Americans. Victorious rebel troops killed black soldiers despite their white flags of surrender, prompting a congressional investigation of atrocities. An undated wood engraving by an unidentified artist shows the "Rebel Massacre of the Union Troops after the Surrender at Fort Pillow" on

April 12, 1864 (PP Graphics File lot 4416 [1864]-N, repro. no. LC-USZ62–33811).

Two black regiments became famous: the Black Brigade of Cincinnati, known as the first group of northern blacks organized for military purposes, and the 1st South Carolina Volunteers, later named the 33d South Carolina. In *The Black Brigade of Cincinnati* (Cincinnati: Boyd, 1864; E474.3.C59 Ton Coll, Rare Bk), Peter H. Clark provides a muster roll of its members and explains its organization. More than twenty-five Civil War regimental histories in the Library's collections include full-length books about the first black regiments to be established and those that engaged in crucial battles.

But perhaps the most famous black regiment of all in the Civil War is the 54th Massachusetts, the first to engage in military action. Several books record the individual acts of bravery shown by the men, especially in the siege of Fort Wagner, which resulted in many casualties. Their colonel, Robert Gould Shaw, was killed in the battle and buried with his fallen men. Histories and biographical portraits are found in Paul Burchard's *One Gallant Rush: Robert Gould Shaw and His Brave Black Regiment* (New York: St. Martin's, 1965; E513.5 54thB8) and Luis F. Emilio's *A Brave Black Regiment: History of the 54th Massachusetts Volunteer Infantry, 1863–1865* (New York: Arno Press, 1969; E513.5 54th E 1969). *On the Altar of Freedom, a Black Soldier's Civil War Letters from the Front* (Amherst: University of Massachusetts Press, 1991; E513.5 54th. G66 1991) edited by Virginia Matzke Adams, consists of letters written by Corporal James Henry Gooding, who served with the 54th.

An 1863 Currier and Ives lithograph depicts the "Gallant Charge of the Fifty-fourth Massachusetts (Colored Regiment) on the Rebel Works at Fort Wagner on July 18, 1863" (PP PGA-A Currier & Ives, repro. no. LC–USZ62–7824) and an 1867 engraving from a painting by Thomas Nast entitled "Attack on Fort Wagner" document the

"Storming Fort Wagner." Chromolithograph by Kurz & Allison, copyright 1890. (PP PGA Kurz & Allison, D size. LC-USZC2–1889)

same event (PP Graphics File lot 4416 [1863]-F, repro. no. LC-USZ62–25390). An undated engraving by an unknown artist portrays the entrance of the "Fifty-Fifth Massachusetts (Colored) Regiment" into Charleston on February 21, 1865 (PP Graphics File lot 4422-E, repro. no. LC-USZ62–33247).

Regimental histories for other African-American units include Edwin M. Main's *The Story of the Marches, Battles, and Incidents of the Third U.S. Colored Cavalry: A Fighting Regiment*

in the War of the Rebellion (Louisville, Ky.: Globe Printing Co., 1908; E492.95 3d.M33 1970); John A. Reed's *History of the 101st Regiment of Pennsylvania, Veterans Volunteer Infantry, 1861–1865* (Chicago: Dickey, 1910; E527.5 101st); and Jeremiah Mickley's *The 43rd Regiment of U.S. Colored Troops* (Gettysburg: J. E. Wible, Printer, 1866; E492.94).

The wood engravings "The 1st Loyal Colored Regiment of South Carolina and the 8th Georgia Rifles in Action" and "Drilling Negro Recruits for the 1st South Carolina Regiment in the Streets of Beaufort, South Carolina,'' are among the many images of African-Americans published in *Pictorial War Record: Battles of the Late Civil War* (New York: Stearns & Co., 1881–84; 2 vols. E461.P61).

EMANCIPATED BLACKS IN THE WAR ZONE

Although the Reconstruction period did not officially begin until after the war, some blacks were freed after Union victories early in the fray. Many coastal South Carolina and Georgia African-Americans in the area of Beaufort near Port Royal Sound were emancipated in 1861 when their former owners' properties were confiscated for back taxes. In this region blacks were given or sold land for farms, schools, and churches, but unfortunately no official policy was established for the treatment of the newly freed population. Consequently, independent groups of missionaries, teachers, and philanthropists went to the South to try to help meet the needs of the black population. The papers of Esther Hill Hawks (MSS, papers 1856–67), a teacher for the National Freedmen's Relief Association, and a medical doctor, contain letters relating to the health and education of the emancipated slaves written by Hawks, other members of the association, and her husband, who was also a doctor working with freedmen in the Beaufort region. The papers of Mary Tyler Peabody Mann (MSS, papers 1863–76) include ten letters describing her work as an agent of the U.S. Sanitary Commission at a freedmen's camp in Helena, Arkansas. In her correspondence she comments on disease and deaths among freedmen, their abuse by soldiers and merchants, black life, efforts to organize black regiments, and the acquisition and distribution of supplies for the freed slaves. A June 18, 1863, letter written from Beaufort by Gen. Rufus Saxton (MSS, papers 1862–89) to the American Medical Association thanks the association for its interest in his work in behalf of the freedmen in his department.

The George Bancroft collection (MSS, microfilm 1811–1961), reproduced from originals in the Cornell University Library, contains a few letters he wrote to his wife from Washington, D.C., during the war. In one Bancroft remarks on a visit to the Freedmen's Village and the encampment of black troops. The papers of New York abolitionist James Morrison MacKaye (MSS, papers 1824–1953) include forty-four letters to members of the American Freedmen's Inquiry Commission concerning the condition and treatment of black refugees, the assignment of officers to black regiments, and his employment as a residential superintendent for black refugees. His correspondents include Edward M. Stanton and Charles Sumner. Correspondence relating to visits to freedmen's camps survives in the Low-Mills Family Papers (1795–1959), as does an 1865 certificate appointing Mary Hillard Loines to serve as a teacher for the National Freedmen's Relief Association in Norfolk, Virginia.

The records of the Presbyterian Church in the U.S.A. Presbytery of Washington City (MSS, records 1823–1936) include materials relating to the establishment and growth of black churches during the war. Lectures relating to the education of African-Americans are found in the papers of Julia Ward Howe (MSS, papers 1845–1917), author of ''The Battle Hymn of the Republic.'' The papers of Lucy Salisbury Doolittle (MSS, papers 1864–67) include an 1865 certificate appointing her superintendent of the industrial school in ''Georgetown, D.C.'' under the auspices of the New York-based National Freedman's Relief Association. The ''commission" commends "her to the favor and confidence of the officers of Government, and all persons who take an interest in aiding the Freedmen, or in promoting their intellectual, moral, and religious instruction."

Many of the "freedmen's aid" societies, which were private organizations set up to aid the recently freed people, worked independently at first and then allied themselves with the Freedmen's Bureau after the war. Some of their publications and reports are in the Library's collections, including copies of founding documents as well as publications of the American Freedmen's Union, Western Freedmen's Aid Commission, New England Freedmen's Aid Society, and others. The New England group published the *First Annual Report of the Educational Commission for Freedmen* (Boston: D. Clapp, 1863; LC2703.N423) and *Extracts from Letters of Teachers and Superintendents of the New-England Freedmen's Aid Society* (Boston: J. Wilson and Son, 1864; MicRR 83/6307).

FIRST-PERSON ACCOUNTS

Important sources for the study of blacks during the course of the war are the published diaries, letters, papers, and personal narratives of both black and white observers. These speak for a varied group, including such individuals as those sent to teach freed men and women, military officers who served with colored troops, plantation owners, nurses, and doctors.

The accounts of missionaries or socially conscious northern women who went South to teach former slaves appear in works like *The Letters and Diary of Laura M. Towne* (Cambridge: Riverside Press, 1912; MicRR 37640, or New York: Negro University Press, 1969; E185.93.S7 T7 1969). Written from the Sea Islands of South

Carolina from 1862 to 1884, the diary describes Towne's life on Saint Helena Island, where, as an agent of the Freedmen's Aid Society of Pennsylvania, she devoted her life to teaching the newly freed people. Another account of this kind is Elizabeth Pearson's *Letters from Port Royal Written at the Time of the Civil War* (Boston: W. B. Clarke, 1906; MicRR 37566). In these letters five ardent antislavery workers tell about their work among the former slaves. Towne received a subsistence allowance and transportation to teach and instruct the former slaves. In *Dear Ones at Home: Letters from Contraband Camps* (Nashville: Vanderbilt University Press, 1966; E185.2.S98), selected and edited by Henry L. Swint, two Quaker sisters, Lucy and Sarah Chase, relate their experiences teaching reading, writing, arithmetic, and basic household chores, often with humor. Wishing to overcome the ignorance and satisfy needy, forsaken, and displaced blacks, the two were appointed as teachers by the Boston Educational Commission to work at Craney Island, Norfolk, and Roanoke.

In *A Cycle of Adams Letters, 1861–1865* (Boston: Houghton, Mifflin, 1920; 2 vols. E601.F72), edited by Worthington Chauncey Ford, members of a distinguished American family discuss issues of the day. In an April 6, 1862, letter, Charles Francis Adams, Jr., writes to Henry Adams giving observations of life about him on a South Carolina plantation, "among troopers, missionaries, contrabands, cotton fields and serpents." He discusses the contraband problem, "cotton growing machinery," the "African personality," government policy, and other matters. Assistant Secretary of War Charles A. Dana's *Recollections of the Civil War* (New York: Collier Books, 1902; E470.D18) describes his personal view of the bravery and courage displayed by black soldiers.

Some diaries and journals reflect the views of blacks themselves. One of the books in the Stern Collection of Lincolniana written by Elizabeth Keckley, a black woman who served as Mary Todd Lincoln's seamstress, is entitled *Behind the Scenes; or Thirty Years a Slave, and Four Years in the White House* (New York: G. W. Carleton & Co., 1868; E457.15.K26 Stn Coll, Rare Bk). Keckley, who was born into slavery in Virginia, purchased freedom for herself and her son after thirty years of work as a dressmaker. In the nation's capital she sewed for Senator Jefferson Davis's family, working late on Christmas Eve in 1859 to finish a dressing gown for Mrs. Davis to present to her husband. Observers believed that the abolitionist James Redpath helped Keckley write her account, which focuses mainly on her work and friendship with Mary Todd Lincoln, and that Redpath was responsible for publishing an appendix of unedited letters from Mary Lincoln to Keckley regarding the sale of used clothes to raise money for the widow's support. Keckley hoped her book would raise money to help Mary, but Robert Lincoln had most of the copies recalled. Dorothy Porter Wesley's introduction to a 1968 reprint (New York: Arno Press, 1968; E457.15.K26 1968) argues that Keckley's book, considered scandalous and a stretch of the truth at the time it was published, was eventually considered to be a reliable source of information on the intimate family life of the Lincolns and a credible portrait of Mary.

A parody of the book by an unknown author—but copyrighted by Daniel Ottolengul—entitled *Behind the Seams; By a Nigger Woman Who Took in Work from Mrs. Lincoln and Mrs. Davis* (New York: National News Co., 1868; E457.15K46 Stn Coll, Rare Bk) is held in the Rare Book and Special Collections Division. The implication of this twenty-three-page satire is that Keckley exaggerated her friendship with Mary Todd Lincoln and others.

In her book *A Black Woman's Civil War Memoirs: Reminiscences of My Life in Camp* (New York: Wiener Publications, 1988; E492.94 33d.T3 1988), Susie King Taylor describes her life as a laundry

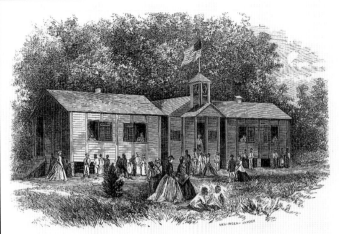

"Education among the Freedmen," illustrated with a picture of "Sea-Island School, No. 1—St. Helena Island; Established April, 1862." (Broadside Collection, Port 157 : 41 Rare Bk. LC-USZ62 – 107754)

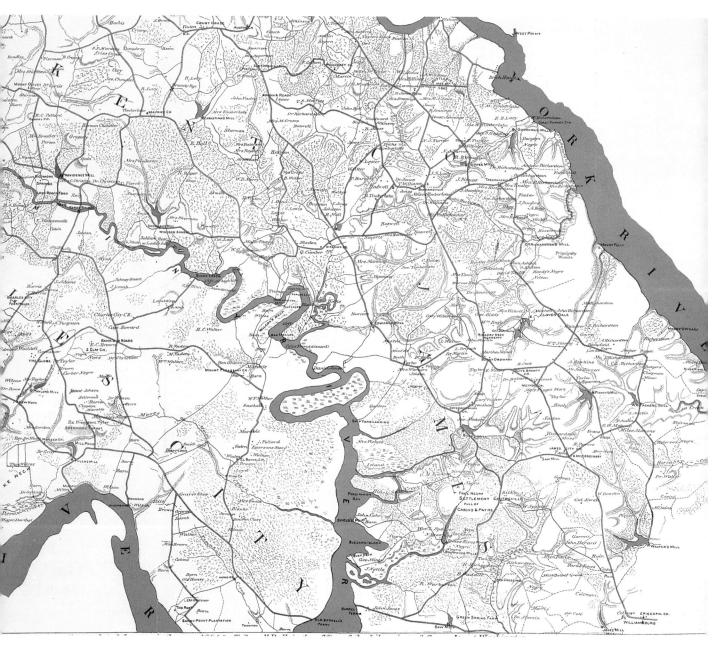

A Confederate map, 1864, of the area northwest of Williamsburg, Virginia, showing plantations along the James River, scattered Negro residences, and an area identified as "Free Negro Settlement Full of Cabins & Paths." (GM Civil War map 626)

woman with the 33d U.S. Colored Troops (formerly called the 1st South Carolina Volunteers) and relates events of the war and Reconstruction, including the failure of the Freedmen's Savings Bank. *The Journal of Charlotte L. Forten* (New York: Dryden Press, 1953; LA2317.F67A3) represents another example of the published views of a black woman. Forten was one of the very few black educated women who went South to teach blacks. An introduction by historian Ray Allen Billington provides biographical information about the Forten family. William Mack Lee's ten-page *History of the Life of Rev. William Mack Lee, Body Servant of General Robert E. Lee, Through the Civil War* (Norfolk, Va.: The Smith Printing Co., 1918; MicRR 41134) presents a brief view of the Confederate perspective from the vantage point of a black man.

A final category of Civil War reminiscences consists of biographical narratives of soldiers— black and white—describing their war service, battles and events in which they participated, and relations with superiors and other soldiers. Examples of this type of memoir are *Notes on Colored Troops and Military Colonies on Southern Soil by an Officer of the 9th Army* (New York: n.p., 1863; E540.N3N9 and E449.D16 vol. 24, no. 2 Mur Pam Coll, Rare Bk); *Army Life in a Black Regiment* (East Lansing: Michigan State University Press, 1960; E492.94 33d.H5 1961) by Thomas Wentworth Higginson; and Norwood P. Hallowell, *The Negro as a Soldier in the War of the Rebellion* (Boston: Little, Brown, and Co., 1897; E449.D16 vol. 24, no. 17 Mur Pam Coll, Rare Bk).

CHARTING THE WAR

Civil War maps provide several levels of information pertaining to black history. The most obvious is the documentation of black participation in military activities. Numerous detailed maps depict the areas where major battles occurred, such as Manassas, Antietam, Gettysburg, Vicksburg, Fredericksburg, Richmond, and Petersburg. Many other sites of military activities are also covered, including Millikens Bend, Mississippi, Fort Wagner, South Carolina, Fort Olustee, Florida, and Port Hudson, Louisiana, where black soldiers played an important role in the fighting. These maps may show fortifications, earthworks, and troop positions.

There are approximately twenty-four thousand maps and seventy-six atlases in the Library's Geography and Map Division pertaining to the Civil War. Full cartobibliographical descriptions for each item are found in Richard Stephenson's *Civil War Maps: An Annotated List of Maps and Atlases in the Library of Congress* (Washington: Library of Congress, 1989; Z6027.U5L5 1989) These maps, prepared by both Union and Confederate army officers, as well as by commercial publishers, consist of reconnaissance maps, field sketches, and theater-of-war maps recording troop positions, movements, and fortifications. Two significant collections of Civil War maps are those assembled and drawn by Maj. Jedediah Hotchkiss, a topographical engineer serving with the Army of Northern Virginia, and maps belonging to Gen. William Tecumseh Sherman. The former collection focuses on Virginia county maps and battlefield maps, and the latter concerns Sherman's military activities in Georgia.

The best single source for military maps is the U.S. War Department's postwar compilation *Atlas to Accompany the Official Records of the Union and Confederate Armies* (Washington: Government Printing Office, 1891–95; G1201.S5U6 1891). Consisting of 176 plates, the atlas reproduces maps compiled by both Union and Confederate officers, many of which are detailed battle maps compiled after the war. Another useful research tool is *Civil War Maps: A Graphic Index to the Atlas to Accompany the Official Records of the Union and*

Confederate Armies (Chicago: The Newberry Library, 1987; G1201.S5U6 1891 Index), compiled by Neil S. O'Reilly, David C. Bosse, and Robert W. Karrow, Jr.

Landownership and topographical maps are the most useful for the study of black settlement patterns at the time of the Civil War. Most battlefield maps, which were prepared as officer's reports immediately after the battles or as historical documentation after the close of the war, were prepared on large-scale base maps. The base maps recorded topography, farmsteads, fields, wooded areas, names of residents, roads, bridges, mills, churches, and towns. Over these detailed depictions of the physical and cultural landscapes, troop positions, movements, and fortifications were indicated.

These maps are useful for black history when African-Americans lived in the vicinity of the major military engagements and when the engineers recorded settlement information. A particularly good example is a map of the vicinity of Richmond, Virginia, prepared by the Confederate engineers under the direction of Capt. A. H. Campbell and published in 1864 (Stephenson, *Civil War Maps*, entries 624–26). The most obvious settlement features depicted on this map are the numerous plantations and farms, including the well-known plantations of Shirley, Westover, Berkeley, Harrison, and President John Tyler's Sherwood Forest along the Charles City County side of the James River. Depictions of these plantations sometimes include notations indicating the location of "quarters" and the "overseer." Several miles west of Richmond and Manchester, a quarry is indicated with "Negro quarters" nearby.

More intriguing, however, are numerous references to free Negro settlements. For example, in Charles City County, there are numerous isolated "Negro houses," a "Freetown" north of Westover, and, a little farther north, a cluster of five "Negro houses." Similarly in James City

County there are a number of isolated Negro residences identified, as well as one which is labeled "Free Negro Settlement Full of Cabins and Paths." In contrast, a map covering much of the same area which was prepared by Union engineers in 1862 under the direction of Maj. Gen. George B. McClellan is much sketchier and does not include any references to black settlements (Stephenson, *Civil War Maps*, entries 594, 594.1, 595). A map of the battlefield of Cold Harbor prepared in 1867 by Maj. J. E. Weiss, however, identifies a "Colored Ch." (Stephenson, *Civil War Maps*, entry 531.2). Since the church is not shown on Campbell's 1864 map, which includes the Cold Harbor area, it is possible that it did not exist at the time of the battle.

WAR IMAGES

Photographs, lithographs, engravings, and woodcuts of African-Americans document the progress of the war and the role blacks played in it. Materials range from caricatures (among the approximately one hundred Civil War images relating to blacks in the PP Graphics File) to political cartoons (PP Graphics File lot 4419), many of which deal with the dilemma of extending full citizenship to blacks, to images from illustrated newspapers (PP Graphics File lot 4422-E), primarily portraying domestic life, contraband activities, and African-Americans in the military. Illustrated weeklies contained images of the African-American experience during the Civil War. A card index for these illustrations in the Prints and Photographs Division includes entries under "Negro" that concern slavery, abolition, and emancipation.

In 1919 J. P. Morgan presented to the Library drawings by a monumental corpus of leading Civil War artists for *Harper's Weekly*, *Frank Leslie's Illustrated Newspaper*, and the New York *Illustrated News*. The Library's collection of six-

"Mustered Out," Little Rock, Arkansas, April 20, 1865, a drawing in pencil and gouache by Alfred R. Waud (1828–1891), published in Harper's Weekly, May 19, 1866. (PP DRWG/US-A, Waud, no. 162. LC-USZ62–175)

teen hundred drawings provides an invaluable record of camp life, marches, and important events of the war. The best represented artist in the collection is Alfred Waud, who primarily followed the Virginia campaigns from 1861 to 1865, producing hundreds of pencil-and-wash drawings for *Harper's* and the *Illustrated News.* A wood engraving that appeared in the January 23, 1864, edition of the illustrated newspaper *Harper's Weekly* shows African-American troops under Gen. Edward Augustus Wild liberating slaves in January 1864 on the North Carolina Terrebee plantation (PP *Harper's Weekly* 8, no. 369, p. 52, Graphics File lot 4422-E, repro. no. LC-USZ62-32314). Selected photographic

copies of eyewitness drawings by Civil War newspaper artists such as Alfred Waud and Edwin Forbes are available in the Prints and Photographs Division Reading Room, where a finding aid for Civil War drawings describes these and other drawings.

Images filed under "Contraband and Slavery" may include more than that and some show the migrations of families, their temporary accommodations, and Freedmen's Village in Arlington, Virginia. Careful examination of images filed under such headings as "camp life" shows blacks working as barber's assistants, cooks, teamsters, and stablemen.

Blacks were also portrayed as a burden to a

moribund southern economy and as a divisive element between planters and white yeoman farmers. One of the most graphic of these cartoons in the Graphics File (filed under "Civil War–Symbolism," lot 4420-L) is an 1861 wood engraving by T. W. Strong called "South Carolina Topsey in a Fix." It depicts Harriet Beecher Stowe's character Topsy on a porch speaking to a seated white woman who holds a flag in her lap. Topsy, a personification of the secessionist state South Carolina, is being chided for disrupting the Union. A male slave is running off the porch saying "Hand us over to ole Abe, eh? Ize off!" (PP PC/US-A 1861.S924.4, repro. no. LC-USZ62–13954). Cartoons about the Confederacy (PP Graphics File lot 4421-E) include contemporary political drawings showing Confederate sentiment toward blacks during the war, and blacks may appear in other political drawings, such as one showing Confederate women rioting over bread shortages at the end of the Civil War, with blacks at the perimeter of the crowds (*Frank Leslie's Illustrated Newspaper* 7, no. 334; PP repro. no. LC-USZ62-42028; "Confederacy—Miscellany," PP Graphics File lot 4421-F). Illustrated envelopes current in Baltimore in 1861 sometimes featured caricatures of blacks, such as "Dis chile's Contraban'." Three volumes of these envelopes in the Rare Book Collection include thirty such caricatures.

A rich source for Civil War images of blacks are cartoons dealing with Abraham Lincoln. Most of them address Lincoln's attempts to give freedom and citizenship rights to blacks. The antiwar Peace Democrats—also known as Copperheads—in their attempts to negotiate an end to the war and continue the institution of slavery generated political images caricaturing blacks. One lithograph by a Copperhead sympathizer is titled "The great American What Is It? Chased by Copper-heads," and was published in 1863 by E.W.T. Nichols. This anti-Lincoln satire shows Lincoln being pursued by three large copperhead snakes as he tears a piece of paper labeled "Constitution and the Union as It Was." Lincoln, who is portrayed as a barefoot backwoodsman, has just dropped a paper titled "New Black Constitution" which is signed "A.L. & Co." The "What-is-it" of the title refers to a deformed African man featured at P.T. Barnum's Museum on Broadway (PP Presidential File; repro. no. LC-USZ62–89615).

Specific subjects treated in contemporary images range from contraband and employment to black children. Stereographs that show African-Americans mostly date from after the Civil War

"He Died for Me!," collector's card no. 12 in "Stephens' Album Varieties: The Slave in 1863," copyright 1864. (PP lot 5174. LC-USZC4–2517; LC-USZ62–28495)

period, but one stereo does show the 1864 convention in Philadelphia known as the Great Sanitary Fair (PP Stereo "Negroes—Conventions—1864"; repro. no. LC-BH8184-10343).

Contemporary photographic coverage of the Civil War can be sampled in a reading room browsing file (PP). A Mathew Brady Studio photograph shows the 107th U.S. Colored Infantry guardhouse and guard at Fort Corcoran, with black soldiers in uniform with weapons (PP lot 4190-F, repro. no. LC-B8184–841). All known images of blacks in the Brady collection are listed in a reference aid, "Photographs of African-Americans during the Civil War, Lots 4161 through 4205," which cites more than one hundred. Subjects include blacks allied with Union troops, contrabands, and African-Americans serving in official capacities.

Included in the Herman Haupt Collection in the Prints and Photographs Division are images made by Capt. Andrew Joseph Russell, the first official U.S. Army photographer, who was hired in 1863 to document the work of the Construction Corps of the U.S. Army Military Railroad. His photographs show black men working on railroads, helping the U.S. Military Construction Corps, and walking on the streets of Richmond and Washington, D.C., the Confederate and Union capitals (PP lot 11486-H, boxes A, C, E, G, H).

George N. Barnard photographed the battleground at Bull Run in 1862 while in the employ of Mathew Brady. His photograph titled "Part of the U.S. Military Establishment at Nashville, Tenn., 1864–65," shows a crowd of black men standing at the doors of the Taylor Depot in downtown Nashville (PP PH-B, Barnard no. 70, repro. no. LC-B8184–10263). Another "City of Atlanta, Ga., no. 1," taken in 1866, shows a well-dressed black man standing on a flat car in a nearly destroyed railyard (PP PH-B Barnard no. 35, repro. no. LC-B8184–10092).

The Clara Barton Collection includes an al-

"To Miss Dinah Dobson of Nashville, Tenn.: Poor Oppressed or the Contraband Schottisch," by E. A. Benson. This satirical cover image shows a glamorized female contraband—the name given to slaves who fled to Union lines—decorating the sheet music for a Scottish round dance, the schottisch. Lithographic music cover, published by C. D. Benson, copyright 1862. (PP lot 10615–13. LC-USZC4–2443)

bum of cartes de visite, the small mounted photographic images exchanged between friends during the nineteenth century. Her cartes, which include images of an aged black woman and several slave children whose skin color and features range from Caucasoid to Negroid, were initially produced for distribution by the National Freedmen's Relief Association to raise funds for freed people like the ones featured on the cartes.

In an extended polemic against the North, Confederate sympathizer and Copperhead Adalbert Volck—also known by the pseudonym V. Blada—published etchings during the Civil War that included caricatures of blacks. A Baltimore dentist, Volck did his artistic work in secret at night and circulated it underground. An 1861 pen-and-pencil drawing by Volck titled "Slaves Concealing Their Master from a Search Party" shows a slave master, pistol in hand, hiding behind a door, while the loyal female slave misleads Yankee soldiers. In the background a well-fed slave child clings to a well-dressed male slave sitting at the fireplace. Part of the Stern Collection, the drawing is reproduced in *Confederate War Etchings* (Baltimore: n.p., n.d.; E647. V92 Stn Coll, Rare Bk). Volck's etching "Enlistment of Sickle's Brigade" (1861, Stn Coll, Rare Bk) depicts black and white soldiers who rallied to war cries as undisciplined scoundrels. His "Free Negroes in the North" and "Free Negroes in Hayti" (both 1864, Stn Coll, Rare Bk) are disparaging portrayals of free blacks.

ENTERTAINMENT AND MUSIC

Minstrel songs continued to be popular during the Civil War, some of them voicing strong antislavery sentiments. For example, "Kingdom Coming," by Henry Clay Work (Chicago: Root & Cady, 1862; M140.W), became widely popular almost overnight, spreading to blacks behind

the Confederate lines within six months. Union soldiers entering Confederate territory were greeted by welcoming freedmen singing it. Another emancipation song was J. C. Wallace's "We Are Coming from the Cotton Fields" (Chicago: Root & Cady, 1864; M1640.W) with its remarkable third verse:

> We will leave our chains behind us, boys
>   The prison, and the rack,
> And we'll hide beneath a soldier's coat,
>   The scars upon our backs.

Both of these illustrate that not all the songs sung by the minstrels projected racist stereotypes. Many of them in their original editions can be located in the Music Division, but published collections may provide a more convenient sampling. Examples are *Our War Songs, North & South* (Cleveland: S. Brainard's Sons, 1887; M1636.06) and *Songs of the Civil War*, compiled and edited by Irwin Silber (New York: Columbia University Press, 1960; M1637.S5S6).

The public in the North enjoyed these songs, but it was almost unaware of the existence in the South of African-American folk music, particularly the spiritual. Not until white Northerners went South on war assignments did knowledge of the spiritual become generally known, although distinctive black religious songs had been described in magazine articles and novels since early in the century. The first spiritual to be published with its music was "The Song of the Contrabands, 'Oh Let My People Go,'" better known today as "Go Down, Moses" (New York: Horace Waters, 1861; M1671.S). This was an awkward arrangement for voice and piano by an English musician, Thomas Baker, who apparently knew little about African-American musical style.

Another song, "Down in the Lonesome Valley: Shout Song of the Freedmen of Port Royal" was published in Boston by Oliver Ditson in 1864 (M1671.D Case). As the war progressed, interest in the freedmen and their music was nourished by descriptions of spirituals with snatches of texts that appeared in newspapers and magazines. Not until 1867, however, did a collection of the songs appear as a separate volume, *Slave Songs of the United States* (New York: A. Simpson & Co., 1867; M1670.A42 Case), edited by William Francis Allen, Charles Pickard Ware, and Lucy McKim Garrison. The editors, who were educated and music-loving Northerners stationed during the war in the Sea Islands, felt a responsibility to preserve the songs before they disappeared. It was a landmark collection in the history of black folk music, but at the time its publication was hardly noticed.

Collections of words of spirituals appear in "Negro 'Shouts' and Shout Songs" in Henry George Spaulding's "Under the Palmetto," *Continental Monthly* for August 1863 (4:196–200; AP2.C73) and Thomas Wentworth Higginson's "Negro Spirituals" in *Army Life in a Black Regiment* (Boston: Beacon Press, 1962, c1869; E492.94 33d.H5 1962).

Over three hundred Civil War songs collected in four bound volumes, one relating to the Confederacy and the three others to the Union, are held in the Rare Book and Special Collections Division. "Battle Song of the Black Horsemen," from Winchester, Virginia, October 1861 (Confed no. 22), "Colored Volunteers" (Union nos. 97, 98), "Colored Brigade" (Union nos. 94, 95), and "Come Back, Massa," distributed by Johnson Publishing, Philadelphia (Union no. 109) are among the songs. "Black Regiment" (Union no. 61) and "Old Shady, a Contraband Song" (Union no. 120) were both published by the Committee for Recruiting Colored Regiments.

Over three thousand nineteenth-century playbills include several with black or blackface casts. A parody of *Uncle Tom's Cabin* was presented in Washington, D.C., in 1854, and standard versions were performed there in 1859 and 1862 and in Philadelphia in 1861. Playbills for *Gems of Minstrelsy* and other minstrel shows in Washington, D.C., in 1860 are also available. A special playbill card file is arranged by title and place of performance (Thr A9–3, A9–31, A10–1, P11–16, Rare Bk).

During the war, a blind African-American pianist, Thomas Greene Bethune, advertised by his former master as "Blind Tom," caused a stir because of his remarkable talents. A piece by Bethune, "Oliver Gallop, by Tom, the Blind Negro Boy Pianist, only 10 Years Old" (New York: Horace Waters, 1860; Music 3087 Item 4) was published as early as 1860. His battle piece, "The Battle of Manassas" (Chicago: Root & Cady, 1866; M20.C58B) included realistic music echoing the sounds of a battle. After emancipation, his former master continued to exploit his abilities, acting as his manager and guardian. When Tom was sixteen, the list from which his evening's program could be selected comprised eighty-two titles, including works by Beethoven, Mendelssohn, Bach, and Chopin and variations on operatic themes, as well as three of his own compositions. He wrote over one hundred songs, many of which were published. A contemporary publication relating to Bethune is entitled *The Marvelous Musical Prodigy, Blind Tom, the Negro Boy Pianist, Whose Performances at the Great St. James and Egyptian Halls, London, and Salle Hertz, Paris, Have Created Such a Profound Sensation* (New York: French & Wheat Printers [1868?]; ML417.B3 M3; E449.D16 vol. 23, no. 23 Mur Pam Coll, Rare Bk). Tom's biography has been written by Geneva H. Southall, *Blind Tom: The Post-Civil War Enslavement of a Black Musical Genius* (Minneapolis: Challenge Productions, 1979; ML417.B78S7 1979).

In spite of hundreds of years of unpaid labor, blood shed in battle, and obvious cultural contributions, African-Americans still faced formidable obstacles to full citizenship during the Reconstruction years.

CHAPTER FIVE

RECONSTRUCTION AND ITS AFTERMATH

Even after the issuance of the Emancipation Proclamation in 1863, two more years of war, service by African-American troops, and the defeat of the Confederacy, the nation was still unprepared to deal with the question of full citizenship for the newly freed black population. *Reconstruction* is a term used to describe the methods of reorganizing the Southern states after the Civil War, to provide the means for readmitting them into the union, and to define the means by which whites and blacks could live together in a nonslave society. President Lincoln wanted leniency for the Southern states, and believed that the colonization of former slaves was desirable, since he feared that blacks and whites could not live together peaceably. Nevertheless, Lincoln proposed that the rebellious states recognize the permanent freedom of ex-slaves and provide education for them. When he was assassinated in April 1865 and Vice President Andrew Johnson succeeded him, the policy changed. Johnson, a Tennessean, had disagreed with the secession of the Southern states but was unwilling either to punish the former Confederates too severely or to sanction full citizenship rights for African-Americans.

The South continued to chafe under its defeat and most Southerners felt humiliated by both the whites and blacks who gained political power and prestige during the Reconstruction era. When the election of 1876 resulted in a disputed contest between Rutherford B. Hayes and Samuel J. Tilden, Northern and Southern Congressmen came up with a compromise. The South would throw its support behind Hayes if the North would remove all troops from the former Confederate states and allow them to direct their own internal affairs. When the compromise was reached, it was obvious that the North was abdicating its responsibility to protect the rights of the newly freed black population.

Among standard histories of the period from the close of the Civil War to the ascendancy of Booker T. Washington in the 1890s are Kenneth Stampp's *The Era of Reconstruction* (New York: Knopf, 1965; E668.S79), John Hope Franklin's *Reconstruction after the Civil War* (Chicago: University of Chicago Press, 1961; E668.F7), and Eric Foner's *Reconstruction: America's Unfinished Revolution, 1863–1877* (New York, Harper, 1988; E668.F66 1988). A condensed version of Foner's book is entitled *A Short History of Reconstruction, 1863–1877* (New York: Harper, 1990; E668.F662 1990). W. E. B. DuBois's *Black Reconstruction in America* (Cleveland: World Publishing Co., [1964, c1962]; E668.D83 1964) provides a history of the

period and discusses Reconstruction historiography. DuBois includes a section on "The Propaganda of History" in which he argues that many previous authors' background and training influenced them to distort facts and report on conditions as they wished them to appear. He includes lists of "anti-Negro" writers, sympathetic white historians, and black historians.

Charles Crowe's *The Age of the Civil War and Reconstruction, 1830–1900: A Book of Interpretive Essays* (Homewood, Ill.: Dorsey Press, 1975; F216.C76 1975), edited with an introduction and bibliographical essay in each chapter, is another general introduction to the period. It attempts to present the explanations of South-

"Emancipation" (Philadelphia: S. Bott, 1865) is Thomas Nast's picture of what the future held for free blacks in the United States. Wood engraving. (PP Reilly 1865–3. LC-USZ62–2573)

RADICAL   RIOTS

SOUTHERN RIGHTS

LINCOLN CHAPEL

WHAT THEY WERE.

ANDREW JOHNSON'S

RECONSTRUCTION,

MEMPHIS.   NEW ORLEANS

TREASON IS A CRIME AND MUST BE MADE ODIOUS, AND TRAITORS MUST BE PUNISHED.

LOVE THINE ENEMIES

JOHNSON. VETOES FREEDMENS BUREAU CIVIL RIGHTS BILL AND THE AMENDMENT TO THE U.S CONSTITUTION OBJECT TO

I AM YOUR MOSES TO

DR.P.B.RANDOLPH A COLORED MAN HAD DINNER, AND A GRATEFUL GLASS OF WINE AT THE WHITE HOUSE.

SEE N.Y. TIMES

PARDON TO REBELS

I AM ONE OF YOUR BEST FRIENDS

VETOES TO UNION MEN

PLANTATION BITTERS GOOD FOR THE CONSTITUTION

OTHELLO. DOST THOU MOCK ME?
IAGO.   I MOCK YOU! NO, BY HEAVEN: WOULD YOU WOULD BEAR YOUR FORTUNES LIKE A MAN.
SHAKSPEARE.

1862.

1866.

HOW IT WORKS.   Th. Nast.

Iago. The Moor is of a free and open nature,
That thinks men honest that but seem to be so;
And will as tenderly be led by the nose,
As asses. . . . . .
Make the Moor thank me, love me, and reward me
For making him egregiously an ass,
And practising upon his peace and quiet
Even to madness. 'Tis here, but yet confus'd:
Knavery's plain face is never seen, till us'd. . . . . .
Though I do hate him as I do hell pains,
Yet, for necessity of present life,
I must show out a flag and sign of love,
Which is indeed but sign. . . . . .
Then devils will their blackest sins put on,
They do suggest at first with heavenly shows,
As I do now. . . . . .
I humbly do beseech you of your pardon,
For too much loving you. . . . . .
I hope, you will consider, what is spoke
Comes from my love,—But, I do see you are mov'd—
I am to pray you, not to strain my speech
To grosser issues, nor to larger reach
Than to suspicion. . . . . .
. . . . O grace! O heaven defend me!
Are you a man? have you a soul or sense—
God be wi' you; take mine office.—O wretched fool,
That liv'st to make thine honesty a vice! . . . . .
O monstrous world! Take note, take note, O world!
To be direct and honest, is not safe.—
I thank you for this profit; and, from hence,
I'll love no friend, sith love breeds such offence. . . . . .
Work on,
My medicine, work! . . . . .

"I have been accused of being inimical to the true interests of the colored people: but this is not true. I am one of their best friends and time, which tries and tests all, will demonstrate the fact. . . . I once said I would be the Moses of your people, and lead them on to liberty—liberty they now have. . . . . . I have been blamed for vetoing the Freedmen's Bureau Bill, and have been also represented as the colored people as having done it because I was their enemy. This is not true. . . . . . The ordinary course of judicial proceedings is no longer interrupted. The courts, both State and Federal, are in full, complete, and successful operation, and through them every person, regardless of race and color, is entitled to and can be heard. The protection granted to the white citizens is already conferred by law upon the freedmen. . . . . It can not be expected that men who have for four years been made familiar with the blood and carnage of war, who have suffered the loss of property, and in no many instances reduced from affluence to poverty, can at once assume the calm demeanor and return of those citizens of the country whose worldly possessions have not been destroyed, and whose political hopes have not been blasted, and the worst view of this subject affords no parallel in violence to similar outrages that have followed all civil commotions, always less in magnitude than even. But I do not believe that this is to be represented state of things will last long."—Andrew Johnson.

ern behavior described by nineteenth- and twentieth-century historians and treats "The Meaning of Reconstruction," "The Issues of Reconstruction," and "The Retreat of Reconstruction," as well as "The Black Experience beyond Slavery."

Another guide to the literature is Milton Meltzer's excerpted essays, reports, and documents, illustrated with photographs and drawings, entitled *In Their Own Words: A History of the American Negro, 1865–1916* (New York: Crowell, 1964–67; 3 vols. E185.M54). Meltzer argues that the characterization of the period as one of "Negro rule" is mistaken. Although this was the first time that blacks held significant federal and state offices, blacks did not have a monopoly on leadership positions. In fact, blacks had a hard time even being seated in the bodies to which they were elected. During the period 1866 to 1900, only twenty-two blacks actually served in the U.S. Congress.

Scholarly essays, articles, and accounts are found in Emma Lou Thornbrough's *Black Reconstructionists* (Englewood Cliffs, N.J.: Prentice-Hall, 1972; E668.T48) and *Reconstruction in the South, 1865–77: First-hand Accounts of the American Southland after the Civil War by Northerners and Southerners* (New York: Farrar, Straus and Giroux, 1965; E668.W78), edited by Harvey Wish. Thornbrough includes biographical accounts of black congressmen, voicing their concerns, and presents views of black and white Southerners and Northerners from a number of perspectives, giving historical interpretations of Reconstruction scholarship. Important documents such as Gen. Philip Sheridan's observations about the 1866 New Orleans race riot,

Gen. Oliver Otis Howard's report on the efforts of the Freedmen's Bureau in the area of education for African-Americans, and Supreme Court Justice John Harlan's dissenting opinion on the civil rights cases are included.

The *Documentary History of Reconstruction: Political, Military, Social, Religious, Educational, and Industrial, 1865 to 1906* (New York: McGraw-Hill, 1966; E668.F58 1966), edited by Walter L. Fleming with a foreword by David Donald, contains state and federal laws, official reports, political platforms, observations of Northern men and foreigners living or traveling in the South, and accounts of white and black Southerners and Confederate and Union sympathizers. With the exception of laws and political documents, the materials are primarily accounts by individuals who had firsthand knowledge of conditions in the South, most of whom were not favorably disposed to the equal treatment of blacks as citizens. A similar volume, James P. Shenton's *The Reconstruction: A Documentary History of the South after the War, 1865–1877* (New York: Putnam, 1963; E668.S543) consists of addresses, essays, and lectures from the period.

Accounts of leading figures of the age are found in *Black Leaders of the Nineteenth Century* (Urbana: University of Illinois Press, 1988; E185.96.B535 1988), edited by Leon Litwack and August Meier, which includes "Alexander Crummell: Black Nationalist and Apostle of Western Civilization" and "Martin Delany: Elitism and Black Nationalism." *Black Women in Nineteenth Century American Life* (University Park: Pennnsylvania State University Press, 1976; E185.96.B54), edited by Bert James Loewenberg and Ruth Bogin, consists of biographical accounts of such outstanding women as journalist Ida B. Wells-Barnett, missionary Amanda Smith, and Fannie Barrier Williams, who was a leader of the black women's club movement.

A summary of the legislation of the Thirty-ninth through Forty-first Congresses, com-

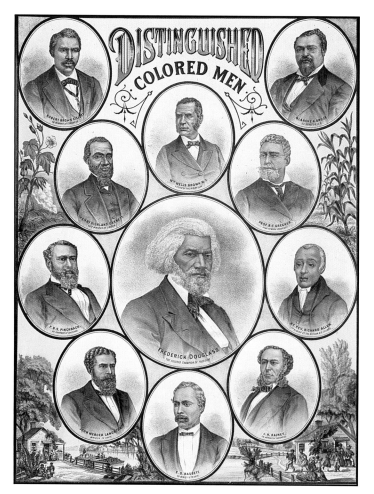

"Distinguished Colored Men." Chromolithograph by Muller & Company, ca. 1883. (PP. LC-USZC4–1561)

PUBLIC OFFICIALS AND AFRICAN-AMERICAN LEADERS

The papers of Andrew Johnson (MSS, microfilm 1814–1947) cover the term of his presidency, a period during which the politics of Reconstruction preoccupied the nation. The Manuscript Division also holds some papers of vocal Radical Republican Congressmen Thaddeus Stevens (MSS, papers 1811–1927) and Benjamin Wade (MSS, microfilm 1832–81). A small collection of Charles Sumner papers (MSS, papers 1841–74) and Sumner correspondence in several other collections including those of President Lincoln (MSS, papers and microfilm 1833–1934), Salmon Portland Chase (MSS, microfilm and papers 1755–1898), Daniel Webster (MSS, microfilm 1798–1900), and Hamilton Fish (MSS, microfilm 1732–1914) augment the Library's Reconstruction holdings. Stevens, Wade, and Sumner were considered radical not only because they wanted to punish the South for its rebellion, but also because they wanted to give full citizenship rights to blacks immediately. They spearheaded legislation designed to protect the rights of blacks, including the Thirteenth Amendment to the Constitution (1865), which outlawed slavery, the Fourteenth (1868), which established that all people born or naturalized in the United States were citizens entitled to due process of law, and the Fifteenth (1870), which granted the vote to all male citizens "regardless of race, color, or previous condition of servitude," as well as the Civil Rights Acts of 1866, 1870, and 1875.

During the Reconstruction period several violent reactionary groups, including the Ku Klux Klan, were organized largely for the purpose of terrorizing blacks into submission to white supremacist governments. The Congress passed several "Force Acts" between 1870 and 1875 to enforce the South's recognition of the freedmen's civil and political rights.

piled by Edward McPherson, clerk of the House of Representatives, is entitled *The Political History of the United States of America during the Period of Reconstruction, April 15, 1865, to July 5, 1870* (Washington: Government Printing Office, 1875; E668.M17). The volume reprints political manuals issued at various periods from 1866 to 1870, addresses the controversies surrounding President Andrew Johnson, and discusses the Fourteenth Amendment, Tenure of Office Act, and other legislation of the period.

Reconstruction public officials such as Ohio Senator and Cabinet member Thomas Ewing (MSS, papers and microfilm 1754–1941), Illinois Representative and Senator John Alexander Logan (MSS, papers 1847–1923), Illinois Senator Lyman Trumbull (MSS, microfilm 1843–94), Virginia Congressman William Cabell Rives (MSS, papers 1694–1939), Secretary of the Treasury Hugh McCulloch (MSS, papers 1855–94), and Attorney General Caleb Cushing (MSS, papers 1785–1906) dealt with various aspects of Reconstruction legislation and politics concerning freed slaves, such as civil and voting rights for African-Americans.

Several black Reconstruction congressmen are represented among Library holdings. John Mercer Langston (MSS, Fisk University microfilm 1853–98), son of a freed slave woman and her former master, served as a U.S. representative from Virginia, a dean of the law school and vice president of Howard University, and a diplomat to Haiti and the Dominican Republic. A small collection of Mississippi Senator Blanche Kelso Bruce papers (MSS, papers 1878–90) is supplemented by Bruce correspondence found in the papers of abolitionist and orator Frederick Douglass (MSS, microfilm 1841–1967) and Ohio politician John Paterson Green (MSS, microfilm 1869–1932). The originals of the Green materials are in the Western Reserve Historical Society in Ohio. Some material relating to another black Mississippi senator, Hiram Revels, is in the Carter G. Woodson collection (MSS, microfilm 1796–1933) along with some undated writings of Mississippi Representative John Roy Lynch and correspondence with South Carolina Congressman Robert Smalls.

Speeches by Charles Sumner about Reconstruction legislation and addresses by black Reconstruction legislators such as Hiram Revels, Joseph Rainey of South Carolina—the first black congressman—and J. T. Walls of Florida are found in a Rare Book Division collection of

congressional speeches (YA5000J17 Rare Bk), dating from 1830 to 1920. A typed guide, "An Inventory of the Library of Congress Collection of Texts of American Speeches," is arranged alphabetically by speaker and identifies broad subject areas.

Another source for speeches is *Black Congressional Reconstruction Orators and Their Orations, 1869 to 1879* (Metuchen, N.J.: Scarecrow, 1976; E185.2.B52), edited by Annjennette McFarlin, which provides a survey of the addresses of black Reconstruction congressmen who served in the Forty-first through Forty-fifth Congresses and includes reprints of the most

"Radical Members of the First Legislature after the War, South Carolina," photograph, 1878. (PP lot 4422. LC-USZ62–28044)

notable speeches. General reference books on African-American representation include Maurine Christopher's *Black Americans in Congress* (New York: Crowell, 1976; E185.96.C5 1976), Samuel D. Smith's *The Negro in Congress, 1870–1901* (Chapel Hill: University of North Carolina Press, 1940; JK1929.A2), and *Black Americans in Congress, 1870–1989* (Washington: Government Printing Office, 1990; E185.96.R25 1990).

Portraits or commemorative prints of black congressional representatives portray "The First Colored Senator and Representatives" (PP PGA-A Currier & Ives, First Colored, repro. no. LC-USZ62-2814), "Heroes of the Colored Race" (PP PGA-D Hoover, repro. no. LC-USZ62-10180), "Distinguished Colored Men" (PP PGA-D Muller, repro. nos. LC-USZ62-7825, LC-USZC4-1561),

"Admission to the United States Supreme Court of the First Colored Lawyer, at Washington, Feb. 2d.," wood engraving in Frank Leslie's Illustrated Newspaper, March 13, 1880. *(PP. LC-USZ62–22105)*

and "From the Plantation to the Senate" (PP PGA-D Watson, repro. nos. LC-USZ62-25259, LC-USZC2-639). An 1868 lithograph by an unknown Louisiana artist features vignette portraits of twenty-nine members of a Louisiana constitutional convention, most of them black. Prominently featured are black lieutenant governors of Louisiana Oscar J. Dunn and P. B. S. (Pinckney Benton Stewart) Pinchback, who served as governor of Louisiana for thirty-six days in 1872 when the white governor was impeached (PP unprocessed DLC/PP-1991:87). An article and illustration in *Frank Leslie's Illustrated Newspaper*, March 13, 1880, about a black lawyer admitted to argue before the United States Supreme Court, details the experience of Samuel Lowry of Huntsville, Alabama (PP Graphics File lot 4422-G; repro. no. LC-USZ62–22105; MicRR 02282). An individual chromolithographic portrait of Hiram Revels was executed by Louis Prang in 1870 from a painting by Thomas Kaufmann (PP PGA-B Prang, repro. nos. LC-USZ62–10181, LC-USZC4-681).

Postwar images of blacks from the Brady-Handy photographic studio in Louisiana include Lieutenant Governor P. B. S. Pinchback (PP Biog., repro. no. LC-BH826-3486) and Congressman Robert Smalls (PP Biog., repro. no. LC-USZ62–99507). Other images of these same individuals include one of Smalls that contains scenes of black life and military service (PP PGA-D Rogan, repro. no. LC–USZ62–36274).

One of the activities of the first Reconstruction Congress was to establish the Joint Committee on Reconstruction. The committee, composed of nine members of the House of Representatives and six senators, was responsible for investigating conditions in the former Confederate states to determine whether the states should be readmitted with full representation in Congress. The U.S. Congress *Report of the Joint Committee on Reconstruction* (Washington: Government Printing Office, 1915; E668.

"The Freedman's Bureau," drawn by Alfred R. Waud for a wood engraving in Harper's Weekly, *July 26, 1868. (PP. LC-USZ62–18090)*

U5844) describes the process of establishing military governments throughout the South. A related publication, *The Journal of the Joint Committee of Fifteen on Reconstruction* (New York: Columbia University, 1914; E668.K33), was edited by Benjamin Kendrick, who describes it as "the most important source of information concerning the process by which the framers of that amendment arrived at the conclusions which they submitted to Congress."

"Laws in Relation to Freedmen," compiled by Gen. Oliver O. Howard, commissioner of the Freedmen's Bureau, is a useful compendium of the black codes governing the behavior of the newly emancipated freedmen in the ten Confederate states. The laws are included in the Freedmen's Bureau's *Assistant Commissioner's Report* (U.S. 39th Congress, 2d Sess. Senate Executive Document no. 6: Serial Set 1276, LL, MicRR). Sample laws include Alabama's act concerning vagrancy and labor contracts and a Florida act legislating the death penalty for assaults on white females.

The Carter G. Woodson collection (MSS, microfilm 1796–1933) includes papers of Benjamin Tucker Tanner, a bishop of the African Methodist Episcopal Church, and Whitefield McKinlay, a successful real estate broker and

Watercolor by Henry L. Stephens (1824–1882). Primarily an illustrator and caricaturist, Stephens lived in Philadelphia and New York and worked for Frank Leslie and Harper Brothers. (DLC/PP—CAI–Stephens, H.L., no. 1, A size. LC-USZC4–2442)

political appointee. Tanner's correspondents include abolitionist and orator Frederick Douglass, Civil War hero Christian A. Fleetwood, diplomat Richard Theodore Greener, Senator Hiram Revels, diplomat Ebenezer Bassett, and South Carolina Secretary of State Francis Lewis Cardozo. A small collection of Francis Lewis Cardozo family papers (MSS, papers 1864–1968) relate, in part, to his career as a South Carolina public official.

RACE RELATIONS AND RACIAL VIOLENCE

Believing that freed blacks would experience difficulties adapting to freedom, Congress established the Bureau of Refugees, Freedmen, and Abandoned Lands in March 1864. The bureau, which existed from 1865 to 1872, was established in the War Department to supervise affairs relating to refugees and freedmen. It assisted in the protection of black farmers and laborers, helped to establish schools for freedmen, regularized marriages, conducted relief work among destitute freedmen, and aided in the search for family members sold in various parts of the South. Free blacks and whites, women, children, soldiers, laborers, and contrabands all needed food, clothing, and shelter, and the Freedmen's Bureau, as it was popularly called, was designed to aid them in the procurement of necessities. Yet the bureau did more. It enforced labor contracts and served as judge and jury in disputes. George R. Bentley's *A History of the Freedmen's Bureau* (Philadelphia: University of Pennsylvania, 1955; E185.2.B4) is considered a standard work. Other useful books include Paul Skeels Peirce's *The Freedmen's Bureau* (Iowa City, Iowa: The University, 1904; E185.2U59 and MicRR 37516), and John Winthrop Chandler's *Freedmen's Bureau* (Washington: Congressional Globe, 1866; MicRR 41166). Daniel A. Novak's *The Wheel of Servitude: Black Forced Labor after Slavery* (Lexington: University Press of Kentucky, c1978; E185.N88) is critical of the bureau. He argues that "the lien concept, originally written into Bureau contracts to protect the worker, became an instrument by which he was bound to the land."

Several manuscript collections provide information about the Freedmen's Bureau. An April 1866 letter from M. H. Doolittle and his wife Lucy Salisbury Doolittle (MSS, papers 1864–67) to a friend states:

Lucy still continues her industrial school, and teaches colored women to sew and knit, &c. . . . The Freedman's Bureau has pretty nearly ceased issuing relief to the "contrabands"; as they are generally able to take care of themselves, now that the winter is over and we do not have to spend so much time looking after suffering among them.

The John Mercer Langston papers (MSS, Fisk University microfilm 1853–98) include information about his work as a traveling representative for the bureau. The papers of Samuel Denham Barnes (MSS, papers 1791–1867) contain material about his work with the Freedmen's Bureau in Mississippi as do those of James Jenkins Gillette (MSS, papers 1857–84), which also yield information about efforts to educate the freedmen.

The American Missionary Association (AMA) (MSS, microfilm 1846–82) was particularly concerned about educating freed blacks. Originals of the AMA papers are located at the Amistad Research Center in New Orleans. The association founded and sustained more than five hundred schools in the South for African-Americans, including Dillard University in Louisiana, Houston-Tillotson College in Texas, Tougaloo College in Mississippi, Talladega College in Alabama, and LeMoyne College in Tennessee. It maintained an interest in Hampton Institute and Fisk and Atlanta Universities.

Images from this period of many of these educational institutions can be found in the "Negroes—Schools and Colleges" category in the Graphics File (PP Graphics File lot 4422-F), which refers the searcher to images of African Free Schools, Hampton Institute, and Freedmen's Bureau schools. An album of wood engravings of the Hampton Normal and Agricultural Institute and the town of Hampton, Virginia, describes an image of four black children as "Young Hopefuls" in 1883 in its caption (PP lot 7969-F). Stone Hall, one of the earliest buildings at historically black Atlanta University, was built in 1882 by architect Gottfried Norrman. Originally used as an administrative building, it became a landmark of the central district of the city because of its tower and elevated location and is documented in the Historic American Buildings Survey by eleven photographs (PP HABS GA, 61-ATLA., 10A-).

"Family Amalgamation among the Men-stealers," woodcut illustration from George Bourne, Picture of Slavery in the United States of America *(Middletown, Conn.: Edwin Hunt, 1834; E449.B772 Rare Bk). (LC-USZ62–30851)*

The antiblack terrorist group known as the Ku Klux Klan had its origins in Pulaski, Tennessee, in 1866. The KKK of the twentieth century and related white supremacist organizations are not directly related to it. William Peirce Randel's *The Ku Klux Klan: A Century of Infamy* (Philadelphia: Chilton Books, [1965]; E668.R18) provides a history of the origin of the Ku Klux Klan, along with bibliographical notes. Randel considered the "most authoritative" book on the Reconstruction Klan to be Stanley F. Horn's *Invisible Empire: The Story of the Ku Klux Klan, 1866–1871* (Boston: Houghton Mifflin, 1939; E668.H78). An important source for details of KKK atrocities before 1871 is the thirteen-volume report *Ku Klux Klan Conspiracy*, officially titled *The Testimony Taken by the Joint Select Committee to Inquire into the Condition of Affairs in the Late Insurrectionary States* (U.S. House of Representatives Rept. 22, parts 1–13; 42d Cong., 2d sess., 1871–72, and U.S. Senate Rept. no. 41; 42d Cong.; serial nos. 1484–1496, MicRR). Excerpts from the hearings are also reprinted in Harvey Wish's anthology, *Reconstruction in the South, 1865–1877* (New York: Farrar, Straus and Giroux, [1965]; E668.W78). Three images of lynchings of blacks by hate groups from 1889–94 are in the Prints and Photographs Division Specific Subject File under "Executions— Lynchings" (PP SSF).

Outbreaks of racial violence between blacks and whites took place in 1866 in Memphis, Tennessee, and New Orleans, Louisiana. A congressional committee appointed to investigate the causes of the riots issued *Memphis Riots and Massacres* (U.S. House of Representatives Rept. 101, 39th Cong., 1st sess.; F444.M5U53 1969). In Memphis hundreds of blacks were killed or wounded and their schools and churches were burned. The New Orleans riot is discussed in *Judge Edmund Abell and the New Orleans Riot of 1866* (Des Moines, Iowa: W.R. Abell, [1986]; F379.N557 A93 1986).

Besides providing further examples of extreme reactions to race during the period, Forrest G. Wood's *Black Scare: The Racist Response to Emancipation and Reconstruction* (Berkeley: University of California Press, 1968; E185.61.W84) asserts that the election of 1864 became a referendum on the national government's policies toward blacks and relates the history of the miscegenation controversy. A contemporary booklet by David Goodman Croly entitled *Miscegenation: The Theory of the Blending of the Races Applied to the American White Man and Negro* (New York: H. Dexter, Hamilton and Co., 1864; HT1581.C7 Rare Bk) also discusses this question.

David Augustus Straker's *New South Investigated* (Detroit, Mich.: Ferguson Printing Co., 1888; F215.S89 Rare Bk) is based on ten years' residence in the South during which Straker, a black lawyer, evaluated changes that occurred after emancipation and the difficult conditions African-Americans faced. He was optimistic that blacks could uplift themselves and effect social change through expanded opportunities in industrial and higher education. Two Straker pamphlets from the 1880s are part of the Murray Pamphlet Collection in the Rare Book and Special Collections Division.

BLACK EXODUS

In addition to publications and documents about the Reconstruction South, the Library has many materials that reflect the movement of blacks to other areas. Migrations took African-Americans to places like Kansas, northern and southern urban areas, and foreign locations such as Liberia. Rev. Charles K. Marshall, a noted white Vicksburg, Mississippi, minister, wrote *The Exodus, Its Effect upon the People of the South* (Washington: Colonization Rooms, 1880; E448.M36 Rare Bk). He reported that after emancipation blacks had "learned their multiplication tables and forgotten their prayers" and were consequently hindering the development of the South by departing to other regions.

The Kansas migration is reported in several books and government documents. One of the most revealing is the published hearing of the *Senate Select Committee to Investigate the Causes of the Removal of the Negroes from the Southern States to the Northern States* (Washington: Government Printing Office, 1880; Senate Rept. no. 693, part 2, serial set). Benjamin "Pap" Singleton, who is

Broadside advertising opportunities for land and homesteading with "Old Pap" Benjamin Singleton, leaving Nashville on April 15, 1878. (PP HABS KS N-6, field photo KS-49-14)

Ho for Kansas!

Brethren, Friends, & Fellow Citizens:

I feel thankful to inform you that the

REAL ESTATE

AND

Homestead   Association,

Will Leave Here the

15th of April, 1878,

In pursuit of Homes in the Southwestern Lands of America, at Transportation Rates, cheaper than ever was known before.

For full information inquire of

Benj. Singleton, better known as old Pap,

NO. 5 NORTH FRONT STREET.

Beware of Speculators and Adventurers, as it is a dangerous thing to fall in their hands.

Nashville, Tenn., March 18, 1878.

One of the many posters calling on southern blacks to leave for Kansas.

frequently credited as the leader of the movement, testified at the hearing, stating, "I have been fetching people; I believe I fetched out 7,432 people." He noted that he had been doing it since 1869. Another migrant said, "We can stand the climate North, East or West as well now as when fleeing from the cruel yoke of bondage. We believe life, liberty and happiness to be sweeter in a cold climate than murder, raping and oppression in the South."

A detailed, well-documented study by Nell Irvin Painter is entitled *Exodusters: Black Migration to Kansas after Reconstruction* (New York: Knopf, 1977; E185.93.K16P34 1977). Other scholarly studies are Robert G. Athearn's *In Search of Canaan: Black Migration to Kansas, 1879–1880* (Lawrence: The Regents Press of Kansas, 1978; E185.93.K16A8) and *At Freedom's Edge: Black Mobility and the Southern White Quest for Racial Control, 1861–1915* (Baton Rouge: Louisiana State University Press, 1991; E185.6.C66 1991), by William Cohen.

Migration patterns can be traced by using maps and atlases. Probably the first atlases to include maps portraying the distribution of blacks in the United States were the statistical atlases that were prepared to illustrate the results of the United States decennial censuses, starting in 1870. *Statistical Atlas of the United States Based on the Results of the Ninth Census, 1870* (New York: Julius Bien, 1874; G1201.G1U53 1874), edited by Francis A. Walker, was the Census Office's first attempt to prepare a cartographic summary of the decennial census. The atlas includes two maps pertaining to the distribution of blacks, one based on density, that is the number of blacks per square mile, and the other showing percentage of total population by county. Both maps emphasize the concentration of blacks in Virginia and Maryland and the southeastern states, with beginning concentrations in northern urban areas—New York City, southeastern Pennsylvania, southern Ohio, central Missouri, and eastern Kansas. One of the graphic devices used is a series of squares drawn proportionately to the population of each state and then divided to show the constituent elements of the population including foreign, native white, and native colored.

The atlas for the 1880 census, *Scribner's Statistical Atlas of the United States* (New York: Charles Scribner's Sons, 1883; G1201.G1H4 1883), edited by Fletcher W. Hewes and Henry Gannett, has only one map showing black population, as a ratio to total population of each county. The atlas for the succeeding census, however, *Statistical Atlas of the United States, Based upon the Results of the Eleventh Census* (Washington: Government Printing Office, 1898; G1201.G1U53 1898), edited by Henry Gannett, includes a greater variety of maps pertaining to the black population, with distribution by density and percentage of total population, age and sex percentages, population pyramids, pie diagrams, and bar charts showing percentage of "colored" and other ethnic groups, and bar graphs for sixteen states showing percentage of blacks from 1790 to 1890. Similar but simpler atlases were compiled for the 1910 and 1920 censuses.

Many blacks relocated during the Reconstruction period. Two especially good sources of cartographic materials for documenting these changing settlement patterns are fire insurance maps and county landownership maps and atlases. Maps and atlases for specific locations that have been published or revised at various intervals during the ensuing one hundred years can provide an excellent source for studying the changing black settlement patterns which started during Reconstruction and continued through the world wars. With these records it is possible to document the black migration from rural countryside to towns, cities, and other rural areas within the South or to urban and rural

settings in the Northeast, Midwest, and Great Plains.

Fire insurance maps, which pertain only to urban areas, provide detailed, large-scale surveys of cities and most major towns throughout the United States from the last quarter of the nineteenth century until the middle of the twentieth century. These maps, most of which were published by the Sanborn Map Company of Pelham, New York, were prepared specifically as a graphic reference tool for insurance underwriters in determining their risk as they wrote individual policies. Consequently, the maps give a wealth of information about the physical condition of the buildings—building outlines, number of stories, construction material (wood, brick, stone, etc.), roof composition, and proximity to water mains and fire hydrants. The function and names of commercial and public buildings (churches, schools, factories, social halls, stores, warehouses, etc.) are also indicated. Dwellings are marked "D" or "Dwg," but the names of residents are not included. House numbers, however, are recorded, so residents may be determined by consulting corresponding city directories.

One example is Selma, Alabama, a city that gained prominence during the civil rights movement in the 1960s, for which there are nine Sanborn fire insurance maps dating from the post-Reconstruction era (1884, 1889, 1893, 1898, 1903, 1907, 1913, 1925, and 1925 corrected to 1949). These maps not only trace the physical growth of the city, but also provide evidence of the growing number of blacks residing in the city. Originally settled in 1817, Selma had a population of approximately 7,500 in 1884 and grew to 23,000 by 1950, at which time 55 percent of the city's population was nonwhite. Comparing the number of public institutions such as churches, schools, or hospitals that are identified in the index to special activities as "colored'' or ''Negro,'' allows the researcher to visualize the growing concentration of blacks within the city. The earliest editions, 1884–98, identify two churches, both African Methodist Episcopal, and one school as ''colored,'' and an examination of individual map sheets shows the location of ''Negro tenements,'' ''Negro shanties,'' ''shanties,'' and a ''Negro female boarding house'' near two cotton warehouses and a foundry by the railroad track. By 1907 there were eleven ''Negro churches'' and three ''Negro schools,'' half of which were clustered in the northwest section of the town near Selma University, a black institution of higher education founded in 1878. A city hospital, Selma Infirmary, had a ''colored ward'' which was constructed of wood, whereas the main building, the women's ward, and a Confederate veterans' ward were constructed of brick. Meanwhile, the ''Negro tenements and shanties'' associated with the cotton warehouses and foundry shown on the earlier editions were replaced on the 1907 map by the growth of the industrial complex. By 1925 the number of institutions identified as ''Negro'' had increased to twenty-seven and included a Benevolent Hall, a Burial Society, Burwell's Infirmary, Queen Esther Society Club House, and Payne University, reflecting the increased concentration of blacks within the city and their increased demand for a variety of public services.

Xenia, Ohio, provides an example of black settlement in a northern city. Settled in 1803, Xenia was a station on the underground railroad before the Civil War. Wilberforce University, one of the nation's first permanent black colleges, was erected two and a half miles northeast of the town. Founded in 1856, it derived its name from the English abolitionist William Wilberforce. The eight fire insurance maps for Xenia date from 1885 to 1950. In that time, the town's population grew from 7,000 to 13,000, when approximately 19 percent of the city's population was classified as nonwhite. The earliest maps (1885, 1890, and 1895) each show one African Methodist Episcopal church and one colored public school, and the 1901 edition is the first to show Wilberforce University. By 1910 there were six Negro churches and two Negro schools, numbers which did not change significantly during the succeeding years. Most of these facilities were located on the eastern side of town, which has been identified as the black section by a local historian, Helen H. Santmyer, in *Ohio Town* (Columbus: Ohio State University Press, 1962; F499.X4S3). Interestingly, the 1931 edition, which identifies the black institutions as ''colored'' rather than ''Negro'' as in the previous editions, shows the location of a Ku Klux Klan lodge. The 1950 corrected edition indicates that this building was later demolished, since a paste-up correction showing a vacant lot was applied over a building identified only as ''Hall.''

Fire insurance maps published by the Sanborn Map Company held by the Library of Congress are listed in *Fire Insurance Maps in the Library of Congress* (Washington: Library of Congress, 1981; Z6026.I7U54 1981), with entries arranged alphabetically by state and city. These maps have been copied on microfilm by the Chadwyck-Healey Company of Alexandria, Virginia, which markets the film to state and local historical and educational institutions. Fire insurance maps produced by companies other than the Sanborn Map Company are also available in the collections.

Another useful resource for black settlement patterns are county landownership maps and atlases. Many of the landownership maps published after the Civil War for the midwestern and Great Plains states were published in atlas format. Atlases acquired by the Library before 1950 are described in *United States At-*

LEFT: *The First Baptist Church of Nicodemus, Kansas, was documented in 1983 by the Historic American Buildings Survey. Home of a congregation first organized in 1878 in the all-black settlement, the native limestone structure was begun in 1907. (PP HABS KS-49-K, sheet 1 of 9 sheets. LC-USZA1–1426)*

BELOW LEFT: *West elevation of the First Baptist Church of Nicodemus, Kansas. (PP HABS KS-49-K, sheet 7 of 9 sheets. LC-USZA1–1432)*

lases (Washington: Library of Congress, 1950; Z881.U5 1950).

Since county landownership maps and atlases were published by commercial companies, usually on a subscription basis, they were produced for the wealthier rural areas where the atlases could be sold profitably. A few landownership maps were published for counties in southern states during the Reconstruction and Booker T. Washington periods. One useful example is a map of Madison County, Tennessee, published by D.G. Beers and Company of Philadelphia in 1877 (GM Landownership 874). Although the map shows the names of landowners throughout the county, there is no indication that any of these owners were black. At least eight "colored" churches and one schoolhouse for blacks, located in county rural areas, are indicated, however. The location of numerous rural cotton gins points to the southern farmer's attempt to preserve the cotton-based economy after the Civil War.

Landownership atlases also document the migration of blacks to the Great Plains. The black community of Nicodemus, established in 1877 in Graham County in the high arid plains of northwestern Kansas, was organized by a group of blacks from Topeka, who encouraged migration from their home state, Kentucky. Although the town did not grow as rapidly as anticipated, the town plats and surrounding landowners are recorded in the 1906 atlas of Graham County, *Standard Atlas of Graham County, Kansas* (Chicago: George A. Ogle Company, 1906; G1458.G403 1906), which, like other county atlases, includes photographic views of prominent buildings and farmsteads and family portraits of subscribing patrons. The final page of the photograph section in this atlas is devoted entirely to black families and individuals. Comparing portraits to the names on the maps, it is possible to locate most of these families in the townships surrounding Nicodemus.

Architectural drawings, photographs, and oral interviews with residents further enrich the study of this community. In 1983, the Historic American Buildings Survey undertook to document the structures in Nicodemus, a national historic landmark black settlement, which had flourished until bypassed by the railroad in 1888. A town-site plan for the years 1877–90, architectural drawings or photographs of forty-two of the buildings, and the HABS field notes with transcripts of oral history interviews with several people who lived in the town and copies of photographs are available for study (PP HABS KANS, 33-NICO, 1–).

The settlement of blacks in Oklahoma, which reflects their close association with the Five Civilized Tribes, can also be documented by using maps and atlases. For example, a series of maps of the Indian Territory published by the General Land Office (GM Titled Collection) in 1876, 1879, 1883, 1885, and 1887 shows a "Negro Settlement" near Purcell on the Canadian River in Cleveland County. Several other black towns, such as Berwyn and Wynnewood, are shown within the Chickasaw Nation. Another source for examining black settlements in association with the resettled Indians in Oklahoma are three landownership atlases published in the early twentieth century. A 1910 atlas, *Has-*

tain's Township Plats of the Creek Nation ([Muskogee, Okla.]: E. Hastain, 1910; G1365.H3 1910) includes symbols identifying those landowners who were Creek (c), freedmen (f), minor freedmen (mf), and native-born freedmen (nbf). Similar atlases [*Township Maps of the Cherokee Nation*] (Muskogee, Okla.: Indian Territory Map Co., [1909]; G1365.I5 1909) and *Hastain's Township Plats of the Seminole Nation* (Muskogee, Okla.: E. Hastain, 1913; G1365.H35 1913) appear to have an "f" by some of the names, but there are no legends explaining this symbol.

BUFFALO SOLDIERS

Some blacks lived among the Indians but others worked to control and contain the native American population. In their role as soldiers in the military, African-American men were instrumental in patrolling the Great Plains, the Rio Grande, and areas of New Mexico, Arizona, Colorado, and the Dakotas. Under acts of Congress, four segregated regiments were established in 1866 to use the services of black soldiers. Two were cavalry regiments and two were infantry units. Black cavalry regiments consisted of the 9th and 10th Cavalry, and the infantry units included the 24th and 25th Infantry divisions.

The exploits and experiences of the *Buffalo Soldiers*, a term used by Indians to describe the black troops, are described in a comprehensive account by William H. Leckie, *The Buffalo Soldiers: A Narrative of the Negro Cavalry in the West* (Norman: University of Oklahoma Press, 1963; UA31 10th L4). Other useful histories are Monroe Billington's *New Mexico's Buffalo Soldiers, 1866–1900* (Niwot, Colo.: University of Colorado Press, 1991; E185.93.N55B55 1991); Fairfax D. Downey's *Buffalo Soldiers in the Indian Wars* (New York: McGraw-Hill, 1969; UA30.D6); *History of the Twenty-fifth Regiment, United States*

Infantry, 1869–1926 (New York: Negro Universities Press, 1969; UA29 25th.N25) by John Henry Nankivell; and Edward Glass's *The History of the Tenth Cavalry, 1866–1921* (Tucson, Ariz.: Acme Printing Co., 1921; UA81 10th).

The Black Infantry in the West, 1869–1891 (Westport, Conn.: Greenwood Publishing Corp., 1971; E185.63.F66) by Arlen Fowler recounts the experiences of black troops in Texas, the Dakotas, and Montana. Theophilus G. Steward, a black chaplain, wrote a historical account entitled *The Colored Regulars in the United States Army* (New York: Arno Press, 1969; E725.5. N3S8 1969). William Sherman Savage's *Blacks in the West* (Westport, Conn.: Greenwood Press, 1976; E185.925.S38) discusses official policies relating to black units, cites examples of exemplary service of soldiers, and discusses problems within the ranks. John M. Caroll's *The Black Military Experience in the American West* (New York: Liveright, 1971; E185.63.C37) also provides information about the troops and their officers.

In 1877 Henry Ossian Flipper became the first black graduate of West Point, after enduring four years of ostracism at the academy. Assigned as a second lieutenant to the 10th Cavalry, he was accused of embezzlement and "conduct unbecoming an officer and a gentleman." Although he was exonerated of the first charge, he was convicted of the second and dismissed from the military. His autobiography is entitled *The Colored Cadet at West Point* (New York: H. Lee & Co., 1878; U410.P1F6 Rare Bk; reprint, New York: Arno Press, 1969). Sara Dunlap Jackson wrote an informative introduction to the Arno reprint.

The cover of the April 21, 1880, illustrated weekly *Puck* is entitled "Running the Gauntlet—A Special Course for Colored Cadets at West Point." The color lithograph shows a stumbling, beaten black man near the end of a run labeled "brutality, torture, persecution, cruelty, and intolerance" and seems to refer to Flipper (PP SSF, repro. no. LC-USZC2–1231). After his dismissal, Flipper continued to work in the West for many years. He recounted these experiences in *Negro-Frontiersman: The Western Memoirs of Henry O. Flipper* (El Paso: Texas Western College Press, 1963; E185.97.F5 1963).

The Edgar Alexander Mearns collection documents activities of the 10th Cavalry, including photographs of a water wagon with a black driver, a black soldier with white officer's children at Fort Verde, Arizona (PP lot 11210–2-⟨F⟩; repro. nos. LC-USZ62-53822, LC-USZ62-105867), and black troopers in Arizona, 1884–87 (PP lot 11210–3-F). A photograph of a celebration at Fort Sill, Oklahoma, in 1891, shows a gathering of black soldiers and a few black women at a well-maintained area with substantial houses lining the green (PP lot 10428-F; repro. no. LC-USZ62–67501). The Historic American Buildings Survey collection documents buildings the black soldiers occupied at Fort Sill (PP HABS OKLA, 16-FOSIL), Fort Riley, Kansas (PP HABS KANS, 81-FORIL, 2), and Fort Bliss, Texas (PP unprocessed HABS TEX 3339). The Fort Sill material contains photographs of an undated drawing of the fort and post headquarters and a description of Sherman House, the original stone building that served as the commanding officer's quarters. Photographs of eleven engravings from Frederic Remington drawings (PP Graphics File lot 4391-G) used for illustrations in an article entitled "A Scout with the Buffalo-Soldiers" in the *Century* (April 1889, vol. 37, p. 906; AP2.C4) are also in the collection.

SOCIAL AND ECONOMIC CONDITIONS

Beyond the politics of the Reconstruction period are the diaries and personal papers of freed slaves. An account of the period immediately

"18421. EMANCIPATION DAY, RICHMOND, V

"Emancipation Day, Richmond, Va.," an annual celebration. Photograph copyright Detroit Publishing Company, 1905. *(PP. LC-D401–18421)*

after emancipation in Georgia appears in Houston Hartsfield Holloway's diary (MSS, journal n.d.). He admitted that the "colord people did not know how to be free and the white people did not know how to have a free colord person about them. . . . We held many meetings as we were not used to being free." Discussing the economic situation for most blacks, he explained: "As for luxuries outside of meat and bread there was none and we wanted none for we was free. Glory to God was our daily cry."

Holloway's diary is also important for the study of African-American religious life in the postwar period, as are the minutes of the Colored Methodist Episcopal Church in America, Virginia Annual Conference (MSS, records 1871–1900); the A.M.E. Bishop Benjamin Tucker Tanner papers in the Carter G. Woodson collection (MSS, microfilm 1796–1933); and the records of the Presbyterian Church in the U.S.A. Presbytery of Washington City (MSS, records, 1823–1936). The work of photographer Charles Milton Bell in the Prints and Photographs Division includes images of black church leaders such as "Rev. Dr. Amos," "Bishop Handy," and L.W. Hillary (PP lot 12261–5-G).

Some former slaves and their former owners made new arrangements for working together. The account book of the Hampton Plantation (MSS, papers 1866–68) in South Carolina, which contains the record of supplies issued to freedmen immediately after the end of the Civil War, indicates that work agreements had been reached between the plantation residents. The Montgomery Family papers (MSS, papers 1872–1938) document the lives of one extended family during the Reconstruction period. Former slaves of Confederate president Jefferson Davis and his brother Joseph, the Montgomerys were literate blacks who had helped with the management of the Davis plantation and who were able to acquire their master's property and successfully farm it for almost a decade. When

they lost the land during hard times, the family moved to Mississippi, where they founded the all-black town Mound Bayou in 1887. These records include a speech by Isaiah Thornton Montgomery, a manuscript by Gladys B. Shepherd entitled "The Montgomery Saga: From Slavery to Black Power," a copy of a master's thesis about Mound Bayou, some biographical sketches of family members, and an 1872 diary kept by Mary Virginia Montgomery that relates some of the difficulties they encountered as plantation owners. She wrote on July 8, 1872: "All mothers hands are out after worms. Brother . . . came up to try coal oil on the cotton, he thinks of trying . . . arsenic, better fight than allow the worms to come now." The papers of the Roberts Family (MSS, papers 1734–1944) of North Carolina and Indiana also include scattered documents relating to African-American life during this period.

Pictorial documents record scenes of the everyday life of African-Americans during the Reconstruction period. A videodisc in the Prints and Photographs Division—an electronic visual index—has approximately 150 book and periodical illustrations of the everyday life from various collections with topics such as dance and music, domestic life, education, work, housing, military service, recreation, and spiritual life, some of which relate to freed blacks and civil rights. Selections from the Cabinet of American Illustration consist of approximately sixty caricatures and serious drawings used in periodical illustrations. Artists represented include André Castaigne, A. B. Frost, Glackens, Arthur Ignatius Keller, E. W. Kemble, Henry Raleigh, William Ludwell, Frederic Dorr, and Herbert Merril.

More than forty prints, drawings, and book illustrations of African-Americans such as portrait engravings of women or cotton and rice production may be located by consulting the "Negroes—Negro Life" category in the Prints and Photographs Graphics file (PP Graphics File lot 4422-D). Caricatures and serious images of political activity from the 1860s and 1870s focus on suffrage for blacks (PP Graphics File lot 4422-H) or civil rights (found under "Negro Leaders"; PP Graphics File lot 4422-G). Described by "Industry-Tobacco" are an advertisement and five wood engravings showing black tobacco workers (PP Graphics File lot 4397-Q).

Stereographs showing black domestic life made by photographer B. W. Kilburn (PP lot 11692-⟨S⟩) of Charleston, South Carolina, portray blacks as maids, vendors, fish and oyster women, and cotton workers or in school groups and street scenes.

An 1873 Washington, D.C., convention for equal rights was shown in a photograph (PP SSF—"Negroes—Civil Rights," repro. no. LC-USZ62-68959). Informal portraits of black men, women, and children join some serious portraits such as "Candy Sam," done by an unknown photographer in 1868, pianist and composer "Blind Tom [Bethune]," photographed in 1880 by John G. Bethune (PP repro. no. LC-USZ62-84287), two portraits of Joe Ballard, done by Theodore Burbaum in 1908 (PP repro. nos.

Watermelon market, Charleston, a wood engraving from a sketch by J.E. Taylor for Frank Leslie's Illustrated Newspaper, *December 15, 1866. (PP. LC-USZ62–37850)*

Bureau of Engraving and Printing. Cyanotype by Frances Benjamin Johnston, 1889 or 1890. (PP lot 8861, no. 6. LC-USZ62–107599)

LC-USZ62-46745, LC-USZ262-46746), and various unidentified portraits by named or unnamed photographers. About twenty portraits of black women made in the late 1800s and early 1900s are filed under this heading as well (PP SSF-Negroes—Portraits).

The American Genetic Association collection has three photographs of men and women working in the cotton industry and two of carriage drivers in Washington, D.C. (PP lot 12261–6). Black workers holding shovels appear among the work crews posing on the construction site of the Pension Building in 1883, in two of the twenty-one photographs from the Montgomery G. Meigs collection (PP lot 8544, repro.

nos. LC-USZ62–59413, LC-USZ62–56364). Photographs that depict construction of the State, War, and Navy Building in the nation's capital portray blacks pushing wheelbarrows and mixing concrete in 1884 (PP lot 10574, repro. nos. LC-USZ62–60465 through 60467).

When Frances Benjamin Johnston photographed the U.S. Bureau of Engraving in Washington she took pictures of several black office workers: a messenger, a cloth sorter, and a laborer tying printed sheets (PP lot 8861, repro. nos. LC-J687-17, LC-J687-32). In Mammoth Cave, Kentucky, she showed blacks working as tourist guides in the cave interiors (PP lot 5020). Charles Milton Bell photographed black train workers in front of Grover Cleveland's presidential train in 1887 (PP lot 12527). Photocopies of caricature drawings showing Washington, D.C., black life, depicting musicians (PP repro. no. LC-USZ62-78425), women quarreling, boys dancing (PP repro. no. LC-USZ62-78426), a huckster, and a family dressing for church can be found in the Colburn collection (PP lot 7694). The George Prince collection documenting Washington, D.C., includes a photograph of two black men in front of George Washington's tomb (PP lot 12508).

Romanticized rustic settings provided a backdrop for a group of seven silver gelatin and platinum photographs of African-Americans made between 1887 and 1906 by Rudolf Eickemeyer. Eickemeyer began photographing blacks in the 1880s at Mount Meiggs, Alabama, at the farm of a family friend (PP PH Eickemeyer). He made a conscious effort to pose his subjects in the style of the French romantic painter Jean François Millet, who heroicized French peasants.

A group of photographs of Mississippi and Ohio River steamboats, 1870–1900, includes three which depict steamers carrying cotton with blacks working or observing on the boats and on shore (PP lot 2938). An interior of a steamboat cabin at dinnertime shows white diners waiting to be served by black waiters lined up along the length of the cabin (PP lot 2938-G, repro. no. LC-USZ62–24291). An image titled "Wayside Scene, Stony Creek, Virginia," by photographer George Barker, shows a black man hauling a load of sacks and quilts in 1887 (PP lot 3282–3, repro. no. LC-USZ62–41945). Charles Martin, a black man who worked for Alexander Graham Bell, appears in some photographs dating from the 1870s through the 1890s in the A. G. Bell collection (PP lot 11533).

Lithographic prints that appeared in illustrated periodicals of the time often were hung in homes for decoration. The Library's best-known collection of this material is described in *Currier and Ives: A Catalog Raisonné* (Detroit: Gale Research Co., 1983; NE2312.C8A4 1983a). When these images show blacks, they are usually comic vignettes, generally presented in pairs, that ridicule black people. Seventy-four entries from the comic Darktown Series date from 1884 to 1897, each title beginning with the word *Darktown*. A brief list of repositories where the images have been located is included in the catalog (see also PP Graphics File lot 4448, for 67 images).

As snapshot photography emerged after 1888, a new genre of depiction of blacks developed. Travel images from before the era of photography convey a curiosity about African-Americans. Similarly, in "Aids to Memory," an album of 593 photos, most of them taken in or around Washington, D.C., amateur photographer George Hall included images of blacks along with his photographs of historic buildings, monuments and markers, natural wonders, and tourists. He photographed a woman with a pipe in her mouth sitting in the open doorway of a log cabin, a man with a team and wagon captioned "Old Va.," and a woman with children sitting on a cabin porch, probably in the vicinity of Richmond (PP lot 9737).

Between 1871 and 1891, amateur photographer Joseph J. Kirkbride made about fifteen thousand photos of his vacations in southern Canada, Cuba, Florida, Georgia, Maine, northern Mexico, New York, Pennsylvania, and Texas. He photographed tourists, guides, and lumber company employees and made other informal portraits. Near Thomasville, Georgia, he photographed cabins, either occupied by blacks or deserted, a chain gang with black convicts and rifle-bearing whites (labeled "Captain and Guard," PP repro. no. LC-USZ62-30089), poorly dressed black children, groups of African-Americans at porch railings and under trees, and an "old slave pen." In the Florida albums there are several photographs of black workers and fishermen (PP lot 7753-C, D, F, G).

RIGHT: *Trade card—"Bread Fruit." Chromolithograph, n.d. (PP lot 6730. LC-USZC4–2445)*

BELOW: *Trade card—"Ayer's Cathartic Pills (The Country Doctor)." Chromolithograph, copyright 1883 by J.C. Ayer & Son, Lowell, Massachusetts. (PP lot 6730. LC-USZC4–2449)*

MATERIAL AND POPULAR CULTURE

Nineteenth-century advertising labels became a part of the Library's collections through copyright deposit and today are held in the Prints and Photographs Division. Blacks were prominently featured on trade cards during the Reconstruction period, principally in advertisements for such products as scouring powder, stove blacking, shoe polish, house paint, liquor, and banjos. Although there are some instances of sympathetic treatments of blacks on the cards, many of them presented blacks as objects of amusement and ridicule. The cigarette cards in the Benjamin K. Edwards collection were given to the Library by Carl Sandburg in 1954. Produced by tobacco companies in New York, Baltimore, Richmond, and Danville, Virginia, between 1880 and 1935, these collectable cards include prints of musicians, black soldiers, and a black man holding the reins of George Washington's horse (PP lot 6593).

The Claude N. Feamster collection contains cards from the 1870s and 1880s, which were distributed with Allen and Ginter cigarettes, Arm & Hammer baking soda, Arbuckle Brothers coffee, and others products. These cards feature lithographic images caricaturing blacks in occupational scenes, playing cards, eating watermelon, or shooting dice (PP lot 6730). The Samuel Rosenberg collection of trade cards includes eighteen portrayals lampooning blacks while marketing food products such as seasonings and garden seeds or rice and items used in domestic occupations such as soap and stove blacking. Many of the goods make either overt or covert reference to color (PP lot 10250).

The Tobacco Labels Collection, with labels dating from 1867 to 1890, contains lithographic images associated with sentimentalized views of the plantation South, such as black men laboring in the field or playing banjos or a black woman smoking a cigar (PP lot 10618–61). The James H. Richardson collection of nineteenth-century wooden blocks used to print book illustrations contains images that ridicule black males (PP lot 8776). In the poster collection for the nineteenth and early twentieth centuries, there are posters featuring images of African-Americans, most frequently advertising products such as soap powders, shoe polish, laundry starch, patent medicine, railroads, sewing machines, tobacco, toilet articles, or sports.

The Music Division holdings, which document a cultural aspect of black Americans' journey into freedom and citizenship, also demonstrate how blacks had to face ridicule and hostility as a free people. In 1870, a new copyright law centralized all deposits of copyrighted works in the Library of Congress. Although the Music Division would not be established until 1897, copyrighted music from 1870 on—much of it by or about African-Americans—is likely to be found in the division.

As changing conditions created a demand for new hymnals, Marshall W. Taylor's *A Collection of Revival Hymns and Plantation Melodies* (Cincinnati: Marshall W. Taylor and W. C. Echols, 1882; M1670.T24) was published. Although *Slave Songs of the United States* had been published in 1867, it was not until the first tour of the Fisk Jubilee Singers in 1871 that spirituals became widely recognized. This tour was the result of a valiant attempt by Fisk University in Nashville to solve its financial problems by sending a specially talented group of students on a tour of northern churches to raise funds. At first the response was disappointing, but when the group reached New York, it achieved a notable success. Demands arose for copies of the spirituals, songs that until then had not been transcribed in musical notation and were virtually unknown in the North. The Jubilee Singers' sponsor, the American Missionary Association, arranged to have the spirituals transcribed by Theodore F. Seward. He produced *Jubilee Songs* (New York: Biglow & Main, 1872; M1670.J825 1872), a pamphlet of twenty-four selections. It was so well received that a full-length book with a musical supplement was prepared by the singers' manager, Gustavus Pike, entitled *The Jubilee Singers and Their Campaign for Twenty Thousand Dollars* (Boston: Lee and Shepard, 1873; ML400.P63). Steady demand required many editions, with increasing numbers of songs, until it was superseded in 1875 by J. B. T. Marsh's *The Story of the Jubilee Singers, with Their Songs* (7th ed., London: Hodder and Stoughton,

1877; ML400.M34 1877), which was also reissued in many editions, with increasing numbers of songs, until after the turn of the century.

The stunning success of the Fisk Jubilee Singers led other schools with similar financial problems to organize groups of singing students and send them on fund-raising tours. Hampton Institute in Virginia sponsored *Cabin and Plantation Songs, as Sung by the Hampton Students*, arranged by Thomas Fenner (New York: G.P. Putnam's Sons, 1874; M1670.H5), and Jacob J. Sawyer arranged *Jubilee Songs and Plantation Melodies (Words and Music), as Sung by the Original Nashville Students, the Celebrated Colored Concert Company* (n.p.: J.J. Sawyer, 1884; M1670. S27). Many other collections of spirituals can be found in the Music Division.

While groups of students popularized the spirituals, other African-Americans entered various forms of public entertainment. Songs document the fact that blacks were able to gain a foothold on the stage by blacking up and participating in caricatures of themselves. As time passed, more and more black minstrel troupes were formed, presenting an increasingly realistic picture of plantation life. Sam Lucas and James Bland were outstanding black minstrel performers who achieved success singing songs of their own composition. Examples of their productions can be found in Lucas's *Careful Man Songster* (Boston: White, Smith & Co., 1881; M1628.L94C3) and Bland's *The James A. Bland Album of Outstanding Songs* (New York: Edward B. Marks Music Corp., 1946; M1620.B638H3). Among Bland's songs were "Oh, Dem Golden Slippers" (1879) and "Keep Dem Golden Gates Wide Open" (1880). Bland also wrote "Carry Me Back to Old Virginny" (1878), which was adopted as the Virginia State song.

Other black musicians whose work is included in the holdings of the Music Division appeared on the concert stage, such as soprano Elizabeth Taylor Greenfield, "The Black Swan,"

and tenor Thomas Bowers. Both were discussed in the first book-length history of music in the United States, a history of African-American music, James Monroe Trotter's *Music and Some Highly Musical People, with Sketches of the Lives of Remarkable Musicians of the Colored Race* (Boston: Lee and Shepard, 1878; ML60.T85). Other musicians discussed by Trotter were the Hyers sisters, Emma Louise and Anna Madah, born in 1853 and 1854 respectively, whose voices were widely praised. After several concert tours, they joined forces with Sam Lucas to produce such musical shows as *Out of Bondage* and *The Underground Railroad*.

Music covers related to African-American music for this period include "Love Among the Roses" (1869) and "Dem Golden Slippers" (1879) (PP lot 10615–62⟨H⟩). Among the graphics material related to Harriet Beecher Stowe's *Uncle Tom's Cabin* (PP lot 4422-B)—a popular commercial entertainment of the period—are music covers (also PP lot 10615-60-⟨H⟩) and engravings of scenes that were used as book illustrations. Photocopies of posters and playbills for Stowe's work may be found in the Prints and Photographs Division's Specific Subject File under the heading "Negro Theater—Minstrel." Twenty-four posters relating to *Uncle Tom's Cabin* can be located by using the card catalog for nineteenth-century U.S. theater posters, which is arranged by title.

Minstrel posters distinguish between black and white performers and provide a rich source for images of African-Americans (PP POS Minstrel). Early minstrel performers were whites who donned blackface to perform for white audiences. The earliest of the approximately 150 minstrel items in the collection, arranged alphabetically by title of musical company, is an 1847 poster for an "Ethiopian" group, but the bulk of the material dates from the 1870s.

Commercial theater performances such as John McCullough's Othello (PP POS-C 19th c.

Theater, 1878 O7 no.1, repro. nos. LC-USZ62-69764, LC-USZC4-2434), sometimes took racial topics as their subject matter. Although the Prints and Photographs Division card catalog for nineteenth-century theater posters contains several entries for plays with titles that suggest African-American subjects—from Dion Boucicault's pre-Civil War smash *The Octoroon* and the ubiquitous stage versions of *Uncle Tom's Cabin* to obscure works like *Coon*—no systematic attempt has been made to locate all that deal with African-American experience.

Although nascent talents of African-Americans began to emerge in the years immediately after the Civil War, growth through educational attainment manifested itself more tangibly in political leadership, literature, and the arts from the decade of the 1890s to the beginning of World War I. By the turn of the century—after decades of legally enforced illiteracy—the majority of the black population could read and write. This was the era during which Booker T. Washington, principal of Tuskegee Institute, was an important political and social leader of the black community. It was also the time during which legislative and social gains were forcibly assaulted by white supremacists.

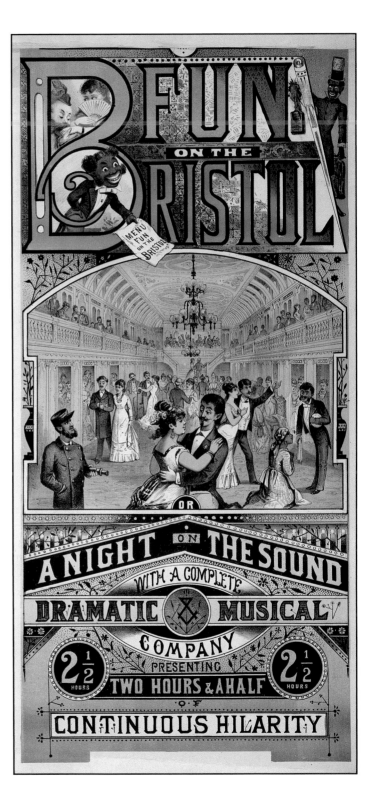

"Fun on the Bristol: A Night on the Sound," a theater poster. Color lithograph, 189–. *(PP Pos—Adv 19c—Misc Adv A01, no. 32, C size. LC-USZC4–2419)*

CHAPTER SIX

THE BOOKER T. WASHINGTON ERA

With the African-American community left by the federal government to fend for itself, almost every appreciable political and social gain began to evaporate. A series of Supreme Court decisions reversed the benefits for blacks in the area of civil rights, and mechanisms to deter blacks from voting such as violence, economic intimidation, ballot fraud and manipulation, literacy tests, grandfather clauses, and poll taxes stymied political gains. Economic and social conditions degenerated to such an extent that historian Rayford Logan characterized the period as "the nadir" of black-white relations, a term still used to describe the era. Peonage, sharecropping, and tenant farming confined vast numbers of southern blacks to an economic bondage that was just short of slavery. African-Americans who were vocal in their protests or who were financially successful were dealt with very severely by terrorist groups such as the Ku Klux Klan.

Yet during this period there also arose a group of men and women of large purpose, leaders who demonstrated the ability to establish and run new institutions, schools, colleges, learned societies, social welfare organizations, and humanitarian and benevolent associations. These exceptional men and women also organized racial conferences to seek ways to improve their condition and that of the society in which they lived.

"Afro-American Monument," a large chromolithograph published for the Tennessee Centennial Exposition in Nashville in 1897 by the Goes Lithograph Company. Eleven vignettes surrounding a central arched medallion show the history of blacks from 1619 to 1897. Peter Salem, Crispus Attucks, Frederick Douglass, and Booker T. Washington are pictured. (PP PGA. LC-USZ62–2239; LC-USZC4–2329 [color])

AFRO-AMERICAN MONUMENT.

Booker T. Washington (1856–1915). Silver gelatin photograph, copyright C.M. Battey. (PP. LC-USZ62–25624)

AFRICAN-AMERICAN EDUCATION AND DEVELOPMENT

Fortunately, the era of racial hatred and violence did not hinder all blacks in their quest for social and economic progress. As the nineteenth century drew to a close, one of the black men who was most interested in establishing a dialogue between whites and blacks was educator, orator, and author Booker T. Washington (MSS, papers and microfilm 1882–1942). He was born into slavery in 1856 in Franklin County, Virginia, but moved with his parents to West Virginia in 1865. He had the opportunity to attend Hampton Institute in 1872 and graduated with honors three years later. He then taught school in West Virginia and at Hampton Institute and attended Wayland Seminary in Washington, D.C. In 1881 Washington became the first principal of the Normal School for Colored Teachers at Tuskegee, Alabama, and served in that capacity until his death in 1915. An excellent public speaker, he soon was in demand before diverse groups, receiving a cordial reception by some white audiences because of his conciliatory attitude toward race relations. Washington wrote in *Up from Slavery: An Autobiography* (New York: Doubleday, Page & Co., 1901; E185.93.W3W4) that the future of the black person rested "largely upon the question as to whether or not he should make himself, through his skill, intelligence, and character, of such undeniable value to the community in which he lived that the community could not dispense with his presence."

The statement that characterized Washington's desire for blacks to accommodate themselves to the American racial climate was espoused most succinctly, however, in his famous 1895 Atlanta Exposition Speech, where he said, "In all things that are purely social we [whites and blacks] can be as separate as the fingers, yet one as the hand in all things essential to mutual progress." A copy of the speech, recorded by Washington in 1908, is available in the Library's Recorded Sound Section. Washington believed that by training blacks in all areas of industry and agricultural economy he would be rendering a service to both races and providing a means for peaceable progress of blacks into full citizenship.

Frederick Douglass died in 1895, on February 20, seven months before Washington's Atlanta Exposition Speech. Within five years after Douglass's death the Frederick Douglass Memorial Association (MSS, records 1900–1989) was formed to plan a fitting memorial for the venerable abolitionist at Cedar Hill, his home in Anacostia, District of Columbia. The records of the association document the successful work, principally by black women's organizations, to make Cedar Hill a national landmark. The void in leadership left by Douglass was filled by several able men and women of whom Booker T. Washington was the best known.

The extensive collection of Booker T. Washington papers in the Manuscript Division, over 300,000 items, document his career, the growth and development of Tuskegee Institute, and the role of blacks in the area of education, political activity, business, and international relationships. The records are divided into personal and family correspondence, general correspondence, photographs, National Negro Business League correspondence, papers relating to the death of Washington, a speech and writing file, and Tuskegee records, which include the principal's office correspondence, department head file, student file, employment applications, donation letters, lecture engagements, extension work file, clippings, scrapbooks, and printed matter.

As Washington traveled around the country to raise funds for his school, he established relationships with many wealthy and powerful individuals. Eventually, he became a trusted ad-

viser to several presidents on issues relating to the black population, and his recommendations for patronage positions were generally sought after by blacks and respected by those in office. The Washington papers include correspondence with a number of government officials. Other correspondents are educators Robert R. Moton, Hollis B. Frissell, and George Washington Carver; benefactors George Peabody, Anson Phelps Stokes, John D. Rockefeller, Julius Rosenwald, and Andrew Carnegie; black leaders Frederick Douglass and W. E. B. DuBois; and many others. Many of these correspondents were members of Tuskegee's board of directors.

Selected correspondence from the Washington papers has been published in a multivolume work edited by Louis R. Harlan entitled *The Booker T. Washington Papers* (Urbana: University of Illinois Press, 1972–89; 14 vols. E185.97.W274). For each correspondent a helpful biographical sketch is included, making this work an invaluable reference tool for the period. The final volume is an extensive cumulative name and subject index to the published papers. While they were working on the volumes, Harlan and his staff prepared a manuscript index to the papers, a copy of which is in the Manuscript Reading Room.

A few Washington letters are found in the papers of Presidents Grover Cleveland (MSS, microfilm 1859–1945), Benjamin Harrison (MSS, microfilm 1787–1938), and William McKinley (MSS, papers 1847–1901), and a large number in the papers of Theodore Roosevelt (MSS, microfilm from various repositories 1759–1921) and William Taft (MSS, microfilm 1784–1930). The papers of industrialist Andrew Carnegie (MSS, papers 1803–1935) and those of banker and philanthropist George Foster Peabody (MSS, papers 1894–1937) also include Washington correspondence. The Carter G. Woodson collection (MSS, microfilm 1796–1933) includes Booker T. Washington correspondence along with materials relating to other Tuskegee staffers such as Margaret Washington, Emmett J. Scott, Robert R. Moton, Monroe N. Work, and George Washington Carver.

The Library's general collection includes over 150 volumes by and about Washington. Some of Washington's own works are *Black-Belt Diamonds: Gems from the Speeches, Addresses, and Talks to Students of Booker T. Washington* (New York: Fortune and Scott, 1898; MicRR 37520 E; reprint, New York: Negro Universities Press, 1969; E185.W314 1969), *Working with the Hands* (New York: Doubleday, Page, and Co., 1904; E185.97.W32; MicRR 37567E), *The Negro in Business* (Boston: Hertel, Jenkins & Co., 1907; HD8081.A65W37 1907, also MicRR 37631 HD), *Frederick Douglass* (New York: Greenwood Press, [1969, c1906]; E449.D75W37 1969b), *The Negro in the South: His Economic Progress in Relation to His Moral and Religious Development* (Philadelphia: G.W. Jacobs & Co., [1907]; E185.6.W316), *The Story of the Negro: The Rise of the Race from Slavery* (New York: Doubleday, Page, 1909; 2 vols. MicRR 52009; reprint, New York: P. Smith, 1940; 2 vols. E185.W316 1940), and *My Larger Education* (Garden City, N.Y.: Doubleday, Page, 1911; MicRR 52059 E).

Next to Booker T. Washington, the most prominent person at Tuskegee was George Washington Carver (MSS, microfilm from various repositories 1894–1975), who was born a slave in Missouri just before the end of the Civil War. An orphan, he spent much of his young life roving in search of an education. In 1896 after attending Simpson College and Iowa State, he was invited by Washington to come to Tuskegee to work with the needy black farmers there and to continue his agricultural experimentation. Although Carver is best known for his work with the peanut, he also studied flowers, trees, soils, grasses, and other plants and was a competent artist. The Carver papers include memorabilia, correspondence, and writings by and about Carver. Papers of the third president of Tuskegee, Frederick Douglass Patterson (MSS, papers 1926–88), contain some Carver materials, including information about the scientist's posthumous induction into the New York Hall of Fame. Also among the division's holdings is a manuscript biography of Carver by Rackham Holt (MSS, undated), who interviewed Carver as well as people who knew him, including some of his friends and teachers in Iowa. The work was published as *George Washington Carver, an American Biography* (Garden City, N.Y.: Doubleday, Doran and Co., 1943; S417.C3H6).

Sanborn fire insurance maps for the town of Tuskegee, Alabama, located in the Geography and Map Division, date from 1885. The 1885 and 1891 editions show only the Tuskegee Female College located in the town, but the 1897 edition shows the Tuskegee Normal and Industrial Institute located one mile southwest of the town. By 1903 two map sheets displayed the institution's extensive grounds and buildings and identified the functions of each. The maps indicate the various trades taught in the Boys and Girls Trade Buildings. These include woodworking, carpentry, foundry work, and shoemaking for the boys and dressmaking, ironing, plain sewing, cooking, and basketry for the girls, underscoring the vocational nature of the curriculum in the early twentieth century.

One of the more interesting sets of photographs documenting Tuskegee Institute in the Prints and Photographs Division is a group of nine photomontage prints of sixty-one photographs made by the Shepherd Photo Company in Saint Paul, Minnesota, in 1899. The photos show classroom and field activities, buildings, the homes of Booker T. Washington and J. N. Calloway, and general views. These images were displayed as part of the American Negro Exhibit at the Paris Exposition of 1900 (PP lot 11293).

Washington's publicity efforts on behalf of

Tuskegee Institute attracted the attention of major photographers. One of the most prominent was Frances Benjamin Johnston, who, in the period 1902–6, made 631 photographs documenting the institute. Her photographs include indoor and outdoor class activities, buildings, portraits, and images of branch and vicinity schools (PP lot 2962–1 to 5). Johnston's collection also includes graphs and pamphlets about Tuskegee (PP lot 2962-6).

Tuskegee Institute attracted news service attention leading the Underwood & Underwood agency to make twelve stereo photographs of the marching band and of campus exteriors in 1906 (PP lot 11117). More materials relating to Tuskegee in the Prints and Photographs Division are in the Stereo File under the heading "Negroes—Education," where there are two images of classroom and chapel gatherings. The Herman L. Wittemann collection contains photographs made by the Albertype Company in 1913–14, showing buildings, vocational classes, and a commencement day parade, and individuals such as Booker T. Washington, Emmett J. Scott, and Warren Logan (PP lot 7496). Photographs of the Tuskegee facilities between 1898 and 1914 are in the Detroit Publishing Company collection as well (PP lot 9050).

Tuskegee history class. Silver gelatin photograph by Frances Benjamin Johnston, 1902. (PP lot 2962. LC-USZ62–64712)

The Oaks, Booker T. Washington's home, was built by Robert Taylor, one of the first professionally trained African-American architects. The house is documented by eleven sheets in the Historic American Buildings Survey collection (PP HABS ALA, 44-TUSG, 10–). Washington's home and the buildings at Tuskegee can be contrasted with housing for rural blacks by searching the Specific Subject File under rural dwellings and by consulting the Stereo File, which has eight stereos of southern dwellings under the heading "Negroes—Housing."

Materials in the Prints and Photographs Division also document activities at other institutions of higher education. Educational institutions for blacks were becoming increasingly important and photographers were hired to document their advances. Frances Benjamin Johnston's 1899–1900 series on Hampton Institute, Virginia, includes 173 photographs of buildings, classroom scenes, vocational training, farming, carpentry, and shipbuilding (PP lot 11051). By establishing a reputation for industrial education and Christian zeal, Hampton became a model school for educating blacks. The photographs, intended for use in Hampton's public relations and fund-raising activities, were meant to convey the accomplishments unskilled, uneducated blacks could achieve when given vocational education and Christian training opportunities. Johnston also made a few photographs documenting the James Hallowell Elementary School located near Hampton (PP lot 12643–3).

Just as Sanborn fire insurance maps were identified as a useful source for documenting the physical structure and growth of Tuskegee Institute, these same cartographic materials can be used in the study of other institutions of higher learning. Since large-scale maps show the layout, construction, and functions of individual buildings in most urban areas during the first half of the twentieth century, they usually include colleges or universities within their respective urban areas. In addition to Wilberforce University located near Xenia, Ohio, and Selma University in Alabama, which was discussed in the previous chapter, there are numerous other black schools that are portrayed on the fire insurance maps in the Geography and Map Division.

Examples of the earliest maps for other selected schools are Howard University in Washington, D.C., 1903; Miner School in Washington, D.C., 1888; Storer College in Harpers Ferry in 1894; Virginia Normal and Collegiate Institute in Petersburg, 1891; Hampton Normal and Agricultural Institute in Hampton, Virginia, 1885; Princess Anne Academy in Princess Anne, Maryland, 1911; Fisk University, Nashville, Tennessee, 1888; Shaw University, Raleigh, North Carolina, 1896; North Carolina State Agricultural and Mechanical College, Greensboro, 1896; Bennett Colored Seminary, Greensboro, North Carolina, 1888; Claflin University and Colored Normal Industrial, Agricultural, and Mechanical College of South Carolina in Orangeburg, 1904; and Atlanta University, 1906.

The location and development of segregated schools at the primary and secondary levels can often be documented on county maps published during the first two decades of the twentieth century. These basic reference maps are filed geographically in the Geography and Map Division's Titled Collection. One particularly interesting map is *A New and Historical Map of Albemarle County, Virginia* (Richmond: Virginia School Supply Co., 1907; G3883.A3S1 1907.M3) by Frank A. Massie. It not only shows "colored" schools throughout the county, it also indicates a "colored settlement" about five miles south of the county seat of Charlottesville and a "colored college" near Glendower in the southeastern part of the county. Similarly, 1908 and 1909 maps of two Georgia counties, *Map of*

Monroe County, Georgia (Atlanta: Hudgins Co., 1908; GM Titled Collection) and *Map of Jenkins County, Georgia* (Atlanta: Hudgins Co., 1909; GM Titled Collection) identify a number of schools, as well as churches and residents, as "Col." A 1917 Maryland map, entitled *Map of Anne Arundel, Prince Georges Counties, Maryland, and District of Columbia* ([Chicago]: Rand McNally and Company, [1917]; G3843.A5 1917.R3), shows "colored" schools dispersed throughout the two counties.

The papers of industrialist Andrew Carnegie (MSS, papers 1803–1935) include some materials relating to schools for black youths, such as a fifty-one-page copy of the organizational records of the "Negro Rural School Fund." Members of the fund's board included Booker T. Washington, Robert Russa Moton, William H. Taft, and Andrew Carnegie. Several other reports, mostly dated in 1905, yield information about schools for black youths in various parts of the South. A brief study called "Notes on the Progress of the Negro People" (undated) and some statistics about the black population since emancipation are also included in the files. Alabama statesman and educator Jabez Lamar Monroe Curry's collection (MSS, microfilm 1637–1939) contains information about his efforts to assist southern black and white youths in gaining a good education. Some of these reports and other papers concern the John F. Slater Fund for Negro Education, the Peabody Education Fund, and the Southern Education Board.

The papers of banker and philanthropist George Foster Peabody (MSS, papers 1894–1937) include correspondence with both Booker T. Washington and Robert Russa Moton as well as with officials of other schools for black youths. Peabody, who served as a member of the board of directors for several schools for African-Americans, is described in the *Witness, a National Paper of the Episcopal Church* (March 11, 1926) as a "leading layman . . . who interested himself in the work of the Church among Negroes" and who was recognized as a "leading authority on racial problems." Peabody was treasurer and member of the board of trustees of the American Church Institute for Negroes. His records also reflect his interest in the preservation of African-American music as an art form, especially through his correspondence with Natalie Curtis Burlin, who recorded by hand "the actual singing" and "spontaneous harmonies" of freed blacks.

A series of occasional publications relating to the education of African-Americans was sponsored by the John F. Slater Fund. John F. Slater, a wealthy manufacturer of cotton and woolen goods from Norwich, Connecticut, established a million-dollar trust fund to educate newly freed blacks in 1882. Publications such as Jabez L. M. Curry's "Difficulties, Complications, and Limitations Connected with the Education of the Negro" and Alice Bacon's "The Negro and the Atlanta Exposition" are available in the Microform Reading Room (*Occasional Papers*, MicRR 33061–33092).

SOCIAL CONDITIONS AT THE TURN OF THE CENTURY

Reference sources for the turn of the century include guides, histories, documentaries, and biographical dictionaries of leading men and women. Rayford Logan's *The Negro in American Life and Thought: The Nadir, 1877–1901* (New York: Dial Press, 1954; E185.61.L64), which was also published under the title *The Betrayal of the Negro from Rutherford B. Hayes to Woodrow Wilson* (New York: Collier Books, 1965; E185.61L64 1965), and C. Vann Woodward's *Origins of the New South, 1877–1913* (Baton Rouge: Louisiana State University Press, 1951; F215.W85) provide a general introduction to the period and its prominent personalities. Other resources that give the flavor of the intellectual and social ferment around the turn of the century include August Meier's *Negro Thought in America, 1880–1915* (Ann Arbor: University of Michigan Press, 1963; E185.6.M5) and *Negro Social and Political Thought, 1850–1920* (New York: Basic Books, 1966; E185.B876), edited by Howard Brotz. *Black Leaders of the Twentieth Century* (Urbana: University of Illinois Press, 1982; E185.96.B536 1982), edited by John Hope Franklin and August Meier, features essays on journalist T. Thomas Fortune, attorney Charles Hamilton Houston, educator Mary McLeod Bethune, and insurance executive Charles Clinton Spaulding. Another useful source is *A Documentary History of the Negro People in the United States* (New York: Citadel Press, 1951; E185.A58), edited by Herbert Aptheker. An understanding of the origin of the pervasive Jim Crow system may be found in C. Vann Woodward's *The Strange Career of Jim Crow* (New York: Oxford University Press, 1955; E185.61.W86), which has been revised several times since it first appeared in 1955.

Several collections of articles and documents provide an overview of the main issues and concerns for African-Americans at the beginning of the new century and reflect important scholarship and documentation available. They include I. A. Newby's *Jim Crow's Defense: Anti-Negro Thought in America, 1900–1930* (Baton Rouge: Louisiana State University Press, 1965; E185.61.N475); *The Negro's Image in the South: The Anatomy of White Supremacy* (Lexington: University Press of Kentucky, 1967; E185.61.N872), by Claude H. Nolen; *The Segregation Era, 1863–1954* (New York: Oxford University Press, 1970; E185.W434), edited by Allen Weinstein and Frank Gatell; Mary Ellison's *The Black Experience: American Blacks since 1865* (New York: Barnes & Noble, 1974; E185.61.E52 1974), and *Racism at the Turn of the Century: Documentary Perspectives 1870–1910* (San Rafael, California: Leswing Press, 1973; E185.6.D46), edited by Donald P. DeNevi and Doris A. Holmes.

One of the primary resources for information about African-Americans in the labor force is *The Black Worker: A Documentary History from Colonial Times to the Present* (Philadelphia: Temple University Press, 1978–; E185.8.B553), edited by Philip S. Foner and Ronald L. Lewis, which reprints materials from newspapers, journals, conference proceedings, and other sources. Typical is "Why Freedmen Won't Work" from the January 15, 1866, *Boston Daily Evening Voice*. A black worker tells of hiring himself out to a man in Aubeville [South Carolina?] for $12.00 a month for three months, a paltry sum for a man with a wife and two children to support. When he went to settle his account at Christmastime, however, he was given only $22.50. His employer said he had not earned more, although he had worked hard all the time.

Julius Jacobson's *The Negro and the American Labor Movement* (Garden City, N.Y.: Anchor Books, 1968; E185.8.J3) contains a selection of articles describing black relations with trade unions. Marc Karson and Ronald Radosh's "The American Federation of Labor and the Negro Worker, 1894–1949" tells how blacks were excluded from labor unions because their presence reduced the recruitment of white blue-collar workers who preferred not to work with or near blacks. The article also discusses Samuel Gompers, who remained silent about the mistreatment and disenfranchisement of African-Americans and characterized blacks in a stereotypical fashion. A study by W. E. B. DuBois in 1902 showed that "forty-three internationals including the Railroad Brotherhoods" had no black members.

Other historical accounts of black labor include Charles H. Wesley's *Negro Labor in the United States, 1850–1925* (New York: Russell & Russell, 1968; E487.W36 1968), Sterling Spero's *The Black Worker: The Negro and the Labor Movement* (Port Washington, N.Y.: Kennikat Press, 1966, c1959; E185.8.S74 1966), and Daniel A. Novak's *The Wheel of Servitude: Black Forced Labor after Slavery* (Lexington: University Press of Kentucky, 1978; E185.2.N88).

Testimony in U.S. Congress, Senate Committee on Education and Labor, *Report of the Committee of the Senate upon the Relations between Labor and Capital* (Washington: Government Printing Office, 1885; 48th Cong., 2d sess., rept. no. 1262, MicRR 68793) reveals much about the discrimination against black workers in the industrial trades:

Q. For some reason or other the negro [*sic*] is not well adapted to cotton manufacturing, I take it?
A. He is not adapted to the management of intricate machinery.
Q. But this intricate machinery is not so troublesome but what ten-year-old white children can take care of it and run much of it?
A. Oh, colored people can be used in factories if circumstances should make it necessary.

In the same hearing a respondent states: "My wife says she would not have felt so bad about the results of the war if it had only left her negro [*sic*] house servants."

In her photographic retracing of Confederate battles in the Winchester vicinity of upland Virginia around 1900, Frances Benjamin Johnston took photographs of black laborers such as men sawing (PP lot 11728; repro. no. LC-J682-3) and men working on ship's hulls and in blacksmith

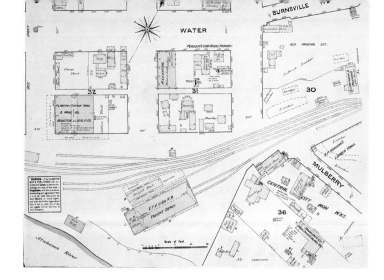

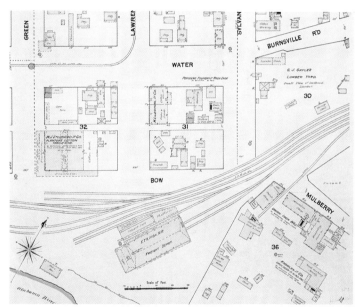

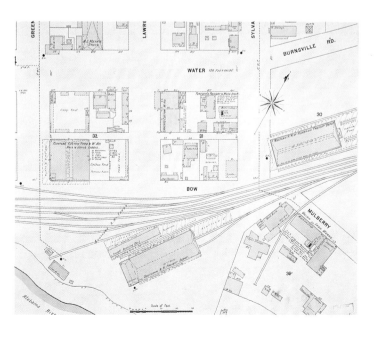

TOP RIGHT: *A fire insurance map of an area in the vicinity of the railroad tracks and a cotton warehouse in block 31 of Selma, Alabama, in 1884, identifies "Negro shanties." (GM Sanborn Fire Insurance Maps, Selma, Alabama, 1884; sheet 5)*

MIDDLE RIGHT: *A map depicting the same area in 1889 identifies these buildings only as tenements and dwellings. (GM Sanborn Fire Insurance Maps, Selma, Alabama, 1889; sheet 2)*

RIGHT: *The 1898 map includes most of the same buildings in block 31 but identifies them as "Negro tenement, Negro f. b. [female boarding], and Negroes." (GM Sanborn Fire Insurance Maps, Selma, Alabama, 1898; sheet 2)*

An oysterer on the Chesapeake Bay shown in Puck, *October 10, 1905. Color lithograph. (AP101.P7 P&P Case X, vol. 58. LC-USC4–2440)*

and machine shops at the Newport News dry docks for the Washington & Norfolk Steamboat Company (PP lot 11750). On her 1903 trip west, she included two images of fishermen (PP lot 11739-1). Early photo services for newspapers are another source of images of black Americans at work. Images of coal passers from 1911 and 1912 are found in the George Bain news service collection (PP lot 10861) and photographs of blacks engaged as laundresses, musicians, farmers, draymen (PP lot 12341–6), and road workers (PP lot 12355–9) were made for the National Photo Company. The Stereo File contains two photos of blacks working as oyster shuckers in Maryland and Virginia (PP Stereo-Industry-Shellfish).

The heading "Negroes as businessmen" in the Prints and Photographs Divisional Catalog refers to photographs showing various tasks at the T.B. Williams Tobacco Factory in Richmond, Virginia (PP lot 11302). Other black businesses appear in materials for the Paris Exposition of 1900. The Specific Subject File heading "Negroes—Business enterprises" indicates the location of photocopies of images depicting black men using sulfur-heating equipment at Mound Bayou, Mississippi.

Most rural blacks were engaged in agricultural work. Stereographic photographs show black people raising cotton, rice, or sugar cane and working in mines. One stereograph pictures black men tending tobacco crops in Alabama. Other photographs about "plantation crops" include images of blacks working in cotton, sugar cane, and tobacco. In 1901 Samuel E. Rusk of Newport News, Virginia, copyrighted a photograph of a black man with an ox and plow. A black farmer in Rocky Mount, Virginia, is the subject of a photograph registered for copyright in 1908 by L. W. Stewart. Another group of photographs of blacks working in cotton fields date from 1900 to 1928 (PP lot 4728). Erwin E. Smith (1886–1947), who recorded ev-

Illustration by Edward Henry Potthast for "A Funny Little School," by Ruth McEnry Stuart, in St. Nicholas magazine, November 1897 (24:45). Wash drawing. (PP CAI–Potthast no. 2, D size. LC-USZ62–107500)

eryday life on the ranches of the Texas Panhandle, photographed black cowboys roping animals, riding horseback, and doing ranch work. Four of his photographs show black men and women on a parade float in the Negro Fair, held at Bonham, Texas, sometime between 1908 and 1910 (PP Erwin E. Smith Collection—Negroes).

Photographer Barnell M. Clinedinst made an image of cooks working in the U.S. Senate kitchen in 1911 (PP lot 12526). The Detroit Publishing Company collection includes some photographs of African-American iron workers and blacks among groups in street scenes in various cities, including Birmingham, Alabama (PP lot 9050). Twenty-five photographs of southern blacks portray various occupations including a fish vendor and an ox cart driver, 1900–1910 (PP lot 6350-F; repro. no. LC-D4-13308).

Black domestic life at the turn of the century is documented to some extent by photographic portraits and images of children, though many of these are caricatures and stereotypes, and the photographs are often accompanied by derogatory captions.

In 1897 white photographer F. Holland Day, a pioneer American art photographer, began his

ABOVE: *The character Simon Pure, featured on this poster from about 1870, was invented by the English playwright Susanna Centlivre (1667?–1723) and appeared in her play* A Bold Stroke for a Wife *(1718). (PP POS Adv 19c Misc Adv A01 no. 30, D size. LC-USZ62–107751; LC-USZC2–150)*

RIGHT: *Unidentified woman at Hampton Institute, Hampton, Virginia. Platinum photograph (possibly with gum) by F. Holland Day, 1905. (PP Day, unprocessed. LC-USZ62–52944)*

Nubian Series, which juxtaposed light and dark subjects. He dressed his models in exotic robes and skins. In 1905 Day made a group of portraits of black men, women, and children in street clothes. The Prints and Photographs Division has more than twenty of these portraits. One is a gum platinum print entitled "Black Girl with Broad White Collar" (PP unprocessed).

The D. E. Boswell collection in the Prints and Photographs Division includes seven lantern slide proofs of posed tableaux with caricatures of blacks with captions such as "Coon, Coon, Coon" (PP repro. no. LC-USZ62-35743), "I Had My Face Enameled," and "I Wish My Color Would Fade" (PP lot 10295). Caricatures of blacks are also among the works submitted by Asheville, North Carolina, photographer John H. Tarbell for copyright deposit between 1897 and 1904 (PP lot 11826). Further examples occur in the Nace Brock collection, from the period

1900 to 1904, which contains a photograph of a black woman cooking and one of a small building captioned "Uncle Tom's Cabin" in Asheville (PP lot 12050).

Other photographs document the civic and social activities of African-Americans. Black boxer John Arthur ("Jack") Johnson, who lived from 1878 to 1946, is shown in a commanding pose in a cabinet card photograph by Otto Sarony (PP PR 4 (B) Portraits J-K; repro. no. LC-USZ62–26385), and other photographs show blacks engaged in boxing and cock fighting (PP SSF—Sports; repro. no. LC-USZ62-51629) and as Freemasons of Lodges 1 and 2 in 1897 (PP SSF Negroes; repro. nos. LC-USZ62-38123, LC-USZ262-80591). Graphics in the Prints and Photographs Division's Popular Graphic Arts collection that document a sense of appreciation for black history include a large lithograph called "Afro-American Monument," published in 1897 by Goes Lithograph Company (PP PGA-D Goes; repro. nos. LC-USZ62–22397, LC-USZC4-2329).

THE SPANISH-AMERICAN WAR

Many black men pursued a military career after the Civil War. During the next major conflict—the Spanish-American War—the 9th and 10th Negro Cavalry, known since 1866 as the Buffalo Soldiers, distinguished themselves in the charge of San Juan Hill in Cuba and the 25th Negro Infantry took part in the Battle of El Caney, capturing a Spanish fort. Because Africa has a tropical climate, many believed blacks were immune to tropical diseases and disorders like yellow fever. Black troops therefore were among the first sent to war. They participated in military campaigns in Cuba, Puerto Rico, and the Philippines. Accounts of their war service are found in Willard B. Gatewood, Jr.'s "Smoked Yankees" and the Struggle for Empire: Letters from Negro Soldiers, 1898–1902 (Urbana: University of Illinois Press, 1971; E185.63.G38), which re-

produces pertinent correspondence that black soldiers sent to black newspapers such as the Richmond Planet, the Broad Ax, the Freeman (Indianapolis), and the Iowa State Bystander. Freedom and Jim Crow, 1865–1917, volume 3 of Blacks in the United States Armed Forces; Basic Documents, edited by Morris J. MacGregor and Bernard C. Nalty (Wilmington, Del.: Scholarly Resources, 1977; 13 vols. E185.63.B55), includes documents concerning African-American men in the military before and during the Spanish-American War and the two Texas controversies involving black soldiers, the Brownsville Affray, 1906, and the Houston Riot, 1917.

Black views of their military service are also expressed in Herschel Cashin's Under Fire with the Tenth U.S. Cavalry (New York: Arno Press, 1969; E725.45 10th.C3 1969); Miles V. Lynk's Black Troopers (New York: AMS Press, 1971; E725.5.N3L9 1971); and Edward A. Johnson's A School History of the Negro Race in America from 1619 to 1890, Combined with the History of the Negro Soldiers in the Spanish-American War (New York: AMS Press, 1969; E185.J622 1969). African-American opinions on American foreign policy during the war are discussed in George P. Marks's The Black Press Views American Imperialism, 1898–1900 (New York: Arno Press, 1971; E713.M35) and in Willard Gatewood's Black Americans and the White Man's Burden, 1898–1903 (Urbana: University of Illinois Press, 1975; E721.G27).

Stereo photographs of African-American soldiers are scattered among nearly one thousand photographs of the Spanish-American War in the Prints and Photographs Division. Photos of El Caney, the 23rd Kansas Volunteers, the 24th U.S. Colored Infantry, and Troop A–9th Cavalry Mounted are available (PP lot 12300-3). Twenty-six stereos of camp life and training situations are filed under "Negroes in the Military," and most of these are also included in the division's videodiscs. Photographs of the large colored lithograph of the Battle of Quasimas, which shows the 9th and 10th Colored Cavalry, and the original in the Popular and Applied Graphic Arts Collection (PP PGA-D-Kurz & Allison, repro. nos. LC-USZ62–134, LC-USZC4-508) are available for study.

Five black members of the 10th U.S. Cavalry received the Congressional Medal of Honor and two black members of the U.S. Navy received the Navy Medal of Honor for bravery during the Spanish-American War. Portraits of the medalists and a composite photograph made from fifteen separate photographs showing blacks who won these medals during the Spanish-American War and other conflicts are in the collections (PP Reading Room). Some early silent films in the Library's collection, like *Colored Troops Disembarking* and *9th U.S. Cavalry Watering Horses*, are from the Spanish-American War.

Buffalo Soldiers were trained as cadets at the artillery barracks located at West Point. The barracks were built between 1904 and 1908 by the firm Cram, Goodhue, and Ferguson. Three exterior photographs of the barracks are in the Historic American Buildings Survey collection (PP HABS NY, 36-WEPO, 1/27–). Military images from the W. E. B. DuBois exhibit at the 1900 Paris Exposition include Company D, 8th Battalion, Illinois Volunteer Regiment, which was led by black officers (PP lot 11308). A 1915 panorama of the 9th Cavalry Camp at Douglas, Arizona, is also in the collections. The Edgar Alexander Mearns collection contains images of blacks working at the U.S. Army 3d Division hospital and in the crematory, stables, water closets, and kitchens at Camp Hamilton, Kentucky, in 1898 and 1899 (PP lot 11211).

LYNCHING

In spite of military service to their country, blacks continued to be harassed by white supremacists. If not the primary reason that blacks and concerned whites decided a concerted effort against lawlessness was necessary, lynching was certainly a very important one. This form of mob justice was an outgrowth of the sparsely settled frontier where law enforcement personnel were few and punishment was uncertain. Once indulged in, the practice frequently became a way to mete out punishment for any unpopular offense or alleged crime. The peak period for lynching in the United States was from 1889 to 1922. The practice was not restricted to men or blacks, but African-Americans were the primary victims.

The Library of Congress has vast resources on lynching. Access to the general collections may be readily obtained by using the catalog term *lynching* or *lynch-law*. Many important race leaders, authors, and orators commented on the practice. Noteworthy items include the study by the National Association for the Advancement of Colored People entitled *Thirty Years of Lynching in the United States, 1889–1918; Annual Reports, 1919–1936* (New York: Arno Press, 1969; HV6457.N3 1969b). These reports indicate that 3,224 people were killed in the thirty-year period. Of these, 702 were white and 2,522 were black. Among the reasons given for the lynchings were "using offensive language, refusal to give up land, illicit distilling," and others. Studies of lynching include James Cutler's *Lynch-Law: An Investigation into the History of Lynching in the United States* (New York: Longmans, Green, and Co., 1905; HV6457.C8). Junius Early's *An Eye for an Eye or the Fiend and the Faggot* (Paris: Marshall's Printing House, J. M. Early, 1893; HV6466.T4 1893), a work in favor of lynching, has the following inscription on its title page: "To every Father and Mother, in all the Earth who can say to those who Executed the Murderer of Little Myrtle Vance 'Well Done, Thou Good and Faithful Servant,' the author dedicates this book."

Ida B. Wells, pictured in The Afro-American Press and Its Editors, *by I. Garland Penn (Springfield, Mass.: Willey & Co., 1891; PN4888.N4P4 Rare Bk). (LC-USZ62–107756)*

Black journalist Ida B. Wells-Barnett's condemnatory pamphlets have been reprinted in *On Lynchings: Southern Horrors; A Red Record; Mob Rule in New Orleans* (New York: Arno Press, 1969; HV6457.B37). The reprint volume is in the general collections and the original works are in the Rare Book Collection. A number of important pamphlets written during this period are now available on microfilm as a collection, with the title *Miscellaneous Pamphlets*. Although originally cataloged separately, they were assembled by the Library and include Frederick Douglass's *Why Is the Negro Lynched?* (1895; MicRR 41285) and Francis Grimké's *The Lynching of Negroes* (1899; MicRR 41286).

More recent publications on lynchings and other forms of racial violence include Michael and Judy Ann Newton's *Racial and Religious Violence in America: A Chronology* (New York: Garland Publications, 1991; HN90.V5R33 1991), which lists occurrences by place and date. In Herbert Shapiro's *White Violence and Black Response* (Amherst: University of Massachusetts Press, 1988; E185.2.S52 1988) the author describes racial violence in New York City in 1900 and in Atlanta in 1906. Atlanta was considered a modern progressive southern city, having been rebuilt after the devastation of the Civil War. Yet massive violence erupted when a gubernatorial candidate campaigned for black disenfranchisement.

Daniel T. Williams's *Eight Negro Bibliographies* (New York: Kraus Reprint Co., 1970; Z1361.N39W54), in the Main Reading Room reference collection, includes perhaps the most comprehensive bibliography on lynching available today. Entitled "The Lynching Records at Tuskegee Institute," it gives statistics by state and race from 1882 to 1968 and lists over 313 relevant publications, most of which are found in the Library's collections.

Lynchings and other manifestations of racial hatred were fostered by a host of negative racial stereotypes prevalent during this era. These attitudes are documented by many of the materials in the Prints and Photographs Division. Illustrations in *Judge* and *Puck* magazines, for example, often targeted blacks as objects of ridicule. Prints and Photographs Division videodiscs (nos. 1 and 2) contain images created as illustrations for short stories or as photographic caricatures. Most of the 148 images on the videodiscs relating to African-Americans from the turn of the century to World War I include derogatory poses, captions referring to blacks by first names only or as "Aunt" or "Uncle," or visual puns that generally include watermelons.

RACE LEADERS AND THEIR SUPPORTERS

Nannie Helen Burroughs (MSS, papers 1900–1963), who thought that Booker T. Washington was "the wisest man of his generation," founded the National Training School for Women and Girls (later called National Trade and Professional School for Women and Girls), located in Washington, D.C., and continued as its principal until her death in 1961. She also served as secretary and president of the women's auxiliary of the National Baptist Convention. Burroughs wrote that in addition to the three R's—readin', ritin', and 'rithmetic—blacks needed the three B's—the Bible, the bath, and the broom. She explained that the B's represented clean lives, clean bodies, and clean homes. Armed with the biblical teaching "If you do not work, you do not eat," and the Tuskegee philosophy, Burroughs trained her students and the young women in the Baptist convention to work diligently. One of her publications, which is in her papers in the Manuscript Division, is entitled *Twelve Things the Negro Must Do for Himself—Twelve Things White People Must Stop Doing to the Negro* (n.p., n.d.). Her correspondents included Robert R. Moton, Emmett J. Scott, Mary McLeod Bethune, Daisy Lampkin, Adam Clayton Powell, Sr., Adam Clayton Powell, Jr., Oscar DePriest, and Anson Phelps Stokes.

The photographs that accompanied her papers are in the Prints and Photographs Division and document the painstaking work that went into creating educational opportunities for black girls. Eighty snapshots show students at the National Trade and Professional School, some with parents and teachers identified. One photo shows tennis professional woman Althea Gibson as a young girl at the segregated Sparrow's Point Beach in the Maryland suburbs near Washington, D.C. (PP lot 12569). Others depict school activities, buildings and grounds, and a variety of groups at the school (PP lots 12571, 12574). A group of portraits collected between 1905 and 1958 include classmates, faculty, and administrators at the school and activities and outings such as church conventions and organized recreation (PP lot 12572).

Educator and club woman Mary Church Terrell (MSS, microfilm 1851–1962) was initially opposed to the Booker T. Washington school of thought, although her husband, Robert Heberton Terrell (MSS, microfilm 1870–1925), was a supporter. Robert Terrell was a Harvard graduate, teacher, lawyer, and judge. As a political appointee he appreciated the support that Washington was able to lend. Some of Terrell's correspondence relates to his service as a judge in the Municipal Court in Washington, D.C., for almost twenty-five years as the appointee of four presidents. His correspondents include Charles Anderson, Congressman John R. Lynch, Emmett J. Scott, Booker T. Washington, and Presidents William McKinley, Theodore Roosevelt, William Howard Taft, and Woodrow Wilson. A number of Terrell letters are among the Booker T. Washington collection (MSS, papers and microfilm 1882–1942).

Mary Church Terrell, who was a charter member of the National Association for the Advancement of Colored People (NAACP), changed her opinion about the Washington philosophy when she had an opportunity to visit Tuskegee and see the students in action. Her papers focus primarily on her career as an advocate of both women's rights and equal treatment for blacks. Terrell's papers contain materials relating to women's suffrage, the Equal Rights Amendment, desegregation in the District of Columbia, the National Association of Colored Women, the National Women's Party, and Republican politics. Manuscripts of her autobiography, *A Colored Woman in a White World* (Washington: Ransdell, Inc., [c1940]; E185.97.T47), and information about her terms as a member of the District of Columbia Board of Education are among her papers. Her correspondents include Jane Addams, Mary McLeod Bethune, Benjamin Brawley, Nannie H. Burroughs, Carrie Chapman Catt, Oscar DePriest, W. E. B. DuBois, Christian A. Fleetwood, W. C. Handy, A. Philip Randolph, Haile Selassie, Anson Phelps Stokes, William Monroe Trotter, Oswald Garrison Villard, Booker T. and Margaret Washington, H. G. Wells, and Carter G. Woodson. A name index to the Terrell papers is available in the Manuscript Division.

In 1898 while Terrell was president of the National Association of Colored Women, she addressed the fiftieth anniversary meeting of the National American Women's Suffrage Association. The Rare Book Collection includes a printed copy of her remarks entitled *The Progress of Colored Women* (Washington: Smith Brothers, 1898; E449.D16, A:13 Mur Pam Coll, Rare Bk). The Prints and Photographs Division holds some images of Mary Church Terrell and her family and friends (PP lot 12257). A few letters from Robert R. Church, Terrell's father (MSS,

In Lausanne, in October 1888, Mary Church Terrell writes in her diary about being sick with an abscessed tooth in a foreign country, where there is so much marble in the house that one's feet are always cold. (Mary Church Terrell papers, MSS)

MMC 1875, Carter G. Woodson microfilm, 1796–1933), a wealthy Tennessee businessman, are in the holdings of the Manuscript Division.

The Manuscript Division has microfilm publications of the papers of two black Ohio political leaders who were active during the Booker T. Washington era: George A. Myers (MSS, microfilm 1890–1929) and John Paterson Green (MSS, microfilm 1869–1910). The originals of the Myers papers are in the Ohio Historical Society and Green's in the Western Reserve Historical Society.

Green was a lawyer, a justice of the peace, and an Ohio state legislator. His papers relate to financial aid for Wilberforce University, travels in Europe, his speaking tours in support of William McKinley's presidential campaign, his appointment as a U.S. postage stamp agent, and conditions imposed upon southern blacks. His correspondents include Senator Blanche K. Bruce, African-American lawyer and writer Charles Waddell Chesnutt, black journalist T. Thomas Fortune, George Myers, Ralph W. Tyler, and Marcus A. Hanna. Correspondence with Green is also found in the Booker T. Washington papers (MSS, papers and microfilm 1882–1942).

Myers was a member of the Ohio Republican State Executive Committee and a shopkeeper. His correspondence relates to Ohio and national politics, especially to the Republican party and its candidates, convention campaigns and issues, appointments and activities of the Marcus A. Hanna-William McKinley faction in the years 1892–1904, and the role and attitude of blacks in the Republican party. His correspondents include Secretary of War Newton D. Baker, politician Marcus A. Hanna, African-American journalist Ralph W. Tyler, and Booker T. Washington. There are also Myers letters in the Booker T. Washington (MSS, papers and microfilm 1882–1942) and Carter G. Woodson (MSS, microfilm 1796–1933) collections. In an

August 19, 1921, letter, George A. Myers wrote to Woodson about John Paterson Green:

If you desire any information relating to the early Negro population of Cleveland, I would suggest that you consult Hon. John P. Green. . . . Mr. Green is one of the descendants of an early family and thoroughly conversant with circumstances attendant to their settlement here.

Ray Stannard Baker (MSS, microfilm 1875–1947), a white author and journalist, published a series of articles called "Following the Color Line" in the *American Magazine* (AP2.A346, also MicRR 05422) from 1906 to 1908 and later combined them in his book *Following the Color Line: American Negro Citizenship in the Progressive Era* (New York: Doubleday, Page, & Co., 1908; E185.61B16). Here he offers an analysis of the post-Reconstruction racial climate and makes suggestions about improving race relations. His speech and writings file in the Manuscript Division includes articles about various aspects of "the Negro problem." In one piece contrasting Robert Russa Moton—Booker T. Washington's successor at Tuskegee—and Washington, Baker says that Washington "came like a prophet preaching the glory of duty, of work, of quiet growth, of service, of catching up," whereas Moton is described as the "solidifier and conservator." Baker, whose correspondents include Washington and DuBois, was a participant in the organizational meetings of the NAACP.

ORGANIZATIONAL INITIATIVES FOR EQUAL RIGHTS

African-American leaders held conferences to consider solutions for problems affecting the black population. One of the more notable meetings called by black church leaders in Atlanta in 1902 is recorded in a published report, *The United Negro: His Problems and His Progress,*

Containing the Addresses and Proceedings of the Negro Young People's Christian and Educational Congress (New York: Negro Universities Press, 1969; E184.5.N44 1902b) edited by I. Garland Penn and J. W. E. Bowen. The proceedings present a summary of black social and educational achievement, with articles on such topics as "The Negro's Contribution to His Own Development," "The Effect of Secret and Benevolent Societies upon the Life of the Race," and the "Present Religious Status of the Race." Educator Nannie Helen Burroughs contributed an article on "The Colored Woman and Her Relation to the Domestic Problem." Photographs of early black churches such as St. James Protestant Episcopal Church of Baltimore, Maryland, and Ebenezer Methodist Episcopal Church of Washington, D.C., are included. The Washington Conference on the Race Problem in the United States held a similar session in the nation's capital in 1903. The proceedings are entitled *How to Solve the Race Problem* (Washington: Beresford Printer, 1904; E185.5.W3 1903).

Although Booker T. Washington was a very influential leader, some prominent blacks were strongly opposed to the Tuskegee philosophy of racial accommodationism and a dedication to vocational training. One of these was W. E. B. DuBois (MSS, microfilm 1803–1965), who believed that in matters of lynching and other forms of denial of due process, blacks should speak out forcibly. DuBois, who received his doctorate from Harvard University, was an educator, writer, civil rights leader, and sociologist. His papers, available on microfilm, cover most aspects of his life and work and reflect his academic and political endeavors to achieve equal treatment for blacks in the United States, Africa, and other parts of the world. The original papers are at the University of Massachusetts at Amherst. W. E. B. DuBois's activities eventually led to the organization of several Pan-African Congresses and other national and interna-

tional political gatherings. He was an early participant in the work of the National Association for the Advancement of Colored People (MSS, records 1909–82).

In 1905 W. E. B. DuBois and black militant journalist William Monroe Trotter organized a meeting of black intellectuals and professionals in Niagara Falls, Canada, for the purpose of initiating aggressive action for full citizenship rights for African-Americans. The group subsequently met in Harpers Ferry and Boston. They intended to work for legal redress and demanded freedom of speech and criticism, an "unfettered and unsubsidized" press, abolition of race and color distinctions, recognition of the principle of human brotherhood, the right of the best training available for all people, and belief in the dignity of labor.

The Niagara Movement, as it was called, was opposed to the Tuskegee conciliatory philosophy in that it provided for legal and written confrontation against injustice. Some of the movement's participants later became leaders in the NAACP. DuBois's book *Souls of Black Folk: Essays and Sketches* (17th ed., Chicago: A. C. McClurg & Co., 1931; E185.5.D81 1931) originally published in 1903, argued forcibly against the Tuskegee school of thought and for the classical training of the "talented tenth" of the black population who would then provide leadership for other members of the race. In this work DuBois prophesied that "the problem of the twentieth century" would be "the color line." The Booker T. Washington papers (MSS, papers and microfilm 1882–1942) include correspondence with and about DuBois that reflects their philosophical differences.

The Library holds over 150 volumes by and about DuBois discussing various aspects of his views on racial issues. A series of twenty-four scientific studies about African-Americans which he initiated while on the staff of Atlanta University is available in the Microform Read-

At its headquarters, 69 Fifth Avenue, New York, the NAACP flew a flag to report lynchings, until, in 1938, the threat of losing its lease forced the association to discontinue the practice. (Silver gelatin photograph, NAACP Collection, PP. LC-USZ62–33793)

ing Room (MicRR 04171, Guide K-4). The studies include full-length books, which are also available in the general collections, on subjects such as *The Negro Artisan* (Atlanta, Ga.: Atlanta University Press, 1902; E185.5.A88 no. 7), *The Negro American Family* (Atlanta, Ga.: Atlanta University Press, 1908; E185.5.A88 no. 13), *The Negro Church* (Atlanta, Ga.: Atlanta University Press, 1903; E185.5.A88 no. 8), and *Some Efforts of American Negroes for Their Own Betterment* (Atlanta, Ga.: Atlanta University Press, 1898; E185.5.A88 no. 3; MicRR 04171). All of these volumes have extensive bibliographies.

The members of the Niagara Movement lacked the necessary "power, money, and influence" to implement their recommendations.

Their leadership, however, led to the convening of the National Negro Conference of 1909 (also called the Committee on the Negro or the Committee of Forty), which later assumed the name National Association for the Advancement of Colored People. The proceedings are cited as *National Negro Conference* (New York: Arno Press, 1969; E184.5.N3 1909). The NAACP was organized mainly by whites who invited a few articulate blacks concerned about the treatment of the black population in America to join their effort. The primary interests of the association in its formative years were equal treatment of African-Americans before the law, nullification of Jim Crow laws, the abolition of lynchings, and the end of all forms of discrimination and segregation. Limited photographic coverage of the early work of the organization and portraits of some of the founders are found in the NAACP collection in the Prints and Photographs Division (PP lot 10647).

Three important formative steps for the NAACP in 1910 were the beginning of an antilynching campaign, entrance into the Pink Franklin court battle over equal justice before the law, and the publication of *The Crisis: A Record of the Darker Races* (E185.5.C92; reprint, New York: Arno Press, 1969; E185.5.C89), edited by DuBois. An *Analytical Guide and Indexes to the Crisis, 1910–1960* (Westport, Conn.: Greenwood Press, 1975; 3 vols. E185.5.C923 R67 1975) was prepared by the Rose Bibliography Project at George Washington University. Between 1911 and 1914, fifty branches of the NAACP were organized in cities throughout the United States, largely because of the interest in the NAACP generated by the *Crisis*, which was edited by DuBois for twenty-four years. Two publications that contain selected DuBois materials from the *Crisis* are *The Emerging Thought of W. E. B. DuBois: Essays and Editorials from the Crisis with an Introduction, Commentaries, and a Personal Memoir by Henry Lee Moon* (New York: Simon and Schuster, 1972; E186.97.D73A25 1972) and *Selections from the Crisis*, edited by Herbert Aptheker (Millwood, N.Y.: Kraus-Thomson Organization, 1983; 2 vols. E185.97.D73A25 1983).

The NAACP *Annual Report* (E185.5.N275) provides a periodic review of the association's work and is particularly informative in the area of legal initiatives. Many of the NAACP's cases were matters pertaining to discrimination against individuals. These cases were often undertaken with the hope that the points of law established by successful cases would ultimately provide the precedents necessary to overturn all discriminatory laws. For example, the 1912 annual report discussed the case of a black New York City organist who was denied admission to the

Palisades Amusement Park but who won—with NAACP aid—a season ticket and three hundred dollars in damages.

The January 1913 *Annual Report* states that "The Association now has under consideration two important cases which will test both the Grandfather Law and the 'Jim Crow' law; both cases have been appealed to the Supreme Court of the United States" (p. 8). In the year that Booker T. Washington died—1915—the Supreme Court ruled in the first of many major NAACP legal victories, *Guinn vs. The United States*, that the grandfather clause—which provided that an illiterate man could vote only if his grandfather had—violated the Fifteenth Amendment. The extensive NAACP collection (MSS, records 1909–82) in the Manuscript Division includes only a few materials relating to the organization's formative years.

Moorfield Storey (MSS, papers 1847–1930), first president of the NAACP, acted as a secretary to radical Republican Massachusetts senator Charles Sumner from 1867 to 1869 and had participated in the attempt to impeach President Andrew Johnson. His papers in the Manuscript Division reflect his support of minority groups, indicate some aspects of his service as NAACP president, and document his leadership in the opposition to the exclusion of blacks from freshmen dormitories at his alma mater, Harvard University, in 1922–23. Of special interest are files relating to Edward Brown, a black man who faced discrimination at Harvard Medical College, and an antilynching file dated 1910–22. Storey's correspondents include Charles Francis Adams, William Howard Taft, Charles Evans Hughes, James Weldon Johnson, William E. Borah, William Gibbs McAdoo, Joel E. Spingarn, Walter White, Mary White Ovington, and George W. Wickersham.

William LePre Houston (MSS, papers ca. 1901–35) was a lawyer and educator who in 1891 married Mary Ethel Hamilton, a teacher trained at Wilberforce University. Together they moved to Washington, D.C., where William worked as a clerk in the War Department. One son, Charles Hamilton Houston, who lived from 1895 to 1950, would eventually serve as dean of Howard University's law school and the general counsel of the NAACP. The papers in the Manuscript Division document the elder Houston's establishment of his own law firm in 1921 and its expansion into a partnership with his son in 1924 after Charles graduated from Harvard Law School. The papers show the firm's work in behalf of African-American workers and organizations and the Houstons' active role in politics. Many of the papers reveal the everyday life of an urban black middle-class family. Some correspondence from Margaret Gladys Moran, the woman who became Mrs. Charles Houston in 1924, is included. Besides correspondence, the collection consists of legal briefs, pamphlets, printed matter, financial papers, scrapbooks, clippings, records of the Odd Fellows Lodge, financial accounts, diaries, photographs, and memorabilia. A full-length treatment of Charles Houston's life, entitled *Groundwork: Charles Hamilton Houston and the Struggle for Civil Rights* (Philadelphia: University of Pennsylvania Press, 1983; KF373.H644M3 1983), by Genna Rae McNeil discusses his role in the civil rights struggle, as does Richard Kluger's epic history, *Simple Justice: The History of Brown v. Board of Education and Black America's Struggle for Equality* (New York: Knopf, 1975; KF4155.K55 1976).

About the same time the NAACP was established, another organization important for the development of the black community was being formed. Founded in 1910 through a merger of several welfare organizations, the National Urban League (NUL, MSS, records 1910–85) was originally known as the National League on Urban Conditions among Negroes. Its aim was to promote the improvement of the industrial, eco-

nomic, social, and spiritual conditions in black communities. The NUL also attempted to facilitate the migration of blacks from rural to urban areas. Although some of the records relate to the organization's first decade, most date from a later period.

BLACK BIBLIOPHILE DANIEL ALEXANDER PAYNE MURRAY

Besides taking organizational initiatives, blacks were developing expertise in various professional avenues. Daniel Alexander Payne Murray (MSS, microfilm 1881–1966) was a successful businessman, librarian, and historian who worked for the Library of Congress for fifty-two years. Murray's papers, including draft bibliographic sketches, notes, and correspondence were given to the State Historical Society of Wisconsin in 1966 and the microfilm edition of that collection is available in the Library's Manuscript Division. His papers include correspondence, drafts of writings, and research materials chiefly relating to his unpublished "Historical and Biographical Encyclopedia of the Colored Race." The collection is composed of research notes, biographical sketches, annotated clippings and reviews, photographs, bibliographies, and material relating to Murray's attempts to publish his encyclopedia. There are some files relating to his civic and social activities in Washington, D.C., his work as an assistant to Librarian of Congress Ainsworth R. Spofford, his activities in Republican party politics, and family matters, including information about his wife, Anna Jane (Evans) Murray.

Another small collection of Daniel Alexander Payne Murray (MSS, Miscellaneous Manuscripts Collection 1970) materials in the Manuscript Division consists of an unpublished book by Murray entitled "Paul Jennings and His Times, President Madison's Biographer and Valet."

Born a slave, Jennings worked for Madison and, after Madison's death, for Daniel Webster, from whom Jennings purchased his freedom. Information relating to Murray's career at the Library of Congress can be found in the Library of Congress collection (MSS, records 1800–1987), which also include materials relating to Murray's work with an exhibit of works by and about blacks for the Paris Exposition of 1900.

Murray's collecting of African-American materials, both at the Library and privately, became a lifelong quest. Convinced that "the true test of the progress of a people is to be found in their literature," he collected works which would demonstrate the achievements of black people in all fields of endeavor. Murray bequeathed his personal collection of nearly fifteen hundred books and pamphlets to the Library in 1925. Although much of that material has been integrated into the general collections, pamphlets dating primarily from 1870 to 1920 were kept intact in the Library's Rare Book and Special Collections Division. The Murray Pamphlet Collection is also available on microfilm (MicRR 90/3001).

The Murray Pamphlet Collection includes about 350 items and reflects some of the most significant aspects of African-American life during the fifty years following emancipation. The central role of the church in the black community is illustrated by the numerous sermons encouraging racial pride and political activism, as well as by reports documenting charitable and social activities organized through churches. Progress in education and community development can be traced through academy and college catalogs, graduation orations, and the histories of Hampton Institute and Wilberforce University. Annual reports and convention proceedings record the aspirations and activities of local and national organizations working for political and social advancement. Included are poems, plays, songsters, and assorted ephem-

era used for entertainment or information. Biographies, slave narratives, and historical summaries record past contributions of African-Americans, while campaign literature and political speeches show the attempt by African-Americans to chart courses for the twentieth century.

The publications donated in the Murray bequest are representative of the local, national, and international aspects of his collecting interests. The bibliographies Murray compiled and the books and pamphlets on African-American history and culture that he acquired for the Library, both in his professional capacity and through his legacy, honor his desire to demonstrate "the wisdom of both emancipation and enfranchisement."

For example, P. Thomas Stanford's sermon *Imaginary Obstructions to True Spiritual Progress* (West Somerville, Mass.: Davis Square Printing Co., 1898; E449.D16, E:18 Mur Pam Coll, Rare Bk), which is included in the Murray collection, discusses the means by which African-Americans could overcome obstacles to development. Born a Virginia slave and educated in Connecticut and England through the efforts of Henry Ward Beecher, Stanford was pastor of the North Cambridge Union Industrial Church and Strangers' Home in Massachusetts. The pamphlet collection also includes John Edward Bruce's *Blood Red Record: A Review of the Horrible Lynchings and Burning of Negroes by Civilized White Men in the United States* (Albany, N.Y.: Argus Co., 1901; E449.D16, 17:18 Mur Pam Coll, Rare Bk), in which the author chastises northern whites for ignoring the outrageous violations of the human rights of southern blacks and warns that "danger to the Republic is not past as long as lawlessness is permitted to exist in any part of this land."

In another pamphlet, *A National Appeal: Addressed to the American Negro and the Friends of Human Liberty* (Oskaloosa, Iowa: n.p., 1892?

E449.D16, C:3 Mur Pam Coll, Rare Bk), journalist George Taylor urges blacks to use the power of their votes to support policies that will be good for them and other labor interests, and recommends that the free coinage policy of William Jennings Bryan makes the Democratic party the better choice in the 1896 election. The agenda of topics and participants outlined in the *Official Programme, First Annual Meeting of the Afro-American Council at the Metropolitan Baptist Church* (Washington: National Afro-American Council, 1898; E449.D16, 16:9 Mur Pam Coll, Rare Bk) reveals an impressive congregation of the most prominent African-American leaders and reflects the issues they considered most vital to their advancement.

Principal authors in the Murray Pamphlet Collection include Benjamin W. Arnett, Alexander Crummell, Frederick Douglass, black congressmen John R. Lynch and John M. Langston, Emanuel K. Love, Kelly Miller, Booker T. Washington, and Frances E. W. Harper. About fifty books and separately bound pamphlets from the original Murray bequest have been recovered from the Library's general collections and form part of the Murray Collection (Rare Bk). They include sermons, speeches, biographies of Bishop James Shorter and Rev. David Smith, church histories, proceedings of the conference of the African Methodist Episcopal Church, and the history of the town of Sandy Spring, Maryland. A commemorative history of the National Association for the Relief of Destitute Colored Women and Children, *Fifty Years of Good Works*, by Winfield S. Montgomery (Washington: Smith Brothers, 1914; HV3181.N32 Mur Coll, Rare Bk), credits the efforts of spirited women of both races with instituting and sustaining the work of this national charity dedicated to the "relief, uplift, and salvation" of destitute black women and children. An additional 346 pamphlets by or about African-Americans have been selected from a huge miscellaneous nineteenth-century pamphlet collection in the Rare Book and Special Collections Division by matching names found in Murray's collection and in bibliographies he compiled. This collection complements the Murray pamphlets and is strong in antislavery literature. A checklist is available (E185.A254; African American Pamphlet Collection, Rare Bk).

MURRAY, DUBOIS, AND THE PARIS EXPOSITION OF 1900

In late 1899 the U.S. commissioner general asked the Library of Congress to organize a display of literature about black Americans for the Paris Exposition of 1900. Daniel Murray was assigned to the task and worked swiftly to publish a preliminary list of 270 titles by January 1900 that incorporated a shorter list that was compiled in 1893 for the U.S. Bureau of Education (10/3/1900, Murray Papers, MSS microfilm 1888–1966, 1:84–100). Disappointed in the response to his initial appeal to certain black educators to donate copies of these works and identify additional titles, Murray corresponded by hand with four thousand educators nationwide. This persuasive "personal appeal" yielded 1,100 additional titles and a "large number of unsolicited letters proffering books and pamphlets and information," which allowed Murray to acquire 500 works. Of these, 216 were selected for display at the Paris Exposition, along with a subject catalog listing 980 titles (10/3/1900, Murray Papers, MSS microfilm 1888–1966, 1:84–100).

DuBois, who had recommended that a "Negro exhibit" be included in the Paris Exposition, subsequently won a gold medal for his social study of Georgia exhibited there. In an article entitled "The American Negro at Paris" in *American Monthly Review of Reviews* (July-December 1900, 22:575–77; AP4.R4) DuBois describes the various components of the exhibit and stresses the significance of its being done by blacks. "This is an exhibit of American Negroes," he wrote, "planned and executed by Negroes, and collected and installed under the direction of a Negro special agent, Mr. Thomas J. Calloway."

One of the most significant groups of photographic material for this period is the set of images collected by Dubois for display at the Paris Exposition. The images, which came to the Library as a part of the Murray bequest and are now in the Prints and Photographs Division, represent various aspects of the daily lives of African-Americans, illustrating people, homes, churches, and educational facilities. DuBois intended that the four volumes of images would demonstrate the economic and social progress accomplished by "the Negro race in the United States since its emancipation" (PP lot 11930).

Most of the photographs were made along the central eastern seaboard from New York to Florida, going inland as far west as Memphis and Chicago. There are about four hundred images grouped principally by location. As DuBois is credited with making the special studies, he may have taken the photographs himself. It is one of the earliest instances noted to date of the use of photographs as sociological documents. In the *American Monthly* article DuBois refers to the exhibit as "sociological in the larger sense of the term—that is an attempt to give, in as systematic and compact a form as possible, the history and present condition of a large group of human beings." He cites the major categories as the history of black Americans, the present condition of the group, and their education and literature.

The *Report of the Commissioner-General for the United States to the International Universal Exposition, Paris, 1900* (Washington: Government Printing Office, 1901; 6 vols. T804.G1U6) describes the section of the exhibit that included photographs of Hampton Institute and Atlanta, Fisk, and Howard Universities submitted by DuBois. In compiling the albums he sent to Paris, DuBois included extensive documentation of these and other educational institutions for blacks. For example, twelve photographs of Claflin College in Orangeburg, South Carolina, show male and female students in the manual training shop, the printing shop, and the library. There are also photographs of the marching band, athletic events, the woodwork shop, the printing plant, and a sweet potato harvest (PP lot 11298). Hampton Institute photographs depict classes in military history and training (PP lot 11931); and others portray Howard University President Andrew Rankin and his home, Howard classroom and library scenes, and students studying dentistry, bacteriology, chemistry, pharmacy, carpentry, printing, and law (PP lot 11294). Photographs of Morris Brown College, founded in 1885 by the African Methodist Episcopal Church, consist of portraits of students enrolled in the academic, theology, and teacher training classes. Photographs of the library and other buildings document activities at historically black Roger Williams College in Nashville (PP lot 11307).

Other historically black colleges and universities represented in the DuBois albums include North Carolina Agricultural and Technical College in Greensboro, with twenty photographs of classes in blacksmithing, mechanical drawing, dressmaking, biological research, food production, and water and soil analysis (PP lot 11296), and racially integrated Berea College in Kentucky, with images of buildings, student groups, and classroom scenes in cooking and woodworking (PP lot 11297). For Fisk University in Nashville, Tennessee, there are thirty-four photographs of the campus showing formal group portraits of students, teacher training at a model school, choir performances, and a baseball game (PP lot 11299). Haines Industrial Institute in Augusta, Georgia, is documented with sixteen photographs of teachers, cadets, a sewing class, and a kindergarten (PP lot 11300). Shaw University in Raleigh, North Carolina, is represented by campus views and shots of individual buildings (PP lot 11301).

DuBois also included photographs of black-owned businesses such as a newspaper in Richmond, Virginia (PP lot 11295), and a store in Chicago (PP lot 11308). The images documented the work of black women's groups like a day nursery established by the Women's League of Newport, Rhode Island (PP lot 11304), and a number of homes owned by blacks in Richmond, Virginia (PP lot 11295), Atlanta, Georgia (PP lot 11305), Wilberforce, Ohio (PP lot 11308), Washington, D.C. (PP lot 11303), and Chattanooga, Knoxville, and Memphis, Tennessee (PP lots 11306, 11307). DuBois also included a three-volume 184-page copy of the entire black code of Georgia governing the behavior of slaves and free blacks, dating from 1732 to 1899 (PP lot 11932). Other DuBois photographs and charts in the Prints and Photographs Division, which are a part of a bequest from Daniel A. P. Murray, are too fragile to examine in the original (photos, PP lot 11930; charts, PP lot 11931).

In addition to working with DuBois on the Paris Exposition and becoming a collector of works by and about blacks, Daniel Murray also worked for many years on a black history encyclopedia. The prospectus for this monumental work, entitled *Murray's Historical and Biographical Encyclopedia of the Colored Race Throughout the World* (Washington: World's Cyclopedia Company, 1912; Mur Coll, Rare Bk), describes his efforts to compile an exhaustive record of black achievement throughout history and includes sample entries for the volume. Murray collected subscriptions for his proposed six-volume work between 1911 and 1914 and subsequently returned the money, when the amount collected proved insufficient to underwrite the publication.

In "Bibliographia-Africania," a Murray article appearing in *Voice of the Negro* in 1904 (1: 186–91; E185.5.V88 Rare Bk), he discusses earlier efforts to identify the writings of black authors and describes some of the rarest items on his list of over two thousand titles, including works by Richard Allen, Phillis Wheatley, Noah Cannon, and Peter Williams.

Murray collected sentiments in support of his encyclopedia (Correspondence, Mur Coll, Rare Bk). Edward H. Morris, Chicago attorney and "grand master of Odd Fellows (Colored)," wrote on February 23, 1914:

As soon as your book is out I will take a copy for myself. I feel that you have done a great service to not only the race, but to the world. Those who would know the truth may thru your book know where to find it—and to prove it.

Dr. R. Wellesley Bailey, a Germantown, Pennsylvania, physician wrote an encouraging letter to Murray on July 4, 1914:

How are your volumes progressing? I have had several foreign queries concerning their publishing. . . . Their appearance is eagerly looked for by many well-wishers and collectors of ethnological data.

Murray's tireless devotion to collecting information and writings on black achievement should logically have culminated in the publication of his monumental "Historical and Biographical Encyclopedia of the Colored Race." In his 1904 "Bibliographia-Africania" article, Murray reports that his unremitting search for works by black writers has increased his list to 2,200, just double the number he had identified by the close of the Paris Exposition. In the 1912 subscription prospectus for the encyclopedia, Murray reported that his master work was complete and was composed of a bibliography of 6,000 titles of books and pamphlets, as well as 25,000 biographical sketches, 5,000 musical compositions, and 500 plot synopses of fictional works treating the race problem. Although Murray received a steady stream of correspondence from across the country over a period of years inquiring about the encyclopedia and urging him to publish it, his massive notes and drafts remained unpublished at his death in 1925. They are available today on microfilm (10/3/1900, Murray Papers, MSS microfilm 1888–1966, 1:84–100).

ART, LITERATURE, AND SCIENCE

During the Booker T. Washington era, blacks were active in the arts and their contributions can be documented in the Library's collections. In the fine arts, Henry Ossawa Tanner, an African-American painter who worked between 1881 and 1936, studied under Thomas Eakins at the Pennsylvania Academy of the Fine Arts. Tanner went on to develop his own personal, semi-abstract style of expression that relied on subtle blendings of colors and brushstrokes to capture the essence of his subject. Much of his work depicts biblical characters, possibly reflecting the influence his minister father had on Tanner during his childhood. But Tanner also painted family, friends, and ordinary people wherever he was—the American South, Jerusalem, North Africa, and France, where he made his home as an adult. One of his best known works is *The Banjo Lesson*, a painting showing an elderly black man instructing a black child. A biography of Tanner by Marcia M. Mathews entitled *Henry Ossawa Tanner, American Artist* (Chicago: University of Chicago Press, [1969]; ND237.T33M3) and two exhibit catalogs, *The Art of Henry O. Tanner, 1859–1937* (Washington: The Institute, [1969]; N6537.T35A4 1969), from an exhibit organized by the Frederick Douglass Institute in collaboration with the Smithsonian Institution's National Collection of Fine Arts, and *Henry Ossawa Tanner* (Philadelphia: Phila-

delphia Museum of Art; New York: Rizzoli International Publications, 1991; ND237.T33M3), by Dewey F. Mosby and Darrel Sewell, in the Library's collections document his life and work. Black-and-white glass negatives of two of Tanner's paintings made by the Detroit Publishing Company for commercial sales are held by the Prints and Photographs Division. They show *The Holy Family* and a painting of Christ in the home of Mary and Martha (PP repro. nos. LC-D416–747, LC-D416–783; both reproduced on videodisc no. 1).

James Van Der Zee was the first black master photographer to survey the Harlem community in which he lived by photographing many of its members and many of their activities at his studio. The Library has four portraits of various family members and neighbors made during the Booker T. Washington period (PP PH-Van Der Zee Portfolio). A 1907 Van Der Zee image depicts the Whittier Preparatory School in Phoebus, Virginia, a prep school for the Hampton Institute in Hampton, Virginia.

Paul Laurence Dunbar (MSS, microfilm 1873–1936) and Charles Waddell Chesnutt (MSS, microfilm 1889–1932) were African-American literary giants at the turn of the century. The originals of the Chesnutt papers are at the Western Reserve Historical Society in Cleveland, and the Dunbar papers in the Ohio Historical Society in Columbus. Dunbar was a favorite among many both for his dialect and for his rhymed verses. He created dialect verse in his poem "A Negro Love Song":

> Seen my lady home las' night,
>   Jump back, honey, jump back.
> Hel' huh han' an' sque'z it tight,
>   Jump back, honey, jump back.
> Hyead huh sigh a little sigh,
>   Seen a light gleam f'om huh eye,
> An' a smile go flittin' by—
>   Jump back, honey, jump back.

Dunbar's prose, poetry, and lyrics as well as financial and legal records, notebooks, and scrapbooks form these records. Though he died at the age of thirty-four, Dunbar received national recognition for his work and was able to publish both prose and poetry. His collection also includes correspondence, diaries, other writings, and financial records of Dunbar's wife, Alice Dunbar Nelson, herself an author of prose and poetry.

For a brief period Dunbar worked at the Library of Congress, and from time to time he did public readings. For example, when a reading room for the blind was opened at the Library in November 1897, one of the first programs featured Dunbar reading his poems. In one Dunbar letter, dated October 26, [1898?], in the Library of Congress collection (MSS, records 1800–1987), he asks for a leave of absence because he finds himself "completely broken down both in health and spirits."

Dunbar's works in the Rare Book Collection include *Folks from Dixie* (New York: Dodd, Mead and Co., 1898; PZ3.D911Fo3 Rare Bk, MicRR 47117 PZ), *Lyrics of Lowly Life* (New York: Dodd, Mead and Co., 1896; PS1556.L6 1896 Rare Bk, MicRR 30818), and *Poems of Cabin and Field* (New York: Dodd, Mead and Co., 1899; PS1556.P6 1899 Rare Bk). In addition to his printed works in the general and rare book collections, there are Dunbar materials in the Booker T. Washington (MSS, papers and microfilm 1882–1942) and Carter G. Woodson (MSS, microfilm 1796–1933) collections in the Manuscript Division.

Charles W. Chesnutt, an Ohio lawyer, wrote novels, short stories, and articles on race relations, often publishing in the *Atlantic Monthly* (1857–, AP2.A8; and MicRR 03388) and several other magazines. *The Conjure Woman, The Wife of His Youth, and Other Stories of the Color Line* (New York: Houghton, Mifflin and Co., 1899; PZ3.C4253C) received a notable number of complimentary reviews. Chesnutt's realistic and artistic accounts are enhanced by his experiences in the South during the Reconstruction period.

Chesnutt's *Marrow of Tradition* (Boston: Houghton, Mifflin and Co., 1901; PS1292.C6M3 1901, Rare Bk; MicRR 79320 PZ) is based on the 1898 race riots in Wilmington, North Carolina, and portrays the realities of racism in the New South, showing scant improvement over the Old South. The microfilm collection of his papers in the Manuscript Division consists of writings, literary manuscripts, correspondence, memorabilia, clippings, and photographs. His correspondence includes one or more letters each between Chesnutt and Carter G. Woodson, William Monroe Trotter, Booker T. Washington, Emmett J. Scott, George A. Myers, Oscar Micheaux, and W. E. B. DuBois.

Frances Ellen Watkins Harper's works for this era include *Enlightened Motherhood* (Brooklyn: Brooklyn Literary Society, 1892; E449.D16, 19:6, Murr Pam Coll, Rare Bk) and *Light Beyond the Darkness* (Chicago: Donohue and Henneberry, 189–?; E449.D16, B:13, Murr Pam Coll, Rare Bk). Harper's *Iola Leroy, or Shadows Uplifted* (Philadelphia: Garrigues Brothers, 1892; PS1799. H716 Anthony Coll, Rare Bk) was written to demonstrate to black Sunday School youth the capacity of their race for social and intellectual uplift. This was the first novel by a black person to treat the Reconstruction period, and it brought the message to middle class blacks to work for the betterment of their people. Harper, who lived from 1825 to 1911, was a teacher at Union Seminary and an outstanding antislavery and universal suffrage lecturer.

Over three thousand manuscript plays dating from 1870 to the early twentieth century were acquired by the Library through copyright deposits. These works are housed in the Rare Book and Special Collections Division and can be accessed by author's name. In the collection, there are probably more titles about blacks by whites than there are by African-American authors. *Otille, the Octoroone; Tragedy in Five Acts* (Manuscript Play Collection, Rare Bk), for ex-

ample, was written by white author Sara Gro-
enevelt in 1893. Among almost six thousand
published plays in the Reserve Storage Drama
Collection are many from DeWitt's Ethiopian
and Comic Drama series including John Arnold's *Gripsack* (New York, 1873), *Glycerine Oil*
(New York, 1874), and other short plays like
Aunty Chloe, or Down to Massa's Home (New
York: Happy Hours Co., 1875), which were intended for use by minstrel troupes or amateur
performers.

The need to demonstrate that blacks could
excel in literature, arts, and sciences led to the
formation on March 5, 1897, of the American
Negro Academy, the first black learned society.
Alexander Crummell was its founder and first
president. The academy had as its major purposes the production of scholarly works; assisting youth in attainments reflecting higher
culture; the dissemination of truth; and the
vindication of the Negro through raising the
level of intellectual pursuits. A general history
of the organization is given in Alfred Moss's
*The American Negro Academy: Voice of the Talented
Tenth* (Baton Rouge: Louisiana State University
Press, 1981; E185.5.A53M67). The organization
existed from 1897 to 1928, and during this time
published *Occasional Papers* (Washington: American Negro Academy, 1897–1924; MicRR 22533–
23443), which are described in a guide by Ardie S. Myers entitled "Afro-Americana in the
Microform Reading Room" of the Library of
Congress. Representative papers are "Civilization, the Primal Need of the Race," Alexander
Crummell's 1897 inaugural address, Charles C.
Cook's "Comparative Study of the Negro Problem" (1899), and Archibald Grimké's "Ballotless
Victim of One-Party Governments" (1913). A
reprint edition, available in the general collections, is the American Negro Academy's *Occasional Papers*, nos. 1–22 (New York: Arno Press,
1969; E185.5.A51 1969).

African-Americans who made important sci-

entific contributions are listed in "Blacks in Science and Related Disciplines," by Vivian O.
Sammons and Denise P. Dempsey (*LC Science
Tracer Bullet*, TB 89-9, December 1989) and "Inventions and Inventors," by Constance Carter
(*LC Science Tracer Bullet*, TB 87-11, November
1987), which cites works about African-Americans. *Black Pioneers of Science and Invention* by
Louis Haber (San Diego: Harcourt, Brace, Jova-
novich, 1991; Q141.H2 1991), *Blacks in Science
and Medicine* by Vivian O. Sammons (New York:
Hemisphere Publishing Co., 1990; Q141.B58
1990), *Seven African-American Scientists* by
Robert C. Hayden (Frederick, Md.: Twenty-
First Century Books, c1992; Q141.H37 1992),
and Patricia Carter Ives's *Creativity and Inventions: The Genius of Afro-Americans and Women
in the United States and Their Patents* (Arlington, Va.: Research Unlimited, 1987; T21.I84
1987) also discuss the subject.

As segregation and discrimination became
ever more rigid during the Booker T. Washington era, African-American musicians created
new genres of music of great popular appeal.
White and black audiences alike responded
with enthusiasm to ragtime and syncopated
musicals. At a time when the minstrel show's
popularity was waning, talented composers
and lyricists created full-length black musicals
to compete with operettas and other kinds of
musical shows on Broadway. The first successful all-black show, *Clorindy; or, the Origin of the
Cakewalk* (New York: Witmark, 1898; M1508.C),
was composed by Will Marion Cook in collaboration with the poet Paul Laurence Dunbar.
Thereafter Cook wrote a series of successful
musical shows as well as many single songs.
Excerpts from the shows can be found in the
Music Division (M1508.8), arranged by the
name of the show. Typical of Cook's songs was
"Swing Along" (New York: G. Schirmer, 1912;
M1621.C).

J. Rosamond Johnson formed a song-writing

team with his brother, James Weldon Johnson, and Bob Cole that contributed songs to white musicals and produced shows independently. J. Rosamond Johnson is best remembered for the individual songs he composed, like "Li'l Gal" (New York: J.W. Stern & Co., 1902; 79635) and the stirring "Lift Ev'ry Voice and Sing: National Hymn for the Colored People of America" (New York: J.W. Stern, 1900; M1630. J Case). Ernest Hogan, an extremely versatile entertainer who performed his own songs, drew much applause singing in his show *Rufus Rastus*, in 1905, for which excerpts can be found in the Music Division (M1508.8.H).

Contemporary with the first all-black shows in New York was the publication of the earliest piano rags. "Harlem Rag" (1897) by Thomas Turpin was reputed to be the first piano rag by a black composer to be published. It was followed by the much more successful "Maple Leaf Rag" by Scott Joplin (Sedalia, Mo.: John Stark & Son, 1898; M31.J). Turpin's "St. Louis Rag" (1903; M31.T) earned him the title "Father of St. Louis Ragtime." The catchy syncopation of ragtime took the country by storm, permeating all forms of popular music, from songs to military marches and dance music. Although ragtime was eclipsed for a time by jazz, its revived popularity was demonstrated in many of the collections published years later, such as Rudi Blesh's *Classic Piano Rags* (New York: Dover, 1973; M21.B58C6) and *The Collected Works of Scott Joplin*, edited by Vera Brodsky Lawrence (New York: New York Public Library, 1971; 2 vols. M3.J66.L4).

In contrast to the more conventional transcriptions of spirituals that were published earlier, some newer collections made a greater effort to reproduce the music as it was performed. Emily Hallowell's *Calhoun Plantation Songs* (Boston: C.W. Thompson & Co., 1901; Microfilm Music 2161), transcribed from the singing of students at the Calhoun Colored

School in Lowndes County, Alabama, attempted to preserve "the peculiarities of rhythm, melody, harmony and text." Greater appreciation of the distinctive character of black performance style appeared in Jeanette Robinson Murphy's *Southern Thoughts for Northern Thinkers and African Music in America* (New York: Bandanna Publishing Co., 1904; ML3556. M97). Black composers issued their own arrangements, such as that of Nathaniel Clark Smith with his *New Jubilee Songs for Quartette, Choir or Chorus: Concert, Church* (Chicago: Jubilee Music Co., 1906; M1670.S65). Walter Rose Whittlesey, who in 1897 became the first chief of the Library of Congress Music Division, set himself to the task of preparing a card index of the collections of spirituals in the Library, a catalog that is still in use.

Another stream of black folk music that moved from the rural South to the urban centers was the blues. In contrast to the spiritual, which was usually a group performance with solo and chorus frequently alternating, the blues was a solitary expression of trouble and misery. Its roots probably extended far back into the time of slavery and, earlier still, to Africa. Since these were essentially improvised utterances, the earliest blues were never written down and so were lost. The first published version of the blues was W. C. Handy's "Memphis Blues, Better Known as Mister Crump" (Memphis: Handy Music Co., 1912; M31.H). A 1914 copy of Handy's "St. Louis Blues" in his own hand is in the Music Division (ML96.H2685 Case).

The division also holds extensive writings on the blues that recount its origin and history, analyze texts and music, or describe the lives of blues musicians. Examples are Samuel Charters's *The Roots of the Blues: An African Search* (Boston: M. Boyars, 1981; ML3521.C5) and Paul Oliver's *The Story of the Blues* (Philadelphia: Chilton Book Co., 1969; ML3561.J3047). A periodi-

961—"Ise de Happiest Little Coon in de Cotton Field."

A Whiting View Company (Cincinnati, Ohio) photograph for its Twentieth Century Series of stereopticon slides (no. 961), copyright 1900. (PP Stereo. LC-USZ62–107530)

cal, *Living Blues: A Journal of African-American Blues Tradition*, began in Chicago in 1970 but was subsequently published at the Center for Southern Culture of the University of Mississippi (ML1.L57).

Improvised instrumental music that had developed along with the blues and ragtime came to be known as jazz. The early performers in New Orleans in the 1890s can be known only by reputation as they were neither recorded nor their music written down. An excellent discussion of what is known of these early jazz musicians can be found in Gunther Schuller's *Early Jazz: Its Roots and Musical Development* (New York: Oxford University Press, 1968; ML3561.J3S3295). The earliest recordings of jazz were made in 1917.

Composers who wrote for the concert hall and the church emerged during this period. Harry T. Burleigh attended the National Conservatory of Music in New York in 1892 where

he studied with Antonin Dvorak, the great Bohemian composer, who praised the spiritual as America's natural folk music in an interview in the *New York Herald* for May 25, 1893, saying: "I am now satisfied that the future music of this country must be founded upon what are called negro [*sic*] melodies. This must be the real foundation of any serious and original school of composition to be developed in the United States."

For fifty-two years Burleigh was baritone soloist at Saint George's Episcopal Church in Manhattan. His ballads and art songs were performed by leading singers like John McCormack, but his greatest success was as an arranger of spirituals for various combinations of voices, including *Negro Spirituals Arranged for Solo Voice* (New York: G. Ricordi & Co., 1917–25; 47 vols. M1671.B). The Murray Pamphlet Collection in the Rare Book and Special Collections Division holds the program notes for the

Samuel Coleridge-Taylor Choral Society's first performance of "Hiawatha" at the Metropolitan African Methodist Episcopal Church in Washington, D.C., on April 23, 1903. Black composer Coleridge-Taylor was in his mid-twenties when he composed this choral work based on Longfellow's poem.

In 1902–3 black musicians in Washington issued their own periodical, the *Negro Music Journal* (reprint, Westport, Conn.: Negro Universities Press, 1970; ML1.N2 1970), which is available in the Music Division. A cross-section of the musical activities of the period, including reviews of the singing of Sissieretta Jones, known as the "Black Patti," can be found in the special Bicentennial number of the *Black Perspective in Music* for July 1976 (ML3556.B6 vol. 4).

The 1880s saw the appearance of a new kind of race-based popular song called the "coon" song. This song received fresh impetus at the turn of the century by incorporating the rhythms of ragtime; it disappeared during World War I with the emergence of the blues. As minstrel songs reflected white ideas of the life of black people in the era of slavery, the coon songs mirrored white ideas of African-American life in the post-Civil War era. Most songs in the style used the word coon prominently, often in the title—climaxing in 1901 with Leo Friedman's "Coon! Coon! Coon!" (M1622.F). Some later songs rely on subject matter, such as Hughie Cannon's "Bill Bailey, Won't You Please Come Home?" (M1622.C), to establish race. An example of the use of dialect to establish race is Harry von Tilzer's "Alexander" (M1622.V), with its refrain starting, "Can't you see the wind and hail am fastly falling?" Illustrated music covers also are useful for establishing racial designations of composers.

A fairly comprehensive collection of coon songs may be found under composer's name in the Music Division's collections for the period 1870 to 1923 (M1622). Coon songs were a standard genre at the turn of the century, written by black songwriters as well as white. An occasional coon song by a black composer can be seen as a comment on social mores, like Bert Williams's "She's Getting More Like White Folks Every Day" (M1622.W) and "White Folks Call It Chantecler But It's Just Plain Chicken to Me" (M1622.W). Songs by ethnic writers include titles such as Irving Jones's "St. Patrick's Day Is a Bad Day for Coons" (M1622.J). Some songs are love songs in blackface, including Barney Fagan's "My Gal Is a High-Born Lady" (M1622.F) and "My Rag-Time Gal" (M1622.E). But most trade on stereotypes, from the bland titles like Irving Jones's "All Birds Look Like Chickens to Me" (M1622.J) to "May Irwin's 'Bully' Song" by Charles E. Trevathan (M1622.T).

The Library acquired its first sound recording in 1904 but did not begin systematically collecting until 1925. Once the process began, however, the Library attempted to collect even the earliest recordings. One of the first African-American recording artists, George Washington Johnson, who lived from 1846 to 1910, wrote and performed minstrel or coon songs and comedy routines, as did many of the early recording artists. Johnson's recordings and those of the Dinwiddie Colored Quartet, Bert Williams, and Williams and Walker as well as some mixed groups such as Polk Miller and his Old South Quartet are among the holdings of the Motion Picture, Broadcasting, and Recorded Sound Division. Recordings by the Fisk Jubilee Singers on the Victor label include titles such as "Brethren Rise, Shine," "Good News," "Shout All Over God's Heaven," "Swing Low, Sweet Chariot," "Golden Slippers," and "Steal Away to Jesus."

Nearly all of the Library's commercially released recordings are shelved by manufacturer's label name and number. Of these, fewer than

10 percent are represented in bibliographic systems and therefore access is gained primarily through the use of published discographies or manufacturer and industry catalogs. Published discographies devoted to genres of African-American music include Patricia Turner's *Afro-American Singers: An Index and Preliminary Discography of Long-Playing Recordings of Opera, Choral Music, and Song* (Minneapolis: Challenge Productions, 1977; ML156.4.V7T9 1977), *Blues & Gospel Records, 1902–1943* (3d ed., Essex, U.K.: Storyville Publications, 1982; ML156.4.B6D6 1982) compiled by Robert M. W. Dixon and John Godrich; and *Black Music* (Littleton, Colo.: Libraries Unlimited, 1979; ML156.4.P6T8) by Dean Tudor and Nancy Tudor. The Library's

forty thousand hours of field recordings in the Archive of Folk Culture are filed primarily by name of collector and geographic area.

Photographs of three banjo players by V. G. Schreck, a formal dance, and a family music scene with dancing children are filed under the subject "Negroes—Dance and Music" in the Prints and Photographs Division (SSF). Stereo photographs show blacks dancing to accordion music. Glass lantern slides made for use at sings in about 1900 show posed tableaux using blacks to dramatize song titles such as "You Told Me I Need Never Work No More." The J. D. Cress collection has photographic proofs of 135 of these (PP lot 10242).

Minstrel shows continued during the Booker

"Al W. Martin's Mammoth Production: Uncle Tom's Cabin." Color lithograph, copyright 1898. (PP POS Minstrel-Martin 1898 no. 1, C size. LC-USZ62–520; LC-USZC4–2425)

T. Washington era. Posters showing Negro banjo players and other African-American minstrel companies are indexed in the Prints and Photographs Division poster card file under "Minstrel—Miscellaneous Companies" and entries for posters advertising specific companies are filed by the name of the minstrel company. Lew Dockstader, who was one of the most popular white performers of black music at the turn of the century, appears on such a poster (PP POS Minstrel. Prim & Dock 1898, no. 1 [C size]). Poster advertisements, wood engravings, and colored lithographs of circus scenes and tableaux for *Uncle Tom's Cabin* and other productions with black casts date from about 1912 (PP lot 3971). Photographs of turn-of-the-century stage productions of *Uncle Tom's Cabin* record unidentified actors in the cottonfield, the death of Little Eva, Eliza's escape, Eliza's arrival, the auction scene, and Uncle Tom at the whipping post (PP lot 10547).

Silent motion pictures first flickered on the screen in 1893. The moving pictures, as the medium was known, were widely produced in Europe and America, with each country's images frequently appearing on foreign screens in a developing, universal visual language. The first films were only about a half-minute in length but reached an average of ten to fifteen minutes in length by 1910.

Most initial productions were brief comedy scenes or "actualities," snapshots of real life that displayed the essential movement never available to still photography. Some blacks were featured in such actualities as *Dancing Darkey Boy* (1897) or Edison's four-part Native Woman series of 1903, photographed in the Virgin Islands, one of the titles of which is *Native Woman Coaling a Ship and Scrambling for Money*. In the first decade of the 1900s, black boxer Jack Johnson appeared in a series of films portraying his bouts, and the Library's Motion Picture, Broadcasting, and Recorded Sound Division holds

several of them. Similiar to these films was *A Scrap in Black and White* (1903), showing a bout between two boys, one black and the other white.

A unique collection of this early period in cinema is the Library's Paper Print Collection. Before 1950, 35-mm motion picture film was manufactured on a highly flammable and dangerous nitrate base. To avoid handling this incendiary material, the Copyright Office accepted paper records rather than the actual film for copyright deposit: synopses, scripts, stills, and, in a particularly interesting period before 1912, paper prints. These were paper spools submitted in place of nitrate film, contact-printed with the image of the entire film, recording a succession of small pictures. Eventually these paper prints outlasted many of the actual nitrate films, and today the paper has been rephotographed, frame by frame, to reconstruct the original films from the paper record.

The paper prints provide a wide cross-section of the type of films made during these early years, both fiction and nonfiction, in dramas and comedies. These stories range from Civil War sagas such as *The Guerilla* (1908), showing a black servant helping to save a woman from the unwelcome advances of a Confederate, to D. W. Griffith's 1911 *His Trust* and *His Trust Fulfilled*, in which a slave cares for the wife and daughter of his former master, killed in battle. Many of the comedies, on the other hand, displayed demeaning stereotypes. Among these are the *Watermelon Contest* (1900); *A Hard Wash* (1903), showing a black infant being given a bath; *Laughing Ben* (1902), a close-up of a laughing elderly black man; and *Who Said Chicken?* (1903), in which a black chicken thief hides in a coal bin. In *A Kiss in the Dark* (1904), a man tries to kiss a woman but her eager mammy is substituted as he closes his eyes. A similar event unwittingly occurs in *What Hap-*

pened in the Tunnel (1903) as a man, a woman, and her maid are on a train. *The Mis-directed Kiss* (1904) and *Under the Old Apple Tree* (1907) both show old white men without their glasses making the same faux pas. Similarly, in *How Charlie Lost the Heiress* (1903), a black woman asks a white man to watch over her baby carriage for a minute, but a moment later his fiancée walks by and draws the wrong conclusion.

Stage and vaudeville were an influence on moving pictures, and black images on the screen often reflected theatrical conventions and performance styles, as in *Cake Walk* and *Comedy Cake Walk* (both 1903). Most identified with this era was the frequent use of minstrel show routines using blackface, usually for comedy effect. Such films at the Library include *A Close Call* (1912), *Dark and Cloudy* (1919), and the Lew Dockstader hit, *Everybody Works But Father* (1905), shot with white characters and the same cast in blackface. In *A Bucket of Cream Ale* (1904), a black actor gets a laugh at the expense of a white one.

Film adaptations of the famous novel *Uncle Tom's Cabin* featured white actors portraying the black Uncle Tom. This was true of versions made in 1903, 1910 (that year saw three separate productions, by Vitagraph, Pathé, and Thanhouser), and 1918. Not until 1914 and 1927 (in a Universal Pictures version which was rereleased in 1928 with sound effects and a musical score) would black actors, Sam Lucas and James Lowe, respectively, play Uncle Tom. The Library's collection includes several of these versions: the 1903 Edison film, a reissue of the 1910 Vitagraph feature, the 1914 World Producing Corporation feature, and both the silent and sound versions of the 1927 Universal production. A number of parodies of the novel were made as well, among them *The Barnstormers* (1905) and *Uncle Tom's Cabana* (1947).

In 1910 the first films featuring black actors and aimed specifically at black viewers, rather than seeking broad audience appeal, were produced. The first such films were a result of the formation in Chicago of the Will Foster Moving Picture Company, later known as the Foster Photoplay Company. William Foster, a veteran of horse racing and theater, became the first African-American to produce films featuring black casts. Foster's early efforts demonstrate the interest blacks were taking in films. The movement toward a cinema directed primarily at blacks was under way and would flourish by the late teens. An additional factor provided further impetus toward the creation of a black cinema, however. This was the need to overcome the overtly racist sentiments conveyed in the burgeoning Hollywood industry, epitomized in 1915 with the release of *The Birth of a Nation*.

Based on novels and plays by Thomas Dixon, *The Birth of a Nation* riveted audiences—including President Woodrow Wilson—through its visual presentation of an idyllic Old South, contrasted with a rapacious view of Reconstruction. The fiftieth anniversary of the end of the Civil War had brought a resurgence of interest in the myths of the conflict, resulting in many portrayals of blacks in demeaning roles. *The Birth of a Nation* carried the conventionalized view of the post-Civil War South to a new extreme by identifying its villains with black dominance and miscegenation, while presenting the Ku Klux Klan in a heroic ride to the rescue.

The fact that the film's director, D. W. Griffith, traced the roots of Reconstruction problems beyond Carpetbaggers to racial incompatibility, and portrayed the Klan as the proper response, still sets *The Birth of a Nation* apart from many other motion picture reenactments of the Civil War, such as *Gone with the Wind* (1939). *The Birth of a Nation*, since its creation, represents the rare situation of a work of art, acknowledged as a masterpiece, which rests on

the framework of a racist ideology. Subsequent films about the war and Reconstruction, such as *The Crisis* (1916), avoided the virulent racial politics of *The Birth of a Nation*. In its own way, *Gone with the Wind* would mark an important turning point in Hollywood history. Just as *The Birth of a Nation* had reflected attitudes of its time toward race and the Ku Klux Klan, *Gone with the Wind* would indicate a new willingness on the part of Hollywood to acknowledge that blacks played an important, positive historical role.

The Library holds several versions of *The Birth of a Nation*. Initially shown as *The Clansman* in a version lasting over three hours, the motion picture was quickly retitled and, over the years, edited down to a shorter running time. Although the film has never been officially restored to its full length, the Library has several 35-mm versions from the original release, as well as 16-mm copies from the 1930 edited reissue with sound added. The Library also has several contemporary versions, partially restored and with musical scores added, and a revealing interview with D. W. Griffith in which he discusses the making of the picture.

Even in its own time, *The Birth of a Nation* caused protests among audiences because of its racist sentiments. Black audiences began to show organized concern for the image portrayed on the screen in 1915, when the newly formed NAACP addressed the problem through its journal, the *Crisis*, calling for censorship. Many concerned groups called for blacks to re-

"D. W. Griffith's Immortal Masterpiece 'The Birth of a Nation,' First Time in Sound!," a poster issued in December 1936. Halftone and color lithograph. (PP POS Mot Pic B42, no. 1, C size. LC-USZC4–2427)

spond not only by condemning *The Birth of a Nation* but by creating a black film aesthetic. Blacks realized that they needed to reply to negative images from the film industry through more than protest. DuBois prompted others to create films starring black casts for black audiences as an alternative form of filmmaking, demonstrating that blacks could play responsible roles. Many records relating to the NAACP's fight against the film are held in the Library's Manuscript Division.

The first organized reply to *The Birth of a Nation*, however, was a fiasco. Progressive groups joined together to produce a response, to be entitled *The Birth of a Race* or *Lincoln's Dream*. The Birth of a Race Photoplay Corporation was formed in 1916, initially to produce a history of the African-American. With the coming of United States's involvement in World War I,

however, the theme was expanded to include the various factors that led to this nation's development and the idea of democracy. By the time of its release, the Armistice had been signed, and the producers of *The Birth of a Race* were experiencing grave financial difficulties. The resulting film was a mélange of biblical and historical scenes, climaxing in a story of German-American loyalties during World War I. The Library holds a complete print of this film.

The era in which blacks were too often portrayed as buffoons was drawing to an end. By the time that Booker T. Washington died in 1915, the Great War had commenced in Europe. Although it would be several years before the United States was drawn into the fray, events were beginning to occur that would alter the racial climate in the United States.

PART THREE

AND THE PURSUIT
OF HAPPINESS

Color offset poster, designed by Paul Davis. From the 1976 New York Shakespeare Festival Production of For Colored Girls Who Have Considered Suicide When the Rainbow Is Enuf. Copyright 1976 the New York Shakespeare Festival, New York, New York. Reproduced with permission. (PP POS US D395, no. 11, C size. LC-USZC4–2429)

Much of the twentieth century was characterized by an increasingly aggressive effort on the part of blacks to achieve full citizenship rights in the United States. Individual and organizational efforts to end discrimination and segregation that began during the world wars culminated in the civil rights and black power movements of the 1960s and 1970s. As blacks achieved higher educational levels and were exposed to more opportunities at home and abroad, many scholars, novelists, poets, writers, artists, and musicians developed their talents, which resulted in an outpouring of African-American expression on the world scene. The Harlem Renaissance in the 1920s, various government projects during the Depression, and the black aesthetic movement of the 1960s fostered a blooming of talent. The Library's holdings for this period provide a mosaic for the study of African-American life and history.

CHAPTER SEVEN

WORLD WAR I AND POSTWAR SOCIETY

Events during World War I would begin to change the quality of education for blacks in America. Many youths were drawn out of the rural schools of the South to be educated in the urban centers of the North during the great migration period. Blacks began settling in urban areas to seek jobs in war industries or to take jobs deserted by whites who had been drawn into defense efforts. Not only did blacks move north in search of educational opportunities and defense jobs, but thousands of black men entered the military. Blacks who remained in the South, too, began to distance themselves from Washington's accommodationist philosophies.

EDUCATION

Robert Russa Moton (MSS, papers 1867–1991), who became president of Tuskegee Institute after Booker T. Washington's death in 1915, served during the war years when blacks were becoming more outspoken about their status in America. Moton was born in 1867 in Amelia County, Virginia, the only child of former slaves Booker and Emily (Brown) Moton. In 1885 Moton went to Hampton Institute, where he gravitated to both teaching and law. Ultimately, after graduating in 1890, he was convinced to stay at Hampton to become the commander in charge of the disciplining of cadets, a position "Major" Moton would hold for twenty-five years. He worked directly with students but also accompanied Hampton's president on fund-raising tours. These tours sometimes brought him into contact with Booker T. Washington, and the two occasionally collaborated on fund-raising

Poster from World War I. Copyright 1918 by Charles Gustrine, Chicago. Color offset. (PP POS US J5.F31 "Negro History—WWI." LC-USZC4–2426)

efforts and became allies in some political endeavors.

Upon Washington's death, Moton was chosen as his successor as president of Tuskegee. Under Moton's able leadership, Tuskegee developed from a vocational and agricultural high school to a fully accredited collegiate and professional institution encompassing the agricultural and mechanical arts, skilled trades, home economics, natural sciences, applied research in agricultural chemistry, health sciences, community service extension, teacher training, and liberal arts. In 1935, after twenty years of service at Tuskegee, during which he nearly quadrupled the institute's endowment, Moton retired to his home on the York River in Capahosic, Virginia, where he died five years later.

Among a number of printed biographical materials relating to his life and work, the collection of Moton materials in the Library includes his autobiography *Finding a Way Out* (Garden City, N.Y.: Doubleday, Page & Co., 1920; E185.97.M9, MicRR 37704E) and his volume *What the Negro Thinks* (Garden City, N.Y.: Garden City Publishing Co., 1929; E185.61.M934 1942). Most of the correspondence in his papers dates from his retirement at Capahosic, but the collection also contains materials relating to the many boards and committees on which he served dating back to the 1920s, and some of his personal financial records date from his Hampton years. Moton was a member of the board of the National Negro Business League, the National Urban League, and several black-owned banks. There are a few printed items relating to his investigation of the condition of black troops in France during World War I, his resistance to Ku Klux Klan threats during the staffing of the Tuskegee veterans' hospital in 1923, and the distribution of relief supplies and funds to blacks after the 1927 Mississippi River flood.

The Moton papers include a number of correspondence files belonging to his wife Jennie Dee Booth Moton, who worked as the director of women at Tuskegee, as an official with the Agricultural Adjustment Administration during the 1930s, and as the president of the National Association of Colored Women's Clubs from 1937 to 1941. Papers of Charlotte Moton Hubbard, Moton's daughter, are also included. She was born in Hampton in 1911 and retired as an assistant secretary of state in 1970. Moton family photographs in the Prints and Photographs Division document their years at Hampton and Tuskegee (PP unprocessed).

Frederick Douglass Patterson, Sr. (MSS, papers 1861–1988), Moton's successor as president of Tuskegee, married one of Moton's daughters—Catherine—and edited a volume about Moton's life entitled *Robert Russa Moton of Hampton and Tuskegee* (Chapel Hill: University of North Carolina Press, 1956; E185.97.M92H8). Patterson was born in 1901 in Anacostia, Washington, D.C., and named after the famous civil rights advocate. He came to Tuskegee in 1928 to serve as the head of the veterinary division and was subsequently promoted to the directorship of the School of Agriculture. In 1935 he accepted the presidency of Tuskegee. During Patterson's tenure, he founded the schools of veterinary medicine and engineering and initiated graduate instruction in agriculture, home economics, and education. In 1943 the United Negro College Fund was born when Patterson convened a meeting of the presidents of black colleges to consider ways of uniting their solicitation efforts.

A contemporary of both Moton's and Patterson's, Mary McLeod Bethune (MSS, microfilm 1923–42), born in 1875, was an educator who received national attention for her community work. The Bethune microfilm reproduces original papers at the Amistad Research Center in New Orleans. A leader in the civil rights and women's rights movements, she served as a vice president of the NAACP, as a member of the Executive Board of the National Urban League, and as president of the Association for the Study of Negro (later Afro-American) Life and History. Her papers include correspondence, travel diaries, speeches, writings, invitations, programs, clippings, and photographs. The materials relate to Bethune's work as founder and president of Bethune-Cookman College in Daytona Beach, Florida, her leadership in the work of the National Association of Colored Women's Clubs and the National Council of Negro Women, and her receipt of the NAACP's Spingarn Medal in 1935. The papers document her busy speaking schedule, especially as a guest of black churches, Young Women's and Men's Christian Associations, segregated high schools, and historically black colleges and universities. She also spoke before numerous interracial gatherings. Her correspondents include John Hope, Frank Smith Horne, Mary White Ovington, Adam Clayton Powell, Sr., Walter White, and Roy Wilkins.

Bethune, who was much sought after because of her oratorical ability, stated in her lengthy last will and testament that if she had a legacy to leave her people, it was her philosophy of living and serving:

I leave you love. Love builds. It is positive and helpful. . . . I leave you hope. . . . Yesterday, our ancestors endured the degradation of slavery, yet they retained their dignity. . . . I leave you a thirst for education. Knowledge is the prime need of the hour. . . . I leave you faith. . . . Faith in God is the greatest power, but great, too, is faith in oneself. . . . I leave you racial dignity. . . . I leave you a desire to live harmoniously with your fellow men. . . .

These words appear on a monument in Bethune's honor at Lincoln Park in Washington, D.C. A useful bibliography on black female educators like Bethune and other African-American women of note is Janet Sims-Wood's *The Progress of Afro-American Women: A Selected Bibliography and Resource Guide* (Westport, Conn.: Greenwood Press, 1980; Z1361.N39S52).

A microfilm edition of the papers of John and Lugenia Burns Hope (MSS, microfilm 1898–1947)—from originals housed at Atlanta University—is available in the Manuscript Reading Room. John Hope, the first black president of Morehouse College and later president of the Atlanta University complex, was active in civil rights and international relations as well as education. His wife, Lugenia, was a leader in various social service programs and held prominent positions in the National Council of Negro Women and the Southern Women's Conference against Lynching.

Documentation in the Prints and Photographs Division shows the buildings, grounds, and work of some historically black institutions, including Howard University's Founders Library, built in 1934 (PP HABS—D.C., WASH, 236A–). The exterior of Miner Hall, a dormitory at Howard University, was photographed by an African-American photographer from the black-owned Scurlock Studio, in Washington, D.C., and these views are accompanied by two portraits of educator Myrtilla Miner, for whom the hall was named (PP lot 12045).

Images of the National Training School for Women and Girls in Washington include scenes of domestic life showing youths cooking, eating, playing music, and engaging in educational activities through the war years (PP lot 12571). Documentation of seven open-air schools includes several photographs of young black children at Miner Normal School, also in Washington (PP lot 5338).

The war effort helped the development of African-American educational initiatives in several ways. Moving north, blacks were often able to obtain a better education. Likewise, military and defense industry work offered opportunities to black adults that previously had been closed to them.

Black nurses actively campaigned to serve in the armed forces during World War I, but only a few were able to successfully surmount the military's racial barriers. Sara Fleetwood with fellow graduates of the first class of Freedmen's Hospital Training School of the Howard University School of Nursing, 1896. She is in the top row, far left. (Christian A. Fleetwood papers, MSS)

THE MILITARY AND THE HOME FRONT

Several bibliographies cover World War I and the entire spectrum of black participation in the military, including Lenwood Davis and George Hill's *Blacks in the American Armed Forces, 1776–1983: A Bibliography* (Westport, Conn.: Greenwood Press, 1985; Z1249.M5D38 1985) and the U.S. Army Military History Research Collection's bibliography on *The U.S. Army and the Negro* (Carlisle Barracks, Pa.: Author, 1971; Z1361.N39U39 1975) and its supplement, *U.S. Army and the Negro* (Carlisle Barracks, Pa.: Author, 1977; Z1361.N39U39 1975 suppl.).

Other useful reference books are Jesse J.

Johnson's *A Pictorial History of Black Soldiers (1619–1969) in Peace and War* (Hampton, Va., 1970; E185.63.J64 1970b) and the U.S. Defense Department's overview and biographical compilation *Black Americans in Defense of Our Nation: The Military Heritage of Black Americans* (Washington: Government Printing Office, 1985; UB418. A47B54 1985). Besides covering black participation in the military, the Defense Department volume contains accounts of black generals, blacks in military academies, Medal of Honor winners, black women in the military, and black civilians who have made significant contributions to the military history of the United States.

Morris J. MacGregor and Bernard C. Nalty's *Blacks in the United States Armed Forces: Basic Documents* (Wilmington, Del.: Scholarly Resources, 1977; 13 vols. E185.63.B55) provides an extensive compilation of primary sources, histories, laws, and regulations. Volume 4, subtitled *Segregation Entrenched, 1917–1940*, covers World War I and the postwar years. The Great War provided the first systematic opportunity for the training of black officers. MacGregor and Nalty's *Blacks in the Military: Essential Documents* (Wilmington, Del.: Scholarly Resources, 1981; UB418.A47B55 1981), a one-volume condensation of the previous work, restricts itself "to tracing the evolving racial policies of the army, navy, air force and marine corps" using materials selected from the National Archives, other official sources, and records of the NAACP. Nalty, who edited these document collections, is also the author of *Strength for the Fight: A History of Black Americans in the Military* (New York: Free Press, 1986; UB418.A47N35 1986).

Books on the black experience in World War I are Florette Henri's *Bitter Victory: A History of Black Soldiers in World War I* (Garden City, N.Y.: Doubleday, 1970; D639.N4H37) and Kelly Miller's *History of the World War for Human Rights* (Washington: Austin Jenkins Co., 1919; D523.M46). The first sets forth in a straightforward manner the general facts concerning World War I, recounting the mood of black soldiers and describing Woodrow Wilson's betrayal of black interests as evidenced in his segregation policies. Miller's history provides a general overview of the entry of the United States into World War I and reports on black participation in the army's segregated units. A separate chapter deals with naval service. Although black sailors served on the same ships as whites, they were assigned to positions as messboys and stewards.

Emmett J. Scott, who was appointed special assistant for Negro affairs to the secretary of war, Newton Baker, wrote *Official History of the American Negro in the World War* (Chicago: Homewood Press, 1919; D639.N4S3), detailing aspects of black military service at home and abroad as well as civilian home front activities. Another history of blacks in World War I is William Allison Sweeney's *History of the American Negro in the Great World War* (New York: Negro Universities Press, 1969; D639.N4S8 1969). In addition, Walter W. Delsarte's *The Negro, Democracy, and the War* (Detroit: Wolverine Printing Co., 1919; D639.N4D4) describes attempts to test black soldiers' loyalty. Besides the general histories, some special volumes are also available. Miles V. Lynk's *The Negro Pictorial Review of the Great World War* (Memphis: Twentieth Century Art Company, 1919; D639.N4L8) is a "visual narrative" designed to set forth the "aims, aspirations and accomplishments" of African-Americans during the war.

The *Complete History of the Colored Soldiers in the World War* (New York: Bennett & Churchill, 1919; D639.N4C6) provides an inside view of blacks who served as soldiers overseas. The book contains individual stories, regimental histories, and photographs taken at battle sites. Addie D. Hunton and Kathryn M. Johnson's *Two Colored Women with the American Expeditionary Forces* (New York: AMS Press, 1920; D639.N4H8 1971) adds another perspective. For about fifteen months the authors observed the performance and treatment of black men who served as laborers and engineers in France with the American Expeditionary Forces.

Black participation in World War I is also documented in collections of personal papers in the Manuscript Division. Although black scholar and activist Rayford Whittingham Logan (MSS, papers 1926–80) did not begin keeping his diaries until 1943, he often referred back to earlier events in his life, such as his military service in France during World War I. In 1917, immediately after his graduation from Williams College, Logan enlisted in a segregated army unit, eventually attaining the rank of first lieutenant through a competitive examination. Logan wrote in 1943:

I believe that it was exactly twenty-five years ago, June 13 (Friday), 1918 that I barely escaped death in the Argonne Forest at thirteen o'clock! Too young to go to the Colored Officers Training Camp in Des Moines, I had enlisted July 9, 1917 in . . . Washington. I was promoted to corporal a short time thereafter. . . . While stationed near Harper's Ferry, guarding a bridge at Woodbine, the squad under my command got drunk. I tried to arrest them, they beat me thoroughly and I ducked a few bullets then!

While stationed in France, Logan was troubled by the treatment of African-American soldiers and affronted by the slights he received as an officer, especially from white enlisted men who refused to salute him. Angered by American race relations in general, Logan applied for and was granted a discharge in France, which he was granted. He remained there as an expatriate for five years, preferring the continent's less polarized racial scene. Logan's diaries offer some information about the social and political environment for blacks in the United States and in Europe in the period between the world wars. Logan mentions his work as a translator for Dr. W. E. B. DuBois at the Pan African Conferences in 1921, 1923, and 1927.

Black regiments in World War I were usually accompanied by bands. The most famous was the band of the 369th Infantry, led by James Reese Europe, a prominent musician whose syncopated style animated the dancing of Vernon and Irene Castle, creating a craze for social dancing. Black army bands became immensely popular, both among American troops and the French public, introducing many Europeans to ragtime rhythm and black performance style. A personal memoir of World War I in the records of the NAACP (MSS, records 1909–82) is a 1942 manuscript by Noble Sissle entitled "Memoirs of 'Jim' Europe." A black jazz pioneer, James Reese Europe decided during World War I to join the young men fighting "to make the world safe for democracy." After en-

listing, Europe was asked to recruit a band to serve with the all-black 369th regiment. Sissle, Europe's good friend, and a talented actor, singer, and musician in his own right, had worked with Europe's civilian band and decided that he would be a part of the military band also. When the regiment was sent to France, the band played at a number of locations. The French were so receptive to their jazz sound that the band was acclaimed wherever it appeared. At the war's end, the 369th, with Europe's band in the lead, paraded triumphantly down New York's Fifth Avenue. Although the musicians played martial songs when they were downtown, they broke into jubilant jazz when they arrived in Harlem.

The best known collection of photographs of black soldiers for this period in the Prints and Photographs Division is that of Gen. John J. Pershing. Ostensibly a record of Pershing's military career, following his rise to the rank of general of the armies, the collection unintentionally documents racial segregation in the American military both in the United States and in its missions abroad. The Pershing collection of over four thousand photographs in fourteen albums were made primarily by the U.S. Army Signal Corps or other official photographers, and shows activities of military importance between 1902 and 1921, some of which include black soldiers. Photographs of black American men who served in France in 1918 and 1919 show the type of huts built in French towns by the Construction Department of the Young Men's Christian Association-American Expeditionary Forces. Black men are shown digging trenches, playing musical instruments, and relaxing (PP lot 7708). Images portray blacks in combat training, as railroad porters, wearing gas masks, and marching in bands. Some depict African-American troops doing menial labor, waiting tables on trains, boxing, marching in formation, building railroad tracks, or unloading supply ships. Two photographs show black soldiers working at a veterinary hospital and one portrays a black cavalry unit. Other photos include black prisoners and white men in black-face (PP lots 7729–1, 2, 4, 6, 11, 13, 14).

Photographs made by the International Film Service document Pershing in Europe and New York in 1919 show black soldiers congregating and as railroad crew members (PP lot 7709). A black soldier holding a horse at Fort Monroe, Virginia, and an informal portrait of an unidentified black family are among a group of eighty-eight news service photographs collected between about 1918 and 1930 by Pershing, showing him with patriotic organizations like the American Legion drum and bugle corps (PP lot 8853).

Pershing's presentation album, which was probably compiled in 1919 by the Battle Creek, Michigan, Chamber of Commerce, contains photographs of blacks at nearby Camp Custer. They show soldiers studying French, the Colored Soldiers' Club of Battle Creek, and black waiters standing ready to serve the white guests at the opening banquet of the Roosevelt Community House (PP lot 7714). An unidentified black American soldier winning a track event is the only photograph of blacks included in an album of two hundred pictures showing the Inter-Allied games held at Pershing Stadium in France in 1919 (PP lot 7711). Among the two hundred photographs of a Texas visit by General Pershing during the 1920s, there are three photographs of black men singing in Mexia, Texas (PP lot 8837). An album presented to Pershing in about 1920 relating to Puerto Rican activities includes photographs of blacks at Camp Las Casas and black troops at a Young Men's Christian Association (YMCA) (PP lot 7727).

World War I albums compiled by Ernest K. Coulter parallel the topics documented in the Pershing albums. They include a photograph of the black 301st Labor Battalion singing in

Gièvres, France, and one of the all-black cooks for the 302d Stevedore Regiment at Bordeaux. These form part of an album of fifty-nine photographs collected to serve as a photographic supplement to the historical record of the activities of the U.S. Army Quartermaster Corps, American Expeditionary Force, Remount Service (PP lot 8289). Other images include black grave diggers at Missy-aux-Bois, an all-black battalion of the graves registration service, and two of grave diggers at Fere-en-Tardenois, France (PP lot 8295). Additional photographs portray black cooks, waiters, porters, and service personnel working on Pershing's special train, 1918–19 (PP lot 8283).

Photographs of camp life and training include a shot of a YMCA military library for blacks at St. Nazare, France, 1919. Postwar photographs include three of blacks driving a horse-drawn cart carrying President Woodrow Wilson in an Armistice Day Parade in November 1921 and one of black laborers breaking ground for the grave of the unknown soldier at Arlington Cemetery (PP lot 12286).

The Library has one of the few posters available showing black doughboys. "True Sons of Freedom—Colored Men, the First Americans Who Planted Our Flag on the Firing Line," which has a profile of Abraham Lincoln in the upper right corner, was created by Charles Gustrine in Chicago in 1918. Doughboys in the left foreground push back Germanic-looking troops on the right (PP Pos US J5/F31).

Shortly before the United States was drawn into World War I, blacks saw active military service in the expedition to punish Pancho Villa. The Underwood and Underwood news photo service collection contains thirty photographs of the 24th Infantry Regiment in Mexico in 1916, showing white officers, camp life, Villista prisoners, field day events, the band, and construction projects (PP lot 11924–2). Several films surviving in the Library's motion picture collections from the Gaumont Graphic series depict the black 15th Regiment returning to a hero's welcome after World War I. Other films concerning black contributions to World War I include the documentaries *From Harlem to the Rhine* (1918) and *Our Hell Fighters Return* (1919) and the fictional films *Injustice* (Sidney Dones, 1920) and Democracy Photoplay Corporation's *Loyal Hearts* and *Democracy, or a Fight for Right* (both 1919).

Black Workers in the Era of the Great Migration, 1916–1929 (Frederick, Md.: University Publications of America, 1985; MicRR 85/269) is a collection on twenty-five microfilm reels that documents the movement of blacks into northern and urban areas to find employment. It reproduces pertinent records of such government agencies as the Department of Labor, the Bureau of Employment Security, the U.S. Coal Commission, the Department of Justice, the Women's Bureau, and the Census Bureau.

A work by Florette Henri that draws on government publications is *Black Migration: Movement North 1900–1920* (Garden City, N.Y.: Anchor Press, 1975; E185.61.H489). The Department of Labor, Division of Negro Economics, issued two pertinent publications, *The Negro at Work During the World War and During Reconstruction* (Washington: Government Printing Office, 1921; E185.8.U57) and *Negro Migration in 1916–17* (Washington: Government Printing Office, 1919; MicRR 37748; and New York: Negro Universities Press, 1969; E185.8.U58 1969).

The Great Migration in Historical Perspective: New Dimensions of Race, Class, and Gender (Bloomington: Indiana University Press, 1991; E185.86.G65 1991), edited by Joe William Trotter, Jr., and *The Promised Land: The Great Black Migration and How It Changed America* (New York: Alfred A. Knopf, 1991; E185.6.L36 1991), by Nicholas Lemann, are recent assessments of the period. Other migration studies are Henderson Hamilton's *The Negro Migration of 1916–1918* (Washington: Association for the Study of Negro Life

and History, 1921; MicRR 64627) and Carter G. Woodson's *A Century of Negro Migration* (Washington: The Association for the Study of Negro Life and History, 1918; E185.9.W89).

Volume 5 of the series *Black Communities and Urban Development in America, 1720–1990* (New York: Garland Publishing, 1991; E185.5.B515 1991), edited by Kenneth L. Kusmer, is entitled *The Great Migration and After, 1917–1930*. It includes articles such as James R. Grossman's "Blowing the Trumpet: The Chicago Defender and Black Migration During World War I," Lillian S. Williams's "Afro-Americans in Buffalo, 1900–1930: A Study in Community Formation," and "The Black Migration to Philadelphia: A 1924 Profile," by Fredric Miller. An important survey of the African-American community, Herbert G. Gutman's *The Black Family in Slavery and Freedom, 1750–1925* (New York: Pantheon Books, 1976; E185.86.G77 1976) provides an overview of almost two centuries of the black experience in America, including information about population movements.

POSTWAR POLITICAL AND SOCIAL CONDITIONS

Black soldiers in uniform were harassed by segregationists at home and abroad. One of the worst series of racial clashes in American history occurred during the "Red Summer" of 1919, upon the soldiers' return, when at least twenty-five American cities experienced bloody street battles. Blacks were less willing than before to let racial slights go unanswered, and many whites proved unwilling to accept the changes in the racial status quo that returning African-American soldiers wanted.

These race riots have generated a number of studies. Arthur Waskow's *From Race Riot to Sit-in, 1919 and the 1960s* (Garden City, N.Y.: Doubleday, 1966; E185.61.W24), a general work, studies the relationships between conflict and violence, covering incidences of violence in Washington, D.C., Elaine, Arkansas, and Chicago, Illinois. Other riot studies are Lee E. Williams and Lee E. Williams II's *Anatomy of Four Race Riots: Racial Conflict in Knoxville, Elaine (Arkansas), Tulsa, and Chicago, 1919–1921* (Jackson: University and College Press of Mississippi, 1972; E185.61.W736) and Lee E. Williams II's *Post-War Riots in America, 1919 and 1946: How the Pressures of War Exacerbated American Urban Tensions to the Breaking Point* (Lewiston, N.Y.: The Edwin Mellen Press, 1991; HV6477.W55 1992).

A comprehensive report of the riots is contained in a volume edited by J. Paul Mitchell called *Race Riots in Black and White* (Englewood Cliffs, N.J.: Prentice-Hall, 1970; E185.61.M673), which describes seventeen riots, including those in Atlanta, Georgia, Springfield and East Saint Louis, Illinois, and Houston, Texas. A detailed work entitled *The Negro in Chicago: A Study of Race Relations and a Race Riot in 1919* (New York: Arno Press and the New York Times, 1968; F548.9.N3I2 1968) is the report of the Chicago Commission on Race Relations, a state-sponsored commission designed to uncover the causes of violence and make recommendations to prevent future clashes. The report investigated conditions such as housing, employment competition, increase in black population, and lack of recreational facilities.

The Microform Reading Room holds several collections with separately published guides which are particularly useful for studying race relations during the war period. One is *The East St. Louis Race Riot of 1917* (MSS, microfilm 1917; Frederick, Md.: University Press of America, 1985; MicRR 85/270), which contains material from the National Archives describing the outbreak and spread of racial violence in East Saint Louis that resulted in a high death toll and prompted a congressional investigation.

Books specifically on Detroit riots include Alfred McClung Lee and Norman D. Humphrey's *Race-Riot* (New York: Dryden Press, 1934; F574.D4L4); David Allan Levine's *Internal Combustion: The Races in Detroit 1915–1926* (Westport, Conn.: Greenwood Press, 1976; F574.D4L45); and Ray C. Rist's *The Quest for Autonomy: A Socio-Historical Study of Black Revolt in Detroit* (Los Angeles: University of California, 1972; F574.D4R57). These analyze the conditions in that city which led to racial violence.

Nearly five thousand photographs, cartoon drawings, posters, engravings, and illustrations, dating mainly from 1914 to the 1960s, form the NAACP collection in the Prints and Photographs Division. Commercial portraits of NAACP members and leaders, both formal and informal, were often made at public gatherings or meetings. Portraits include James Weldon Johnson, Mary White Ovington, Adam Clayton Powell, Sr., John Shillady, Arthur Spingarn, and Joel Spingarn. Photographs document the organization's campaigns against racial violence, segregation in schools, the military, and housing, and employment discrimination, as well as activities to protect the franchise for blacks (PP unprocessed, RR).

Records of the NAACP (MSS, 1909–82) for World War I and the Depression provide a wealth of information about the social, economic, and political position of African-Americans. They also document the organization's active efforts not to be classified with any radical group, especially the Communists. World War I folders filed under "military," often relate to segregation and discrimination within the armed forces. Many of them contain complaints of individual servicemen who wrote to the NAACP soliciting help in racial matters. In addition to correspondence the collection includes a number of clippings describing problems and accomplishments of black troops. Major concerns of the NAACP in the postwar years were crimes by whites against blacks—especially lynching—treatment of African-Americans by the courts, the effects of Marcus Garvey's back-to-Africa movement, educational

*Marcus Garvey, in uniform. Autographed silver gelatin photograph, Toussaint Studio, New York, New York, 1926. (*New York World Telegram *portrait file, PP. LC-USZ62–107995)*

and employment opportunities, housing, voting rights, peonage, and various legal cases including the Scottsboro trials. Also of concern were donations to the association, awarding of the Spingarn prize to blacks of outstanding achievement, accomplishments of talented blacks, reviews of radio programs and movies by or about blacks, and commentaries about published materials relating to blacks.

The association waged a concerted media effort in the area of race relations. In the continuous campaign against lynching, for example, an NAACP press release dated September 26, 1924, states that James Weldon Johnson, NAACP secretary:

recently invaded a stronghold of the Ku Klux Klan with a fiery denunciation of the organization and a message to colored citizens that they must "smash the Klan." . . . Every Negro who has an ounce of wisdom should make it a point to vote against any candidate who is a Klansman or is backed by the Ku Klux Klan, whether he be Democrat or Republican. It is a matter of self-preservation that the Negro do this.

During the war era some blacks espoused separatist and nationalistic theories of racial self-determination in the United States. Others believed that Communism and Socialism offered a more equitable way of life for African-Americans. *Federal Surveillance of Afro-Americans, 1917–1925* (Frederick, Md.: University Publications of America, 1985; MicRR 86/100; Guide 105–7), a collection of documents on twenty-five reels of micromfilm edited by Theodore Kornweibel, covers World War I, the Red Scare, and the Marcus Garvey back-to-Africa movement. The documents are drawn from federal records which detail the efforts of the Justice Department and the Federal Bureau of Investigation and its predecessor organizations to target black Americans for harassment because of alleged or supposed Communist or radical activities after World War I.

Two bibliographies available on black nationalism are *Black Separatism: A Bibliography* (Westport, Conn.: Greenwood Press, 1976; Z1361.N39J45), compiled by Betty Lanier Jenkins and Susan Phillis, and *Afro-American Nationalism: An Annotated Bibliography of Militant Separatist and Nationalist Literature* (New York: Garland, 1986; Z1361.N39H47 1986), by Agustina Herod and Charles C. Herod. *Afro-American Nationalism* includes extensive annotations of both books and articles, and provides technical definitions of specific forms of nationalistic philosophies. A listing of black philosophy and philosophers in *Blacks in the Humanities, 1750–1984: A Selected Annotated Bibliography* (New York: Greenwood Press, 1986; Z1361. N39J69 1986) by Donald F. Joyce offers additional clarification.

Among the most useful publications on black nationalism are Essien Udosen Essien-Udom's *Black Nationalism: A Search for an Identity in America* (Chicago: University of Chicago Press, 1962; E185.61.E75), Harold Cruse's *The Crisis of the Negro Intellectual* (New York: Morrow, 1967; E185. 82.C74) and Wilson Jeremiah Moses's *The Golden Age of Black Nationalism, 1850–1925* (Hamden, Conn.: Archon Books, 1978; E185.61. M886). About one hundred titles relating to black nationalism can be found in the general collections.

Works on individual black nationalists, such as Marcus Garvey, reveal their philosophy and ideas. Significant Garvey studies include Edmund David Cronon's *Black Moses* (Englewood Cliffs, N.J.: Prentice-Hall, [1973]; E185.97.G3 C72 1973), Garvey's *Philosophy and Opinions of Marcus Garvey* (New York: Universal Publishing House, 1923–25; 2 vols. E185.97.G3A248), Tony Martin's *Race First: The Ideological and Organizational Struggles of Marcus Garvey and the Universal Negro Improvement Association* (Westport, Conn.: Greenwood Press, 1976; E185.97. G3M37) and his *Literary Garveyism: Garvey, Black*

Arts, and the Harlem Renaissance (Dover, Mass.: Majority Press, 1983; PS153.N5 M263 1983), and Amy Garvey's *Garvey and Garveyism* (Kingston, Jamaica: n.p., 1963; E185.97.G3G3).

The Marcus Garvey documentary project, edited by Robert Hill and published as *The Marcus Garvey and Universal Negro Improvement Association Papers* (Berkeley: University of California Press, c1983–90; 7 vols. E185.971G3M36 1983), includes a wide range of documents by and about Garvey and his followers in the United States, the Caribbean, and Africa. Materials in volume 1 for the World War I years are arranged in chronological order, allowing the reader to follow the development of Garvey's Universal Negro Improvement Association.

James Van Der Zee, who was Garvey's official photographer, provided a comprehensive visual survey of African-American life in Harlem, including images that chronicle black separatism. The Van Der Zee portfolio in the Prints and Photographs Division includes a 1924 photograph of Garvey and the Garvey Militia as well as one of a Garveyite family. An additional Van Der Zee work is a portrait of another nationalist group titled "Black Jews, Harlem, 1929" (PP MPH Van Der Zee Portfolio nos. 7, 8, 13).

Several other organizations seeking justice for African-Americans were established in the post-World War I era. The Commission on Interracial Cooperation (CIC; MSS, microfilm, 1919–44) was founded in 1919 to work for full citizenship rights for all Americans, regardless of race, through the establishment of state and local interracial committees. The Manuscript Division holds fifty-five reels of CIC microfilm reproduced from originals at Atlanta University. The commission's efforts were basically concentrated on education and research. After it ceased operation in the 1940s, some of its members formed the Southern Regional Council. The CIC collection consists of administrative and organizational files, correspondence with

Platinum photograph by Doris Ulmann (1884–1934), South Carolina, ca. 1930. (PP PH Ulmann, D., no. 112, A size. LC-USZ62–45747)

churches, annual reports, financial records, publications, research notes, legal records, clippings, and minutes of meetings. The materials relate to a wide range of subjects, such as accomplishments of black Americans, criminal proceedings against blacks, the Ku Klux Klan, peonage, sharecropping, employment of blacks, voting rights, political campaigns, and lynching. Individuals represented in the records include Will W. Alexander, M. Ashby Jones, John J. Eagan, James H. Dillard, Robert R. Moton, and John Hope.

The Association of Southern Women for the Prevention of Lynching (ASWPL; MSS, microfilm 1930–42) was originally founded in the early 1920s as a subcommittee of the Commission on Interracial Cooperation and called the Interracial Committee for Women. In 1930 it became a separate association under the leadership of Jessie Daniel Ames. In its efforts to prevent lynching the ASWPL generated correspondence, minutes of meetings, clippings, pamphlets, legislation, reports, newsletters, press releases, speeches, resolutions, and petitions. The ASWPL records include information about organizations affiliated with it, particularly churches. Correspondents include Mary McLeod Bethune, Charlotte Hawkins Brown, and Maud Henderson.

Employment opportunity for blacks from before World War I through the Depression is a subject found throughout the A. Philip Randolph collection (MSS, papers 1909–79). In 1918 Randolph joined the Socialist party and in 1925 he organized the Brotherhood of Sleeping Car Porters. As its international president, he spoke out not only on the need to end segregation and discrimination in employment but on many aspects of race relations in America. Photographic portraits of Randolph and his wife Lucille and images documenting Randolph's role as a labor organizer are found in the Prints and Photographs Division. Other materials relating to black labor are the Samuel H. Clark papers

(MSS, papers 1912–79), which document Clark's role in organizing and supporting a railroad workers union in the South and Southwest as "Grand President" of the Association of Colored Railway Trainmen and Locomotive Firemen.

Peonage Files of the U.S. Department of Justice, 1901–1945 (MSS, microfilm 1901–45; Frederick, Md.: University Publications of America, 1989), edited by Pete Daniel, describes problems of forced labor that arose from the sharecropping, tenant farming, and criminal justice system in the South. Daniel is also the author of several other works on southern history including *The Shadow of Slavery: Peonage in the South, 1901–1969* (London: Oxford University Press, 1973; HD4875.U5D3 1973) and *Breaking the Land: The Transformation of Cotton, Tobacco, and Rice Cul-*

tures since 1880 (Urbana: University of Illinois Press, 1985; HD9077.A13D36 1985).

Street cleaning, a subject photographed by Frances Benjamin Johnston (PP lot 12553), is one of the exceptional images relating to the jobs available to blacks during the World War period. Subjects such as "Employment" (SSF) identify photographs of blacks as waitresses, fishermen, hygienists, and agricultural workers in the Prints and Photographs Division. Sixty images of the descendants of slaves in the southern Appalachian region of Tennessee made by B. B. Gilbert during the years 1923 to 1943 (PP lot 7689) document daily life and work in the region. Stereograph images show people working with cotton and tobacco crops. Photographs of rural dwellings document housing.

Doris Ulmann, a New York photographer,

"A Southern Baptism," Aiken, South Carolina, ca. 1900–1906. (Detroit Publishing Company photograph, glass transparency, PP. LC-D418–9381; LC-USZ62–107755)

undertook in 1929 a project to photograph the black people living on Lang Syne Plantation in South Carolina. Many of these people were former slaves. The photographs were intended to illustrate the book *Roll Jordan Roll* (New York: R.O. Ballou, 1933; E185.6.P47), by Julia Peterkin, whose family owned the plantation. Seventeen prints of Ulmann's portraits of men, women, and children, including a few musicians, are in the Prints and Photographs Division. Characteristic of Ulmann's style is her sympathetic imagery. Also characteristic is the lack of identifying names, places, and dates to document each shot, making the photographs difficult to use for research purposes (PP PH-A Ulmann, D. nos. 97, 113–14, 116–29). A copy of *Roll Jordan Roll*, illustrated with photogravures and signed by the photographer, is in the Rare Book Collection and an unsigned copy is in the Prints and Photographs Division's case book collection.

Areas of African-American community life such as religion and recreation are documented in a panoramic view of "The International Religious Congress of Triumph, the Church, and Kingdom of God in Christ." The congress lasted fifty days, beginning July 20, 1919, and Elder E. D. Smith, apostle, was a participant (PP PAN—SUBJECT-E—Groups, no. 150). A portrait of black religious leader Daddy Grace by James Van Der Zee (PP PH Van Der Zee Portfolio, no. 18) dates from 1938. Portraits of participants in the National Baptist Convention are found in the Nannie Helen Burroughs collection (PP lot 12572, 12574). Frances Benjamin Johnston photographed a Louisiana baptism and depicted other aspects of spiritual life in that state (PP lot 12624). A manuscript collection relating to spiritual activities during this period is the Papers of African-American missionary William H. Simons (MSS, family papers 1886–1982), which relate to his work as an international secretary for the Young Men's Christian Association and his association with the Baptist Foreign Mission. Si-

Panoramic silver gelatin photoprint of the International Religious Congress of Triumph, Indianapolis, Indiana, July 10, 1919. Copyright by E.D. Smith. (PP PAN SUBJECT Groups no. 150, E size. LC-USZ62–107501)

mons worked in Africa, India, and the United States, and he kept periodic diaries and corresponded with various individuals and organizations, such as Ambassador Mercer Cook and lawyer and writer Pauli Murray and the American Baptist Foreign Mission Society.

Noteworthy examples of images of African-Americans in sports include an image of Jesse Owens competing in the running broad jump in Berlin in the ninth Olympics in 1936. The original appears in an album that photographer Leni Riefenstahl presented to her patron Adolf Hitler as a Christmas gift. Another important figure, black boxer Tut Jackson, is depicted in a 1922 Acme News Feature portrait (PP Biographical File). Participation of blacks in professional sports and recreational activities is also documented in the NAACP Collection (PP lot 10647) and in a James Van Der Zee Portfolio, which includes a photograph of a swim team in Harlem in 1925 (PP PH Van Der Zee Portfolio no. 11).

"Tut Jackson's Reach," Acme News Features, silver gelatin photograph, copyright 1922. (PP Biog File–Jackson, Tut. LC-USZ62–105319)

BLACK ARTISTS, WRITERS, AND HISTORIANS

The Harmon Foundation (MSS, records 1913–67) was established in 1922 by means of endowments and provided playgrounds throughout the country, tuition payments and vocational guidance for students, educational programs for nurses, and awards for "constructive achievement among Negroes." The competition for blacks was open in nine fields: business, education, farming, fine arts, literature, music, race relations, religious service, and science. The purpose of these awards was to stimulate creative achievement, to acquaint the public with work being accomplished by blacks, and to provide economic opportunity for talented but unknown African-Americans. A portion of the collection held by the Manuscript Division contains the records of art exhibitions featuring black artists that were held throughout the country.

The individual files for candidates for these awards vary greatly in content. Some contain simply an application form and a few documents but others include substantial collections of letters of support, brochures, and other materials sent to influence the judges. The Lucy Craft Laney folder, for example, includes the nomination forms for the education award, photographs of Laney and the school she established—Haines Institute in Augusta, Georgia—her sponsor's justification for the nomination, letters of support, biographical information about Laney, and brochures about Haines Institute.

The applications were to be submitted to George E. Haynes, a black sociologist, who worked as the secretary of the Commission on the Church and Race Relations, Federal Council of Churches, in New York City. Business candidates included Maggie Walker, C. C. Spaulding, Truman Gibson, Albon Holsey, and A. Philip Randolph. Mary McLeod Bethune,

Robert Russa Moton, Arthur Schomburg, Benjamin Brawley, Thomas Campbell, Monroe Work, Charlotte Hawkins Brown, Henry A. Hunt, Mordecai Johnson, and Alain Locke were among the candidates for the Harmon education award.

Fine arts contestants included Laura Waring, Hale Woodruff, Charles Johnson, Archibald Motley, Meta Warwick Fuller, Sargent Johnson, Augusta Savage, William H. Johnson, Richmond Barthé, Lois Mailou Jones, Hilyard Robinson, and Palmer Hayden. The Harmon Foundation collection also includes records relating to traveling exhibits of the works of black artists held in metropolitan centers throughout the United States, as well as correspondence files relating to various aspects of the artists' careers. A few of the many artists for whom there is correspondence are Charles H. Alston, Selma Burke, Aaron Douglas, Jacob Lawrence, Hughie Lee-Smith, Horace Pippin, James Porter, Charles Sebree, Henry O. Tanner, and Charles White.

Some of the candidates for literature awards were Hallie Brown, Countee Cullen, W. E. B. DuBois, Jessie Fauset, Claude McKay, Arna Bontemps, Sterling Brown, Langston Hughes, Eslanda Robeson, and Walter White. Harry T. Burleigh, William Levi Dawson, R. Nathaniel Dett, Carl Diton, Harry Lawrence Freeman, W. C. Handy, Roland Hayes, Eva Jessye, Hall Johnson, J. Rosamond Johnson, William Grant Still, Clarence Cameron White, and John Wesley Work were among the candidates for the Harmon music awards. Race relations award applicants included African-Americans such as Eugene Jones, Howard Thurman, Channing Tobias, and Charles Johnson; among white recipients of racial harmony awards were Mary W. Ovington, George Peabody, Julius Rosenwald, Clark Foreman, and Will Alexander. Two of the nominees for religious service awards were Max Yergan and Jesse Moorland. Science award candidates included George Washington Carver, Charles H. Wesley, Ernest Just, and Cortez Peters.

Art materials from the Harmon Foundation are held in the Prints and Photographs Division. Most significant in this material is the collection of fine art materials given to the foundation by artists it sponsored. Artists represented by original works include Albert Smith, Hale Woodruff, James L. Wells, William H. Johnson, and, by photomechanical reproductions, the sculpture of Richmond Barthé. Silent motion pictures of the artists standing next to their work at the openings of annual Harmon Foundation art exhibitions in the later 1920s are in the Library's motion picture collections. Photographs document the Harlem Art Workshop established for young artists ages ten to twelve, a workshop that was a precursor to the Work Projects Administration arts projects for children. Twenty-three woodcuts produced by the children are also in the collections. Harmon Foundation subject files cover art, African art, black American artists, a proposed educational and religious films project, the Harlem Art Workshop, and photographs and clippings about nursing, student loans, and racially integrated playground programs (PP unprocessed).

Records of the American Council of Learned Societies (MSS, records 1919–89) include correspondence with African-American historians and others writing about famous blacks for the *Dictionary of American Biography* (New York: Charles Scribner's Sons, 1927–; E176.D563). The council's Committee on Negro Studies included Melville J. Herskovits, Sterling Brown, Lawrence D. Reddick, Lorenzo D. Turner, and Eric Williams. An informative file relates to the capitalization of the word *Negro*. A folder of correspondence labeled "Association for the Study of Negro Life and History" (ASNLH) is primarily with Carter G. Woodson, and other folders relate to African studies. Biographical files of no-

table black leaders include Booker T. Washington, Henry Ossawa Tanner, Marcus Garvey, Mary McLeod Bethune, Canada Lee, and Mary Church Terrell.

Background information about some of the black historians who worked with the American Council of Learned Societies can be located in *Black History and the Historical Profession, 1915–1980* (Urbana: University of Illinois Press, 1986; E184.65.M45 1986) by August Meier and Elliott Rudwick. The authors provide biographical and historiographical information about Carter G. Woodson, John Hope Franklin, Benjamin Quarles, Rayford Logan, and Lorenzo Greene. Works by Earl E. Thorpe—*Black Historians: A Critique* (New York: Morrow, 1971; E175.T5 1971), *The Mind of the Negro: An Intellectual History of Afro-Americans* (Westport, Conn.: Negro Universities Press, 1970; E185.82.T5 1970), and *The Central Theme of Black History* (Durham, N.C.: Seeman Printery, 1969; E175.T48)—also discuss African-American historians and their work.

HARLEM RENAISSANCE

During the 1920s African-American art and literature was recognized as a significant part of world culture. Many blacks from the South and the Caribbean moved to the Harlem section of New York City where the blending of cultures led to a flowering of the arts. This literary phenomenon provided an outlet for creativity in the African-American community. Although some black writers had previously demonstrated their mastery of literary forms and created their own poetry, novels, and other literary writings, there was such a prodigious amount of literature created by blacks during the 1920s and 1930s that the period is frequently heralded as a rebirth of the African-American arts—the Harlem Renaissance.

Black writers who gained prominence during this period, also referred to as the New Negro period, are the poets Countee Cullen, Langston Hughes, Arna Bontemps, and Claude McKay. Prose writers Zora Neale Hurston, Nella Larsen, Jessie Fauset, Walter White, Eric Walrond, Rudolph Fisher, Wallace Thurman, and Jean Toomer came out of the Harlem Renaissance. Examples of works published during the era are Langston Hughes's *The Weary Blues* (New York: Knopf, 1926; PS3515.U274W4 1926 Rare Bk) and *Fine Clothes to the Jew* (New York: Knopf, 1927; PS3515.U274F5 1927 Rare Bk); *Banjo* (New York: Harper & Brothers, 1929; PS3525.A24785B3 1929 Rare Bk), *Harlem Shadows* (New York: Harcourt, Brace and Co., 1922; PS3525.A24785H3 1922), and *Home to Harlem* (New York: Harper, 1928; PZ3.M1926 Ho) by Claude McKay; Rudolph Fisher's *The Walls of Jericho* (New York: Arno Press, 1969; PZ3.F5367 Wa) and *The Conjure-Man Dies* (New York: Covici, Friede Co., 1932; PZ3.F5367 Co), and Jean Toomer's *Cane* (New York: Boni and Liveright, 1923; PZ3.T6184 Ca).

In the 1980s published works relating to these writers proliferated, but before 1971 the Harlem Renaissance was not recognized as a Library of Congress subject heading. Since the publication of Robert Hemenway's *Zora Neale Hurston: A Literary Biography* (Urbana: University of Illinois Press, 1977; PS3515.U789Z7) and Alice Walker's anthology and articles about Hurston, publishing interest in the Harlem Renaissance has multiplied. Alice Walker, an African-American writer herself, collected Hurston's short stories and articles in *I Love Myself When I Am Laughing . . . and Then Again When I Am Looking Mean and Impressive: A Zora Neale Hurston Reader* (Old Westbury, N.Y.: The Feminist Press, 1979; PS3515.U789A6 1979). In recognition of the increased interest, a conference on the subject was held at Hofstra University in 1985. Papers presented there by scholars of the

period are published in *The Harlem Renaissance: Revaluations*, edited by Amritjit Singh, William S. Shiver, and Stanley Brodwin (New York: Garland, 1989; PS153.N5H264 1989).

Several reference sources are now available to assist readers and scholars in finding their way through the maze of materials. A general overview of the personalities and works of the Harlem Renaissance may be found in Margaret Perry's *The Harlem Renaissance: An Annotated Bibliography and Commentary* (New York: Garland Publishing, 1982; Z5956.A47P47 1982). Bruce Kellner's *The Harlem Renaissance: A Historical Dictionary for the Era* (Westport, Conn.: Greenwood, 1984; NX511.N4H37 1987) defines terms and describes the personalities and their works, as does the biographical dictionary *Afro-American Writers from the Harlem Renaissance to 1940* (Detroit, Mich.: Gale Research, 1987; PS153.N5A396 1987), edited by Trudier Harris, with Thadious Davis, richly detailing the writings and commentary on major black writers and including several critical essays which offer a context for understanding the period.

Nathan Huggins's pioneering study *The Harlem Renaissance* (New York: Oxford University Press, 1971; NX512.3.N5H8) appeared in the early seventies. Later histories include David Lewis's *When Harlem Was in Vogue* (New York: Knopf, 1981; NX511.N4L48 1981), Jervis Anderson's *This Was Harlem: A Cultural Portrait, 1900–1950* (New York: Farrar Straus Giroux, 1982; F128.68.H3A65 1982), and Cary Wintz's *Black Culture and the Harlem Renaissance* (Houston: Rice University Press, 1988; PS153.N5W57 1988). Among the biographies and special studies of the Renaissance that have appeared are Wayne Cooper's *Claude McKay, Rebel Sojourner in the Harlem Renaissance: A Biography* (Baton Rouge: Louisiana University Press, 1987; PS 3525.A24785Z63 1987); Faith Berry's *Langston Hughes: Before and Beyond Harlem* (Westport, Conn.: Lawrence Hill, 1983; PS3515.U274Z617

1983), and Arnold Rampersad's award-winning work *The Life of Langston Hughes* (New York: Oxford University Press, 1986–88; 2 vols. PS3515.U274Z698 1986); Gerald Early, editor, *My Soul's High Song: The Collected Writings of Countee Cullen, Voice of the Harlem Renaissance* (New York: Doubleday, 1991; PS3505.U287A6 1991), a new collection of Countee Cullen's poetry; and *The Harlem Renaissance Re-Examined* (New York: AMS Press, 1987; PS153.N5H25 1987), edited by Victor A. Kramer. Numerous new editions and reprints of the works of Langston Hughes, Claude McKay, Countee Cullen, and reprints of novels of the period attest to the movement's continuing interest to scholars and researchers.

Prominent collections of personal papers, diaries, and other manuscript materials relating to the Harlem Renaissance are at Yale University's Beinecke Library, the New York Public Library's Schomburg Center, Fisk University's Special Collections, Harry Ransom Humanities Research Center at the University of Texas at Austin, and Howard University's Moorland-Spingarn Research Center. The Library of Congress holds a microfilm of the papers of Countee Cullen (MSS, microfilm 1921–69) made from originals at the Amistad Research Center in New Orleans and has scattered Langston Hughes items from the papers of the NAACP (MSS, records 1909–82), the National Urban League (MSS, records 1910–85), the Miscellaneous Manuscript Collection (Hughes folder, MSS, papers 1939–41), and the Melvin B. Tolson papers (MSS papers 1932–75). Photocopies of many Hughes documents can be found in the Faith Berry papers (MSS, papers 1963–84), many of which she collected while researching her book on Hughes, mentioned above.

Several drafts of a Hughes poem commenting about the life and work of Booker T. Washington are in the Miscellaneous Manuscript Collection. The final draft, dated June 1, 1941, and signed by Hughes in Monterey, California, reads:

Booker T.
Was a practical man.
He said, Till the soil
And learn from the land.
Let down your bucket
Where you are.
Your fate is here
And not afar.
To help yourself
And your fellow man,
Train your head,
Your heart, *and your hand*.
For smartness alone's
Surely not meet—
If you haven't at the same time
Got something to eat.
Thus at Tuskegee
He built a school
With book-learning there
And the workman's tool.
He started out
In a simple way—
For yesterday
Was *not* today.
Sometime he had
Compromise in his talk—
For a man must crawl
Before he can walk—
And in Alabama in '85
A joker was lucky
To be alive.
But Booker T.
Was nobody's fool:
You may carve a dream
With an humble tool.
The tallest tower
Can tumble down
If it be not rooted
In solid ground.
So, being a far-seeing
Practical man,
He said, Train your head,
Your heart, *and your hand*.
Your fate is here
And not afar,
So let down your bucket
Where you are.

The Library's NAACP collection (MSS, records 1909–82) includes coverage of writers such as W. E. B. DuBois, Jessie Fauset, James Weldon

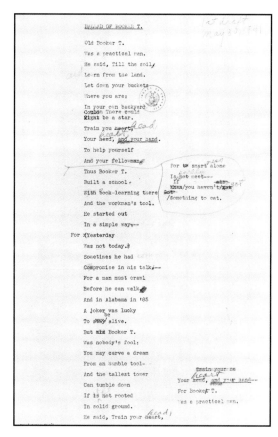

Langston Hughes's first draft of "Ballad of Booker T.," dated May 30, 1941. (Langston Hughes Papers, MSS)

Johnson, and Langston Hughes. The NAACP, the National Urban League, and the Brotherhood of Sleeping Car Porters each sponsored national magazines which contained poetry, essays, and articles by Renaissance writers like Zora Neale Hurston, Langston Hughes, and Claude McKay. They wrote for the NAACP's *Crisis* (E185.5.C92), the National Urban League's *Opportunity* (E185.5.06), and the Brotherhood of Sleeping Car Porter's *Messenger* (MicRR 5062). Library copies of these publications are available in the *Black Journals: Periodical Resources for*

Afro-American and African Studies (Westport, Conn.: Greenwood Publishing Corp., 1970; MicRR 5062). Materials in these collections may be used to complement and round out the information found in general collections. Coverage of periodical literature is discussed in Theodore Vincent's *Voices of a Black Nation: Political Journalism in the Harlem Renaissance* (San Francisco: Ramparts Press, 1973; E185.V56 1973). Abby and Ronald Johnson's *Propaganda and Aesthetics: The Literary Politics of African-American Magazines in the Twentieth Century* (Amherst: University of Massachusetts Press, 1979; PS153.N5J6; reprint, 1991; PS153.N5J6 1991).

Miscellaneous Collection of Radical Newspapers and Periodicals, 1917–1921 (MicRR 122) reproduces newspapers and periodicals transferred from the U.S. Department of Justice. Issues of the *Negro World* for 1920 are included in the collection, as are the *Broad Ax*, published in Chicago, and the *Chicago Defender*. A more extensive collection of Garvey's newspaper *Negro World* (MicRR 03748), filmed by the Library's Photduplication Service from a collection at the New York Public Library, includes issues from February 24, 1923, to October 17, 1933.

The Harlem Renaissance was not an isolated phenomenon. There was a Philadelphia Renaissance, a Chicago Renaissance, and even a Memphis Renaissance. Black literary expression often began with poetry but also found form in novels, drama, folktales, and other literary genres. The papers of Claude Barnett (MSS, microfilm 1918–67), the founder of the Associated Negro Press, a syndicated news service, fill almost two hundred reels of microfilm. Filmed from originals at the Chicago Historical Society, the Barnett papers include news releases, organizational files of the Associated Negro Press, and an extensive subject file on black Americans. Subjects treated include agriculture, colleges and universities, economic conditions, medicine, the military, philanthropic and social organizations, politics and the law, race relations, and religion. Entertainers, arts, and authors are the subject of one file. Claude A. Barnett's personal files are also on the film. Barnett's wife, Etta Moten Barnett, was a singer, actress, and lecturer. Langston Hughes, Eslanda Robeson, and others periodically wrote for the Associated Negro Press.

A new surge of popularity for all-black musicals was inaugurated in 1921 by *Shuffle Along*, composed by Eubie Blake. Twelve vocal excerpts from it were published that same year (New York: M. Witmark & Sons, 1921; M1508). A manuscript of Blake's "Charleston Rag," dated 1917, is also to be found in the Music Division (ML96.B595 Case). A relevant study is *Black Music in the Harlem Renaissance*, edited by Samuel A. Floyd, Jr. (New York: Greenwood Press, 1990; ML3556.8.N5B6 1990).

The Manuscript Division holds a microfilm edition of the papers of actress and singer Fredi Washington (MSS, microfilm 1925–79) reproduced from originals at the Amistad Research Center in New Orleans. From 1922 to 1926 Washington was a chorus dancer in *Shuffle Along* and in 1926 she played the feminine lead in *Black Boy* opposite Paul Robeson. She remained active as a dancer during the postwar period. Paul Robeson also achieved critical acclaim as a singer and actor during the Harlem Renaissance. Notable biographies about him are Marie Seton's *Paul Robeson* (London: D. Dobson, 1958; ML420.R73S4) and Martin B. Duberman's *Paul Robeson* (New York: Knopf, 1988; E185.97.R63 D83 1988).

In the late 1920s, dance and drama critic Carl Van Vechten, also an amateur photographer, used his Leica camera to photograph his famous friends, including many from the Harlem scene, the jazz world, and the civil rights movement. His career, spanning the years 1932 to 1964, is described by Bruce Kellner in *Carl Van Vechten and the Irreverent Decades* (Norman:

University of Oklahoma Press, 1968; PS3543.A653Z77). The Van Vechten photo archive includes portrayals of Pearl Bailey, Cab Calloway, Countee Cullen, and Bessie Smith (PP lot 12735).

MUSIC AND ENTERTAINMENT

Other types of music also flourished during the war and in the postwar era. In 1914, Henry Edward Krehbiel, music critic for the New York *Tribune*, published *Afro-American Folksongs: A Study in Racial and National Music* (New York: G. Schirmer, 1914; ML3556.K9), which demonstrated the African elements in Afro-American music through an analysis of melodic and rhythmic patterns. Krehbiel's study, which is available in the Music Division, was not superseded by more advanced investigations for half a century.

A new form of religious folk song was developing in black America: gospel. In 1916 Charles Albert Tindley published his *New Songs of Paradise* (Lansing, Mich.: E.T. Tindley, 1916; M2198.N5329). He had been writing songs since the turn of the century, but with this publication his songs became enormously popular, setting a pattern for future gospel song writers. A volume of religious songs was issued by the National Baptist Convention Sunday School Board, entitled *Gospel Pearls* (Nashville, 1921; M2193.N24). White songleader Homer A. Rodeheaver published his gospel music as *Rodeheaver's Plantation Melodies* (Chicago: Rodeheaver Co., 1918; M1670.R7P5). Among the many other books on gospel in the Music Division is Anthony Heilbut's *The Gospel Sound: Good News and Bad Times* (New York: Simon and Schuster, 1971; ML35556.H37).

After the First World War, jazz swept the world, giving the postwar era the name the Jazz Age. Beginning in 1917, people who could not hear the music live could listen to recordings. Though the earliest recordings to be called "jazz" were made by the Original Dixieland Jazz Band from New Orleans, a white band, before long, black groups recorded distinctive jazz styles in Chicago, Kansas City, and elsewhere. Among the influential band leaders who moved from New Orleans to Chicago was Joseph "King" Oliver, who recorded extensively. The Music Division holds an enormous literature about jazz: biographies, histories, bibliographies, discographies, and every conceivable kind of discussion. Since much jazz was improvised, recordings are the primary documents in its history. Jazz is the first form of music to be circulated primarily by recording rather than by published music. The Recorded Sound Reference Center has an unparalleled collection of early jazz on 78 rpm disc recordings. Some jazz has been transcribed in musical notation (see M25, M1350, and M1356). Besides Gunther Schuller's *Early Jazz*, cited earlier, examples of serious work that has been done on jazz include Bernhard Hefele's *Jazz-Bibliography: International Literature on Jazz, Blues, Spirituals, Gospels, and Ragtime* (Munich: K.G. Saur, 1981; ML128.J3H43) and Frank Tirro's *Jazz: A History* (New York: W.W. Norton & Co., 1977; ML3561.J3T5). The *Journal of Jazz Studies* was established in 1973 by the Rutgers Institute of Jazz Studies then in New Brunswick, New Jersey, and now in Newark (ML1.J58).

Much early jazz was deposited for copyright, most of it in the form of "lead-sheets"—melody lines with occasional accompaniment. But some copyright registration deposits are in the form of abbreviated arrangements from which a performance can be reconstructed. A special collection of Jelly Roll Morton's copyright deposits, some in his own hand, is available on microfilm. Recordings of his music are available in the Library's Recorded Sound Reference Center.

Parallel to the development of jazz in the

years after World War I is the emergence of the blues. The earliest published blues, including W. C. Handy's "St. Louis Blues" and "Memphis Blues," had been issued before World War I. It was the success of Mamie Smith's 1920 recording of "The Crazy Blues" that started the release of a stream of blues records aimed primarily at a black audience—the so-called race records. Two principal styles of blues records emerged. One, sung most often by a man to his own guitar accompaniment, includes among its major performers Blind Lemon Jefferson, Blind Willie McTell, and Robert Johnson. The other was usually sung by a woman accompanied by one or more other musicians. Principal performers in this style include Bessie Smith, Ida Cox, Clara Smith, Victoria Spivey, and Sippie Wal-

Composer's manuscript of Eubie Blake's Charleston Rag. *(ML96.B595 Case. LC-USZ62–107766)*

Bessie Smith, Columbia phonograph artist, on the sheet music cover for "Gulf Coast Blues" by Clarence Williams. (Music Division)

lace. Paul Oliver's *The Story of the Blues* (Philadelphia: Chilton Book Co., 1969; ML3561.J3047) is a good introduction.

Like jazz, the blues circulated more often in the form of recordings than as printed music. The Library's Recorded Sound Reference Center has an excellent collection of early blues recordings represented by original 78-rpm discs as well as later reissues. Since the sale of a copyrighted record earned a royalty, there was considerable motivation for songwriters to deposit their songs for copyright: thus many blues are represented in the Music Division by some kind of notes-on-paper, either printed or manuscript.

Research in black folk music is exemplified

by the Music Division's manuscript collection of Natalie Curtis Burlin's descriptive commentaries and musical transcription (ML96.B928 Case) made in preparation for her *Hampton Series of Negro Folk Songs* (M1670.B93, vols. 1–4, 1918–19), based on the singing of students at Hampton Institute. Over twenty of Burlin's cylinder recordings of the Hampton Singers are located in the Archive of Folk Culture. Correspondence and articles relating to Burlin's work are also found in the papers of George Foster Peabody (MSS, papers 1894–1937) in the Manuscript Division.

In 1925 the Coolidge Auditorium at the Library of Congress was opened. On December 17, 1926, the Hampton Institute Choir directed by R. Nathaniel Dett was presented in a concert there, performing both European religious music and traditional black spirituals, continuing the Music Division's tradition of interest in black music begun by Walter Whittlesey.

The Johnson brothers, J. Rosamond and James Weldon, who had pioneered earlier in the century in writing black musicals and who participated in the Harlem Renaissance, also contributed to the history of the spiritual with carefully crafted arrangements for voice and piano. James Weldon Johnson edited *The Book of American Negro Spirituals* (New York: Viking Press, 1925; M1670.J67) and the *Second Book of Negro Spirituals* (New York: Viking Press, 1926; M1670.J672), and J. Rosamond Johnson edited *Rolling Along in Song* (New York: Viking Press, 1937; M1670.J65R6).

Other creative arrangers of black folk music included Camille Nickerson, who resided in New Orleans and specialized in Creole French folk song. A photostat of the manuscript (1934) of her arrangement of "M'schieu Banjo (Monsieur Banjo)" (M1668.8.N) is in the Music Division. John Wesley Work III, the third generation of his family active in music at Fisk

University, produced an important collection, *American Negro Songs and Spirituals: A Comprehensive Collection of 230 Folk Songs, Religious and Secular* (New York: Howell, Soskin & Co., 1940; M1670.W93A6). His selection of songs and his extensive commentary represented the best of African-American folk song scholarship of that period.

In striking contrast to most other collections of black songs published between the wars, Lawrence Gellert's *Negro Songs of Protest* (New York: American Music League, 1936; M1670.G32N4), described as "the living voice of the otherwise inarticulate resentment against injustice," documents black voices which were not content to be passive in the face of injustice. Many scholars of the period considered Gellert's collection to be eccentric, driven by Gellert's own political convictions, but the civil rights struggles of the sixties testified to their legitimacy.

After World War I an increasing number of black artists entered the concert field, achieving careers of great distinction. Roland Hayes made his New York debut in 1923 after studying at Fisk University and abroad. For the next fifty years he sang classical songs and arrangements of spirituals that never failed to move his audience. The Music Division holds two of his arrangements: "Carol of the Brown King" (1959; M2114.5.H Case) and "Roll, Jordan, Roll" (manuscript, 1958; ML96.H369 Case), as well as his book *My Songs: Aframerican Religious Folk Songs* (Boston: Little, Brown, 1948; M1670.H4M9). Recorded sound holdings include several unpublished Hayes recordings.

Hayes's remarkable career paved the way for other singers who followed. Marian Anderson, born in 1897, sang in Washington as a very young woman. Programs of her Washington recitals from 1924 and 1925 are in the Music Division (ML42.W3A785), preceding the European tours that began her triumphant career.

An overview of her life can be found in Janet Sims-Wood's *Marian Anderson, an Annotated Bibliography and Discography* (Westport, Conn.: Greenwood Press, 1981; ML134.5.A5S5). Her autobiography, *My Lord, What a Morning* (New York: Viking Press, 1956. ML420.A6A3), gives her personal account of her life.

Brian Rust's *Jazz Records, 1897–1942* (New Rochelle, N.Y.: Arlington House, 1978; 2 vols. ML156.4.J3R9 1978 Case) and Patricia Turner's *Dictionary of Afro-American Performers: 78 RPM and Cylinder Recordings of Opera, Choral Music, and Song, c. 1900–1949* (New York: Garland Publishing, 1990; M106.U3T82 1990) provide discographies that give access to materials by African-American artists in the Library's Recorded Sound Reference Center. Other useful reference tools include *Bibliography of Discographies: Jazz* (New York: R.R. Bowker Co., 1981; ML156.2.B49 vol. 2), by Daniel Allen, *Biographical Dictionary of Afro-American and African Musicians* (Westport, Conn: Greenwood Press, 1982; ML105.S67 1982), by Eileen Southern, *Blues Who's Who: A Biographical Dictionary of Blues Singers* (New York: Da Capo Press, 1981; ML102.B6H3 1981), by Sheldon Harris, and *The New Grove Dictionary of Jazz* (New York: Macmillan Press, 1988; 2 vols., ML102.J3N48), edited by Barry Kernfeld.

THE MOVIES

The Library of Congress houses the nation's largest moving image archive, both as the recipient of film and television copyrights since 1942 and through acquisitions of movies from the past. Since the early 1970s, the Library, in collaboration with the American Film Institute, has collected early black films as part of an intensive effort to gather and preserve America's endangered film heritage. The Library's moving image material related to black studies also has an international focus, and the assemblage of foreign films continues to grow year by year.

Blacks have been represented, and have represented themselves, in all categories of filmmaking. These span classical Hollywood features, short films, animation, documentary films, avant-garde cinema, and television, from the beginning of movies through the present. Overall, blacks have become a recognized part of the moving image industry and compelled filmmakers and audiences to examine black issues and the problems of racial injustice. Their broad goal has been pursued in many different ways. On the one hand, black filmmakers and actors, particularly stars, have sought to become part of the Hollywood industry. On the other, filmmakers, both out of a desire to create their own movies and in frustration with Hollywood practices, have often sought to set up an alternative cinema, aimed predominantly at black audiences. The Library's collection includes newsreels, evening news broadcasts, and a host of different documentaries compiled from various sources.

Books about blacks and films have tended to concentrate on interpretations of black images in the cinema over time. Some examples are Donald Bogle's *Toms, Coons, Mulattoes, Mammies, and Bucks* (New York: Viking, 1973; PN1995.9.N4B6), Daniel Leab's *From Sambo to Superspade* (Boston: Houghton, Mifflin, 1975; PN1995.9.N4L4), and Jim Pines's *Blacks in Films* (London: Studio Vista, 1975; PN1995.9.N4P48). Anthologies such as Richard Maynard's *The Black Man on Film* (Rochelle Park, N.J.: Hayden, Murray, James, 1974; PN1995.9.N4M34) and Lindsay Patterson's *Black Films and Filmmakers* (New York: Dodd, Mead, 1975; PN1995.9.N4B5) have the same emphasis. Books dealing with black filmmakers published in the 1970s include James P. Murray's *To Find an Image* (Indianapolis: Bobbs-Merrill, 1973; PN1995.9.N4M8) and Edward Mapp's *Blacks in American Films* (Metuchen,

N.J.: Scarecrow, 1972; PN1995.9.N4M3 1972) and *Directory of Blacks in the Performing Arts* (Metuchen, N.J.: Scarecrow, 1978; PN1590.B53M3 1990). Useful historical surveys on blacks and films are James R. Nesteby's *Black Images in American Films, 1896–1954: The Interplay between Civil Rights and Film Culture* (Washington: University Press of America, 1982; PN1995.9. N4N4), Gary Null's *Black Hollywood* (Secaucus, N.J.: Citadel, 1975; PN1995.9.N4N8), and Thomas Cripps's two books, *Slow Fade to Black* (New York: Oxford University Press, 1977; PN1995. 9.N4C7) and *Black Film as Genre* (Bloomington: Indiana University Press, 1978; PN1995.9. N4C68).

Phyllis Klotman's *Frame by Frame: A Black Filmography* (Bloomington: Indiana University Press, 1979; PN1995.9.N4K57) is a germinal catalog using the sociological approach to list thousands of films containing appearances by black performers or treating black concerns. Henry Sampson's pioneering work, *Blacks in Black and White* (Metuchen, N.J.: Scarecrow, 1977; PN1995.9.N4S2), synthesizes scarce and disparate information from early black periodicals in a reference guide that is also a history of black cast filmmaking during the first half of the twentieth century. Marshall Hyatt's *The Afro-American Cinematic Experience* (Wilmington, Del.: Scholarly Resources, 1983; PN1995.9. N4H9) is a useful bibliography, especially for the 1960s and 1970s. Donald Bogle's *Blacks in American Films and Television* (New York: Garland, 1988; PN1995.9.N4B58 1988) and James Robert Parish and George H. Hill's *Black Action Films* (Jefferson, N.C.: McFarland, 1989; PN1995.9.N4P37 1989) contain discussions of a variety of titles.

Rebuttals to racial stereotyping in *The Birth of a Nation* (1915) and other Hollywood films echoing similar sentiments came with the first cycle of black cast films in the late teens through the 1920s. By 1916, the Lincoln Motion Picture

Company, owned and operated by blacks, had formed in Los Angeles. Lincoln was initially headed by the noted actor Noble Johnson, already a star at Universal studios. Lincoln's slogan on an early release was:

Colored Moving Pictures . . . Your first opportunity to see a picture owned, written, acted and produced entirely by Negroes. Don't fail to see it.

The Library holds portions of the Lincoln Motion Picture Company's last film, *By Right of Birth*, starring Clarence Brooks.

A different effort ensued from another black-owned concern, the Ebony Motion Picture Company of Chicago. Ebony attempted to create an interracial audience of whites and blacks through a series of ten-minute comedies, released monthly in 1918. The Library holds prints of most of Ebony's products, including *A Reckless Rover, The Comeback of Barnacle Bill, A Black Sherlock Holmes, Mercy the Mummy Mumbled, Two Knights of Vaudeville,* and *Spying the Spy*. The Library's collection also includes *The Very Last Laugh* (1970), a four-part documentary telling the history of the Ebony company and its pictures through interviews with participants. Despite the intentions of their makers, these films invoke many of the timeworn comical stereotypes, such as frantic fear resulting from superstition.

In 1918, perhaps the single most prolific black filmmaker emerged on the movie scene. Oscar Micheaux was an entrepreneur and author before turning to motion pictures. In addition to some of Micheaux's films, the Library holds a number of his novels. His first book, *The Conquest* (Lincoln, Nebr.: Woodruff Press, 1913; E185.97.M62 1913) was sold door to door to both blacks and whites. Micheaux followed a similar pattern with his movies, personally marketing them to southern theaters. Micheaux's third novel, *The Homesteader* (College Park, Md.: McGrath Publishing Co., 1969, c1917; PZ3.

M5809 Ho), was a rewrite of *The Conquest*, itself a semiautobiographical account of Micheaux's experiences as a rancher in South Dakota. George P. Johnson read *The Homesteader* and wanted to purchase the rights to film it. Micheaux, however, demanded supervision of the film, and Johnson refused, given Micheaux's complete lack of film experience.

Out of this impasse emerged a competitor that would outlast the Lincoln Motion Picture Company—Micheaux Pictures Corporation, with Oscar Micheaux as writer, director, and producer, frequently adapting his own novels to the screen. Micheaux's approach to films was similar to his approach to writing. He was entirely self-taught, unlettered in form but manifestly able to express his message and supremely self-confident of his ability to find an audience.

Micheaux sold stock in his company until he had raised the capital to film *The Homesteader* (1918), the first black cast feature-length film. Micheaux was undaunted by the new medium or by his lack of familiarity with Hollywood or filmmaking methods. Although he never mastered the language of cinema in a manner commensurate with the practitioners of the classical Hollywood style, he devised a technique in keeping with his low budget. Micheaux's films, for example, regularly reveal the fact that there was never time or money for retakes. The final films frequently include mistakes in camera work or errors by performers, many of whom were unpaid amateurs. Although audiences appreciated seeing an all-black cast, they were also frustrated by Micheaux's inability to equal the quality that Hollywood films had conditioned them to expect. His primitive technique, however, was compensated for by his determination to approach explicitly black themes and problems. Micheaux was less interested in either the visualization of his story or its narrative coherence than in its racial implications. The original motion picture version of *The Homesteader* has not been found, but Micheaux frequently remade his films, and the story of *The Homesteader* was retold as *The Exile* (1931).

The Exile was the first black-produced feature film with sound, and the Library holds a copy of it. The story concerns a black man who flees the immoral vices of city life for the isolated life of a midwestern rancher. He takes in a man and his daughter, both white, but soon he and the daughter have fallen in love. The black man, however, refuses to marry her, fearing the social consequences, until her father reveals that she also is, in fact, properly considered black—since that was her late mother's race.

Micheaux continued in this controversial vein, often facing considerable censorship difficulties, knowing that such publicity could also bring audiences to the theater. The Library holds a print of the only surviving copy of Micheaux's second film, *Within Our Gates*, recently found in the national film archives of Spain in Madrid under the title *La Negra*. The film attracted notoriety equal to its predecessor, *The Homesteader*, by depicting a lynching. Micheaux produced some two dozen other pictures during the silent era, often reissuing films under new titles or reediting old films into new ones.

Micheaux, however, was not alone; the silent period evolved into a golden era for black filmmakers. Some eighty feature films with black casts were made during the 1920s. By comparison with the complications of sound in later periods, making and exhibiting silent films was a relatively easy task, one that could be accomplished on a minimal budget. Despite the quantity of films by black filmmakers, however, very

few of them survive today. Among those in the Library's collection, one of the most notable is the Colored Players' *Scar of Shame* (1926), a skilled social melodrama analyzing black caste stratification. One of two films by Detroit filmmaker Richard Maurice survives, *Eleven* P.M. (1927), which portrays racial intermarriage, presenting its narrative as the dream of an author.

Most black companies were less dedicated to arousing controversy than Micheaux or the Colored Players but were more successful in imitating the seamless Hollywood technique. Many such companies producing black cast films were not black owned but were either run by whites or represented a cooperative, integrated effort, a persistent pattern in the 1930s and 1940s. Hence, perhaps more typical of the features of the time is *The Flying Ace* (1928), produced in Florida by the Norman Picture Manufacturing Company, one of the few black filmmaking concerns whose corporate papers survive (at Indiana University). *The Flying Ace* concerns a pilot who becomes a detective in order to clear up a mystery. Nonetheless Norman, like many companies making black films, as well as many of Hollywood's white enterprises, went bankrupt with the twin blows of sound films and the Great Depression.

The motion picture industry was just one of the many businesses that were adversely affected by the economic upheavals of the 1930s. Although the Depression was an era of great deprivation, black creativity during the New Deal and African-American political activities during World War II nevertheless resulted in beneficial changes for the black community.

CHAPTER EIGHT

THE DEPRESSION, THE NEW DEAL, AND WORLD WAR II

The stock market crash of 1929 caused soup lines to become the order of the day for the skilled and unskilled alike. Father Divine's "heavens" in Harlem, for example, provided inexpensive, nutritious meals to thousands in need. Black Americans, many of whom were already in precarious economic situations, suffered greatly. When Franklin Delano Roosevelt was elected in 1932, he promised a "new deal" for all Americans that would provide them with security from "the cradle to the grave." Although there were inequities in the New Deal programs that were established, many blacks had opportunities to receive benefits and obtain employment. These New Deal programs generated numerous documents that found their way to the Library's collections. One of the distinguishing features of programs of this era was that they tended to make use of a broader definition of culture than had previously pertained in the United States. Programs addressed three centuries of accomplishments of African-Americans and other ethnic groups as well as European contributions to national development. The New Deal programs celebrated ethnic groups, marginal groups, the financially and politically disenfranchised, the geographically dispossessed, and women and children.

NEW DEAL PROGRAMS

In 1935 Roosevelt formed the Works Progress Administration (WPA) to create jobs at every skill level, to maintain and even advance professional and technical skills while helping individuals maintain their self-respect. Work relief programs functioned under this basic design from 1935 to 1939 when the WPA was renamed the Work Projects Administration. The WPA functioned until 1944 when national emphases shifted and employment soared as the country entered the Second World War. Materials generated by the WPA and other programs that Roosevelt's New Deal administration supported are represented in the many divisions of the Library of Congress and consist of written histories, oral histories, guidebooks, fine prints, plays, posters, photographs, and architectural histories.

Allen Kifer's doctoral dissertation, "The Negro under the New Deal, 1933–1941" (University of Wisconsin, 1961; no. 61–3124; MicRR), uses archival sources from the Civilian Conservation Corps, the National Youth Administration, the Farm Security Administration, and programs of the Works Progress Administration to assess the impact of the New Deal on African-Americans. He found that New Deal policies toward blacks were neither consistent nor uniform. Agency heads who seemed most willing to assist blacks were Harold Ickes, secretary of the interior, Hallie Flanagan of the Federal Theatre Project, and Will Alexander of the Farm Security Administration. In addition to "traditional political appointments," about thirty to forty blacks served in an advisory capacity during the New Deal. Kifer also discusses the "Black Cabinet," the group of African-American officials hired by various New Deal agencies to aid in the administration of programs in the black community.

Names of these influential blacks are listed in *Roosevelt: His Life and Times, an Encyclopedic View* (Boston: G. K. Hall, 1985; E807.F69 1985 MRR/Ref) edited by Otis L. Graham, Jr., and Meghan Robinson Wander. *Farewell to the Party of Lincoln* (Princeton, N.J.: Princeton University Press, 1983; E807.W44 1983) by Nancy J. Weiss provides an analysis of black politics during the Roosevelt administration. Also treating the Black Cabinet are Bernard Sternsher's *The Negro in Depression and War: Prelude to Revolution, 1930*

"*Books Are Weapons: Read about the Negro in National Defense . . . at the Schomburg Collection of the New York Public Library.*" Color silkscreen, New York War Services, 1941–43. (PP POS B WPA NY P06 2. LC-USZC2–1124)

"Cavalcade of the American Negro, the Story of the Negro's Progress during 75 Years," a W.P.A. poster for the Illinois Writers' Project. (PP POS B WPA III C44.1. LC-USZ62–97018; LC-USZC2–1180)

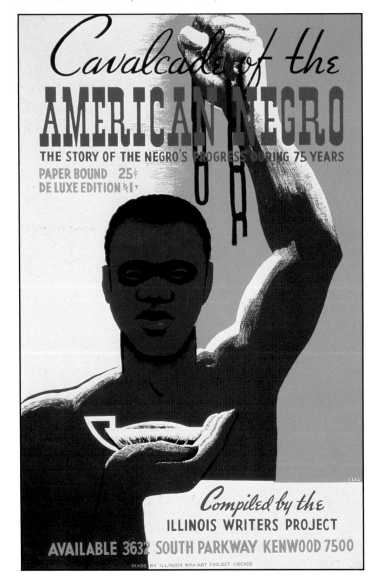

to 1945 (Chicago: Quadrangle Books, 1969; E185.6.S75 1969), Ralph J. Bunche's *The Political Status of the Negro in the Age of FDR* (Chicago: University of Chicago Press, 1973; E185.61.B93 1973), and John B. Kirby's *Black Americans in the Roosevelt Era: Liberalism and Race* (Knoxville: University of Tennessee Press, 1980; E185.6.K548).

Effects of New Deal programs on blacks are discussed in Nancy Grant's study of the Tennessee Valley Authority entitled *TVA and Black Americans: Planning for the Status Quo* (Philadelphia: Temple University Press, 1990; F217.T3 G73 1990), *Women and Minorities during the Great Depression* (New York: Garland, 1990; HN57.W66 1990), edited by Melvyn Dubofsky and Stephen Burwood, and *Negroes and the Great Depression: The Problem of Economic Recovery* (Westport, Conn.: Greenwood Publishing Corp., 1970; E185.6.W85 1970), by Raymond Wolters. The first section of *A New Deal for Blacks: The Emergence of Civil Rights as a National Issue* (New York: Oxford University Press, 1978; E185.61.S596), by Harvard Sitkoff, specifically focuses on the Depression.

Other works relating to blacks during the New Deal years may be found in the bibliographies *Black Labor in America: 1865–1983* (New York: Greenwood Press, 1986; Z7164.L1W54 1986), by Joseph Wilson, which provides an annotated listing of sources, and *Economic Status and Conditions of the Negro* (Bloomington: Indiana University Libraries, 1969; Z1361.N39M43), by Thomas Michalak. An important documentary collection, *New Deal Agencies and Black America in the 1930s* (Frederick, Md.: University Publications of America, 1983; MicRR 86/201, Guide 105–79), edited by John B. Kirby, was filmed from the holdings of the National Archives. It includes information about New Deal programs at federal agencies, including the Office of Education, the National Youth Administration, the Civilian Conservation Corps, the United States Employment Service, and the

National Recovery Administration. The papers of New Deal Secretary of the Interior Harold LeClaire Ickes (MSS papers and microfilm 1815–1969) contain information about Ickes's interaction with the black community, including the memorable 1939 Marian Anderson concert at the Lincoln Memorial which Ickes authorized after the Daughters of the American Revolution refused to allow Anderson to perform at Constitution Hall.

The WPA projects fostered the development of African-American talent. Marguerite D. Bloxom's bibliography *Pickaxe and Pencil* (Washington: Library of Congress, 1982; Z663.28.P5) includes many references to studies about the WPA. In a study specifically addressing writers, *The Dream and the Deal: The Federal Writers' Project, 1935–1943* (Boston: Little, Brown, 1972; E175.4.W9 M3), Jerre Mangione states that the Writers' Project "helped to promote the first Negro studies to be conducted in the United States on an extensive scale." Some of the works blacks produced for the project later formed the basis for creative works such as novels or short stories. Zora Neale Hurston published three of her books while she was employed on the Florida project. Arna Bontemps published his novel *Drums at Dusk* (New York: Macmillan, 1939; PZ3.B64376 Dr) and Claude McKay based his book *Harlem: Negro Metropolis* (New York: E. P. Dutton and Co., 1940; F128.68.H3M3) on materials he gathered in his work on the project.

The collection of slave narratives, transcribed oral interviews with former bondspersons, was one of the major WPA projects. Initially the work was undertaken by employees of the Federal Emergency Relief Administration but later was expanded by adding the staff of the Federal Writers' Project under the direction of John A. Lomax. *Weevils in the Wheat: Interviews with Virginia Ex-Slaves* (Charlottesville: University Press of Virginia, 1976; E444.W37), edited by

Charles L. Purdue, Jr., Thomas E. Barden, and Robert K. Phillips, is one of a number of volumes drawn from the WPA slave narrative material. The slave narratives and other African-American resource materials that were collected by various WPA projects are now in the U.S. Works Projects Administration records (MSS, records 1627–1940), a collection comprising 100,000 items.

Sterling Brown, poet and professor at Howard University, served as Negro affairs editor for the WPA Federal Writers' Project. Brown supervised writers working on various projects, such as the preparation of a section of the WPA state guidebooks devoted to "racial and ethnic" elements of the population. Besides this treatment in guidebooks, Brown instituted field projects to examine black history and folklore in greater depth. A striking example of this was the volume produced by the Virginia Writers' Project, entitled *The Negro in Virginia* (New York: Hastings House, 1940; E185.93.V8W7). Other studies of African-Americans initiated by the Federal Writers' Project included the pamphlet *Cavalcade of the American Negro* (Chicago: Diamond Jubilee Exposition Authority, 1940; E185.6.W92), the *New York Panorama* (New York: Random House, 1938; F128.5.F38), and the *New York City Guide: A Comprehensive Guide to the Five Boroughs of the Metropolis* (New York: Random House, 1939; F128.5.F376). Some of the materials were also used in Roi Ottley's history of African-Americans in New York, *New World A-Coming: Inside Black America* (Boston: Houghton Mifflin Co., 1943; F128.9.N3O75 1968).

The Louisiana Writers' Project gathered folk materials from conversations with black and white Orleanians in *Gumbo Ya-Ya* (Boston: Houghton Mifflin, 1945; GR110.L5G85), a term meaning "everybody talks at once." Two other significant studies incorporating materials about African-Americans are *These Are Our Lives* (Chapel Hill: University of North Carolina

Press, 1939; F210.F45), a collection of oral histories which describe the social life and customs of blacks during the Depression, and *Drums and Shadows: Survival Studies among the Georgia Coastal Negroes* (Athens: University of Georgia Press, 1940; E185.93.G4W7).

Black authors such as Ralph Ellison and Richard Wright were hired by the Federal Writers' Project. Their works are included in several anthologies about the New Deal era, including Harvey Swados's *The American Writer and the Great Depression* (Indianapolis: Bobbs-Merrill, 1966; PS536.S9), which includes an excerpt from Richard Wright's *Twelve Million Black Voices: A Folk History of the Negro in the United States of America* (London: L. Drummond, 1947; E185.6.W9 1947), and Ann Banks's collection of life stories, *First-Person America* (New York: Vintage Books, 1981; E169.F56 1981). Transcribed interviews in *First-Person*—including some conducted by Ralph Ellison—describe the lives of Jim Barber, a laborer; Jim Cole, a packinghouse worker; Izzelly Haines, a conch fishing village resident; and a woman who describes rent parties. Local histories of cities where the black population was large are also part of the writers' project material. George Edmund Haynes's study *Negro Newcomers in Detroit* (New York: Arno Press, 1969; F574.D4H3) was completed while he was employed by the project.

Aaron Siskind's collection of photographs which was exhibited and published as *Harlem Document: Photographs 1932–1940* (Providence, R.I.: Matrix Publications, 1981; F128.68.H3S57 1981) also resulted from work on the project. A white photographer, Siskind portrays everyday life in Harlem, center of the arts for black America during the first half of the twentieth century. In his foreword to the 1981 catalog for Harlem Document, African-American photographer Gordon Parks referred to Harlem as "a city of blackness crammed inside a white city where, when you walked out the door, you

became a stranger." Parks ascribed the vivid nightlife of Harlem to its denizens' sense of hopelessness and exhaustion in the effort to meet basic needs: "In evenings they gave in to whatever their bodies wanted and, without shame, broke into laughter, song and dance to kill the memories of the day; to keep alive what little hope there was left; and to help fill those empty spots in their souls." The Library has in its collections a number of photographs from Siskind's project (PP PH Siskind Portfolio).

Not until the era of the WPA did black artists find favorable conditions outside of their own communities to develop their art. According to Leslie King-Hammond's work *Black Printmakers and the W.P.A.* (Bronx, N.Y.: The Gallery, 1989; NE539.3.A35 K56 1989), black printmakers demonstrated remarkable artistic and technical levels of proficiency between 1935 and 1945. The fine prints program gave black artists the opportunity to earn a living in their chosen fields and to exhibit their work before a wider, multiethnic audience.

In Philadelphia African-American artist Dox Thrash supervised the art project's graphics division, which specialized in printmaking. Both black and white printmakers in that division addressed African-American themes. Although the Library's holdings of works from this project are partial, the Library of Congress began to buy for its collections the work of African-American artists formerly funded or trained by the WPA immediately after the New Deal era and has continued since then to pursue work dealing with the black experience. The Prints and Photographs Division's collections of WPA fine prints includes works by black artists or about African-American subjects. Artists represented include Raymond Steth, Lawrence Smith, Samuel Joseph Brown, Elizabeth Olds, William E. Smith, and Joseph Vavak. Lithographer Prentiss Taylor dealt with politically sensitive issues in his *Eight Black Boys in a Southern*

Jail (PP FP XX T243.A9), and his *Scottsboro Limited*, 1931 (PP FP XX T243.A5), both of which dealt with the Scottsboro rape trial. The latter is signed, dated, and dedicated to Langston Hughes.

Social-documentary art characterizes the WPA poster collection, which contains approximately one thousand original silkscreen posters produced by the WPA between 1936 and 1941. Most of these are display posters produced to promote government-supported art exhibitions and plays. Others deal with social problems such as housing, health, education, and crime.

The collection—which documents the design style, cultural events, and social climate of the period—includes many works by unidentified artists. A book-length study entitled *Posters of the WPA* (Los Angeles: Wheatley Press in association with the University of Washington Press, 1987; NC1807.U5D46 1987) by Christopher DeNoon gives a historical account of this project.

Posters that deal with blacks include those produced for all-black Federal Theater Project (FTP) productions. Sixteen African-American theater units were formed by the FTP and were

Sunday Morning, 1939, lithograph by Thomas Hart Benton (1889–1975). Federal Art Project. (PP XX-B478–A19. LC-USZ62–107758)

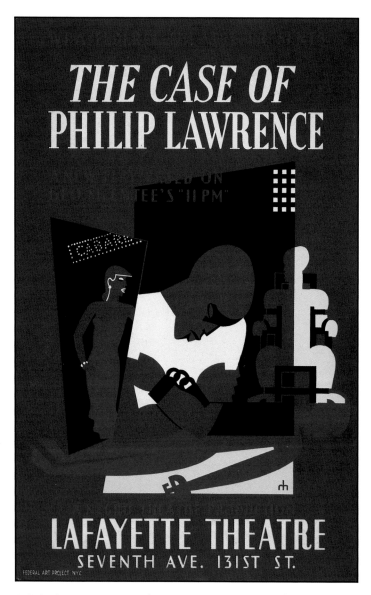

A Federal Art Project poster by Harry Herzog advertises the Negro Theatre production of The Case of Philip Lawrence *at the Lafayette Theatre in New York. Silkscreen, 1937. (PP POS S WPA NY H47 12)*

composed of both performers and technicians. Posters were created to advertise their plays, among them *Haiti, Run Little Children,* and *Swing Mikado.* Other posters deal with such diverse topics as *Cavalcade of the American Negro,* which advertises an Illinois Writers' Project book covering the "story of the Negro's Progress during 75 years." Another poster announces a "Colored Band Concert" sponsored by the WPA Federal Music Project. The Library's Federal Theatre Project collection (MSS, papers 1935–43), which is on deposit at George Mason University in Fairfax, Virginia, includes much information relating to black actors and performances. The surveys and studies file, for example, includes seven folders of "Negro Material." The Living Newspaper records include materials on Father Divine, and the information file includes materials relating to "prejudice and minority groups." Other records consist of playscripts, production information, and personnel files.

The WPA Federal Music Project hired unemployed musicians to give public concerts. Performing groups were segregated, and WPA presentations were exclusively ensemble performances. The music project tended to be most active in states where concerts were popular before the Depression. Performance programs for the Federal Music Project are available in the Music Division arranged by year and then by state. Within the limits of the project's mandate they show a rich variety of African-American musical activity, from the Negro Military Band of New Orleans to Lillian Floyd's Jubilee Singers of San Diego, California.

The National Youth Administration was established as part of the Works Progress Administration in 1935 to conduct work programs and professional development projects for needy youth. Black educator Mary McLeod Bethune was appointed head of the National Youth Administration's Division of Negro Affairs. She

Electric phosphate smelting furnace in a Tennessee Valley Authority chemical plant near Muscle Shoals, Alabama, June 1942. Photograph by Alfred Palmer. (FSA–OWI Collection, PP. LC-USW36–333 [Kodachrome]; LC-USW361–333 [repro. no.])

Fourth of July, Saint Helena Island, South Carolina, a photograph by Marion Post Wolcott, June 1939. (FSA–OWI Collection, PP. LC-USF35–199 [Kodachrome]; LC-USF351–199 [repro. no.])

Going to town on Saturday afternoon, Georgia, May 1941. Photograph by Jack Delano. (FSA–OWI Collection, PP. LC-USF35–91 [Kodachrome]; LC-USF351–91 [repro. no.])

was responsible for the coordination of activities affecting black young people and the development of projects to provide employment opportunities for them. Bethune used publicity about agency programs to try to offset the general invisibility of black Americans. Photographs document Bethune's tours of agency programs and her interest in documenting black performance and leadership and the ability of whites and African-Americans to work together (PP lots 953, 1617, 3469, 5479, 5344, 7263, 7264, 7267, 7268, 53, 127, 146, 595, 682, 683, 688, 795, 1817, 1842, 1964).

A pictorial record of American life in the 1930s was created by the Farm Security Administration (FSA), which was established during the Depression to improve farming operations and give guidance in farm and home management. These photographs document the effect of the Depression and federal relief projects on all segments of the population including thousands of African-Americans. Initially the FSA staff photographed the lives of sharecroppers in the South and migratory agricultural workers in the midwestern and western states. Later they documented rural conditions throughout the country, life in urban areas, and the domestic impact of the war effort.

The Farm Security Administration produced more than eighty thousand photographs, organized into two thousand subject groupings, which were transferred to the Library of Congress in 1944. Although only a few black photographers—Gordon Parks and Roger Smith among them—worked for the FSA project, many of the staff photographers were sympathetic to blacks and their economic and social conditions, as was project director, Roy Stryker. Gordon Parks is responsible for a group of photos on the subject of civil rights. He photographed the activities of black civic groups, including church-based and labor-union-based efforts to abolish the poll tax (PP lot 269). In other photographs by Russell Lee, civil rights activism is an issue, for instance, a 1939 series about black and white sharecroppers organizing in Oklahoma (PP lot 534).

African-American religion is the topic of many FSA photographs. Gordon Parks documented the supportive function religion played in the life of charwoman Ella Watson, who cleaned government offices in Washington, D.C., on the 5:30 P.M. to 2:30 A.M. shift for twenty-six years to support a succession of children and grandchildren (PP lot 156). Episcopal, Catholic, Baptist, Pentecostal, and storefront churches on Chicago's South Side are depicted (PP lots 54, 241). Black Marines attending chapel in North Carolina and abandoned churches in Mississippi were photographed by FSA staff (PP lots 1823, 1638).

Photographers portrayed black children playing amid debris in an African-American neighborhood of Chicago in 1941 (PP lot 1079) and collecting scrap rubber for a war materials drive in Virginia in 1942 (PP lot 1935). Black tenancy was documented largely in southern states, but also in New Jersey, showing problems in housing, health, soil conservation, nutrition, and animal husbandry. Unionization, entertainment and music, eviction, purchase and maintenance of equipment, and raising crops on marginal and submarginal land are the subjects of FSA photographs (PP lots 534, 1192, 1208, 1318, 1499, 1500, 1520, 1545, 1616, 1645, 1649, 1657, 1673). Problems of African-American migrant workers such as fruit pickers are represented in photo-

graphs that show their working conditions, company shacks, poor land, and inadequate equipment (PP lot 1318).

Intended as documentation of deplorable conditions that the federally funded programs were established to improve, FSA photographs depict vermin-ridden shacks in Oklahoma in 1939, evicted black and white sharecroppers in Missouri in 1939, and a former slave in a home in which the walls are covered with newspaper. To demonstrate that government projects between 1936 and 1940 had been effective, some series depicted "improved" conditions, showing the home of a black tenant active in a 4-H Club in 1940 in Oklahoma and a black sharecropper's new home in North Carolina in 1936 (PP lots 526, 1207, 1624, 527, 1485).

Housing was the subject of FSA photographs that depict urban blacks, many shots showing such aspects of city dwellings as outside privies, dilapidated stoves, overcrowding, makeshift plumbing, and inadequate kitchens (PP lots 160, 1081). To demonstrate that some urban conditions improved as the result of FSA programs, photographers portrayed the Ida B. Wells housing project for blacks on the South Side of Chicago in 1942 and the Lakeview Cooperative FSA project for blacks in Arkansas in the 1930s and 1940s (PP lots 49, 1666).

Other New Deal programs that affected African-American housing included an effort to eliminate alley dwellings in Washington, D.C., by 1944. For this, an Alley Dwelling Elimination Act was enacted in 1934. Under the auspices of the Resettlement Administration, photographic documentation of alley life was compiled in the mid-1930s, showing alley residents, most of whom were poor blacks (PP lots 1395 to 1398).

Some of the federally funded housing projects in the New Deal era included provisions for blacks, both as architects and as residents. In fact, however, blacks were specifically excluded from the carefully screened applicants selected

196 THE DEPRESSION AND WORLD WAR II

for the new town of Greenbelt, Maryland, just outside Washington, D.C., and were even banned from visiting the community. Instead, a single racially segregated, federally funded project was built for blacks in the nation's capital. *Greenbelt: History of a New Town, 1937–1987* (Norfolk, Va.: Donning Co., 1987; F189.G7W55 1987), edited by Mary Lou Williamson, is a pictorial work on the subject. Washington-based black architect Hillyard Robinson, working for the Public Works Administration, designed Langston Terrace to afford better housing for black low-income families. Photodocumentation of this housing complex was undertaken by Washington photographer Theodor Horydczak (PP lot 12106, binder 3). Robinson also designed a house for African-American political scientist and diplomat Ralph Bunche, photographs of which are included in the Horydczak collection (PP lot 12106, binder 1). Drawings of Bunche's home are also available (PP HABS DC, Wash, 232–).

The Historic American Buildings Survey, another product of Franklin Roosevelt's New Deal, officially began in 1933 when the National Park Service, the American Institute of Architects, and the Library of Congress joined to initiate this project to preserve through graphic and written records the heritage of America's built environment. Initially, the program made little effort to document the contribution of blacks to America's architectural heritage. Early work did establish precedents by including in HABS records information about where ordinary people—including blacks—lived and worked. Homes of some prominent African-Americans were also recorded.

Some wealthy African-Americans were able to live in buildings of fine design, materials, and workmanship that were selected to be included in architectural surveys. For example, actor Paul Robeson's apartment building at 555 Edgecomb Avenue in Harlem is documented in the His-

toric American Buildings Survey (PP HABS NY, 31-NEYO,117–) as is the apartment building of band leader Edward Kennedy "Duke" Ellington at 935 Saint Nicholas Avenue in Harlem (PP HABS NY, 31-NEYO,119- and 119A-). Villa Lewaro, in Irvington, Westchester County, New York, was an example of a housing development for the emerging black middle class. Built in 1918 by Vertner Woodson Tandy, the first black architect licensed in New York, and owned by Madame C. J. Walker, pioneer black businesswoman in cosmetics, the Villa is also included in the Historic American Buildings Survey (PP HABS NY, 60–IRV, 5–).

The buildings survey also documented the Odd Fellows Hall in Gainesville, Hall County, Georgia, which was built in 1914 by black architect James Dawson O'Kelley (PP HABS GA, 70-GAIN,1-). Lockefield Garden Apartments, four-story apartment public housing in Indianapolis built in 1934, was located in an area which had been a center for the black community since the early 1800s, according to architects William Earl Russ and Merritt Harrison. The Historic American Buildings Survey records relating to the apartments include thirty-eight exterior photographs, sixty-six photocopies of Public Works Administration (PWA) drawings, and other documents (PP HABS IND, 49-IND, 32–).

Closely related to these surveys are a series of atlases entitled *Housing: Analytical Maps*, each with its own call number, that were produced by the New York City office of the WPA in conjunction with the U.S. Bureau of the Census. Based on block statistics gathered in the 1940 census, the maps in these atlases portray such topics as average rent, major repairs, bathing equipment, persons per room, owner occupancy, and mortgage status, as well as percentage of nonwhite households per block. There are copies of eighty atlases from this series in the Library's collections, ranging from Akron to Youngstown, Ohio, with most other states represented by one or two atlases. Cataloging records for both sets of atlases are available in the Geography and Map Division's atlas catalog under the main entry heading "U.S. Works Projects Administration."

SOCIAL AND ECONOMIC CONDITIONS

Architect-designed buildings leave a record of segregation in the drawings themselves as well as in the buildings that resulted from them. The work of one Washington, D.C., architect, Arthur B. Heaton, whose drawings are among the

holdings in the Prints and Photographs Division, is a case study. His design drawings for a Washington Railway and Electric Company building depict segregation, by sex, race, and hierarchy within the trade. The plans include rooms labeled "toilet room colored," "toilet for conductors and motormen," "white barnmen's locker room," "colored barnmen's locker room," "toilet room white," "locker room for conductors and motormen," and "women's room" (PP ADE-D UNIT 524, no. 2).

Heaton's design drawings for the Alexander, Barcroft & Washington Transit Company bus garage show separate bathrooms for white and colored men (PP ADE-E UNIT 967, no. 8) and

Map of the United States showing the distribution of African-American population based on the 1950 census. (GM US—Ethnography—1956)

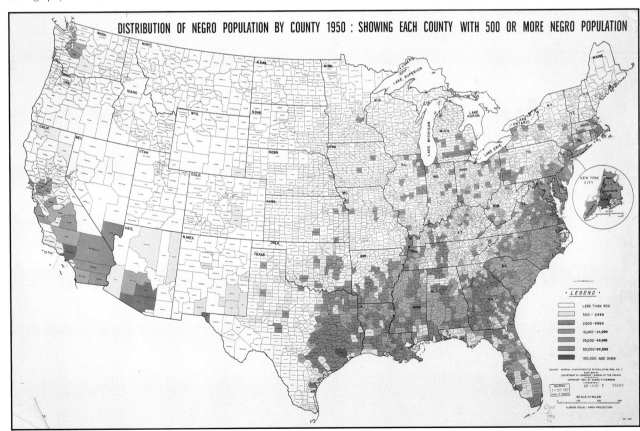

those for his Auto Laundry, built in 1931–32, indicate a "Colored Toilet" and one for "Ladies and White Men" (PP ADE-E UNIT 897, nos. 14–15). A Heaton drawing of the Capitol Garage includes a "colored men's locker room" (PP ADE-E UNIT 1008, no. 63). Another drawing, this time for architect George N. Ray's garage building designed in 1928 and 1929 for William E. Furey at Fourteenth and Church Streets, Northwest, Washington, D.C., shows an area labeled "colored toilets" (PP ADE unprocessed).

Patterns of residential segregation can be traced through sources available in the Geography and Map Division. The interwar years are represented by two sets of closely related atlases that were created as part of the WPA projects. Numerous state offices conducted real property surveys of their major cities, with the results recorded at the block level in limited edition atlases. These surveys, which were designed to provide a picture of urban housing conditions during the Depression, recorded a variety of statistics including age of structure, owner occupancy, persons per room, mortgage status, and race of household. The last was often expressed as a percentage of nonwhite households but in some cases as black households per block. Real property surveys in the Library of Congress are available for eighteen cities ranging from Bessemer, Alabama, to Seattle, Washington.

The Geography and Map Division's Titled Collection, which is essentially a collection of uncataloged maps accessioned before 1968, contains several miscellaneous maps that are of interest for this period. Although these maps have not been cataloged, they are arranged according to a geographical hierarchy (world, continent, country, state, county, and city) and within these geographical categories, there are often subject classifications as well as chronological sequencing. One subject classification that has been used fairly consistently as a sub-

division for many geographical areas is the topic "ethnology."

Maps showing the distribution of various ethnic groups were most often filed under this category. For example, there are several maps showing the distribution of blacks throughout the United States filed under the category "United States—Ethnology," including some based on the 1890 and 1950 censuses. A 1946 pictorial map entitled "Americans of Negro Lineage" illustrates places associated with "outstanding Negroes in American life and history," and a 1961 Associated Press Newsfeature map of blacks moving out of the South. Under the category "United States—Lynchings" is a map showing the distribution of lynchings throughout the United States. Published in 1931, the map is based on data from the Research Department of Tuskegee Institute.

The National Negro Congress (MSS, microfilm 1933–47) was founded in Chicago to agitate for the rights of African-Americans and to find a means of alleviating the impact of the Depression on them. Over eight hundred delegates representing almost six hundred organizations attended the initial meeting of the Congress which was held February 14–16, 1936. A. Philip Randolph, who was elected president of the Congress, later withdrew from the organization because of its leftist politics. The records, which are reproduced from originals at the Schomburg Center for Research in Black Culture, include correspondence, financial and administrative records, and publications. The Library also holds *The Official Proceedings of the National Negro Congress . . . 1936* (Washington: The Congress, 1936; MLCS 83/11215[H], *Resolutions of the National Negro Congress . . . 1936* (n.p. MLCS 83/11214[H]), and *Second National Negro Congress: Official Proceedings, October 15, 16, 17, 1937, Metropolitan Opera House, Philadelphia, Pennsylvania* (Washington: The Congress, n.d.; MLCS 83/7175). A small amount of material relating to the

Congress is among the papers of A. Philip Randolph (MSS, papers 1909–79).

Significant holdings in radical pamphlet literature, ranging from 1870 to 1980, but especially strong for the period from 1930 to 1949, are found in the Rare Book and Special Collections Division. The collection includes works by major leaders of American Communism and Socialism. Pamphlets directed at blacks after 1928 relate to lynchings, sports participation, and segregation in the military and industry. Blacks represented include James Ford, executive secretary of the Harlem Division of the Communist party and vice presidential candidate in the 1930s, William Patterson of the Civil Rights Congress, labor activist A. Philip Randolph, and actor-activist Paul Robeson. Among a collection of two thousand pamphlets gathered by the House of Representatives Committee on Un-American Activities relating to suspected radicals are twenty-six pamphlets filed under the heading "Negro." They discuss black participation in sports, movies, war, and politics, and include historical surveys by Herbert Aptheker.

The changes wrought by the Depression and World War II did not stop forward movement in the area of higher education for African-Americans. As a matter of fact, many thousands were able to attain college degrees with the help of the G.I. Bill. Some black institutions began to cooperate in the area of fund-raising. The United Negro College Fund (UNCF) (MSS, microfiche 1944–65) began its work as a cooperative funding agency for black colleges and universities during the war years. (In 1972 the fund developed the popular slogan, "A mind is a terrible thing to waste.") A microfiche copy of the collection is available in the Manuscript Reading Room as are the papers of one of the organization's principal founders, Frederick Douglass Patterson (MSS, papers 1861–1988).

The diaries of Rayford Logan (MSS, papers 1926–80) chronicle his professional life at Howard University. As a dean and department chairman as well as a history professor, Logan encountered a large number of administrators, faculty, staff, and students. He records in the diaries information about various meetings and gives accounts of his interaction with Mordecai W. Johnson, the first black president of Howard, and discusses his numerous lectures throughout the United States. He usually traveled by train and regularly commented about his accommodations and treatment by white passengers and railroad workers. Always extremely affronted by the indignities of "humiliating, degrading, tomfoolery." Much of Logan's travel was related to his role as president of the collegiate fraternity Alpha Phi Alpha. On other trips, he presented lectures—with such titles as "The White Man's Distress Is the Black Man's Gain" and "Confessions of an Unwilling Nordic"—at academic institutions or before community groups.

Some activities at black educational institutions are graphically documented by photographs. In the 1930s Hubert W. Peet made black-and-white lantern slides depicting educators and schools and colleges such as Tuskegee and Hampton Institutes for use in an international Quaker publication based in London (PP—unprocessed). An album compiled by an unidentified student of the National Trade and Professional School for Women and Girls in the Lincoln Heights section of Washington, D.C., includes photographs showing campus educational, spiritual, and leisure activities for the years 1937 to 1959 (PP lot 12569). Other images of the school include scenes of domestic life portraying youths cooking, eating, playing music, and engaging in educational activities, taken from 1911 to 1956 (PP lot 12571). Other photographs depicting education include a 1943 image of Randall Junior High School by black photographer Roger Smith.

Daddy Grace, a silver gelatin print by James A. Van Der Zee, 1938. Courtesy of Donna Mussenden VanDerZee. (PP PH–Van Der Zee Portfolio. LC-USZ62–107757)

RELIGIOUS MOVEMENTS

Two of the most prominent religious leaders during the Depression were Father Divine and Daddy Grace. Born George Baker, Father Divine founded a church on Long Island, in New York, but later moved its headquarters to Harlem. He drew a large following, which was augmented by the people he fed in his "heavens," or soup kitchens, during the Depression. Although Father Divine's movement was centered in Harlem, heavens were also established in other cities. In *Father Divine: Holy Husband* (Garden City, N.Y.: Doubleday, 1953; BX7350.H37), Sara Harris begins her first chapter, "John Doe, Alias God," by stating:

Father Divine claims that twenty million people call him God. He says "I am their life's substance! I am their energy and ambition. They recognize my deity as that which was in the imaginary heaven, and if they can only get a word with me, they feel like they are in heaven!"

Other works dealing with this charismatic leader are Jill Watts's *God, Harlem U.S.A.* (Berkeley: University of California Press, 1992; BX7350.W38 1992), Mother (Mrs. M. J.) Divine's *The Peace Mission Movement* (Philadelphia: Imperial Press, 1982; BX7350.Z5M68 1982), and Robert Weisbrot's *Father Divine and the Struggle for Racial Equality* (Urbana: University of Illinois Press, 1983; BX7350.A4W44 1983).

Daddy Grace, born Charles Emmanuel Grace, established "Houses of Prayer" for his followers in various cities. Another charismatic leader, he contended with Father Divine for spiritual leadership in Harlem. Lenwood Davis's *Daddy Grace: An Annotated Bibliography* (New York: Greenwood Press, 1992; Z8364.D38 1992) lists various references, including newspaper and magazine articles, about Daddy Grace. Articles on Daddy Grace may also be found in the *Dictionary of American Religious Biography*

(Westport, Conn.: Greenwood Press, 1977; BL72.B68), compiled by Henry Warner Bowden, and in an article on storefront churches in *Religion in Life: A Christian Quarterly* (vol. 28, Winter 1958–59; BR1.R28). Richard R. Mathison's *Faiths, Cults, and Sects of America: From Atheism to Zen* (Indianapolis: Bobbs-Merrill, 1960; BR516.5.M29) includes a chapter on Grace.

Several reference books which document religious movements are Charles Edwin Jones's *Black Holiness: A Guide to the Study of Black Participation in Wesleyan Perfectionist and Glossalalic Pentecostal Movements* (Metuchen, N.J.: ATLA, 1987; Z1361.N39J66 1987) and Sherry DuPree's *Biographical Dictionary of African-American Holiness Pentecostals, 1880–1990* (Washington: Middle Atlantic Regional Press, 1989; BX8762.Z8D86 1989), which contains an extensive listing of Pentecostal leaders and writers. In her work, DuPree lists publications and explains the beliefs and practices of these religions.

Arthur Fauset's *Black Gods of the Metropolis: Negro Religious Cults of the Urban North* (Philadelphia: University of Pennsylvania Press, 1944; BR563.N4F3 1949a) examines five black religious groups: the Mount Sinai Holy Church of America, the United House of Prayer for All People, the Church of God, the Moorish Science Temple of America, and Father Divine's Peace Mission Movement. Raymond Julius Jones's *A Comparative Study of Religious Cult Behavior among Negroes* (Washington: Howard University, 1939; BR563.N4J6 1939a) is a similar study. Milton C. Sernett's edited collection *Afro-American Religious History: A Documentary Witness* (Durham: Duke University Press, 1985; BR563.N4A37 1985) also contains examples of the rural and urban religious expression.

Not only did African-Americans join Pentecostal and Holiness churches, they were also drawn to traditional Baptist and Methodist denominations. Ethel Williams's *The Howard Uni-*

versity *Bibliography of African and Afro-American Religious Studies* (Wilmington, Del.: Scholarly Resources, 1977; Z1361.N39W555) lists publications that deal with various denominations. Marilyn Richardson's *Black Women and Religion: A Bibliography* (Boston: G.K. Hall, 1980; Z1361.N39R53) provides titles of studies about black women's concerns. In addition, Wardell J. Payne's *Directory of African American Religious Bodies: A Compendium by the Howard University School of Divinity* (Washington: Howard University Press, 1991; BR563.N4D57 1991) gives a historical overview of black religion and includes a review article on African-American Holiness and Pentecostal churches. The *Black Americans Information Directory* (Detroit: Gale Research, 1990–; E185.5.B513) provides historical accounts of black denominations and a summary of their beliefs and practices.

General works on the black church during this period include Benjamin Elijah Mays and Joseph Williams Nicholson's *The Negro's Church* (New York: Negro Universities Press, 1969; BR563.N4M3 1969b), E. Franklin Frazier's *The Negro Church in America* (New York: Schocken Books, 1974; BR563.N4F7 1974), and William Harrison Pipes' study *Say Amen, Brother!* (New York: William-Frederick Press, 1951; BR563.N4P53), which discusses black ministers' sermons and methods of persuasion. The question of African linguistic and cultural survivals in African-American culture, particularly religion, is addressed in Melville J. Herskovits's *The Myth of the Negro Past* (New York: Harper, 1941; HT1581.H4).

POPULAR CULTURE AND THE FINE ARTS

Musicians, dancers, artists, people involved in the literary arts, actors and actresses have all been captured in photographs now held in the

Library's collections. Black entertainers were photographed by New York photographer Carl Van Vechten between 1932 and 1964. His subjects included Pearl Bailey, Ethel Waters, Dizzy Gillespie, Joe Louis, Sammy Davis, Jr., and Marian Anderson (PP lot 12735, microfilm). Images of entertainers and sports figures such as Lena Horne, Jackie Robinson, and Count Basie are part of the NAACP collection (PP).

Boxer Joe Louis, known as the "Brown Bomber," was a hero to many during the 1930s and 1940s. The *Joe Louis Scrapbooks* (Alexandria, Va.: Chadwyck-Healey, 1986; MicRR 88/252) reproduced from a collection at the Smithsonian Institution, is available in the Library's Microform Reading Room with an accompanying publication entitled *Guide to the Julian Black Scrapbooks of Joe Louis* by Robert S. Harding (Washington: National Museum of American History, 1987; Z6611.B74N37 1987). Joe Louis won the heavyweight championship during his thirty-sixth professional fight, and he defended his title twenty times before World War II. When inducted into the army during World War II, his presence helped to boost morale, because many African-Americans saw him as a symbol of black prowess. Retiring undefeated March 1, 1949, he reentered the ring as a heavyweight champion in 1950, winning eight more fights before losing to Rocky Marciano on October 26, 1951. The collection includes full-length articles, brief sketches, cartoons, photographs, and statistics from newspapers.

Music by and about African-Americans continued to be an important source of artistic expression during the Depression. The Archive of American Folk Song was established in the Library's Music Division in 1928 to collect folk songs of all kinds—including African-American—on cylinders, and discs, and later on magnetic wires and tapes, with related field notes, photographs, and other manuscript and printed materials. Now called the Archive

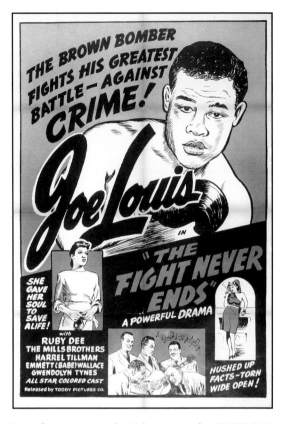

Poster for *Joe Louis* in The Fight Never Ends. *(PP POS DLC/PP/1984:326. LC-USZ62–107761)*

of Folk Culture and situated in the Library's American Folklife Center, it holds a rich variety of material relating to African-American culture.

From materials in its collection, the archive has published over eighty recordings for sale to the public. Typical releases were *Afro-American Blues and Game Songs* (1942, AFS L4), *Animal Tales Told in the Gullah Dialect* (1955, AFS 3 vols. L44, L45, L46), and *Afro-American Spirituals, Work Songs, and Ballads* (1942, AFS L3). The last, recorded in the southern states by John and Alan Lomax from 1933 to 1939, published with a seventeen-page brochure, includes selections such as "Lead Me to the Rock,' sung by Wash Dennis and Charlie Sims, "The Blood-Stained Banders," sung with four-string banjo by Jimmie Strothers, and "Run Old Jeremiah," sung by Joe Washington Brown and Austin Coleman. A catalog, *Folk Recordings Selected from the Archive of Folk Culture* (Washington: Library of Congress, 1989) is available from the American Folklife Center.

Three field projects conducted in the 1970s that include extensive documentation of African-American traditional expressive culture are the South-Central Georgia Folklife Project, Blue Ridge Parkway Folklife Project, and Chicago Ethnic Arts Project. Bibliographies, finding aids, and vertical files are available for recordings of Negro spirituals by various individuals and groups, oral slave narratives, the legend of John Henry and other specific topics, blues singer Huddie "Leadbelly" Ledbetter, and Ferdinand "Jelly Roll" Morton.

In the spring of 1938 recorded oral history got a start on the stage of the Coolidge Auditorium in the Library of Congress when Alan Lomax, in charge of the Library's Archive of American Folk Song, got Ferdinand "Jelly Roll" Morton to tell the story of his life and music for the archive's disc recording machine. What emerged was a distinctly "Mortoncentric" view of the evolution of jazz, blues, and ragtime, in which Jelly Roll was the inventor of every important style of black American music later than the spiritual and earlier than soul. Jazz historians and ethnomusicologists are still dealing with this material—obviously slanted—yet with a richness rare for any comparable figure. It has also provided material for books and shows such as Alan Lomax's *Mister Jelly Roll: The Fortunes of Jelly Roll Morton, New Orleans Creole and "Inventor of Jazz"* (New York: Duell, Sloan and Pearce, [1950]; ML410.M82L6) and *Jelly's Last Jam*, which premiered at the Mark Taper Forum, Los Angeles, on March 6, 1991.

When John Lomax and his son Alan toured the South collecting on paper and recordings the songs of American folksingers for the Library's archive, they took approximately four hundred black-and-white snapshots. Held in the Prints and Photographs Division, those relating to African-Americans show a group of prisoners at Angola, Louisiana, and singers, dancers, and banjo players in various southern states (PP lot 7414). In Belle Glade, Florida, where migrant workers came to harvest crops, additional photographs were made (PP lot 7414). A group of images of prison camps and state farms includes seventeen of Reed Camp, South Carolina, made in December 1934, and twenty-four of Darrington, Sugarland, Lufkin, Jasper, Benton, and San Antonio, Texas (PP lot 7414-E, F).

Writer and folklorist Zora Neale Hurston shot ten rolls of motion pictures in the southern United States in 1927–29 to document logging, children's games and dances, a baptism, a baseball crowd, a barbecue, and Kossula, last of the Takkoi slaves. The American Playhouse biographical drama "Nora Is My Name!", by and with Ruby Dee, was adapted from Dee's play based on Hurston's books *Dust Tracks on a Road: An Autobiography* (Philadelphia: J.B. Lippincott Co., 1935; GR103.H8) and *Mules and Men* (Philadelphia: J.B. Lippincott Co., 1935; GR103.H8). In 1939 when Hurston was in Eatonville, Florida, to collect folk songs for the Library of Congress, photographs documented her work (PP lot 7414-C). The Archive of Folk Culture has a vertical file and a published finding aid about Zora Neale Hurston, which describes programs, readings, correspondence, articles, and other items. The recordings include a collection of 227 disc recordings made by the Lomax-Hurston-Barnicle expedition in Georgia and Florida during the summer of 1935 (AFS 309–385). Additional materials relating to Hurston are in the WPA (MSS records 1627–1940) collection in the

Woman photographed by Alan Lomax, probably Zora Neale Hurston in Eaton-
ville, Florida, 1935. Silver gelatin photograph. (PP lot 7414G. LC-USZ61–
1859)

Manuscript Division. Other collections with scattered materials relating to Hurston include Margaret Mead (MSS, microfilm 1838–1980), Countee Cullen (MSS, Amistad microfilm 1921–69), NAACP (MSS, records 1909–82), and Lawrence Spivack (MSS, papers 1927–73).

The nation's continuing interest in black music is documented by such photographs as one that shows a quintet called "Billy Gardner's Famous Piccaninny's" at Billy Gardner's Restaurant, Milford, Connecticut (PP SSF, "Music—Small Groups"). Farm Security Administration photographs include images of community sings, accordion players, a juke joint, and chain gang singers. Many other forms of music are documented as well, including Marian Anderson in concert and children playing violins and pianos. One particularly interesting series of photographs, taken by Gordon Parks, documents the Ellington Orchestra playing at the Hurricane Club in Manhattan (PP lots 1085, 1081, 850, 819).

Maude Cuney Hare's *Negro Musicians and Their Music* (Washington: Associated Publishers, 1936; ML3556.H3N4) was the first history of black musicians in the United States to be published since Trotter's 1878 volume. Hare, who lived from 1874 to 1936, recounted the careers of a number of distinguished black composers of concert and operatic music, among them William Grant Still, R. Nathaniel Dett, Florence Price, Clarence Cameron White, and William Levi Dawson. All of them are represented in the Music Division's collections. The manuscript of Florence Price's *Rhapsodie Nègre* (ML96.P8328 no. 8 Case) and a photostatic reproduction of her manuscript of *Sonata in E Minor* for piano (M23.P9 E minor Case) illustrate her skill and talent. The score of William Levi Dawson's 1963 revision of his *Negro Folk Symphony* (M1001. D246N4) is in the collections, as is the miniature score published by Shawnee Press in 1965 (M1001.D246N4 1965). William Grant Still's historic *Afro-American Symphony* (New York: J. Fischer & Bro., 1935; M1001.S835A5), the first work by a black composer to be performed by major symphony orchestras, is to be found in a full score, reproduced from the manuscript that is in the holdings of the Music Division. A later composer, Margaret Bonds, who lived from 1913 to 1972, is represented by her songs, *Three Dream Portraits*, to poems by Langston Hughes (New York: G. Ricordi, 1959; M1621.B).

Few individual performers equaled Paul Robeson in popularity. His reputation abroad equaled or exceeded that in the United States, as witnessed by *Paul Robeson Songs for Peace* (Berlin: Lied der Zeit Musik Verlag, 1963; M1977. P4P3) and Martin B. Duberman's *Paul Robeson* (New York: Knopf, 1988; E185.97.R63D83 1988).

First page of the Sonata in E minor for pianoforte by Florence Price. Photostat of composer's manuscript. (M23P9 E min Case LC-USZ62–107765)

Besides numerous commercial holdings in the Library's recorded sound archives, Robeson recordings are also in special collections such as the National Broadcasting Company, Office of War Information, Voice of America, and National Public Radio collections. Robeson recordings for occasions such as an Emancipation Day Celebration in 1944 are also in the Library (LWO 1759). Coca-Cola radio programs featured Robeson singing in June 1941 "Calm as the Night" and "Deep River" and in October "Ezekiel Saw de Wheel" and "All Through the Night" (T5855, 9B1 and 12B2). Numerous published discographies in the Recorded Sound Reference Center provide access to the Library's Robeson recordings.

In 1924 Paul Robeson appeared in one of Oscar Micheaux's silent black films, *Body and Soul* (1924). In 1930 Robeson narrated the documentary *Africa Speaks*. He gained fame in the theater, and he eventually reprised two of his most famous stage roles on film, in *The Emperor Jones* (1933) and *Show Boat* (1936). Based on the acclaimed play by Eugene O'Neill, *The Emperor Jones* was the most lavishly produced black film of the 1930s, and it was released through United Artists.

Soon afterward, Robeson, believing that the British film industry would offer better roles to blacks than Hollywood did, left the United States to work in England. Robeson's first British movie dashed these hopes. *Sanders of the River*, based on Edgar Wallace's stories of colonial Africa, was originally entitled *Bosambo*. A sympathetic, positive portrayal of a native ruler was anticipated, with Nina Mae McKinney playing the queen. Instead, as the change in title implies, the focus was shifted to the British imperial hero, as he installs Bosambo in power and teaches him how to govern. Feeling betrayed, Robeson disowned the picture.

The coming of sound to motion pictures in 1927 posed aesthetic and technical challenges to the motion picture industry. A silent film that might have been produced for as little as three thousand dollars now cost around fifty thousand dollars if it was made with sound. As a result, independent black filmmakers were devastated. Production fell drastically, and only a few silents continued to be made. Eight black cast films were made in 1928, but only three appeared in 1929.

Although these factors understandably impeded the production of black cast filmmaking, the major studios that had heretofore overlooked its commercial possibilities took up the challenge of black filmmaking. In the years immediately after the coming of sound, Metro-Goldwyn-Mayer (MGM) made *Hallelujah!* (1929), a story contrasting the temptations of the city with the values of family and the rural community. One white director, Dudley Murphy, established a substantial part of his reputation in short musical films such as *Black and Tan* with Duke Ellington and *St. Louis Blues* with Bessie Smith, both in 1929. Murphy also directed the feature film *The Emperor Jones.*

Other shorts in the Library's collection are *Sissle and Blake* (1925), *Eubie Blake at the Piano* (1926), *Low Down, a Bird's Eye View of Harlem* (1929), *A Night in Dixie* (1926), with Abbie Mitchell, James P. Johnson's musical *Yamekraw,* and a series of Warner Bros. shorts. Many musical and comedy shorts were produced by Warner Bros., and such filmmaking continued well into the 1930s and beyond, from *Bubbling Over* (1934), with Ethel Waters, and *The Black Network* (1936), with Nina Mae McKinney and the Nicholas brothers, through *Dixie Jamboree* (1946), with Cab Calloway. From the mid-thirties through the mid-fifties musical shorts were regularly produced by the major studios. Dudley Dickerson teamed with white comedian Hugh Herbert in a series of Columbia shorts in the 1940s. Some of the black musical shorts combined jazz and an avant-garde camera style to create a truly artistic film, such as Warner

Bros.' *Jammin' the Blues* (1944), directed by Gjon Mili, a noted still photographer. Shorts made by Universal featured Duke Ellington, Lionel Hampton, Count Basie, Billie Holiday, and the Mills Brothers. Several featured Nat King Cole, and although most shorts were in black and white, Universal's pseudobiography *The Nat "King" Cole Musical Story* (1955) was produced in widescreen and technicolor, as was *Nat "King" Cole and Russ Morgan's Orchestra* (1953). Black cast filmmakers also produced many short sound films with black stars in stage or musical routines, and such pictures continued to appear through the 1940s.

Black cast filmmaking was slow to recover from the conversion to sound. Through the first years of the 1930s, black films continued to be either silent or only "part-talking," including some of those produced by Micheaux Pictures Corporation and the Harlem-based Paragon Pictures. Many films that were released receded further from the mainstream. For instance, the two 1933 silent religious features by Eloise and Robert Gist, *Hellbound Train* and *Verdict: Not Guilty/Not Guilty in the Eyes of God,* were widely shown in black churches. Only fragments of these films are in the Library's holdings. Reports ordered by Roy Wilkins on the exhibition of the Gist films are in the NAACP collection (MSS, records 1909–82).

One of the few black filmmaking businesses to overcome the obstacles of sound was Oscar Micheaux Pictures Corporation. By the summer of 1929, Oscar Micheaux had bounced back, writing, producing, and directing *A Daughter of the Congo,* released in the next year as the first part-talking black feature. Micheaux quickly followed it with the all-talking film *The Exile* (1931).

Many of Micheaux's subsequent films were not sophisticated productions, however, because he could not afford more than one take of any shot. Exacerbating his stylistic problems

was Micheaux's affinity for melodrama in performance and plot, characteristics clearly displayed in two of Micheaux's subsequent films,
Ten Minutes to Live (1932) and *The Girl from Chicago* (1933), both in the Library's collections. *Ten
Minutes to Live* is largely silent, and in it Micheaux apparently attempted to edit together
two separate stories, conceived and shot separately. The resulting film is nearly incoherent in
its plotline. The Library also holds Micheaux's
1932 musical comedy short, *Darktown Revue*, a
record of the performances of the Donald Heywood Choir and comedy routines by Tim
Moore, Andrew Trible, and Amon Davis. Also,
"trailers," previews of coming attractions, exist
on many Micheaux sound titles, and indicate
the advertising strategy used to attract movie-
goers.

During this period, Micheaux, unlike many
of his contemporaries, copyrighted his work
sporadically. The Library's motion picture copyright records, held on microfilm by the Motion
Picture, Broadcasting, and Recorded Sound Division, provide information on many Micheaux
films of the time. For instance, *Harlem after Midnight* (1934) is apparently a "lost" film, but the
copyright files contain a rough script.

Although only a small number of Micheaux's
total output of over three dozen films still exist,
most Micheaux films made after 1935 do survive
and are included in the Library's collection. For
instance, the Library holds *Murder in Harlem*,
a reissue version of the 1935 Micheaux movie
originally entitled both *Lem Hawkin's Confession*
and *Brand of Cain*. The film, one of his most ambitious, relates how a white man tries to frame
his black employee for murder. Among later
Micheaux films at the Library are *Underworld*
(1937), a gangster story, *Swing!* (1938), a musical, *Lying Lips* (1939), a mystery, and *The Noto-
rious Elinor Lee* (1940), an account of boxing
racketeers. Some of Micheaux's films deal directly with social issues. *Birthright* (1939), a re-

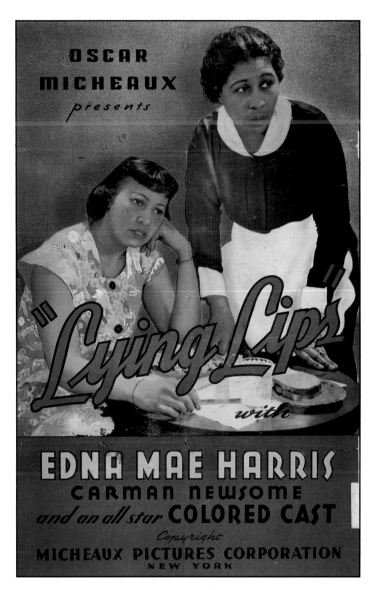

*"Oscar Micheaux Presents 'Lying Lips' with Edna Mae Harris, Carmen Newsome,
and an all star Colored Cast." 1939. Color offset and lithograph. Copyright
Micheaux Picture Corporation, New York. (PP POS Mot Pic Blk Film L95 no. 1,
C size. LC-USZC4–2431)*

make of a Micheaux silent film, is an account of the racism facing a university-educated black who tries to return to his hometown and open a school, only to find prohibitions on the black ownership of property. The Library holds a recently discovered and preserved copy of *Birthright*.

Micheaux was not alone in using film to address black social issues. Typical of other such political films is a 1932 movie *The Black King*, of which the Library holds a reissue version entitled *Harlem Hot Shot*. This black cast picture based on Donald Heywood's play was controversial. Taking a sharp, satiric look at the back-to-Africa movement, A. B. Comathiere portrays a problematic leader who is a fraud and an exploiter of his own race.

In 1937, black filmmaking changed considerably, adopting much of the Hollywood style and technique to create black films that could compete with the industry and attract wider audiences, including whites. The magnitude and success of this new approach were soon clear. In the seven years from 1930 to 1936, only twenty-three black cast films were made, but the next four years, from 1937 to 1940, would see the production of over fifty films. The event that triggered this sudden increase was the formation in Hollywood in 1937 of a promising new black firm, Cooper-Randol, shortly to become Million Dollar Productions. The same year saw the release of eight black films, marking the resurgence in black filmmaking that became a cycle that would continue unabated until the Japanese attack on Pearl Harbor and American involvement in World War II.

Million Dollar Productions had its genesis in 1936, when performer Ralph Cooper was brought to Hollywood by Fox. Slated to appear in a Shirley Temple movie, Cooper was dropped because he did not fit the desired stereotype. Cooper united with another black, George Randol, to produce and star in *Dark Manhattan* (1937), the first of a series of popular black gangster films of the 1930s. The next year Cooper broke with Randol and formed Million Dollar Productions with Harry Popkin, an independent white producer. Between 1937 and 1941 Cooper continued starring in and coproducing films. An example in the Library's collections is *The Duke Is Tops/Bronze Venus/The Bronze Nightingale*.

Although his film career was brief, Cooper had a profound impact. The black filmmaking cycle of the late thirties began as a result of the successful formula and box office receipts from *Dark Manhattan*. Million Dollar Productions starred performers who appealed to a wide audience, such as Cooper, Louise Beavers, and Mantan Moreland. The films depict a wholly black realm, without white influence, in which all the characters, villains and heroes alike, behave with dignity in clear opposition to the standard Hollywood stereotypes. Offering blacks a cinematic world of their own was a powerful statement on behalf of equality, articulating racial consciousness and pride.

The Cooper films in particular, and Million Dollar Productions generally, were a clear departure from earlier black films, using the expertise and equipment available in Hollywood to improve production standards. For instance, *Dark Manhattan* was shot at the Grand National studios rather than in the private homes often used in Micheaux efforts. For the first time, a whole series of black films, instead of a few isolated examples, sustained a professional production style. Not only did Million Dollar Productions secure an important economic niche in Hollywood, but so did the other half of the original Cooper-Randol team. Cooper's former partner, George Randol, was only slightly less successful, merging with two white independents, the brothers Bert and Jack Goldberg, to form International Road Shows in Hollywood. They produced a number of films which echoed the tendencies of Million Dollar, although they were never as well produced. The Library has all five of the Randol-Goldberg films: *Double Deal* (1939), *Midnight Shadows* (1939), *Paradise in Harlem* (1939), with Frank Wilson, *Mystery in Swing* (1940), and *Broken Strings* (1940). The Goldbergs had previously been associated with black stage productions and such films as *Harlem Is Heaven*/*Harlem Rhapsody* (1932). Remaining active, the Goldbergs produced some of the polished black musicals that would highlight such filmmaking in the 1940s.

Whereas Micheaux's films tended toward melodrama, the films of Million Dollar and International Road Shows and their many smaller, less successful counterparts clustered around the crime, musical, and comedy genres, which they usually placed in a black context. Each used generic formulas already well established in mainstream Hollywood B films. For instance, the Library's collection includes a crime film, largely filmed in a nightclub setting, *Moon Over Harlem* (1940). Other genres were represented. Sports films dealing with football and boxing heroes were common, including one of the most prestigious black cast films, the Grand National production of *The Spirit of Youth* (1938), with Joe Louis portraying himself.

Black cast films of the late 1930s even tried the singing cowboy genre, a form popularized by Gene Autry and Roy Rogers. The black response to Autry and Rogers was Herb Jeffries, a black singer and emcee who was still active more than fifty years later. Four black musical westerns were produced featuring Jeffries, of which the Library holds three: *The Bronze Buckaroo*, *Harlem Rides the Range* (both 1939), and *Two Gun Man from Harlem* (1940). Each demonstrates the multiple purposes fulfilled by the Jeffries films. On the one hand, they sought to remind audiences, particularly the young, of the important role played by blacks in the settling of the West, through featuring an all-black cowboy

cast living in black-owned ranches and towns. Simultaneously, the films were light-hearted in their narratives, providing ample opportunity for singing by Jeffries and the Four Tones, along with comedy relief by Lucius Brooks and Mantan Moreland. Most of these films were directed by Richard Kahn, who is also represented by a 1940 musical short in the Library's collection, *The Toppers Take a Bow*.

Outside of black filmmaking, the images presented in Hollywood generally were far different. Black cast films tended to star individuals who otherwise seldom appeared in movies. The reverse was also true; since the early days of Noble Johnson and the Lincoln Motion Picture Company, Hollywood's established black stars made few appearances in black cast films. For instance, Clarence Muse starred in two 1940 black cast films, *Broken Earth*, a short, and *Broken Strings*, a feature, both of which are in the Library's collections. This was, however, an exception. Muse generally played in mostly white Hollywood films whose plots had little relevance to black concerns. Nina Mae McKinney only began to appear in black cast films when she was having difficulty finding roles elsewhere. The Library holds a print of one of her black films, *Straight to Heaven* (1939). The famous musical entertainer, Bill "Bojangles" Robinson, often portrayed a southern butler and dancer. A typical film of his is the short *King for a Day* (1934). Robinson, however, starred in only one black cast film, *Harlem Is Heaven* (1932), portions of which survive in the Library. All these performers were widely known to audiences of all ethnicities but were primarily seen as supporting players in Hollywood studio films and occasionally as the movie's costars, as Robinson was in these musicals.

Working primarily overseas and, like Paul Robeson, failing to find an American market for her European films, Josephine Baker appeared in several French films during the late 1920s and

Josephine Baker, Paris, October 20, 1945. Silver gelatin photograph by Carl Van Vechten. (PP lot 12735 no. 77. LC-USZ62–93000)

early 1930s. Among these are *Princess Tam-Tam* (1935) and *Zou-zou* (1934), both in the Library's collection. Movies, however, proved unable to capture the charisma of the live stage performances that had made Baker a star in the European musical theater.

Only one black cast film was made at a major studio during the thirties, a situation that would change little in the 1940s. In 1936, Warner Bros. produced a prestigious version of the famous spiritual play *The Green Pastures*. The popular radio series, "Amos 'n' Andy," was once transferred to the screen as a popular, amusing novelty by RKO in 1930 as *Check and Double Check*. The show's white radio stars, Freeman Gosden and Charles Correll, played the lead roles in blackface. The Manuscript Division holds over four hundred "Amos 'n' Andy" scripts dating from 1926 to 1937, acquired by copyright deposit, and the Library's Recorded Sound Reference Center includes information about several "Amos 'n' Andy" recordings.

Hollywood sometimes treated black social issues, but typically in a coded fashion that demonstrated a fear of confronting racism directly. A brief antilynching cycle overtly opposing mob violence included *Fury* (1936) and *They Won't Forget*, both of which are in the Library's holdings. Casting whites in the role of victims, the films largely ignored the fact that most of those who were lynched were black. Only *They Won't Forget* touched on the readiness of some whites to conveniently and routinely pin any crime on a black. Indeed, at this time films set in the South still tended to have an idyllic tone, glossing over racial tensions. One of the few exceptions was the 1936 version of *Show Boat*, with its mulatto character and miscegenation subplot.

Often blacks in Hollywood films not only played supporting roles but were comedians. Lincoln Perry and Willie Best, respectively known as "Stepin Fetchit" and "Sleep 'n' Eat," were, like similar performers, generally lauded by the black community for their success in a predominantly white industry despite their use of stereotypes. For example, Lincoln "Stepin Fetchit" Perry regarded himself as the first black to enter the studio through the front gate. Perry deliberately cultivated a reputation with his lazy, slow, rambling screen persona, featured in such Hollywood films as *The Ghost Talks* (1949) and in the black cast 1940s sound shorts *Big Timers* and *Miracle in Harlem* (1948), made after

A color offset poster for WNEW AM 1130 in New York shows Louis Armstrong, 1985. (PP POS US A01 159, C size. LC-USZC4–2423)

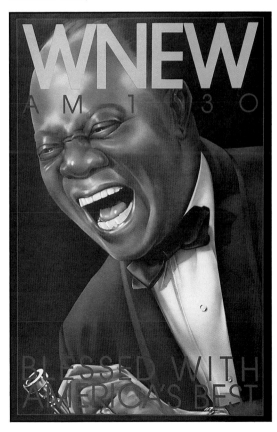

his star status had faded. Willie "Sleep 'n' Eat" Best cultivated a broader but similar persona in such films as *Minstrel Days* (1931).

At Monogram, Mantan Moreland costarred in a series of melodramas with Frankie Darro, including *Let's Go Collegiate* (1941). When Monogram took over the Charlie Chan series, Moreland was a regular as the chauffeur providing comedy relief. Moreland became Hollywood's most prolific black performer in the studio era, appearing in over three hundred films.

Not all black supporting players were confined to the problematic niche of comedians. Performers such as Louise Beavers and Hattie McDaniel offered dramatic portrayals, frequently indicating in subtle ways their personal superiority over their social position. Beavers and McDaniel are most often associated with their roles as maids and cooks, many of which their skill endowed with special significance. Beavers appeared in the 1935 box office hit *Imitation of Life*, a film in which Fredi Washington, playing Beavers's daughter, attempts to pass for white. A microfilm reproduction of the Fredi Washington collection (MSS, Amistad Research Center microfilm 1925–79) is available. Hattie McDaniel immortalized her role as a maid in *Gone with the Wind* (1939), becoming the first black performer to receive an Academy Award. Among McDaniel's film appearances in pictures held by the Library are such varying titles as *Hypnotized* (1932), *Alice Adams* (1935), and *Racing Lady* (1937).

In Hollywood recognized black stage and music stars acted in numerous cameo roles. For instance, Louis Armstrong satirized superstition in the haunted house routine, "Skeleton in Your Closet," in *Pennies from Heaven* (Columbia, 1936) and Etta Moten sang the memorable social commentary number, "Remember My Forgotten Man," in Warner's hit musical *Golddiggers of 1933.*

Duke Ellington, orchestra leader, at the Hurricane Club, New York, May 1943. Silver gelatin photograph by Gordon Parks. (FSA–OWI Collection, PP. LC-USW3–23953)

Duke Ellington was fifth-billed in the Paramount mystery musical *Murder at the Vanities* (1934). Duke Ellington's career is documented in the Library's extensive Valburn/Ellington Collection (M/B/RS). Ellington and his band were featured in different types of motion pictures at various studios, from Paramount and MGM to Columbia and Republic. Yet Ellington's presence and music were most strongly felt in such Hollywood short films as *Black and Tan* (1929), *A Bundle of Blues* (1933), *Symphony in Black* (1934), *Symphony in Swing* (1949), and *Salute to Duke Ellington* (1950). Such appearances were indicative of the thirties: blacks were cast in an increasing variety of roles as stereotypes slowly began to give way to the greater realism in the 1940s.

MILITARY AND HOME FRONT ACTIVITIES OF WORLD WAR II

Remembering the experiences they had had in World War I, black soldiers were no longer willing to quietly accept a segregated army or the discriminatory conditions they had previously endured. To assure blacks that their service was valuable, a special advocate and adviser was appointed as a watchdog on their behalf. William H. Hastie, dean of the Howard University Law School, was chosen as civilian aide to the secretary of war. Phillip McGuire, who captured some of the sentiments of African-American troops in his documentary *Taps for a Jim Crow Army: Letters from Black Soldiers in World War II* (Santa Barbara, Calif.: ABC-Clio, 1983; D810.N4M38 1983), also wrote a biography of Hastie, entitled *He, Too, Spoke for Democracy: Judge Hastie, World War II, and the Black Soldier* (New York: Greenwood Press, 1988; KF373.H38M35 1988). The Manuscript Division holds over a hundred reels of the William Hastie Papers (MSS, microfilm 1916–76) reproduced from the originals at Harvard University.

Several general histories of blacks in World War II are available in the Library. Among the most useful are A. Russell Buchanan's *Black Americans in World War II* (Santa Barbara, Calif.: Clio Books, 1983; D810.N4B82), Neil A. Wynn's *The Afro-American and the Second World War* (New York: Holmes and Meier, 1976; D810. N4W93 1976), and Ulysses Lee's *The Employment of Negro Troops* (Washington: Office of the Chief of Military History, U.S. Army, 1966; D810. N4L4). Each of these volumes discusses the plight of the African-American soldier and tells of the various means used to ensure that blacks could participate in all units of the military. *The Employment of Negro Troops* traces the development of policies relating to the use of black troops. The author notes in a preface that it is "in no sense a history of Negro troops in World War II." He believed that it was impossible to write a history of black involvement in a single volume.

Selections concerning black soldiers from the *Annals* of the American Academy of Political and Social Science, entitled "Minority Peoples in a Nation at War" (Philadelphia: The Academy, 1942; vol. 223; H1.A44), include articles on the war by William H. Hastie, Robert Weaver, Walter White, Lester Granger, and Horace Mann Bond. The subject of blacks in the defense industries, and especially barriers to employment, is also considered.

Black journalists played a decisive part in focusing public attention on the problems associated with black participation in the military. African-American war correspondents covered black troops on duty overseas. The role of the black press correspondent is discussed in John D. Stevens's "From the Back of the Foxhole: Black Correspondents in World War II," in *Journalism Monographs* (no. 27, February 1973;

"Above and Beyond the Call of Duty—Dorie Miller receives the Navy Cross at Pearl Harbor, May 27, 1942." Color offset poster. (PP POS US M372 2, C size. LC-USZC4–2328)

PN4722.J6). Stevens provides a listing of black correspondents, the papers they represented, their reporting in the various theaters of operation, and an assessment of their impact on the war. Another book on the black press is Lee Finkle's *Forum for Protest: The Black Press During World War II* (Rutherford, N.J.: Fairleigh Dickinson University Press, 1975; PN4888.N4F5). C. L. R. James's *Fighting Racism in World War II* (New York: Monad Press, 1980; D810.N4J35) includes articles from African-American newspapers.

The various services are considered in Dennis D. Nelson's *The Integration of the Negro into the U.S. Navy* (New York: Farrar, Straus and Young, 1951; E185.63.N4 1951) and Jean Byers's *Study of the Negro in Military Service* (Washington: Department of Defense, 1950; D810.N4B93). Desegregation of the armed services is the subject of Lee Nichols's *Breakthrough on the Color Front* (New York: Random House, 1954; E185.63.N5), Richard J. Stillman's *Integration of the Negro in the U.S. Armed Forces* (New York: Praeger, 1968; E185.63.S7 1968), and Richard M. Dalfiume's *Desegregation of the U.S. Armed Forces: Fighting on Two Fronts, 1939–1953* (Columbia: University of Missouri Press, 1969; E185.63.D3).

Specific branches of the armed services and the methods the country devised to deal with racial problems came together in the training of black pilots. Alan Osur's *Blacks in the Army Air Force During World War II: The Problem of Race Relations* (Washington: Office of Air Force History, 1977; D810.N4O76) tells the story of black flying units and the official decision to permit blacks to fly. Charles E. Francis's *Tuskegee Airmen* (Boston: Bruce Humphries, 1956; D810.N4F76 1976) provides a firsthand account of the experience of fliers and airmen in World War II. Similarly, *Benjamin O. Davis, Jr., American: An Autobiography* (Washington: Smithsonian Institution Press, 1991; UG626.2.D37A3 1991) expresses his view of the experiment with blacks in the Air Force.

The Rayford Wittingham Logan (MSS, papers 1926–80) diaries in the Manuscript Division chronicle his efforts as chair of the Committee on Participation of Negroes in the National Defense Program. This committee was especially concerned that black aviators be trained to serve in the Army Air Force. As chairman, Logan had the opportunity to testify before congressional committees and meet with President Roosevelt. The committee successfully pressured the army to train African-American pilots, but the trainees were segregated at the Tuskegee Air Base in Alabama.

Gen. Noel Parrish (MSS, papers 1894–1987), whose papers are also housed in the Manuscript Division, is best known as the World War II commander of the Tuskegee air base where black airmen were trained by the army air corps for the first time. Parrish was officially stationed at Tuskegee airfield in 1941 as flight trainer and in 1942 became field commander. His Tuskegee material includes speeches, photographs, clippings, correspondence, reunion yearbooks, copies of the camp newsletter *Hawks Cry*, and some printed matter including a camp songbook. Correspondence with Dr. Frederick Douglass Patterson, who was president of Tuskegee during the time that the airfield was developing, is among the papers. Patterson wrote to Parrish on September 14, 1944, saying, "In my opinion, all who have had anything to do with the development and direction of the Tuskegee Army Air Field and the Army flying training program for Negroes in this area have just cause to be proud. . . . The development had to take place in a period of emergency and of interracial confusion." The papers of Frederick Douglas Patterson (MSS, 1861–1988) are also in the Manuscript Division. A photograph of troops training at Tuskegee taken by World Wide Photos is in the Prints and Photographs

Division with the caption, "the cadets will make up the first organized Negro aviation squadron in the Army" (PP SSF—"World War, 1939–45—Negro Troops—1942"). Posters urging black support for the war include "Keep Us Flying," published by the U.S. Treasury, which shows Maj. Robert Dies of the Tuskegee Squadron, who participated in the bond drive (PP POS US WWII J8.F31).

In March 1945, as part of a publicity project sponsored by the U.S. Army, fashion photographer Toni Frissell became the first professional photographer permitted to photograph the all-black 332d Fighter Pilot Squadron in a combat situation. She traveled to their air base in southern Italy, from which the airmen made sorties into southern Europe and north Africa. There she took photographs of squadron officers, pilots, and ground crew preparing for active duty. Best known of those Frissell photographed was Col. Benjamin O. Davis, seen briefing pilots. Almost 250 of Frissell's images in the Prints and Photographs Division record planes in formation, aerial views of airfield and city, goats on the airfield, and men gathered for an evening's entertainment and playing cards and chess in the officers' club (PP lot 12447).

Blacks as soldiers (PP lots 26, 47, 56, 60, 789, 818, 953, 1823, and 2203) and in the Coast Guard (PP lot 1966) were also recorded on film. At Camp Funston, Kansas, black troops are portrayed in 1942 parading and serving as color guard (PP lot 26). Black photographer Roger Smith made pictures of black coast guardsmen at a training station in New York in 1943. The all-black 41st Engineers at a North Carolina camp in 1942 developed their fitness and survival skills by taking advanced training in ju-jitsu and marksmanship and learning the use of gas masks (PP lot 47). Other 1942 photographs show the training of a black cavalry unit in maneuvers and bivouacs on difficult terrain, ma-chine gun and rifle platoons in sham battles at Fort Riley, Kansas, and black soldiers performing tasks such as shoeing horses (PP lot 56). The Office of War Information (OWI) collection in the Prints and Photographs Division has twenty-three groups of photographs dealing with blacks during World War II. Among them are images of black women in the role of "Rosie the Riveter" (PP lot 773) and civil defense training classes in Washington, D.C. (PP lot 238).

Blacks in uniform were a favorite subject of film documentaries during World War II. Among the Library's film holdings produced by the federal government are *The Negro Soldier* and *The Negro College in Wartime* (both 1943). Carlton Moss's *The Negro Soldier* was an account of black military contributions in American history designed to promote racial cooperation. A long and short version exist but the Library holds a print of the long one only. Several collections in the Library's recorded sound archive—particularly the Armed Forces Radio Service and the Office of War Information—include war programming directed toward blacks.

POLITICAL AND SOCIAL CONDITIONS OF THE WAR YEARS

The papers of A. Philip Randolph (MSS, papers 1909–79) document his protests against segregation in the United States with a particular emphasis on segregation in the armed forces and defense industries during the war years. Randolph led a successful movement during World War II to end segregation in defense industries. He threatened to bring thousands of blacks to protest in Washington, D.C., in 1941. The threatened "March on Washington" prompted President Franklin D. Roosevelt to issue Executive Order 8802 stating that there should be "no discrimination in the employment of workers in defense industries or Government because of race, creed, color, or national origin." The Committee on Fair Employment Practices (FEPC) was established to handle discrimination complaints. Randolph's files include records relating to the operation of the FEPC as well as circulars and clippings about its operations. Randolph's papers also include materials relating to his involvement with the Committee to End Jim Crow in the Armed Services.

The Farm Security Administration includes documentation of defense workers such as skilled munitions workers in California engaged in assembling the USS *George Washington Carver*, the second Liberty ship to be named for a black leader (PP lot 2071).

ARTS FOR VICTORY

As individual citizens began making personal efforts to contribute to the nation's defense, black artists, some of whom had been employed during the Depression by the WPA, began to focus their talents on supporting the war effort. By January 1942, various artists united to form Artists for Victory, Inc., an integrated organization whose purpose was "to render effective the talents and abilities of artists in the prosecution of World War II and the protection of their country," according to Ellen G. Landau (*Artists for Victory: An Exhibition Catalog* [Washington: Library of Congress, 1983; NE508.A77 1983]). By the beginning of 1943, the organization had a national membership of over ten thousand individual painters, sculptors, designers, and printmakers.

Artists for Victory sponsored competitive exhibitions in all media. The second annual exhibition, in 1943, focused on works that conveyed the impact of the war on the life of the Ameri-

can people. A number of the entries selected for the exhibition, which opened simultaneously at various sites throughout the United States, were by black artists or treated black themes. The only complete set of exhibition prints extant is at the Library of Congress, where the exhibition was recreated and hung again in 1982. *Swing Shift* by Will Barnett shows a black man in Harlem working at a sewing machine (PP FP XX B232.A11; repro. no. LC-USZ62-89034). Carolina Wogan Durieux's *Bourbon Street, New Orleans*, pictures two black women singing at a microphone for uniformed servicemen (PP XX FP D910. A4; repro. nos. LC-USZ62-88026, LC-USZC2-3688), and *Next of Kin*, by Helen L. Johann, makes a cynical commentary on American racism by juxtaposing a newspaper headline about a Detroit race riot with one announcing "Allies Take Base" (PP FP XX J65.A1; repro. no. LC-USZ62-88047).

In 1942 heavyweight boxing champion Joe Louis appeared on a World War II poster (PP POS U.S. J44 F31/1942; repro. nos. LC-USZC4-1334, LC-USZ62-67814) and Dorie Miller, hero at Pearl Harbor, on another (PP POS C/U.S./M372 2; repro. no. LC-USC4-2328). The Office of War Information issued a series of informational posters as propaganda for civilian personnel (PP POS C/U.S. L502.1 1943). "United We Win," produced by the War Manpower Commission, uses details of a photograph by Howard Liberman showing a black man and white man working together on an airplane engine (PP OWI POS 38 C/U.S. L502.1; repro. no. LC-USZC4-943), mixing media to achieve a new effect. "Twice a Patriot," a poster released by the War Production Board (poster no. A-37) depicts ex-private Obie Bartlett. Released from the military in 1941 after losing his left arm at Pearl Harbor, Bartlett, by 1943, was employed as a welder at a West Coast shipyard (PP POS DOC-WWII U.S. J71.F31 1943). A 1944 incentive poster produced by the Government Printing Office states "Supply lines are life lines—they depend on You." The image includes an African man stripped to the waist in the foreground working with white soldiers wearing uniforms and helmets (PP POS DOC-WWII U.S. J71.J22 1944). In his book *The Posters That Won the War* (Osceola, Wisc.: Motorbooks International, 1991; D743. 25.N45 1991), author Derek Nelson includes most of these examples of war propaganda posters that picture black Americans.

The growing importance of black culture in American life was recognized by a series of exhibits and concerts in the Library of Congress beginning December 18, 1940, commemorating the seventy-fifth anniversary of the proclamation of the Thirteenth Amendment to the Constitution of the United States, which abolished slavery. The exhibit of "books, manuscripts, music, paintings and other works of art" celebrated "the contribution of the American Negro to American culture." Four concerts on December 18, 19, 20, and 21 in the Coolidge Auditorium presented "A Festival of Music," including "two of the greatest of Negro singers,"—Roland Hayes and Dorothy Maynor, "a selection of the magnificent folk music of the Negro race," performed by the Golden Gate Quartet, with Joshua White on guitar, and "a selection of chamber music composed by Negroes or composed on Negro themes." A recording of Dorothy Maynor's December 18, 1940, concert in the Library's Coolidge Auditorium was released as the first in the series of Library of Congress Historical Performances (1991, LCM 2141).

The National Negro Opera Company made its first appearance in 1941 at the annual meeting of the National Association of Negro Musicians in Pittsburgh with Verdi's *Aida*. Its archives in the Music Division document through programs, photographs, and papers the history of this company. The group continued to per-

Lillian Evanti as Violetta and William Franklin (?) as the elder Germont in act 2 of La Traviata, produced by the National Negro Opera Company, 1944. (Music Division. LC-USZ62–107767)

form until 1961, presenting such works as R. Nathaniel Dett's *The Ordering of Moses* (New York: J. Fischer & Bro., 1937; M2003.D48307) and Clarence Cameron White's *Ouanga!*, based on a Haitian drama (manuscript 1932; M1503.W58708).

Innumerable published works deposited for copyright join with many manuscripts of musical works, including works by such black composers as William Grant Still, Ulysses Kay, Louis Armstrong, David Baker, J. Rosamond Johnson, and Jeffrey Mumford, in the Music Division. Manuscript correspondence from such notables as R. Nathaniel Dett, Jester Hairston, Roland Hayes, Ulysses Kay, William Grant Still, Clarence Cameron White, Katherine Dunham, Zora Neale Hurston, James Weldon Johnson, Bill Robinson, Eubie Blake, Noble Sissle, and Paul Laurence Dunbar is also in the collection.

At the end of the 1930s black concert composers became less of a rarity. William Grant Still wrote the theme music for the New York World's Fair of 1939. The Library has the holograph—done on music typewriter—of the theme music, entitled "Rising Tide" (ML96.S915 Case). Still consolidated his place as a composer with *Plain Chant for America* (M1613.S86P5) and *And They Lynched Him on a Tree* (M1553.3.S85A6), both in 1941, and *In Memoriam: The Colored Soldiers Who Died for Democracy* (M1045.S855I5) in 1943.

Under the influence of the war, big band music came to be regarded as a symbol of American optimism and determination. Recordings available in the Library of Congress are the best sources for this music. Much of it was published in the form of "stock" arrangements, which gave a local band a chance to play what the recorded bands were playing, and the Music Division also has lists of holdings of two particularly important sets of stocks for the period: the arrangements of the Count Basie orchestra published by Bregman, Vocco, and Conn, and the Leeds Manuscript Series, which published representative arrangements of some black orchestras. *Bebop*, the new jazz style for small groups, was less reducible to publishable form. The Music Division does, however, have some important bop pieces in the form of stocks, including *Anthropology, Man Teca, Ool Ya Koo* (all M1356.G [Gillespie]), *Confirmation, Ornithology, Scrapple from the Apple*, and *Yardbird Suite* (all M1365.P [Parker]).

Gospel music continued to grow in popularity as Thomas Dorsey, who lived from 1899 to 1993, produced such timeless favorites as "Take My Hand, Precious Lord" (Chicago, 1938; M2146.D) and "He Is the Same Today" (Chicago, 1949; M2199.D). The Music Division has virtually every gospel song deposited for copyright, beginning with the single sheets of the Chicago period and continuing to the present day. Library recordings of much of this music are available.

Some motion pictures during the war presented minority groups as integral members of the Allied fighting forces. Blacks were given dignified, heroic supporting roles in such wartime pictures as *Bataan* (1943) and *Lifeboat* (1944), or in stories set outside of the combat zone, as seen in Dooley Wilson as Sam in *Casablanca* (1943). In stories set far from the conflict, the major studios again produced black cast films for the first time since *The Green Pastures* (1936). In 1943, MGM produced a noted musical with famous black stars, *Cabin in the Sky*. Yet progress was tentative at best. Only a few years later, *The Song of the South* (1946) combined live action and animation to retell the Uncle Remus stories.

Wartime saw the emergence of two black musical stars in Hollywood, Hazel Scott and Lena Horne. Horne was the first black female performer to be glamorized as a star in her own right, not playing opposite whites. Horne had already appeared in a number of early 1940s black cast shorts, such as *Bip Bam Boogie* and *Harlem Hot Shots*. Hazel Scott nearly always played herself, never a character role. Examples are *Rhapsody in Blue* (1945) and *The Heat's On* (1943), both in the Library's collection. In otherwise white movies, Horne and Scott, along with the Nicholas Brothers, Cab Calloway, and Dorothy Dandridge, were usually featured in isolated musical numbers.

Another musical form allowed black entertainers onto a different type of screen. Soundies were musical short subjects produced during the 1940s, each between two to five minutes in length and featuring a single song that gave the short its title. Soundies were for use in Panorams, jukebox style devices that were coin operated and about the size of television screens. Later, soundies were combined into quarter-hour films and made available for home rental and sale. Soundies combined musical and comic routines in a manner similar to short films; in fact many soundies were excerpts from longer works, and the Library has examples of both in its collection. Incredibly cheap and fast to produce because they avoided union regulations, over two thousand soundies were made during World War II.

Although regarded as not quite "respectable" as musical art, soundies recorded the performances of many outstanding artists, some three hundred of them featuring black performers. Soundies even became the refuge of white experimental filmmakers like Josef Berne and of Dudley Murphy, director of *Black and Tan* (1929) and *The Emperor Jones* (1933). In the 1950s, Snader Telescriptions—much like soundies but made for television—featured veteran soloists and groups in popular music standards; a few of these are also held by the Library.

Animated black caricature films in the Library's motion picture archive begin with the "Amos 'n' Andy" cartoons of the early 1930s and go through George Pal's animated puppet films of the 1940s: *Jasper and the Watermelons, Jasper and the Haunted House, Shoe Shine Jasper,* and *A Date with the Duke,* which combined puppets with live action of Duke Ellington playing his "Perfume Suite." The Warner Bros. cartoons that had mostly black characters were the "Inki" series, *Coal Black and de Sebben Dwarfs* (1943), with caricatures of Fats Waller and Stepin Fetchit as two of the dwarfs, and *Goldilocks and the Jivin' Bears* (1944), with Vivian Dandridge's voice on the soundtrack.

In the 1940s, Spencer Williams began to direct black cast films, and he became the decade's principal black director. Williams had wide experience in the industry and was well-known to audiences as an actor. After a foundation in stage acting, Williams had entered filmmaking as a technician for early sound films. He became a coauthor of scripts for Al Christie comedies, many of them based on the stories of Octavus Roy Cohen. Possessing multiple talents, Williams also acted in many black cast films in the 1930s, before adding directing to his repertoire. Williams eventually reached his widest audience in the early 1950s as Andy on the "Amos 'n' Andy" television series.

The Library's collection contains all of Williams's fictional films from the 1940s, most of which he not only directed but also wrote and performed in. Between 1941 and 1947 Williams, working under a number of corporate banners, directed *Go Down, Death!, The Blood of Jesus, Of One Blood, The Girl in Room 20, Beale Street Mama, Dirtie Gertie from Harlem, U.S.A., Jivin' in Be Bop,* and *Juke Joint*. Williams's efforts were hindered by low budgets that allowed for only minimal sets and photography, generally precluding time for retakes or careful work. Many of Williams's films reflect an interest in religious themes that were otherwise rare in black cast filmmaking. In 1991 *The Blood of Jesus* was chosen for the National Film Registry at the Library of Congress.

Dominating the production of black cast films from a commercial point of view after 1945 were independent white producers, including veterans of the 1930s. Most were individuals involved in the making of "quickie" productions on Hollywood's "poverty row." Ted Toddy, often using the corporate names Consolidated National Film Exchange or Dixie National Pictures, was one of the most prolific distributors of black films during the 1940s. He retitled and kept in release most of the Million Dollar Productions films.

By contrast, producer William Alexander was black. He organized Associated Producers of Negro Pictures in New York City, producing eight black cast features, both fiction and documentary, between 1946 and 1948. Among those held by the Library are *Jivin' in Be Bop* (1946) with Dizzy Gillespie, *That Man of Mine* (1947) with Ruby Dee, and *Souls of Sin* (1949) with Savannah Churchill and William Greaves. Vaudevillian Eddie Green founded the Sepia Art Picture Company in 1938, making shorts, and his work is represented in the Library's collection by his last film, *Mr. Adam's Bomb* (1948).

Low-budget "states rights" releases were distributed through a regional distribution system to small or rural theaters. Dewey Markham, who acquired the nickname "Pigmeat" while working in minstrel shows, starred in many shorts and features from 1938 on, and among his features in the Library's collection is *Junction 88*. Like many states rights releases, the precise date of *Junction 88* is unknown (probably between 1943 and 1948). Astor Pictures, an independent clearinghouse for pictures intended for the states rights trade, picked up low-budget films from various sources, including *Tall, Tan,*

and Terrific (1946), starring Mantan Moreland and Cab Calloway, which is in the Library's collections. Astor released a series of films starring the charismatic Louis Jordan at the height of his popularity as a musical entertainer. *Caldonia* (1945), a short, exploited Jordan's hit record of the same title and was followed by the features *Beware!* (1946), *Reet, Petite, and Gone* (1947), and *Look Out, Sister* (1948). An equally popular singer, Dusty ("Open the Door, Richard") Fletcher, appeared in such films as *Hi-de-ho* (1947) and *Killer Diller* (1948).

Jack Goldberg, another white independent producer of black films, founded Hollywood Pictures in 1945 and produced *Beale Street Mama* with Spencer Williams. The next year, Goldberg organized Herald Pictures to produce *Boy, What a Girl* (1946), *Sepia Cinderella* (1947), and *Miracle in Harlem* (1948), with Lincoln Perry, William Greaves, and Juanita Moore. The Library holds prints of all three titles. *Sepia Cinderella* is a model of the late 1940s black film: a lively musical, following the standard boy-meets-girl formula. The fact that it was intended for both black and white audiences is underlined by a guest interview with former child star Freddie Bartholomew in an integrated nightclub set where the concluding show takes place.

By the end of the 1940s, budgets for black motion pictures, although still limited, had grown significantly. Consolidating the gains made by Million Dollar Productions in the 1930s, black filmmaking achieved an aesthetic that was fully compatible with the classical Hollywood style. Simultaneous with the achievement of this quality, the third cycle of black cast filmmaking came to an end, owing to several factors. With the end of segregated theaters, black films had achieved sufficient quality and commercial success to move beyond a parallel, underground economy. Hollywood could no longer ignore the dramatization of black concerns, clearly both a palatable and a potentially profitable source of screen entertainment. As a result, major studios and producers adapted black themes in a resurgence of topical and sociological subject matter in the 1950s and 1960s. The advance of civil rights and the move toward integration turned the focus away from black cast films toward adopting these themes in Hollywood "social consciousness" films dealing with black issues. In this way, Hollywood absorbed for a time much of the drive that formerly fostered independent black cast filmmaking, reflecting a trend in race relations that would lead to many changes on the American scene.

CHAPTER NINE

THE CIVIL RIGHTS ERA

The collections of the Library of Congress provide an in-depth history of the twentieth-century civil rights movement. The work of individual activists, rights organizations, and jurists are well represented. Together the collections provide sources for the study of the struggle to obtain equal rights and opportunities for all people regardless of race, creed, sex, or religion.

INDIVIDUAL AND ORGANIZATIONAL INITIATIVES FOR EQUAL RIGHTS

During the civil rights era both the National Association for the Advancement of Colored People (MSS, records 1909–82) and the National Urban League (NUL, MSS, records 1909–85) became increasingly important vehicles for the advancement of civil rights among blacks in the United States. While the NUL tended to focus its programs on obtaining opportunities for blacks in employment and housing, the NAACP, moving forward on many fronts, concentrated its most forceful thrust in the effort to obtain equal protection before the law for all Americans. Association records in the Manuscript Division document its struggle for the abolition of segregation, discrimination, lynching, and other forms of racial oppression.

The NUL records consist of almost a million items from the headquarters and southern regional offices. The materials include correspondence, minutes of meetings, financial papers, speeches, reports, surveys, statistical data, NUL publications, and press releases relating to the programs and policies of the National Urban League and its affiliates. Subjects include community service, housing, industrial relations, public relations, research, vocational services, the training of black social workers, civil rights,

race relations, sit-in demonstrations, job placement, improvement of employment opportunities for black workers, urban renewal, housing,
medical care, fund-raising, and other league efforts in the field of social welfare.

Also with the NUL records are papers of Lester B. Granger, executive director from 1941 to
1960, and files relating to many others who
were active in the league and in the wider civil
rights arena, such as George Edmund Haynes,
Eugene K. Jones, Truman K. Gibson, George
Weaver, A. Philip Randolph, and Langston

Hughes. The Southern Regional Office records
(MSS, records 1912–79) include personal pa-
pers of the office's first director, Jesse O.
Thomas. Correspondents include Claude A.
Barnett, Mary McLeod Bethune, John Hope,
Benjamin E. Mays, Robert Russa Moton,
Forrester B. Washington, Monroe Work, and
Whitney Young. In addition to the two major
NUL collections, there are records relating to the
league in the Library's Carter G. Woodson pa-
pers (MSS, microfilm 1796–1933). The Prints and
Photographs Division holds NUL photographic

*Civil rights march on Washington, D.C., at the Lincoln Memorial, August 28, 1963. (U.S. News and World Report silver
gelatin photograph, PP. LC-U9–10360-23)*

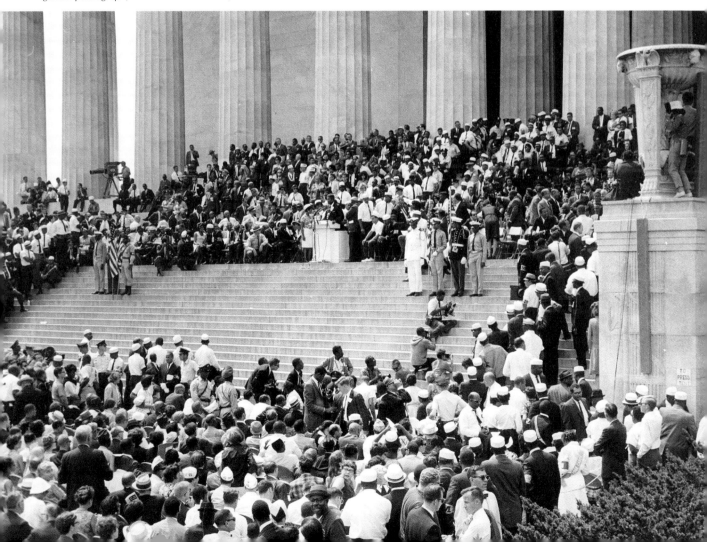

material, consisting of images depicting adult education and league activities and leaders (PP unprocessed).

Books on the National Urban League include Guichard Parris and Lester Brooks's *Blacks in the City: A History of the National Urban League* (Boston: Little, Brown, 1971; E185.5.N33P3), Nancy J. Weiss's *The National Urban League, 1910–1940* (New York: Oxford University Press, 1974; E185.5.N33W44), and the league's own *Black Americans and Public Policy: Perspectives of the National Urban League* (New York: The League, 1988; E185.86.N37 1988).

The NAACP collection of headquarters and Washington bureau records consists of two million items that provide source materials for the social history of black Americans in the second half of the twentieth century. Minutes of the board of directors, annual reports, office and administrative files, branch files, legal briefs, trial transcripts, congressional and legislative files, speeches, and copies of NAACP publications like the *Crisis* and the *Bulletin* make up the collection. The NAACP legal files provide a chronicle of civil rights cases tried before various courts, which led to the elimination of Jim Crow laws. Subjects addressed in the postwar administrative files include the Korean War, the Montgomery bus boycott led by Martin Luther King, Jr., freedom riders, the Little Rock Nine, sit-ins, and police brutality. Correspondence of NAACP officials such as Daisy Lampkin, Thurgood Marshall, Clarence Mitchell, Juanita Jackson Mitchell, Arthur and Joel Spingarn, Moorfield Storey, Constance Baker Motley, Walter White, Roy Wilkins, and Oswald G. Villard is in the collection. Photographs held in the Prints and Photographs Division include NAACP images of Roy Wilkins and other officials, materials relating to the Korean War, and scenes of protests and lynchings (PP unprocessed). Twelve cartoon drawings about lynching or antilynching legislation in the NAACP Collection (PP unprocessed, RR) include three by African-

American illustrator Cornelius Johnson. Films from the NAACP collection are in the Library's motion picture archive. Many NAACP recordings relating to conferences, meetings, and televised appearances by prominent African-Americans on programs such as "Face the Nation" and "Meet the Press" are available in the Library's Recorded Sound Reference Center.

Langston Hughes discusses NAACP history in *Fight For Freedom* (New York: Norton, 1962; E185.5.N276H8). Charles Flint Kellogg's *NAACP, A History of the National Association for the Advancement of Colored People* (Baltimore: Johns Hopkins Press, 1967; E185.5.N276 K4), Robert L. Zangrando's *The NAACP Crusade against Lynching, 1909–1950* (Philadelphia: Temple University Press, 1980; HV6457.Z36), Mark V. Tushnet's *The NAACP's Legal Strategy against Segregated Education, 1925–1950* (Chapel Hill: University of North Carolina Press, 1987; KF4155.T87 1987), and Minnie Finch's *The NAACP: Its Fight for Justice* (Metuchen, N.J.: Scarecrow, 1981; E185.5.N276F56) also cover the topic.

Personal papers of some of the individuals who worked closely with the NAACP are available as well: Moorfield Storey (MSS, papers, 1847–1930), the association's first president; Arthur Spingarn (MSS, papers, 1911–64), its third president; Roy Wilkins (MSS papers, 1938–77), executive director of the association for over forty years, from 1931 to 1977; and Nannie Helen Burroughs (MSS, papers 1900–1963), who served as a member of the NAACP board. Microfilm publications of papers relating to NAACP officials from other repositories include W. E. B. DuBois (MSS microfilm, 1803–1965) from originals at the University of Massachusetts at Amherst, Mary McLeod Bethune (MSS, microfilm 1923–42) from the Amistad Research Center, and the William Hastie Papers (MSS, microfilm 1916–76) reproduced from materials at Harvard University.

The papers of United States Supreme Court

Justice Thurgood Marshall (MSS, papers 1961– 91), which span the thirty-year period from 1961 to 1991, document his judicial career as an appellate court judge and solicitor general of the United States and his twenty-four-year tenure as Supreme Court justice. These papers along with other collections in the Manuscript Division—notably the records of the NAACP and the NAACP Legal Defense and Educational Fund, which document Marshall's earlier career as a civil rights lawyer and activist—bring together in the Library a record of a sixty-year career from before the time that Marshall was first admitted to argue cases before the Supreme Court through his tenure as a seasoned justice on that body.

The NAACP headquarters and Baltimore branch files during 1930s reflect Marshall's work, especially his legal efforts to desegregate the University of Maryland's graduate and professional schools. In 1936 Marshall became an assistant to Charles Hamilton Houston, the NAACP's special counsel, and when Houston retired two years later, Marshall succeeded him as the national organization's chief legal officer. In 1939 the NAACP founded its Legal Defense and Educational Fund to raise money to spearhead the organization's legal fight against discrimination. Marshall served as counsel and director of the fund from 1940 to 1961 and was responsible for hundreds of legal actions "to secure and protect full citizenship rights for Negroes, especially voting privileges, justice in criminal proceedings" and attempts to equalize public school expenditures for all children regardless of race.

Many of the records of the NAACP (MSS records, 1909–82) and the NAACP Legal Defense and Educational Fund (MSS records, 1915–68) reveal Marshall's grueling schedule of travel and meetings as well as his acute sense of humor even in the face of threats from whites and distrust by blacks. After the inauspicious beginning of the Texas primary case, Marshall re-

marked, on November 17, 1941: "All agreed that if we did not get another case started all of us would have to leave the U.S. and go live with Hitler or some other peace loving individual who would be less difficult than the Negroes in Texas who had put up the money for the case."

Marshall was so successful as a litigator that in 1946 the NAACP made him the thirty-first recipient of its coveted Spingarn Medal. Other distinguished Americans who have received this award include W. E. B. DuBois, James Weldon Johnson, Marian Anderson, Carter G. Woodson, George Washington Carver, Mary McLeod Bethune, William H. Hastie, Paul Robeson, Bill Cosby, Lena Horne, Duke Ellington, and Rosa Parks.

Marshall's long and successful career as a trial attorney culminated with the 1954 *Brown v. Board of Education of Topeka, Kansas* decision, the NAACP's key victory in the legal battle to dismantle segregation in the United States. In 1961, President John F. Kennedy appointed Marshall to the United States Court of Appeals for the Second Circuit. Four years later President Lyndon B. Johnson named him solicitor general of the United States and subsequently nominated him to the Supreme Court in 1967. Three-fourths of the Marshall papers relate to Marshall's work on the Supreme Court and most of the rest concern the period during which he was circuit judge. Only a small percentage deal with his tenure as solicitor general. About 80 percent of the material is composed of case files and related documents such as case summaries, docket books, hearing lists, orders, and journals. The materials are arranged chronologically usually by court term and include separate folders for opinions written by Marshall, memoranda between justices, and drafts of other justices' opinions.

Other files contain personal and official correspondence and administrative records. Personal correspondence files reflect Marshall's active involvement in professional, community, and fraternal organizations such as the National Bar Association, Alpha Phi Alpha fraternity, the Episcopal Church, the Boy Scouts, and the Masons. The files also contain hundreds of invitations asking Marshall to speak, receive awards and honors, attend conferences, and serve on boards and committees.

The Kenneth Bancroft Clark collection (MSS papers, 1936–76) demonstrates this social psychologist's concern with the psychology of racism, one that brought him into national prominence in the postwar era. Beginning in 1951 with a case in Charleston, South Carolina, Clark worked with Robert Carter, Thurgood Marshall, Jack Greenberg, and other NAACP Legal

Defense Fund attorneys to prepare cases that would eventually bring down the elaborate system of segregation in the South and other parts of the nation. In a series of trials, Clark became increasingly skilled in his presentations about racism before critical prosecutors.

Clark's papers, chiefly 1960–76, document his activities in New York as a university professor, president of the Metropolitan Applied Research Corporation, research director of the Northside Center for Child Development, author, and independent researcher and consultant whose findings were cited in the 1954 Supreme Court decision *Brown v. Board of Education*. His correspondence, speeches, reports,

Thurgood Marshall with Lyndon Baines Johnson, who is signing the Civil Rights Bill, 1968. (U.S. News and World Report silver gelatin photograph, PP. LC-U9–18985-13a)

research notes, book chapters, manuscripts, book reviews, clippings, articles, photographs, printed matter, and tape recordings relate largely to his work in the field of race relations, segregation, discrimination, urban ghettos, black youth programs such as HARYOU (Harlem Youth Opportunities Unlimited), and related social issues. Other material relating to both Clark and civil rights is included in the papers of the American Psychological Association (MSS, records 1912–72).

The NAACP Legal Defense and Educational Fund (MSS, records 1935–80), created by the NAACP in 1939, originally shared some members of the board of directors but later became totally independent. The administrative and legal files of this organization document a systematic series of court battles designed to eradicate discrimination and segregation in the United States. The records, which include some materials relating to the *Brown* case, consist of correspondence, printed matter, legal files, and subject files concerning issues such as desegregation, discrimination, riots, crime, education, fair employment practices, housing, the Ku Klux Klan, labor, police brutality, racial tensions, sit-in demonstrations, discrimination in the military, and segregated transportation. Some of Thurgood Marshall's and Robert Carter's subject files, speeches, and correspondence files are found here. Correspondents include Josephine Baker, Kenneth Clark, Constance B. Motley, Clarence Mitchell, Spottswood Robinson, Walter White, and Roy Wilkins.

Other important civil rights activists and their organizations are also represented in the Manuscript Division collections. The Brotherhood of Sleeping Car Porters (MSS, records 1920–68) was founded by labor leader Asa Philip Randolph in 1925. The records consist of general correspondence, subject files, legal and financial papers, printed matter, and miscellany relating to the operation of the union, chiefly for the period from 1950 to 1968. They include some personal papers of the brotherhood's founder, A. Philip Randolph, and internal papers and files of some of its principal officers. The records document the activities of the union in the areas of civil rights and equal employment opportunity. Some of the correspondence is with labor unions representing dining car employees, locomotive firemen, and railway clerks and with officials of the American Federation of Labor-Congress of Industrial Organizations (AFL-CIO). Records relating to women's auxiliaries of the union and to the work of railroad maids are also included in this collection. Correspondents include Julian Bond, James Farmer, Martin Luther King, Jr., Floyd B. McKissick, Thurgood Marshall, Tom Mboya, Adam Clayton Powell, Jr., George Meany, Bayard Rustin, Walter Reuther, Paul Robeson, Malcolm X, Mary McLeod Bethune, Jackie Robinson, Joseph L. Rauh, Arthur B. Spingarn, Walter White, Roy Wilkins, and Whitney Young.

Writings on the Brotherhood of Sleeping Car Porters include *Tearing Down the Color Bar: A Documentary History and Analysis of the Brotherhood of Sleeping Car Porters* (New York: Columbia University Press, 1989; HD6515.R362B768 1989), edited by Joseph F. Wilson, and *The Brotherhood of Sleeping Car Porters* (New York: Harper & Brothers, 1946; HD6515.R36B83 1946a) by Brailsford Brazeal. Jack Santino's *Miles of Smiles, Years of Struggle: Stories of Black Pullman Porters* (Urbana: University of Illinois Press, 1989; HD6515.R36S26 1989) was made into a film (1982) of the same title, available in the Library's motion picture archive.

Some of the A. Philip Randolph papers (MSS, papers 1909–79) for the civil rights period relate to the operation of the Brotherhood of Sleeping Car Porters, leadership of the March on Washington for Jobs and Freedom in 1963, efforts to establish a permanent federal Committee on

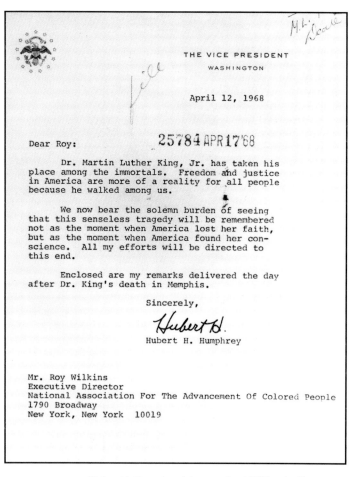

THE VICE PRESIDENT
WASHINGTON

April 12, 1968

25784 APR17'68

Dear Roy:

Dr. Martin Luther King, Jr. has taken his place among the immortals. Freedom and justice in America are more of a reality for all people because he walked among us.

We now bear the solemn burden of seeing that this senseless tragedy will be remembered not as the moment when America lost her faith, but as the moment when America found her conscience. All my efforts will be directed to this end.

Enclosed are my remarks delivered the day after Dr. King's death in Memphis.

Sincerely,

Hubert H.

Hubert H. Humphrey

Mr. Roy Wilkins
Executive Director
National Association For The Advancement Of Colored People
1790 Broadway
New York, New York 10019

Hubert H. Humphrey's letter to Roy Wilkins, April 12, 1968, speaks of the "senseless tragedy" of Martin Luther King, Jr.'s death. (NAACP collection, MSS)

Fair Employment Practices, participation in the White House Conference to Fulfill These Rights, support of the Pan-African movement, and involvement in the planning for various civil rights demonstrations and protests. The collection consists of family papers, general correspondence, subject files, legal papers, speeches and writings, and biographical material. Correspondents include Dwight D. Eisenhower, Hubert H. Humphrey, Lyndon B. Johnson, John F. Kennedy, Rayford W. Logan, Chandler Owen, Eleanor Roosevelt, Wyatt T. Walker, and Harry Truman. A microfilm edition of records relating to Truman's President's Committee on Civil Rights (MSS, microfilm 1946–48), reproduced from materials at the Truman Library in Independence, Missouri, is also available in the Manuscript Division.

The papers of Bayard Rustin (MSS, papers 1937–87) show in action a civil rights strategist who advocated nonviolence and passive resistance. Rustin worked closely with Randolph and other civil rights leaders, including Martin Luther King, Jr., during the 1957 Montgomery, Alabama, bus boycott. He assisted Randolph in the coordination of the practical details for the 1963 March on Washington. His papers relate to the march and to antiwar movements, nuclear weapons protests, school desegregation efforts, the eradication of anti-Semitism, support of African independence, promotion of civil rights, and labor movement activities. Photodocumentation of the August 28, 1963, March on Washington includes images of Rustin and a souvenir portfolio, originally published by the National Urban League, with press releases, handbills, and leaflets (PP lot 10049). The photo archives of *U.S. News and World Report*, also in the Prints and Photographs Division, contains images of the march itself, its preparation, and its aftermath.

Civil rights activists Martin Luther King, Jr., and Roy Wilkins both appeared on "Meet the Press" in televised programs documented in the transcripts and in the papers of radio and television producer Lawrence Spivak (MSS papers, 1927–73). Videotape copies of nearly every "Meet the Press" television program and tape recordings of the radio programs are held in the Motion Picture, Broadcasting, and Recorded Sound Division. Photographs document their appearances (PP lots 13025, 13026). Civil rights is a frequent topic. Spivak's papers also cover a variety of aspects of the civil rights movement.

Records relating to King's murder are included in the United States Federal Bureau of Investigation, Martin L. King Assassination Investigation files (MSS, records 1967–78). This collection consists of FBI records released under the Freedom of Information Act relating to the congressional investigation of the assassination of King. The copy deposited for copyright for King's "I Have a Dream" speech, given at the March on Washington in 1963, is in the Miscellaneous Manuscript Collection MSS, various dates). For photographs of King, the photo archives of *U.S. News and World Report* (PP) are again an especially rich collection.

The Leadership Conference on Civil Rights (LCCR, MSS, records 1952–90), organized in 1949, is a coalition of more than one hundred national civil rights, religious, labor, civic, professional, and fraternal organizations. The records reflect its efforts to bring about legislative and executive measures to ensure full civil rights protection for all Americans regardless of race. The LCCR collection consists of general and legislative correspondence, administrative and subject files, financial papers, organizational files, affiliate group records, government agency correspondence, newspaper clippings, recordings, and printed matter. A few of the component organizations of the Leadership Conference are the African Methodist Episcopal Church, Alpha Kappa Alpha Sorority, Omega Psi Phi Fraternity, National Medical Association, National Council of Jewish Women, National Council of Negro Women, Actors Equity, NAACP, National Organization for Women, Southern Christian Leadership Conference, National Baptist Convention, and National Catholic Conference for Interracial Justice.

Original records of the interracial civil rights advocacy organization, the Southern Regional Council (MSS records 1944–68), are at Atlanta University, and a 225-reel microfilm copy is available in the Library's Manuscript Reading Room. From its origins as the Commission on Interracial Cooperation in 1944, the Southern Regional Council has gathered data and provided financial support to help confront social and economic problems in the postwar South. Correspondence, administrative and reading files, reports, publications, articles, and clippings relating to subjects such as human relations, labor, voter registration and education, women's issues, urban planning, crime and corrections, public education, and community organization make up the collection.

The Center for National Policy Review, a nonpartisan civil rights advocacy group established in 1970 at Catholic University in Washington, D.C., was directed by attorney William L. Taylor, who, with his staff, monitored the efforts of government agencies to enforce the antidiscrimination laws of the 1960s. The center's records (CNPR, MSS, records 1971–86), about sixty thousand items, provide analyses of the civil rights performances of federal and state government agencies during the Nixon, Ford, Carter, and Reagan presidential administrations. The collection consists of reports, publications, studies, clippings, articles, and correspondence relating to civil rights issues studied by the staff, such as employment, transportation, school desegregation, law enforcement, voting rights, capital punishment, judicial and political nominations, legislation, and litigation.

Established in 1942 and originally called the Committee on Racial Equality, the Congress of Racial Equality (CORE) began as an interracial organization committed to the strategy of nonviolent direct action to achieve equal opportunity and access for people of all races. It initially directed its protests against discrimination in public accommodations, but its emphasis later changed to discrimination in employment and housing. By the 1960s CORE's membership included a national body and over one hundred affiliated local groups who participated in free-dom rides on buses in efforts to desegregate public transportation, voter registration proj-ects, sit-ins, and sponsorship of grass-roots political action groups like the Mississippi Freedom Democratic party. James L. Farmer became the national director of CORE in 1961 and Floyd B. McKissick assumed that position in 1966. Records of the Congress of Racial Equality (CORE, MSS, microfilm 1941–68), most dating from 1959 to 1964, have been filmed from originals in the State Historical Society of Wis-consin in Madison and the Martin Luther King, Jr., Center for Nonviolent Social Change in Atlanta. The records include correspondence of the organization's officers, operational rec-ords of the national office and its affiliates, reports, press releases, clippings, pamphlets, publications and copies of the organization's newsletter, the *CORE-lator*, 1947–67.

Several studies available on the congress are August Meier and Elliott Rudwick's *CORE: A Study in the Civil Rights Movement, 1942–1968* (Urbana: University of Illinois Press, 1975; E185.61.M516 1975), Inge Powell Bell's *CORE and the Strategy of Nonviolence* (New York: Random House, 1968; E185.61B37), and James Farmer's *Freedom, When?* (New York: Random House, 1966; E185.61.F19).

In 1960, after four black students from North Carolina Agricultural and Technical College at Greensboro refused to leave a segregated lunch counter, it seemed that students from all over the country traveled south to "sit-in" or held sympathetic protests in other regions for the purpose of hastening the desegregation of all public facilities. Officially named the Student Non-violent Coordinating Committee, SNCC—called "Snick"—was established in 1960 to co-ordinate the student protest movement. Lead-ers of the organization included Marion Barry, John Lewis, H. Rap Brown, James Forman,

and Stokely Carmichael. Under Carmichael's leadership, the organization began to move away from its nonviolent stance and espouse a concept called "black power." The leaders of the organization also began to organize voter education and registration drives, farmers' co-operatives, and aided the work of the Missis-sippi Freedom Democratic Party and other po-litical organizations. The committee established bail funds and freedom schools and monitored developments in the newly independent Afri-can nations. Records from SNCC's Atlanta, New York, and Washington, D.C., offices (SNCC, MSS microfilm 1959–72) are reproduced from originals at the Martin Luther King Center for Nonviolent Social Change and include corre-spondence, clippings, press releases, financial reports, field reports, and administrative and subject files.

The Student Nonviolent Coordinating Com-mittee has spawned a variety of publications, songs, histories, biographies, and poetry. How-ard Zinn's *SNCC: The New Abolitionists* (Boston: Beacon Press, 1964; E185.61.Z49) was the first history to appear. Other works include Cleve-land Sellers's *The River of No Return: The Autobi-ography of a Black Militant and the Life and Death of SNCC* (Jackson: University Press of Mississippi, 1990; E185.97.S44A3 1990), Emily Stoper's *The Student Nonviolent Coordinating Committee: The Growth of Radicalism in a Civil Rights Organiza-tion* (Brooklyn, N.Y.: Carlson Publishing, 1989; E185.61.S876 1989), and Clayborne Carson's *In Struggle: SNCC and the Black Awakening of the 1960s* (Cambridge, Mass.: Harvard University Press, 1981; E185.92C37 1981). Other works include Elizabeth Sutherland Martinez's com-pilation *Letters from Mississippi* (New York: McGraw-Hill, 1965; E185.61.M363), and SNCC's own *Freedom School Poetry* (Atlanta: SNCC, 1965; PS591.N4S8).

Other collections document the work of individuals in various aspects of the civil rights struggle. For example, Fannie Lou Hamer, who, after working for many years as a share-cropper, became an outspoken leader in the southern civil rights movement, was the leader of the Mississippi Freedom Democratic party. Her papers (MSS, microfilm 1966–78), repro-duced from originals at the Amistad Research Center, document her work with Mississippi politics, the Freedom Farm Corporation, the Delta Ministry, Mississippians United to Elect Negro Candidates, the National Council of Ne-gro Women, and Delta Opportunities Cor-poration, relating to voter registration drives, political campaigns, the Poor People's Cam-paign, and civil rights initiatives throughout the South.

The efforts black Americans made in opening the doors of educational opportunity are appar-ent in such documents as the papers of the third president of Tuskegee Institute, Frederick D. Patterson (MSS, papers 1861–1988). The Ray-ford W. Logan collection (MSS, papers 1926–80) documents Logan's struggle to eradicate social and educational barriers based on race. Best known as a historian and a professor at Howard University, Rayford Logan was also active in political matters for much of his life. The same is true of historian Lorenzo J. Greene (MSS, papers 1913–89) who taught for many years at Lincoln University in Missouri. Though his academic work was in the area of African-American history, his papers demonstrate that he was also a strong lobbyist for the social and political rights of black Americans. He worked with state groups such as the Missouri Asso-ciation for Social Welfare, the Missouri Advi-sory Commission, and the Missouri Council of Churches and national organizations like the National Urban League and the National Asso-ciation for the Advancement of Colored People. Greene conducted an extensive study on "De-segregation of Public Schools in Missouri, 1954–59" for the United States Civil Rights Commis-sion and worked with the Missouri legislature on a program to introduce black history in pub-lic schools. Writings and speeches of educator and clubwoman Mary Church Terrell (MSS, mi-crofilm 1851–1962) document her work in com-bating both racism and sexism. She was espe-cially active in the effort to desegregate public facilities in the District of Columbia in the 1950s. Gladys B. Sherrerd's *Mary Church Ter-rell—Respectable Person* (Baltimore: Human Re-lations Press, 1959; E185.97.T47S48) focuses primarily on Terrell's efforts to desegregate Thompson's Restaurants in Washington, D.C.

The papers of two well known political fig-ures, Patricia Roberts Harris (MSS, papers 1950–83) and Senator Edward W. Brooke (MSS, papers 1962–78) chronicle the efforts of black Americans to move into the center of the politi-cal arena. Harris, the first black woman to serve at the Cabinet level, worked as secretary of housing and urban development and secretary of health, education, and welfare (later called Health and Human Services) during the Carter administration. Brooke was the first black to serve as a U.S. senator since the Reconstruction period.

Joseph L. Rauh (MSS, papers 1934–85), a law-yer, civil libertarian, and civil rights activist, was a cofounder of the Americans for Demo-cratic Action in 1947. He served as general counsel for the Leadership Conference on Civil Rights and also worked for the Brotherhood of Sleeping Car Porters. Most of the legal cases represented in his papers pertain to civil rights, government security measures, and labor dis-putes. The Manuscript Division holds papers of many well-known jurists who heard important civil rights cases, such as Supreme Court Jus-tices William O. Douglas (MSS, papers 1801–1980), Earl Warren (MSS, papers 1864–1974),

William Brennan (MSS, papers 1956–80), Felix Frankfurter (MSS, microfilm 1864–1966), Hugo Black (MSS, papers 1883–1976), and Robert H. Jackson (MSS, papers 1853–1974), as well as those of Thurgood Marshall (MSS, papers 1961–91) discussed above.

Biographies and memoirs of individual civil rights activists also add to the depth of information on the period. Examples include Roy Wilkins's memoir, written with Tom Mathews, called *Standing Fast* (New York: Viking, 1982; E185.97.W69A37 1982); James Farmer's *Lay Bare the Heart: An Autobiography of the Civil Rights Movement* (New York: Arbor House, c1985; E185.97.F37A35 1985); Sheyann Webb and Rachel Nelson's *Selma, Lord, Selma: Girlhood Memories of the Civil Rights Days as Told to Frank Sikora* (University, Ala.: University of Alabama Press, 1980; F334.S4W4); Ralph Abernathy's *And the Walls Came Tumbling Down: An Autobiography* (New York: Harper & Row, 1989; E185.97.A13A3 1989), James Forman's *The Making of Black Revolutionaries: A Personal Account* (New York: Macmillan, 1972; E185.97.F715A3); and Daisy Bates's *The Long Shadow of Little Rock* (New York: David McKay, [1962]; F419.L7B3).

Jackie Robinson, the black man who helped break down the barriers to blacks in major league baseball, is one figure among those who appear in several collections detailing desegregation in the area of sports. The NAACP records (MSS, records 1909–82) include clippings and correspondence relating to Robinson and others. There is also information about Robinson and the Negro baseball leagues in the collections of sportswriter Arthur William Mann (MSS, papers 1901–62) and Brooklyn Dodgers' coach Branch Rickey (MSS, papers 1904–65). Mann is the author of *The Jackie Robinson Story* (New York: F. J. Low Co., [1950]; GV865.R6 M3).

The sports arena has been an important facet of the civil rights struggle. Lenwood Davis compiled the bibliography *Black Athletes in the United States: A Bibliography of Books, Articles, Autobiographies, and Biographies on Black Professional Athletes, 1800–1981* (Westport, Conn.: Greenwood, 1981; Z7515.U5D38). Arthur Ashe, himself an award-winning tennis professional, wrote one of the most comprehensive histories of blacks in sports, *A Hard Road to Glory: A History of the African-American Athlete* (New York: Warner Books, 1988; 3 vols. GV583.A74 1988–). Other important volumes on the subject include James A. Page, *Black Olympian Medalists* (Englewood, Colo.: Libraries Unlimited, 1991; GV697.A1P284 1991), *Pioneers of Black Sport: The Early Days of the Black Professional Athlete in Baseball, Basketball, Boxing, and Football* (New York: Dodd, Mead & Co., 1974; GV697.A1C47) by Ocania Chalk; John Holway's *Voices from the Great Black Baseball Leagues* (New York: Dodd, Mead & Co., 1975; V697.A1C47), and Edwin B. Henderson, *The Black Athlete: Emergence and Arrival* (New York: Publishers Co., and the Association for the Study of Negro Life and History, 1968; GV697.A1H38).

In addition to individual pamphlets, books, and periodicals on civil rights, a wealth of information is available in the Library's Microform Reading Room. *Facts on Film* (Nashville: Southern Education Reporting Service, 1954–74; MicRR 03721) presents an indexed collection of documents used by the Southern Education Research Service as it provided regional coverage of news about the campaign to desegregate the nation's schools. Local news stories form the core of a collection that includes copies of public laws, court cases, newspaper clippings, and editorial cartoons. The materials deal not only with public schools but also with desegregation of parks, libraries, other institutions, and public accommodations.

The Mississippi Oral History Collection (Sanford, N.C.: Microfilming Corp. of America, 1981; MicRR 82/302, *New York Times Oral History Guide* no. 3) is part of the New York Times Oral History Program, a series begun at Columbia

University during the 1950s and later funded through the New York Times. Historian Allan Nevins realized that a program to preserve the views and actions of notable figures in American history by recording and transcribing their views would prove valuable to future historians. The Mississippi Oral History Collection was designed specifically to preserve the memory of the civil rights struggle in Mississippi during the twentieth century. The collection contains memoirs of Fannie Lou Hamer; Charles Evers, former mayor of Fayette, Mississippi, a candidate for governor of Mississippi, and brother of slain civil rights worker Medgar Evers; Aaron Henry, a pharmacist and longtime NAACP official and worker; Ruby Magee, a participant in the voter registration campaigns throughout the state; and others. The memoirs vary in length, with some equivalent in size to a full-length book. *The Stanford University Project South Oral History Collection* (Stanford, Calif.: Stanford University Archives, 1965; MicRR microfiche 2479, *New York Times Oral History Guide* no. 1; AI3.07) consists of transcripts of recorded interviews with civil rights workers and participants in the Freedom Summer of 1964 and the Meredith March of 1966.

For a general look at the civil rights period, useful sources are Anthony Lewis's *Portrait of a Decade: The Second American Revolution* (New York: Random House, [1964]; E185.61.L52 1964); John Hope Franklin's *The Negro in Twentieth Century America: A Reader on the Struggle for Civil Rights* (New York: Vintage Books, [1967]; E185.61.F79); and *Eyes on the Prize: Civil Rights Reader* (New York: Viking, 1991; E185.61.E95 1991), containing documents, speeches, and "firsthand accounts from the black freedom struggle, 1954–1990." The reader is based on the book by Juan Williams, *Eyes on the Prize: America's Civil Rights Years, 1954–69* (New York: Viking Press, 1987; KF4757.W52 1987). Copies of the television miniseries with the same title,

aired in 1987, are available in the Motion Picture and Television Reading Room. *Documentary History of the Modern Civil Rights Movement* (New York: Greenwood Press, 1992; E185.61.D64 1992), edited by Peter B. Levy, contains Fannie Lou Hamer's testimony in 1964 before the Democratic National Convention Credentials Committee, Martin Luther King's sermons, and an extensive reading list on the civil rights struggle. The CBS News Reference Book, *Civil Rights: A Current Guide to the People, Organizations, and Events* (New York: Bowker, 1970; JC599.U5A3468), by A. John Adams and Joan M. Burke, is useful in identifying activists and organizations. But bibliographies provide the primary entrée to the plethora of publications relating to the civil rights movement.

Daniel Williams's *Eight Negro Bibliographies* (New York: Kraus Reprint, 1970; Z1361.N39W54) focuses on "The Freedom Rides," "The Southern Students' Protest Movement," "The University of Mississippi and James H. Meredith," and "Martin Luther King, Jr., 1929–1968," one of the first extensive bibliographies to appear after King's death. Other short bibliographies include "Martin Luther King, Jr.: A Selected List of References" (*Library of Congress Information Bulletin* [LCIB], December 23, 1985, pp. 381–88; MRR Ref) and "March on Washington," (*LCIB*, August 29, 1988, pp. 351–55, MRR Ref), both by Ardie Myers.

The establishment of the Martin Luther King holiday in 1983, with national celebrations effective in 1986, led to the publication of bibliographies designed to meet the need for books, articles, speeches, plays, skits, and other activities associated with King and the civil rights movement. Several full-length bibliographies are available, such as *A Guide to Research on Martin Luther King, Jr., and the Modern Freedom Struggle* (Stanford, Calif.: Stanford University Libraries, 1989; Z1361.N39G82 1989), compiled by the editors of the Martin Luther

King Papers project at Stanford University. The volume covers the period after King's death as well. Also useful is *A Testament of Hope: The Essential Writings of Martin Luther King, Jr.*, edited by James Melvin Washington (San Franciso: Harper & Row, c1986; E185.97K5A25 1986). In addition, King's own published books add perspective on his philosophy and thought. They include *Stride Toward Freedom: The Montgomery Story* (New York: Harper, 1958; E185.89.T8K5), *The Trumpet of Conscience* (New York: Harper & Row, 1968; E185.97.K5 1968), a compilation of five radio talks, and *Why We Can't Wait* (New York: Harper & Row, 1964; E185.61K54), which explains why he believed that his nonviolent direct action plan was imperative.

Over three hundred published books and articles in the Library relate to King, including biographies such as Lawrence Reddick's *Crusader without Violence* (New York: Harper, [1959]; E185.97.K5R4); David Lewis's *King: A Critical Biography* (London: Allen Lane, 1970; E185.97.K5L45); David Garrow's *Bearing the Cross: Martin Luther King, Jr., and the Southern Christian Leadership Conference* (New York: Morrow, c1986; E185.97.K5G36 1986); and Taylor Branch's *Parting the Waters: America in the King Years, 1954–63* (New York: Simon and Schuster, 1988; E185.61.B7914 1988).

Two significant oral histories document movement activities. *Voices of Freedom: An Oral History of the Civil Rights Movement from the 1950s through the 1980s* (New York: Bantam Books, 1990; E185.61.H224 1990), compiled by Henry Hampton and Steve Fayer with Sarah Flynn, is based on one thousand transcribed interviews recorded from the "Eyes on the Prize" television documentary project. Howell Raines's *My Soul Is Rested: Movement Days in the Deep South Remembered* (New York: Putnam, 1977; E185.61. R235 1977) provides a record of early interviews with participants in the movement.

Books on the civil rights organizations also richly document the period. Aldon Morris's *Origins of the Civil Rights Movement: Black Communities Organizing for Change* (New York: Free Press, 1984; E185.61.M845 1984) gives a historical account of participating organizations. Morris describes the civil rights activists, the individuals who were involved in the attempts to desegregate buses, restaurants, and other public accommodations. The National Council of Negro Women (NCNW) features in *Women in the Civil Rights Movement: Trailblazers and Torchbearers, 1941–1965*, edited by Vicki L. Crawford, Jacqueline A. Rouse, and Barbara Woods (Brooklyn, N.Y.: Carlson Publishers, 1990; E185.86.B543 1990). It chronicles black women's leadership in the struggle for civil rights. Robert Penn Warren's *Who Speaks for the Negro?* (New York: Random House, 1965; E185.61.W22) is an early record of conversations Warren had with James Farmer, Whitney Young, Stokely Carmichael, Ralph Ellison, and other blacks with differing political views.

Campaigns and movements of the civil rights era are chronicled in such works as Charles Fager's *Selma, 1965: The March That Changed the South* (2d ed., Boston: Beacon Press, 1985; F334.S4F34) and *Selma's Peacemaker: Ralph Smeltzer and Civil Rights Mediation* (Philadelphia: Temple University Press, 1992; F334.S4L66 1987), by Stephen L. Longenecker. *At the River I Stand: Memphis, the 1968 Strike, and Martin Luther King* (Memphis: B&W Books, 1985; HD5325.S2572 1968 M46 1985) is Joan Beifuss's recounting of the events that occurred just before King's death. A listing of books about specific marches may be obtained through searches of the Library's printed and automated catalogs.

Recorded speeches and broadcasts of many civil rights leaders can be heard in the Library's Recorded Sound Reference Center, and a number of films relating to civil rights are available in the Motion Picture and Television Reading Room. A few of the many recordings are

Malcolm X's *Ballots or Bullets* (LP First Amendment Records 100), *Dr. Martin Luther King, Jr.—Speeches and Sermons* (RYA 9128), and a King broadcast of June 3, 1967, by Minnesota Public Radio, dealing with the struggle of blacks to overcome poverty and achieve equal rights.

A map that appeared in the May 11, 1958, issue of the *Washington Post* showing the status of segregated and desegregated schools in the southern and border states is one of several newspaper maps preserved in the Geography and Map Division's uncataloged Titled Collection recording civil rights activities of the late 1950s and the early 1960s. This map is filed under the category "United States—South—Education." Similarly, two Associated Press (AP) newsfeature maps show the desegregated school districts in 1960 and 1961. Another AP newsfeature map filed under "United States—South—Social Problems" shows the routes of ten freedom rides and the associated sites of violence or arrests that occurred in 1961.

Numerous places throughout the United States, many of them associated with a particular black person or a black-related settlement feature, used the word *Nigger* as part of their names. The U.S. Geological Survey topographic quadrangles provide a source for tracing the changing sensitivities to place-names, particularly those with negative ethnic connotations. In the early 1960s there was increased protest against such derogatory names, and Secretary of Interior Stuart Udall recommended to the U.S. Board on Geographic Names, a federal board responsible for determining the proper place-name usage within the federal government, to reconsider its policy on derogatory names. Subsequently, the board decided to change all place-names containing the word *Nigger* to *Negro*. As new maps were prepared for areas including such features, the new name changes could be noted. A peak in Jackson County, Oregon, called "Nigger Ben Hill,"

named after the operator of a blacksmith shop in a nearby mining camp, was changed to "Negro Ben Hill." Near Austin, Texas, there is a feature that was originally named "Niggerhead Hill." Recent suggestions propose that the name be changed from "Negrohead Hill" (as it appears on the 1966 edition of the 1/24,000 Travis Peak, Texas, quadrangle) to a name commemorating a prominent black Texan.

As a result of the civil rights movement, academic geographers and cartographers have shown an increased awareness of African-American related topics when publishing historical, thematic, and regional atlases. An early example that has served as a model, is *Atlas of the Historical Geography of the United States* (New York: American Geographical Society; Washington: Carnegie Institution, 1932; G1201.S1P3 1932), compiled by Charles O. Paullin and John K. Wright. One of the most recent historical atlases covering the nation's history as a whole, the National Geographic Society's *Historical Atlas of the United States* (Washington: National Geographic Society, 1988; G1201.S1N3 1988) is comprehensive in its treatment of black history. For the Reconstruction and Booker T. Washington eras, there are maps showing lynchings, black institutions of higher education, and the distribution of blacks in 1890 as percentages of total population. Maps showing distribution of the black population in 1980, cities electing black mayors, civil rights occurrences, and black population and property ownership in Washington, D.C., are also included.

Thematic atlases, particularly those focusing on the cultural geography of the United States, portray the distribution of various ethnic groups. *This Remarkable Continent: An Atlas of United States and Canadian Society and Culture* (College Station: Texas A&M University Press, 1982; G1201.E1T5 1982), edited by John F. Rooney, Wilbur Zelinsky, and Dean R. Louder, includes a chapter on ethnicity, with maps focusing on topics such as the distribution of African-Americans, black migration patterns, blacks in Charleston, Richmond, Philadelphia, and Lexington, Kentucky, and all-black towns in the United States. Another atlas, *We the People: An Atlas of America's Ethnic Diversity* (New York: Macmillan, 1988; G1201.E1A4 1988), edited by James P. Allen and Eugene J. Turner, devotes a chapter to "People of African Origin," and a new publication, *The Historical and Cultural Atlas of African Americans* (New York: Macmillan, 1991; E185.A8 1991), compiled by Molefi K. Asante and Mark T. Mattson, focuses entirely on black history and culture.

The distribution of blacks at the state level is recorded in *North Carolina Atlas: Portrait of a Changing Southern State* (Chapel Hill: University of North Carolina Press, 1975; G1300.N7 1975) edited by James W. Clay, Douglas M. Orr, Jr., and Alfred W. Stuart. *The Atlas of Georgia* (Athens: University of Georgia, Institute of Community and Area Development, 1986; G1310.H6 1986), edited by Thomas W. Hodler and Howard A. Schretter, and *Atlas of Florida* (Tallahassee: Florida State University Foundation, 1981; G1315.A83 1981), edited by Edward A. Fernald, not only include general distribution maps, both current and retrospective, but they also include maps and graphs pertaining to black population increase, birth and death rates, age and sex composition, urban and rural percentages, employment, public school enrollment, and even automobile ownership. The relevant mapping in other atlases, however, is not as extensive. For example, *Atlas of Alabama* (University, Ala.: University of Alabama Press, 1973; G1340.L5 1973) edited by Neal G. Lineback and Charles T. Traylor, *Atlas of Mississippi* (Jackson: University Press of Mississippi, 1974; G1345.C7 1974), edited by Ralph D. Cross and Robert W. Wales, *Atlas of Michigan* (Lansing: Michigan State University, 1977; G1410.A8 1977), edited

by Lawrence M. Sommers, and *The Atlas of Pennsylvania* (Philadelphia: Temple University Press, 1989; G1260.A86 1989), edited by David J. Cuff and William J. Young, each include only one or two maps showing the general distribution of blacks within the state.

The black population of individual cities has also been mapped in several published atlases. Twenty of the nation's largest cities are included in *A Comparative Atlas of America's Great Cities: Twenty Metropolitan Regions* (Minneapolis: University of Minnesota Press, 1976; G1204.A1A3 1976), edited by Ronald Abler and John S. Adams. Each chapter, devoted to a single city, has a section entitled "The People," which includes a small-scale map showing the distribution of black inhabitants as a percentage of the total population. In contrast to this general treatment, Nathan Kantrowitz's *Negro and Puerto Rican Populations of New York City in the Twentieth Century* (New York: American Geographical Society, 1969; G1254.N4K3 1969) focuses on a single metropolitan area and includes maps showing the distribution of the black population for each census year from 1910 to 1960. From this sequence, the expanding concentrations are quite obvious. In the mid-1970s, the U.S. Bureau of the Census published a series of small atlases entitled *Urban Atlas, Tract Data for Standard Metropolitan Statistical Areas* (GM) for the sixty-five largest metropolitan areas in the United States. Based on population and housing data derived from the 1970 census, each atlas contains twelve maps covering broad classes of demographic and housing characteristics. In each atlas, one map shows the black population as a percentage of the total population.

Several interesting single maps have been prepared for the Los Angeles metropolitan area by the staff and students of the Geography Department at California State University, Northridge. *Ethnic Patterns in Los Angeles, 1980* (Northridge: University of California, Depart-

THE CIVIL RIGHTS ERA

ment of Geography, 1989; GM uncataloged), compiled by Theresa Clemen, Eugene J. Turner, and James P. Allen, provides a series of maps of the city showing the distribution of predominant and secondary ethnic groups. Los Angeles's population is composed of many ethnic groups, but the large concentration of blacks in the south central portion—including Watts—of the city is particularly evident. An earlier map prepared by Turner, *Life in Los Angeles* (Northridge: California State University, 1977; G4364.L8E8625 1971.T8 ACSM 77–13), which was designed to portray the quality of life (including proportion of white population, urban stresses, unemployment, and affluence) in the city, uses a sequence of color-coded faces as symbols. A black face with a frown is applied to the Watts area.

BLACK MILITANCY

Despite efforts on the part of black leaders to wage a nonviolent civil rights movement, urban riots erupted in 1965 in the predominantly black neighborhood of Los Angeles known as Watts. For the next few years, outbreaks spread to other urban centers—Newark, Detroit, Philadelphia, Washington, D.C., and Milwaukee. *Cities under Siege: An Anatomy of the Ghetto Riots, 1964–1968* (New York: Basic Books, 1971; E185.615.B56), edited by David Boesel and Peter H. Rossi, includes articles on individual riots, with one by August Meier and Elliott Rudwick called "Black Violence in the Twentieth Century: A Study in Rhetoric and Retaliation." Other general studies of riots are *Urban Race Riots* (New York: Garland Publishing, 1991; F574.D49N485 1991), Arthur Waskow's *From Race Riot to Sit-Ins, 1919 and the 1960s: A Study in the Connections between Conflict and Violence* (Garden City: Doubleday, 1966; E185.61.W24), and Allen Grimshaw's *Racial Vio-*

lence in the United States (Chicago: Aldine Publishing Co., 1969; E185.61.G89).

In *Rivers of Blood, Years of Darkness* (New York: Bantam Books, 1967; F869.L8C66) Robert E. Conot identifies the patterns of segregation in urban areas and racial division as leading factors causing racial violence. Nathan Cohen's *The Los Angeles Riot: A Socio-Psychological Study* (New York: Praeger, [1970]; F869.L8L58) examines attitudes of blacks about the riot and provides a "white reaction study." The *Testimony before the Governor's Commission on the Watts Riots* (Los Angeles: State Office, 1965; F869.L8C15, vols. 3–18) documents the State of California's attempts to probe the reasons for the riot, and *The Los Angeles Riots* (New York: Arno Press and the New York Times, 1969; F869.L8F62), compiled by Robert M. Fogelson, presents an anthology of reports and studies, including critiques of the Governor's Commission on the Los Angeles riots and Bayard Rustin's article "The Watts 'Manifesto' and the McCone Report."

Examinations of the Detroit riots include Van Gordon Sauter and Burleigh Hines's *Nightmare in Detroit: A Rebellion and Its Victims* (Chicago: Regnery, 1968; F574.D4S18) and Ray C. Rist's *The Quest for Autonomy: A Socio-Historical Study of Black Revolt in Detroit* (Los Angeles: Center for Afro-American Studies, UCLA, 1972; F574.D4R57). Other investigations include one edited by Tom Hayden, *Rebellion in Newark: Official Violence and Ghetto Response* (New York: Vintage Books, 1967; F144.N6H27) and Ron Porambo's *No Cause for Indictment: An Autopsy of Newark* (New York: Holt, Rinehart and Winston, 1971; F144.N6P6). An extensive examination of the causes of violence nationwide is offered in the *United States National Advisory Commission on Civil Disorders Report* (New York: Dutton, 1968; HV6477.A56 1968) popularly known as the Kerner Report (and published by the U.S. Government Printing Office in 1968 with the title *U.S.*

"Today you have a new generation of black people who have come on the scene, who have become disenchanted with the entire system, who have become disillusioned over the system, and who are ready now and willing to do something about it."
—Malcolm X—

Malcolm X (1925–1965). Poster, published by the Militant Publishing Association, copyright 1969. (PP POS 6-US no. 824. LC-USZ62–107760)

Kerner Commission Report). Materials relating to the Kerner Commission are available in the Manuscript Division in the microfilm edition of "Civil Rights during the Johnson Administration" (MSS, microfilm 1963–69), reproduced from originals at the Lyndon Baines Johnson Library in Austin, Texas.

After the Selma March in 1965 there was a change in the racial climate. Although Martin Luther King was still alive, some of the younger activists became less willing to be guided by the nonviolent tactics promoted by King's Southern Christian Leadership Conference. When James Meredith began his walk to Mississippi to demonstrate the changed conditions of the South and was shot just outside of Memphis, the march resumed a few days later with a large group of civil rights marchers. On the march Stokely Carmichael led some participants in shouts for "black power." The shouts marked the establishment of various black militant groups who demanded immediate revolutionary changes in the racial status quo "by any means necessary."

Several books provide a history of these militant tactics and philosophies during the 1960s. August Meier and Elliott Rudwick's *Black Protest in the Sixties* (Chicago: Quadrangle Books, 1970; E185.615.M36 1970) presents a collection of articles that originally appeared in the *New York Times*, which report occurrences from the sit-ins in Greensboro, North Carolina, in 1960, to the marches in Birmingham and Selma. Progressively these articles show the radicalization of the movement owing to unemployment and poverty and to the impact of the Black Muslims. Four hundred riots from 1964 to 1969 fostered the development of black power groups such as the Black Panther party.

The Black Revolt: The Civil Rights Movement, Ghetto Uprisings, and Separatism (Englewood Cliffs, N.J.: Prentice-Hall, 1971; E185.615.G48), edited by James A. Geschwender, brings together analytical essays exploring the black revolt, the civil rights movement, black power, ghetto uprisings, and separatism. Allen J. Matuson's "From Civil Rights to Black Power: The Case of SNCC, 1960–1966," is included in this anthology. Other articles appear in *Conflict and Competition: Studies in the Recent Black Protest Movement* (Belmont, Calif.: Wadsworth Publishing Co., 1970; E185.61.B782), edited by John H. Bracey, Jr., August Meier, and Elliott Rudwick. Robert H. Brisbane's *Black Activism: Racial Revolution in the U.S., 1954–1970* (Valley Forge, Pa.: Judson Press, 1974; E185.615.B72) includes essays on Malcolm X, black power, and revolutionary black nationalism. Stokely Carmichael and Charles V. Hamilton's *Black Power: The Politics of Liberation in America* (New York: Random House, 1967; E185.615.C32) discusses the meaning of the slogan and the purpose of the movement it inspired.

Major figures in the black power movement—Ron Karenga, the founder of the organization US; H. Rap Brown, Stokely Carmichael's successor at SNCC; Eldridge Cleaver, of the Black Panther party, and many more—are introduced in James Haskins's *Profiles in Black Power* (Garden City, N.Y.: Doubleday, 1972; E185.96.H36). Compilations of speeches and writings demonstrate more fully the black power advocates' philosophies. Among these are *The Black Panther Leaders Speak: Huey P. Newton, Bobby Seale, Eldridge Cleaver, and Company Speak Out through the Black Panther Party's Official Newspaper* (Metuchen, N.J.: Scarecrow Press, 1976; E185.615.B546), edited by G. Louis Heath, and *Eldridge Cleaver: Post-Prison Writings and Speeches* (New York: Random House, 1967; E185.615.C63), edited by Robert Scheer.

The activities and thinking of militant or extremist African-American groups is documented in a collection of four thousand pamphlets by suspected radicals gathered by the House Un-American Activities Committee. Arranged by title, it contains postwar publications of organizations such as the American Negro Labor Congress, the Black Panthers, and the National Negro Congress as well as items by Malcolm X, Paul Robeson, and Henry Winston, and twenty-six items filed under the heading "Negro." The Radical Pamphlet Collection includes two thousand pamphlets and other ephemera arranged by author or organization. Materials relating to the National Negro Congress include a 1946 petition to the United Nations urging elimination of political, economic, and social discrimination against blacks in the United States. For the period 1949 to 1950 there are three addresses by Paul Robeson on peace and labor issues. Also included is a 1951 brochure by the National Committee to Defend W. E. B. DuBois, who was indicted with four associates of the Peace Information Center for circulating information about peace activities. A pamphlet by DuBois entitled *I Take My Stand for Peace* (New York: Masses & Mainstream, 1951) is illustrated by a profile drawing of DuBois by black artist Charles White.

SOCIAL AND ECONOMIC CONDITIONS

Increased activism in racial protests is reflected in pictorial materials of the period. Illustrations for an article in the 1958 edition of the *Encyclopaedia Britannica* yearbook (AE5.E363), donated to the Library by the publishers, include five photographs of members of the Prayer Pilgrimage for Freedom at the Lincoln Memorial in Washington, D.C., in 1957; a boycott at a chain store in Tuskegee, Alabama; President Eisenhower with Orval E. Faubus, governor of Arkansas; white supremacist John Kaspar, addressing a crowd in Camden, New Jersey; and the entrance to Central High School in Little Rock, Arkansas, at the time the school was being integrated (PP lot 8718 RR).

Photographs of African-Americans during the Kennedy administration, 1961–63, are avail-

Girls with federal escort on their way to enter Central High School, Little Rock, Arkansas, October 1957. (U.S. News and World Report silver gelatin photograph, PP. LC-U9–1054-E-9)

James Meredith, Oxford, Mississippi, 1962. (U.S. News and World Report silver gelatin photograph, PP. LC-US9–8556-24)

able in a collection assembled by Magnum Photos, Inc. Two photographs cover the 1963 March on Washington, and two show 1963 civil rights demonstrations in Birmingham, Alabama. Single photographs depict Martin Luther King, Jr., blacks in surplus food lines, a black militant bookstore, segregated benches, evictions of black voters, and a freedom riders' bus. There are also some scenes of blacks watching the John F. Kennedy funeral procession and passing by the bier in the Capitol rotunda (PP lot 10499-12 RR).

One of the most useful collections in the Prints and Photographs Division for locating images of blacks during the post-World War II period is the photo morgue of *U.S. News and World Report*, which begins its coverage of nationally important issues and events in 1955. Photographs document black capitalism, the Black Caucus, black churches, segregation, integration, riots, civil disorders, Black Muslims, Little Rock segregation riots, voting rights, registration, and demonstrations outside the White House. The March on Washington, the Poor Peoples March, employment and unemployment, the black middle class, CORE, and the Black Panthers are also subjects of these news photos. Individuals pictured include Malcolm X, Thurgood Marshall, Adam Clayton Powell, Jr., Benjamin O. Davis, Sr., Benjamin O. Davis, Jr., Andrew Young, Whitney Young, John Lewis, James Meredith, Julian Bond, Martin L. King, Sr., Martin L. King, Jr., James Farmer, and Bayard Rustin.

In 1931 two New York newspapers, the *World* and the *Evening Telegram*, merged to form the *New York World-Telegram and Sun*. In 1967 the Library of Congress acquired the newspaper's complete picture files. International in scope, the approximately 1.5 million items in this photograph morgue date principally from the late 1920s to 1966. The bulk of the collection is a biographical file arranged alphabetically by

surname. A topical file contains images relating to politics, transportation, housing, and entertainment. The photographs are dated, captioned, and credited to the owners of the reproduction rights.

Civil rights activists and black militants whose photographs are found in the *New York World* morgue include Martin Luther King, Jr., Ralph D. Abernathy, Shirley Chisholm, Ralph Bunche, Julian Bond, Medgar Evers, Malcolm X, Benjamin O. Davis, Sr., Benjamin O. Davis, Jr., Frankie Freeman, Walter Fauntroy, James Farmer, Mary McLeod Bethune, and Stokely Carmichael. Some artist-activists and other figures of note represented in the collection are James Baldwin, Ralph Ellison, Maya Angelou, Bill Cosby, Cassius Clay, Pearl Bailey, Louis "Satchmo" Armstrong, Julian "Cannonball" Adderly, Wilt Chamberlain, Chubby Checker, Duke Ellington, Ella Fitzgerald, Miles Davis, Sammy Davis, Jr., Billy Eckstine, Althea Gibson, and Berry Gordy, Jr.

Selected political propaganda posters published between 1965 and 1978 were collected by Gary Yanker for his book *Over 1,000 Contemporary Political Posters* (London: Studio Vista, 1972; D44.Y36 1972). Seventy-three posters dealing with African-American themes are among the four thousand items now at the Library of Congress in the Yanker Poster Collection. These include posters published by the NAACP, the National Urban League, the Socialist Workers party, and the Black Panther party. Topics addressed are social and political concerns, such as education, employment opportunities, equal justice, health care, political participation, feminism, gay rights, integration and improved race relations, and African-American art. These images are available on videodisc in the Prints and Photographs Reading Room. Produced for the emancipation centennial, the Crawford Studio collection consists of twenty-one color postcards portraying "notable Negroes" in various fields, including educators, politicians, athletes, and activists, with a biographical sketch of each (PP lot 10502).

In June 1957, photographer Toni Frissell produced twelve black-and-white photographs of black workers picketing the Investment Cafeteria on K Street in Northwest Washington and twelve more of people relaxing at the Tidal Basin (PP lot 12433). Photographs made by Milton Rogovin show storefront churches in Buffalo, New York, as well as portraits of two black women during the 1960s (PP PH-Rogovin nos. 1–10). Selections from Rogovin's later series of people at work portray industrial workers on the job site and at home (PP PH-Rogovin nos. 19–23).

Art photographers of the civil rights era turned their cameras to blacks as subject matter. A bibliography of black photographers in the postwar era by Deborah Willis-Thomas is entitled *An Illustrated Bio-Bibliography of Black Photog-raphers, 1940–1988* (New York: Garland Publishers, 1989; TR139.W55 1989). Roy DeCarava—a black photographer best known for his collaboration with Langston Hughes on *The Sweet Flypaper of Life* (New York: Hill and Wang, 1967; F128.9.N3D4 1967), an illustrated poem about daily life in Harlem—was the first African-American photographer to receive a Guggenheim Fellowship. He began his photographic career in 1946. The Library has a copy of his untitled portfolio containing images of children playing on streets and in a park, studies of people dancing or listening to music, portraits of well-known people like Paul Robeson, and a view of rowhouses at night (PP UNPROCESSED).

William Christenberry made photographs of his native Alabama between 1979 and 1981, including them in his 1981 portfolio of dye transfer color photographs entitled "Ten Southern Photographs." Seven of the photographs show the definite imprint the black presence—and

*Integrated lunch counter, Louisville, Kentucky, June 1963. (*U.S. News and World Report, *silver gelatin print, PP. LC-U9– 9936-12)*

absence—has made on the Deep South. Made in Akron, Demopolis, and Havanna Junction, they include a tree full of martin houses made of gourds, and a cotton gin and cotton warehouses, all deserted, some with solitary black men observing the photographer. All these photographs comment on the former large numbers of blacks and their absence now, a testimony to the urban migration of the twentieth century (PP PH-Christenberry, W., Portfolio).

Jim Goldberg's series "The Rich and Poor of San Francisco, 1978–1983," depicts poor blacks in their homes with their own handwritten comments on the photo margins (PP PH-Goldberg, J., Portfolio). Among the photographs of victims of the 1972 flood in Harrisburg, Pennsylvania, by photographer Terry Husebye are five portraits of blacks (PP PH-A Husebye, T., nos. 2, 6, 8, 10, 11). Richmond Jones includes a black male among his portraits of mentally retarded residents at a Southbury, Connecticut, training school, in his work titled "Friends of Mine, 1975–76" (PP PH-Jones, R., Portfolio). Jerome Liebling's 1976 portfolio (PP PH Liebling, Portfolio) portrays a single black male child, with worn-out shoes. Selections from Danny Lyon's work from 1962 to 1979 include photographs of black males as part of an urban motorcycle gang (PP PH Lyon, D., Portfolio).

In the mid-1960s, photographer Billy E. Barnes produced a group of twenty-six images with captions documenting poverty in North Carolina. Eleven of those images show poor blacks in various small rural communities and urban slums. Some images depict protest marches (PP repro. no. LC-USZ62-61859), sanitation problems, or public signs designating segregated facilities. An image of Sunset Theatre & Cafe, made somewhere in northeast North Carolina in the summer of 1965, depicts an abandoned modern cinderblock building with entrances marked "white" and "colored" (PP lot 10988).

Homes of prominent African-Americans,

Angela Davis. Poster (offset) of the New York Committee to Free Angela Davis, ca. 1971. (Yanker Poster Collection, PP POS G US no. 733. LC-USZ62–107759)

historically black colleges and university facilities, and buildings designed and built by African-Americans are documented in the Architecture, Design, and Engineering (ADE) collections, indexed under "black architecture." The Historic American Buildings Survey, for example, documented a portion of the historic district of Sweet Auburn, the commercial heart of black Atlanta from 1880 to 1950. Documentation consists, in part, of thirty-six measured drawings and sixty-four photographs relating to the historic district (PP GA-1170), the Herndon Building and Atlanta Life (PP GA-1170-A), the Odd Fellows Building and Auditorium (PP GA-1170-B), and street facades on Auburn Avenue (PP GA-1170-C, PP GA-1170-C[SR]).

ARTISTIC EXPRESSION AND THE AFRICAN-AMERICAN COMMUNITY

During the 1940s and 1950s, African-American writers came into their own. The black writers who received public recognition demonstrated a general level of competence and achievement that could not be denied, and soon blacks began to win literary prizes. In 1940 Richard Wright became a best-selling author with the publication of *Native Son* (New York: Harper & Brothers, 1940; PZ3.W9352 Nat). Margaret Walker won the Yale Younger Poets Award for her poem "For My People" in 1942. Gwendolyn Brooks became the first African-American to win a Pulitzer Prize, when she won this prestigious award for her book of poems *Annie Allen* (New York: Harper, 1949; PS3503.R7244A7 Rare Bk). James Baldwin attained critical acclaim for his *Go Tell It on the Mountain* (New York: Knopf, 1953; PS3503.A5527G6). Ralph Ellison's *Invisible Man* (New York: Random House, [1952]; PS3555.L625I5 1952), published in 1952, received the praise of critics for its complexity and use of metaphor.

The Rare Book and Special Collections Division routinely collects first editions of a significant number of African-American twentieth-century literary figures, including Maya Angelou, James Baldwin, Gwendolyn Brooks, Ralph Ellison, Robert Hayden, Chester Himes, Langston Hughes, Claude McKay, Toni Morrison, Alice Walker, and Richard Wright. Several books that deal with African-American writers in the postwar era are *Black American Writers: Bibliograpical Essays* (New York: St. Martin's Press, 1978; 2 vols. PS153.N5B55), edited by M. Thomas Inge, Maurice Duke, and Jackson R. Bryer. The second volume of *Black American*

Writers contains essays on Richard Wright, Ralph Ellison, James Baldwin, and Amiri Baraka. *African American Writers* (New York: C. Scribner's Sons, 1991; PS153.N5A344 1990), a critical anthology, contains biographical essays, selected bibliographies of the authors' works, and biographical and critical writings about them. Among the writers discussed are Sterling Brown, Robert Hayden, and Gwendolyn Brooks. Another work is *Afro-American Writers after 1955: Dramatists and Prose Writers* (Detroit, Mich.: Gale Research Co., c1985; PS153.N5A39 1985). Craig Hansen Werner's *Black American Women Novelists: An Annotated Bibliography* (Pasadena, Calif.: Salem Press, 1989; Z1229.N39W47 1989) indexes periodical articles, books, and some newspaper articles that concern novels of Alice Walker, Gloria Naylor, Toni Morrison, and Paule Marshall.

Works such as Mod Mekkawi's *Toni Morrison: A Bibliography* (Washington: Founders Graduate Library, Howard University Libraries, 1986; Z8595.5.M44 1986) and Therman O'Daniel's *James Baldwin, a Critical Evaluation* (Washington: Howard University Press, 1977; PS3552.A.45Z84) focus on a particular individual. Other surveys and anthologies that include a number of writers are Darwin T. Turner's *Black American Literature: Essays, Poetry, Fiction, Drama* (Columbus, Ohio: Merrill, 1970; PS508.N3T77); Arthur Paul Davis's *From the Dark Tower: Afro-American Writers (1900–1960)* (Washington: Howard University Press, 1974; PS153.N5D33); and James A. Emanuel, compiler, *Dark Symphony: Negro Literature in America* (New York: Free Press, 1968; PS508.N3E4).

Afro-American Poets since 1955 (Detroit: Gale Research Co., PS153.N5A38 1985), edited by Trudier Harris and Thadious M. Davis, and *Black American Poets between Worlds, 1940–1960* (Knoxville: University of Tennessee Press, c1986; PS153.N5B535 1986) provide information about the work of poets Margaret Walker, Melvin B. Tolson, Dudley Randall, Margaret

Danner, and others. Both Gwendolyn Brooks (1985–86) and Robert Hayden (1976–78) served as Library of Congress consultants in poetry. Records of the Library of Congress Poetry and Literary Functions (MSS, records 1934–89) include correspondence with Brooks and Hayden as well as Maya Angelou, Melvin Tolson, Sterling Brown, Ralph Ellison, Ernest Gaines, Alex Haley, and Margaret Walker. *Poetry's Catbird Seat: The Consultantship in Poetry in the English Language at the Library of Congress, 1937–1987* (Washington: Library of Congress, 1988; Z733.U6M38 1988) includes information about Brooks and Hayden as well as other black poets.

The Recorded Sound Reference Center holds many records and tapes of Harlem Renaissance and postwar writers. For example, Arna Bontemps's recording *Anthology of Negro Poetry* (Folkways, 1954, 1961) includes Langston Hughes, Sterling Brown, Claude McKay, Countee Cullen, Gwendolyn Brooks, and Margaret Walker reading their own poems. Another, *Anthology of Negro Poets in the U.S.A.: 200 Years* (Folkways, 196?), is read in its entirety by Bontemps. Langston Hughes is probably the most popular of the Harlem Renaissance writers represented in the Library's recorded sound collections. His recordings include *The Best of Simple* (Folkways, 1969), *Simple* (Caedmon, 1968), *The Dream Keeper* (Folkways, 1955), *The First Album of Jazz for Children* (Folkways, 1961), *The Glory of Negro History* (Folkways, 1955), *Jericho-Jim Crow* (Folkways, 1964), and others. Films relating to the lives of some black writers are available in the Library's motion picture archives.

Black art is the subject of several bibliographies, including Lynn Moody Igoe's comprehensive *250 Years of Afro-American Art: An Annotated Bibliography* (New York: R.R. Bowker Co., 1981; Z5956.A47I38). Yale University art historian Robert Farris Thompson's *Flash of the Spirit: African and Afro-American Art and Philosophy* (New York: Random House, 1983; E29.N3T48 1983), focuses on the continuity of African traditions in art forms created by American blacks. Thompson's students are also making important contributions to understanding African-American art, among them Richard J. Powell, who compiled two books to accompany the major exhibitions he curated, *The Blues Aesthetic: Black Culture and Modernism* (Washington: Washington Project for the Arts, 1989; NX512.3.A35P68 1989) and *Homecoming: The Art and Life of William H. Johnson* with an introduction by Martin Puryear (Washington: National Museum of American Art, Smithsonian Institution; New York: Rizzoli, 1991; ND237.J73P69 1991).

Another contribution to the study of African-American arts and crafts by a student of Robert Farris Thompson is Maude Southwell Wahlman's "Art of Afro-American Quilt-making: Origins, Development, and Significance" (Ph.D. dissertation, Yale University, 1980; MicRR AAC 8300050). Many other recent dissertations can be located in *Dissertation Abstracts International* (Z5053.D57) and by electronic retrieval in the Library's Main Reading Room.

Since World War II, art exhibitions have produced the most important body of literature on African-American art. Many of these exhibits have toured the country, spreading the awareness of black artists' contributions beyond large cultural centers. Mainstream institutions have mounted such major shows, accompanied by scholarly catalogs, as the Metropolitan Museum of Art's *Harlem on My Mind: Cultural Capital of Black America, 1900–1968* (New York: Random House, [1969]; F128.68.H3S3). A groundbreaking bicentennial exhibit publication by David Driskell with Leonard Simon, *Two Centuries of Black American Art* ([Los Angeles]: Los Angeles County Museum of Art; New York: Knopf, distributed by Random House, 1976; N6538.N5D74), looks at the diaspora of black art and extends its view to fine arts, crafts, and architecture. In 1978 the Cleveland Museum of Art produced *The Afro-American Tradition in Decorative Arts* (Cleveland: Cleveland, Museum of Art, 1978; N6538.N5V57) by John Michael Vlach.

Examples from the 1980s include *Sharing Traditions: Five Black Artists in Nineteenth-Century America: From the Collections of the National Museum of American Art* (Washington: Published for the Museum by the Smithsonian Institution Press, 1985; N6538.N5N34 1985) by Lynda Roscoe Hartigan; *Against the Odds: African-American Artists and the Harmon Foundation* (Newark, N.J.: Newark Museum, 1989; N6538.N5R49 1989) by Gary Reynolds and Beryl J. Wright; and *Black Art Ancestral Legacy: The African Impulse in African-American Art* (Dallas: Dallas Museum of Art, 1989; N6538.N5B525 1989) by the Dallas Museum of Art. Another notable exhibition catalog, *Before Freedom Came: African-American Life in the Antebellum South* (Richmond: Museum of the Confederacy; Charlottesville: University Press of Virginia, 1991; E443.B44 1991), was edited by Edward D. C. Campbell, Jr., with Kym S. Rice.

Both large and small institutions have devoted resources to shows and monographs about black American artists. Examples are *Martin Puryear* (Chicago: Art Institute of Chicago, Thames and Hudson, 1991; NB237.P84A4 1991), by Neal David Benezra with an essay by Robert Storr, and *Memory and Metaphor: The Art of Romare Bearden, 1940–1987* (New York: Studio Museum in Harlem, Oxford University Press, 1991; N6537.B4A4 1991), with essays by Mary Schmidt Campbell and Sharon F. Patton and an introduction by Kinshasha Holman Conwill. The Studio Museum in Harlem is one of a number of smaller institutions generating exhibitions.

Artist and writer Adrian Piper exhibited and wrote a catalog for her work *Adrian Piper, Reflections, 1967–1987* (New York: Alternative Museum, 1987; MLCM87/7794⟨N⟩), which was shown at the Alternative Museum in New York.

In 1988, the pioneering Kenkeleba Gallery in New York published a catalog of its exhibition *Three Masters: Eldzier Cortor, Hughie Lee-Smith, Archibald John Motley, Jr.* (New York: Kenkeleba Gallery, 1988; ND238.N5T48 1988). The next year the gallery published *Norman Lewis: From the Harlem Renaissance to Abstraction* (New York: Kenkeleba Gallery, 1989; ND237.L624A4 1989). Regional studies that focus on local artists are *East-West, Contemporary American Art* (Los Angeles: California Afro-American Museum, 1984; N6512.P38 1984), with an essay by Sharon F. Patton; *Fifteen under Forty: Paintings by Young New York State Black Artists* (Albany: Division of the Humanities and the Arts, 1970; ND238.N5F5); *Who'd a Thought It: Improvisation in African-American Quiltmaking* (San Francisco: San Francisco Craft and Folk Art Museum, 1987; NK9112.L46 1987) by Eli Leon; and Bernadine B. Proctor's *Black Art in Louisiana* (Lafayette, La.: Published by the Center for Louisiana Studies, University of Southwestern Louisiana, 1989; N6538.N5P76 1989).

Some exhibition publications provide studies in race and ethnic relations, most notably *Bridges and Boundaries: African Americans and American Jews* (New York: George Braziller, 1992; E185.61.B825 1992) by Jack Salzman with Adina Back and Gretchen Sorin and *Facing History: The Black Image in American Art, 1710–1940* (Washington: Corcoran Gallery of Art, 1990; N8232.M44 1990) by Guy McElroy. *The Image of the Black in Western Art* (New York: Morrow, 1979; 19 vols. N8232.I46) devotes its fourth volume, by Hugh Honour, to African-Americans.

The vast periodical literature on African-American art and artists is indexed by the *Art Bibliographies Modern* (Z5935.L64) and *Art Index* (Z5937.A78). One of the most influential of a number of serials devoted to black art in the Library's holdings is *International Review of African American Arts* (NX164.N4B5), edited by Samella Lewis, issued four to six times a year. Its bio-

The Family. *Color etching and aquatint, 1976, by Romare Bearden (1914–1988). Courtesy of the Estate of Romare Bearden. (PP XX B368 D3)*

graphical sketches of African-American paint- ers and crafts people whose work is featured by galleries are particularly helpful for the profiles they provide of emerging artists.

Building on the New Deal-era initiative of collecting fine prints that deal with black themes by both black and nonblack artists, the Library's Prints and Photographs Division has acquired examples by Romare Bearden, John Dowell, Marion A. Epting, Sam Gilliam, Rich- ard Howard Hunt, Jacob Lawrence, Norma Glo- ria Morgan, Elizabeth Olds, and Charles Wil- bert White.

Complementing the Library's holdings of original works of art on paper are a few short books on black printmakers, including *Prints by American Negro Artists* (Los Angeles: Cultural Exchange Center, 1965; NE508.R6) edited by T. V. Roelof-Lanner; *Contemporary Print Images: Works by Afro-American Artists from the Brandy- wine Workshop* (Washington: SITES, 1986; NE539.3.A35C6 1986); and Leslie King- Hammond's *Black Printmakers and the W.P.A.* (Bronx, N.Y.: Lehman College Art Gallery, City University of New York, 1989; NE539.3.A35K56 1989).

In *The Art of Rock: Posters from Presley to Punk* (New York: Abbeville Press, 1987; ML3534.G78 1987), Paul D. Grushkin discusses the evolution of artwork and design used in printing posters for black music from about 1950 to the mid- 1980s. Posters for early movies, band and singer tours, music festivals, urban blues, gospel and ethnic music, and individual performers like James Brown are considered. Copies of many of the posters discussed in the book are in the Li- brary's Prints and Photographs Division.

A source of portraiture of black entertainers is the performing arts section of the Poster Col- lection, which has approximately seven thou- sand circus, minstrel, magic, vaudeville, bur- lesque, variety, legitimate theater, and specialty act performance posters. Celebrities include

Aretha Franklin, Sarah Vaughan, Sly and the Family Stone, and Louis Armstrong.

The postwar era brought about interesting developments in the African-American music materials collected by the Music Division. With the end of World War II, interest in black music increased, both within and without the black community. Jazz, gospel, and blues continued to flourish, dominating the world of popular music. Black churches decided to revise their hymnals and issue new ones. The African Methodist Episcopal Church published *The Richard Allen A.M.E. Hymnal* (Philadelphia: A.M.E. Book Concern, 1946; M2127.A3R5), and the African Methodist Episcopal Zion Church issued *The A.M.E. Zion Hymnal* (Charlotte, N.C.: A.M.E. Zion Publishing House, 1957; M2131.A35H9).

Serious composers like Howard Swanson found a new public for their works. Swanson had composed *The Negro Speaks of Rivers* (New York: Leeds Music Corp., 1949; M1621.S) to a text by Langston Hughes in 1942, but it re- mained unpublished until Marian Anderson performed it at a recital in New York in 1949. In 1952, his *Short Symphony* (New York: Wein- traub, 1952; M1001.S98S5 1951a) received the New York Music Critics Circle Award.

Louis Armstrong, long a favorite entertainer and jazz trumpeter, wrote his autobiography, *Satchmo: My Life in New Orleans* (New York: Prentice-Hall, 1954; ML419.A75A3). The great jazz composer Duke Ellington also wrote one, *Music Is My Mistress* (Garden City, N.Y.: Dou- bleday, 1973; ML410.E44A3), but as for all jazz musicians, their recordings are their best testi- monial. The Valburn Collection in the Library's recorded sound archives includes eleven thou- sand recordings of jazz giant Duke Ellington on disc. Films, videos, clippings, photos, concert programs, and related magazines also docu- ment Ellington's career. Almost every known commercially released Ellington recording is represented in its original format in the Valburn Collection, which encompasses everything from Ellington's first recording, "It's Gonna Be a Cold, Cold Winter," made in late 1924, to a 16mm color film of the composer's funeral in 1974.

Among the female blues singers who performed most often in the contexts of vaudeville and southern tent shows was pioneer singer Ma Rainey, whose biography by Sandra Lieb, *Mother of the Blues* (Amherst: University of Massachusetts Press, 1981; ML420.R274L5), details her performances throughout the rural South.

A WNEW AM 1130 poster (color offset) pictures Ella Fitzgerald, 1985. (PP POS US A01 162, C size. LC-USZC4–2422)

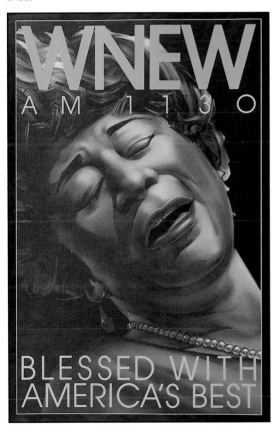

Chris Albertson's *Bessie* (New York: Stein and Day, 1972; ML420.S667A7) chronicles the life of Bessie Smith, "Empress of the Blues." Ethel Waters represents another tradition of performing, described in her autobiography *His Eye Is on the Sparrow* (Garden City: Doubleday, 1951; ML420.W24A3). An important social document, the autobiography begins, "I never was a child," a statement that describes the condition of many who grew up in the urban North at the turn of the century. Waters remained in the United States, but Josephine Baker, slightly younger, left for Paris in the 1920s. *Jazz Cleopatra: Josephine Baker in Her Time* (New York: Doubleday, 1989; GV1785.B3R66 1989) by Phillis Rose tells of her life.

Later generations of women singers were seen as jazz rather than blues figures. Billie Holiday, perhaps the archetypal figure of this group, wrote about her own life in *Lady Sings the Blues* (Garden City: Doubleday, 1956; ML420.H58A3 Case). *Billie's Blues: The Billie Holiday Story, 1933–1959* (New York: DaCapo, c1975; ML420.H58C5 1975c) is an informative and accurate biography by John Chilton.

The *New Orleans Jazz Oral History Collection of Tulane University* (Glen Rock, N.J.: Microfilming Corporation of America, 1978; MicRR 49702) consists of printed transcripts of individual interviews with jazz personalities John Handy, Lillian Armstrong, Omar Simeon, Sing Miller, and others, covering social as well as professional concerns of the musicians. The Newport and Monterrey Jazz Festivals and thousands of other live jazz performances are included in the Voice of America collection available in the Recorded Sound Reference Center. The collection also includes hundreds of interviews with Duke Ellington, Louis Armstrong, Nat King Cole, and other jazz musicians. A new appreciation of black folk music developed after the war, based on a more searching analysis of its rhythmic and melodic patterns. Harold Courlander's *Negro*

Folk Music, U.S.A. (New York: Columbia University Press, 1963; ML3556.C7) is an example of this approach. The complicated interrelationships between the various forms of postwar popular music such as rhythm and blues and rock 'n' roll can best be compared in Music Division books like Arnold Shaw's *Dictionary of American Pop/Rock* (New York: Schirmer Books, 1982; ML102.P66S5 1982).

Not since the antislavery movement before the Civil War did songs play such a prominent role in a political and social movement as they did in the civil rights era. "We Shall Overcome" (New York: Ludlow Music, 1963; M1978.D4S Case)—which was usually sung in a circle with participants holding crossed hands—played a significant role in encouraging the demonstrators and creating a sense of fellowship. Guy and Candie Carawan, of the Highlander Folk School, gathered the songs into two collections: *We Shall Overcome! Songs of the Southern Freedom Movement* (New York: Oak Publications, 1963; M1629.C2W4) and *Freedom Is a Constant Struggle: Songs of the Freedom Movement* (New York: Oak Publications, 1968; M1629.C2F7). Songs were also published in a magazine called *Broadside* published in Los Angeles (ML3544.B76, nos. 17, 30, 46, 51, 57).

With the civil rights movement in the 1960s came the popularity of soul music, the gospel-influenced rhythm-and-blues songs directed to multiracial audiences. Their titles and lyrics often expressed black pride. James Brown's "Say It Loud, I'm Black and I'm Proud" (King 1047) was one hit number that exemplified this quality, as did Nina Simone's "To Be Young, Gifted, and Black" (RCA APL1–1788) and Aretha Franklin's "Respect" (Atlantic LP 8139). "Respect" was originally recorded by its composer, Otis Redding (Atlantic 81762–1). B. Lee Cooper's *A Resource Guide to Themes in Contemporary American Song Lyrics, 1950–1985* (Westport, Conn.: Greenwood Press, 1986; ML156.4.P6C66

1986) includes a chapter entitled "Race Relations" that provides both an essay and a short topical discography. In the discography Cooper includes about thirty titles, such as "We're a Winner" (MCA 1500) and "People Get Ready" (MCA 1500), both by the Impressions.

Black empowerment during the civil rights movement is represented by individuals such as Berry Gordy, founder and president of the Motown record company, one of the most successful black-owned corporations in United States history. Among about twenty books in the Library's collections about Motown, Gordy, and other members of the corporation is *Heatwave: The Motown Fact Book* by David Bianco (Ann Arbor: Pierian Press, 1988; ML156.4.S6B5 1988), which includes chapters on Motown stars, a Motown chronology, a list of Motown and related labels, and Motown discographies for the United States and the United Kingdom. Marvin Gaye, Stevie Wonder, the Jackson 5, the Miracles, the Spinners, the Temptations, the Supremes, Gladys Knight and the Pips, the Marvelettes, and Martha and the Vandellas are among the individual performers and groups discussed.

Other books about Motown include Nelson George's *Where Did Our Love Go? The Rise and Fall of the Motown Sound* (New York: St. Martin's Press, 1985; ML3537.G46 1985); David Morse, *Motown and the Arrival of Black Music* (London: Studio Vista, 1971; ML3556.M7), and Peter Benjaminson, *The Story of Motown* (New York: Grove Press, 1979; ML429.G67B4). These and other volumes on postwar recording companies are available in the Recorded Sound Reference Center.

To many, soul music and its wide acceptance reflected the hopes of the civil rights movement. For the first time since the swing era of the 1930s and the early 1940s the confluence of musical taste seemed to surmount racial boundaries. During a short time in the mid-

1960s *Billboard* magazine (Microfilm MFM [o] 8104 Mus, Performaing Arts Reading Room, and MicRR [o] 83/414) merged its black rhythm-and-blues hits chart "Hot R&R Singles" with its generic "Hot 100" charts in response to the perceived uniformity of tastes.

The Library's original recordings of soul music on such labels as Motown, Atlantic, and Stax are not comprehensive because, until 1972, there was no mandatory copyright deposit for recordings. Today, however, the Library is actively developing its American popular music collection of original discs. Many reissues of the classic recordings of the 1950s and 1960s are held by the Library on compact disc anthologies. The Library's extensive collections of popular music are documented by artist, label, and genre discographies in addition to biographies of artists and histories of American popular music. *Popular Music, 1920–1979: A Revised Cumulation*, an annotated index of over eighteen thousand American songs edited by Nat Shapiro and Bruce Pollack (Detroit: Gale Research Company, 1986, 3 vols; ML120.U5S5 1985), is arranged by song title and yields information about thousands of hit songs, including their composers and original artists.

Among the other resources providing information about African-American recordings during the civil rights era in the Recorded Sound Reference Center is *The Cash Box: Black Contemporary Singles Chart, 1960–1984*, compiled by George Albert and Frank Hoffmann (Metuchen, N.J.: Scarecrow Press, 1986; ML1156.4P6A42 1986), which lists titles and names of performers and gives information on popularity chart ratings.

The civil rights movement led to a demand for black studies in American universities and colleges and an increased interest in all aspects of African-American culture. Illustrative of this growing interest were performances of long ignored works. Scott Joplin's opera *Treemonisha*,

"Packing Up," by the Ward Singers, 1957. (SAVOY MG 14020, Recorded Sound Section collection. LC-USZ62–107764)

published by the composer in 1911, was first performed in 1972 and was made generally available in 1976 (Chicago: Dramatic Publishing Co., 1976; M1500.J77T7 Case).

Growing interest in black history and culture spread from college campuses to the black community and beyond, attracting interest far beyond professional historians. Publications on black music grew from a trickle to a stream as new titles were published and old ones reprinted. Most of these are represented in the collections of the Music Division. Bernard Katz edited an anthology of earlier writings, *The Social Implications of Early Negro Music in the United States* (New York: Arno Press, 1969; ML3556.K28). The following year saw the publication of Arnold Shaw's *The World of Soul:*

Black America's Contribution to the Pop Music Scene (New York: Cowles Book Co., 1970; ML2811.S48).

A major change in the copyright status of recordings occurred in 1972. For the first time in the United States, a recording could be copyrighted. Recordings issued before that date were acquired by the Library of Congress primarily as gifts. Beginning in 1972, they arrived as copyright deposits, increasing the likelihood of their inclusion in the Recorded Sound Archives. That same year saw the publication of the first scholarly journal devoted exclusively to black music: the *Black Perspective in Music* (Cambria Heights, N.Y.: 1973–91; ML3556.B6), edited by Eileen Southern. *Sinful Tunes and Spirituals: Black Folk Music to the Civil War* (Urbana: University of Illinois Press, 1977; ML3556.E8), by Dena J. Epstein, a documented history of black folk music in the United States, traces the development of this music up to the publication of the first collection of spirituals in 1867. Arnold Shaw produced another book the following year, *Honkers and Shouters: The Golden Years of Rhythm and Blues* (New York: Macmillan, 1978; ML3561.B63S53). Edward A. Berlin contributed *Ragtime: A Musical and Cultural History* (Berkeley: University of California Press, 1980; ML3530.B47).

The increasing recognition received by black composers was signaled in 1973 when Columbia Records announced a Black Composer's Series. Between 1974 and 1979 Columbia issued nine recordings of music written by black composers during the eighteenth, nineteenth, and twentieth centuries. In 1990 the series was reissued by the College Music Society. Besides recordings, black composers received increased recognition through the publication of their music. Willis Patterson compiled an *Anthology of Art Songs by Black American Composers* (New York: E.B. Marks Music Corp., 1977; M1619.A72). David Baker edited *The Black Composer Speaks* (Metuchen, N.J.: Scarecrow Press,

1978; ML390.B64). Raoul Abdul wrote *Blacks in Classical Music: A Personal History* (New York: Dodd, Mead & Co., 1977; ML385.A27). Among the compositions by black composers in the Music Division is Ulysses Simpson Kay's *Danse Calinda, a Ballet in Two Scenes* (New York: American Music Center, 1977; M1520.K53D3 Case). George Walker was praised for his *Sonata no. 1 (1953) for Piano* (Hastings-on-Hudson, N.Y.: General Music Publishing Co., 1972; M23.W145 no. 1). Olly Wilson is represented by *Spirit Song* for soprano solo, double chorus, and orchestra (n.p., 1974; M2020.W53S7 fol.).

In southern Louisiana, French-speaking

Sam Cooke, ca. 1964. (New York World Telegram portrait file, silver gelatin photograph, PP. LC-USZ62–107994)

blacks had made their own music for many years, but only in the postwar years did the outside world become aware of it, largely through sound recordings made by small companies that specialized in folk music. The Motion Picture, Broadcasting, and Recorded Sound Division holds numerous recordings of both Cajun and Zydeco music, but little of it has been written down. Two books in the Music Division that discuss this music are Barry Jean Ancelet's *The Makers of Cajun Music = Musiciens Cadiens et Créoles* (Austin: University of Texas Press, 1984; ML3477.A5 1984) and John Broven's *South to Louisiana: The Music of the Cajun Bayous* (Gretna, La.: Pelican Publishing Co., 1983; ML3477.B76 1983).

An attempt to extend bibliographic control over the burgeoning literature was made by Dominique-René De Lerma in his *Bibliography of Black Music* (Westport, Conn.: Greenwood Press, 1981–; ML128.B45D44). In 1983 a second black music journal began publication, the *Black Music Research Journal*, issued by the Center for Black Music Research at Columbia College in Chicago (ML3556.B58).

In 1989 the Center for Black Music Research also began to issue a series of monographs. Number 2 in the series was *Black Music in Ebony: An Annotated Guide to the Articles on Music in Ebony Magazine, 1945–1985* (Chicago: Center for Black Music Research, 1990; ML128.B45V3 1990) by Kimberly R. Vann. Another ambitious reference book appeared in 1990: *African-American Traditions in Song, Sermon, Tale, and Dance, 1600s-1920; an Annotated Bibliography of Literature, Collections, and Artworks* (New York: Greenwood Press, 1990; Z5956.A47S68 1990) compiled by Eileen Southern and Josephine Wright.

Occasional black cast films continued to appear at the beginning of the 1950s, including two about basketball that are in the Library's collections: *The Harlem Globetrotters* (1951) and *Go, Man, Go* (1953). *The Quiet One* (1948), *The Well* (1950), *Bright Road* (1953), and *Take a Giant Step* (1959) all deal with black children. By the mid-1950s, black cast films were no longer relegated to the margins of independent production; these films were produced and released by the major studios as well, including *Carmen Jones* (1954) and *Porgy and Bess* (1959). Black actress Dorothy Dandridge quickly became established as a star after her title role in *Carmen Jones*.

By the early 1950s, studios sought to present different subject matter to lure audiences away from home entertainment and back to the theater. Liberalized censorship regulations opened up movies to unconventional themes. In 1949, a number of fiction feature films with largely white casts dealt with racism, including *Home of the Brave, Intruder in the Dust, Lost Boundaries,* and *Pinky,* all in the Library's collections. *Pinky* was Twentieth Century-Fox's highest grossing film of the year. Both *Lost Boundaries* and *Pinky* dramatize the subject of light-skinned blacks passing for white, with white actors playing light-skinned blacks and African-Americans in supporting roles. This theme was taken up again in *Imitation of Life* (1959)—a remake of the 1930s film—*I Passed for White* (1960), and *Shadows* (1960). *Take a Giant Step* (1959) portrays a black child raised in a white middle-class neighborhood. More commonly, black characters were featured as mentors and friends of white protagonists, as in *The Member of the Wedding* (1952) and *The Breaking Point.*

For the first time, a star system began to operate for black players in Hollywood. Sidney Poitier emerged as the first black leading man in, for instance, *No Way Out* (1950), *The Blackboard Jungle* (1955), *Something of Value* (1957), *The Mark of the Hawk/Accused* (1957), *Island in the Sun* (1957), and *The Defiant Ones* (1958). Poitier played a humane carpenter in *Lilies of the Field,* a performance for which he won the Academy Award for Best Actor in 1963, the first black to win it.

Poitier's films remained popular with both

Bill Cosby, 1965. (New York World Telegram portrait file, silver gelatin print, PP. LC-USZ62–107996)

black and white audiences. Examples in the Library's collections include *A Patch of Blue* (1965), *The Slender Thread* (1965), *Duel at Diablo* (1966), *In the Heat of the Night* (1967) and its sequel *They Call Me Mister Tibbs* (1970), *Guess Who's Coming to Dinner* (1967), *To Sir With Love* (1967), and *For Love of Ivy* (1968).

Another star, Harry Belafonte, appeared in films such as *Bright Road* (1953) and *The World, the Flesh, and the Devil* (1959), a post-Armageddon tale of survival which he also produced. Belafonte played a heavenly messenger in *The Angel Levine* (1970). Sidney Poitier starred with Ruby Dee and Belafonte in *Buck and the Preacher* (1971), a saga of black migration to the West which Poitier also coproduced and directed. *Man and Boy* (1971) presented television star Bill Cosby as a Civil War veteran making a home for his family in Arizona. Proving once again that the participation of the most popular stars was not necessarily a guarantee

of box office success, the Bill Cosby vehicle, *Leonard 6* (1987), was a financial disaster. An important artistic achievement of the 1970s, *Sounder* (1972) made universal the story of a southern sharecropping family in the 1930s through the performances of its black stars, Cicely Tyson and Paul Wingate.

With the rise of the civil rights movement in the 1960s, leads for blacks began to proliferate in Hollywood filmmaking. For instance, *One Potato, Two Potato* (1964) offered a positive portrayal of a racially mixed marriage. *Black like Me* (1964) related the true experiences of a white reporter who used a chemical to turn his skin black in order to experience racial prejudice first hand. Sammy Davis, Jr., starred in *A Man Called Adam* (1966), which particularized racial issues through the experience of a jazz musician. Many of these films followed the conventions of the social consciousness genre. One of these was a 1964 film *Nothing But a Man*, generally considered one of the best evocations of black family life. Traditional genres such as westerns began to depict black characters in leading roles, such as Woody Strode in *Sergeant Rutledge* (1960).

Some of the black cast films of the late 1960s and early 1970s were independent productions exhibited mainly in urban areas with heavily black populations. Often these films took a harsh look at the issues of integration and racism, as did the melodrama *The Bus Is Coming* (1971). Produced with modest means in Watts, California, and directed by Wendell James Franklin, this film depicts a confrontation between racist white policemen and militant blacks.

African-Americans, just over 10 percent of the U.S. population in the 1970s, made up a fourth of the movie-going audience. Films such as *The Split* (1968), costarring Jim Brown and Julie Harris, were aimed at both white and black audiences. Brown, a celebrated football player thanks to television exposure, had turned film actor and would star in a dozen films. Soon the market was inundated by "blaxploitation" films, designed to draw African-American audiences, typically action melodramas like *Superfly* (1972) and the *Shaft* series of the early 1970s. Two Harlem dentists financed *Superfly*. Its popular drug-pusher hero, an unacceptable role model for youth, earned the ire of the NAACP and other black organizations.

Soon the main Hollywood studios began making films with black casts and black themes to attract patrons to their big city downtown theaters. Black action films expanded genres such as westerns, with *Take a Hard Ride* (1975) and other films; horror, with *Blacula* (1972), and, eventually, even science fiction, with *Change of Mind* (1969), starring Raymond St. Jacques. Martial arts was an ingredient in the amusing Motown production *The Last Dragon* (1985), with its character, "Sho'nuff," who aspires to be known as "the Shogun of Harlem."

By 1987, modestly budgeted black-interest films that had grossed a million dollars or more in the United States included *Slaughter* (1972); *Slaughter's Big Rip-Off* (1973); *Blacula* (1972) and its sequel *Scream, Blacula, Scream* (1973); *Sheba, Baby* (1975), in which the queen of the private eyes fights criminals determined to destroy her father's loan company; *Cooley High* (1975); *J.D.'s Revenge* (1976); *She's Gotta Have It* (1986); and *Hollywood Shuffle* (1987). Before interest faded, more than two hundred black films in the action category alone would be produced. Some—like *Gordon's War* (1973) with Paul Wingate—typically follow the actions of returned Vietnam veterans who take on crime in the streets.

Many of these urban action adventures were revenge dramas. *Black Shampoo* (1975), for instance, features a hair stylist who is also a "killing machine." Absurd elements dominate *Steele Justice* (1987), in which a Vietnam veteran finds that a former Vietnamese general has become a drug lord in America. Films such as these were parodied in Keenan Ivory Wayans's spoof, *I'm Gonna Git You, Sucka* (1988). A professional team with Billy Dee Williams and Ben Norton is assembled in *Oceans of Fire* (1987), in which the protagonists fight a corrupt oil company and put out a burning oil rig that is about to blow up.

Literary sources for black films ranged from Chester Himes's police procedurals *Come Back Charleston Blue* (1972) and *A Rage in Harlem* to the plantation fantasies written by white authors, such as *Mandingo* (1975) and *Drum* (1976). Gregory Hines costarred with Billy Crystal in a police movie, *Running Scared* (1986), set in Chicago. Other police movies included *Off Limits* (1988), a police saga set in Saigon in 1968, and *Eve of Destruction* (1991). The most successful example was the *Lethal Weapon* series with Danny Glover and Mel Gibson. Cleavon Little appeared in *The Gig* (1985), and Danny Glover in an adaptation of a Stephen Coonts best-seller thriller, *The Night of the Intruder* (1990).

Several black directors emerged in the seventies, most notably Melvin Van Peebles, who wrote and directed *Sweet Sweetback's Badasssss Song* (1971), which, with its unmistakably black folk hero, was a phenomenal success with black audiences. African-American director Spike Lee reached a large film audience in a sustained, successful series unprecedented for a black filmmaker: *She's Gotta Have It* (1986), *School Daze* (1988), and *Do the Right Thing* (1989). Hollywood was once more forcefully reminded of the possibilities inherent in black stories and themes, evident also in Steven Spielberg's *The Color Purple* (1985). As long as the budget was conservative, black theme films appeared to have a ready audience and a secure profitability. Exceptions to the violent melodramas that proliferated in the 1970s were the commercially successful romantic comedy *Claudine* (1974), starring Diahann Carroll and James Earl Jones, and *Aaron Loves Angela* (1975). *Amazing Grace* (1974) reunited several veteran Hollywood film comics and character actors from the 1930s and 1940s, including Moms Mabley, Butterfly Mc-Queen, and Stepin Fetchit.

Paris Blues (1961) and *Round Midnight* (1986) both dramatized incidents in the life of jazz musician Bud Powell. Another of the fictional dramas based on the lives of actual people was *Brothers* (1977), which featured Bernie Casey playing a character modeled on Black Panther activist George Jackson and Vonetta McGee portraying a character resembling activist Angela Davis. A documentary produced by American Documentary Films, *Angela Davis*, is in the Triangle Labs collection, along with *Huey* and *If There Were No Blacks*. Other documentary biographies in the Library's collections are *King: A Film History from Montgomery to Memphis* (1970) and *Jack Johnson* (1971). *Lorraine Hansberry: The Black Experience in the Creation of Drama* (1975) and *Accomplished Women* (1974), with poet Nikki Giovanni and Shirley Chisholm, present writers as their subjects. Collective television biographies include "The Black Soldier" (CBS, 1968), William Miles's historical documentary "Men of Bronze" (1977), and "Black Rodeo" (1972), which depicts members of the Black Cowboys Association.

Music was a strong element in the appeal of many black films, including musicals such as *The Wiz*, the later series of documentaries of reggae festivals such as *Sunsplash '82*, with groups like Toots and the Mayals, and most influential, the reggae music in the Jamaican crime drama *The Harder They Fall* (1973) with Jimmy Cliff. Reggae also enhanced the Caribbean island adventure film *The Mighty Quinn* (1989). Musicals exploiting the street art of break dancing—an acrobatic style involving rhythmic ground movements—included *Beat Street* and a classical dance academy with choreography by Dennon and Saymber Rawles.

The original black theater film *Cry Freedom* (1987) recounts the circumstances of the death of South African anti-apartheid leader Steve Biko. Television news documentaries covered such subjects as the U.S. ambassador to Kenya, "Ambassador in Shirtsleeves" (ABC, 1965), the head of Kenya, "Jomo Kenyatta" (ABC, 1965), and "A Black View of South Africa" (CBS, 1973). *Glory* (1989), one of the celebrated black cast films made within traditional Hollywood in the late 1980s, chronicles the history of the first black military unit in the Civil War. Denzel Washington won the Academy Award for Best Supporting Actor for his performance in it. Black filmmaker Charles Burnett's student film *Killer of Sheep* (1978) was selected for the National Film Registry at the Library of Congress in 1990.

During the late 1940s, television began to establish itself in American life, joining the living room furniture in most homes by 1952. Black entertainers and themes found an early niche in the new medium, first with variety shows, then with two series inspired by long-running radio programs: "Beulah" and "Amos 'n' Andy."

Unlike radio, however, which featured white performers, the television version of "Amos 'n' Andy" actually cast blacks in the leading roles. "Amos 'n' Andy" operated in a completely black world, similar to the realm found in black cast movies, with Tim Moore playing "the Kingfish," Spencer Williams as Andy Brown, and Alvin Childress as Amos. The situation comedy formula was used to present black leading characters in a popular medium, winning audiences across ethnic lines. Following the standard conventions of sitcoms, however, they ignored contemporary political reality, and both "Amos 'n' Andy" and "Beulah" were condemned by some black opinion leaders for their perceived stereotypes and for overlooking the problems of racial conflict. "Amos 'n' Andy" came in for the bulk of the criticism, and by 1954 both it and "Beulah" had been forced from the airwaves. Records relating to the NAACP effort that eventually resulted in the end of the program are included in that organization's archives, which are held in the Manuscript Division (MSS, records 1909–82).

A television documentary, "Amos 'n' Andy: Anatomy of a Controversy," was produced about the series in 1983. Despite the furor, "Amos 'n' Andy" remained in syndication for many years, and the Library's collection includes most of the shows; the series is also widely available on commercial videotape. Because most television shows are in a series format, whether weekly or daily, the number of individual shows that make up any series may vary. In only a few cases does the Library of Congress television collection contain every program in a series; most often the Library holds a representative sample, from several to dozens of episodes of a given series.

Unfortunately, the move to cancel "Amos 'n' Andy" had a long and chilling effect that prevented new largely black shows from being considered for television. Instead, blacks usually were seen playing supporting roles, whether Eddie "Rochester" Anderson in "The Jack Benny Show" (1950–65), Willie Best in "My Little Margie" (1952–55) and "The Stu Erwin Show" (1950–55), Ruby Dandridge in "Father of the Bride" (1961–62), or Amanda Randolph in "Make Room For Daddy" (1953–64). Variety shows offered the best opening for black talent, and, for instance, the Library holds kinescopes of NBC's "Nat 'King' Cole Show" (1956–57). Otherwise, blacks usually could be seen only in specials, occasional interviews, musical programs, or anthology shows.

By the 1960s, gradual change was evident. Blacks were seen more often in continuing supporting roles: Diahann Carroll appeared regularly on "Peter Gunn" (1958–60), Eartha Kitt was on "Burke's Law" (1963–65), and Cicely Tyson played a secretary to George C. Scott in the short-lived 1963–64 series "East Side, West Side." A year later "I Spy" (1965–68) created a sensation by costarring Bill Cosby opposite Robert Culp in an action series, which portrayed equality and interracial partnership as workable possibilities. The pattern was repeated, usually in more subtle form, in such subsequent series as "Mission: Impossible" (1966–73), with Greg Morris; "Daktari" (1966–69), with Hari Rhodes; "Ironside" (1967–75), with Don Mitchell; and "Hogan's Heroes" (1965–71), with Ivan Dixon. A 1968 episode of the series "High Chapparal" dramatized the work of the black cavalry known as the Buffalo Soldiers.

The first series since "Amos 'n' Andy" to star a black actor in the lead, in a nonservant role, and to portray the life of a black family appeared in 1968. "Julia" was a vehicle for Diahann Carroll, as a self-sufficient Vietnam War widow who was raising her son while working as a nurse in the employ of a doctor played by Lloyd Nolan. Although popular, "Julia" was also criticized as detached from contemporary events in black life; the show was canceled after three seasons. "The Bill Cosby Show" (1969–71) suffered a similar fate and criticisms. Black variety shows also appeared. By 1966, Sammy Davis, Jr., had a short-lived variety show on NBC, "The Sammy Davis, Jr., Show," and a musical variety series, "The Barbara McNair Show," was produced in Canada and syndicated from 1969 to 1970.

With the success of "All in the Family," beginning in 1971, self-conscious racial humor and the use of ethnic types was accepted for exploration in the format of the television series. In 1972, the same team that created "All in the Family" developed "Sanford and Son," which lasted through 1977 and starred Redd Foxx in a situation comedy of a father-son junk dealership in the Los Angeles ghetto, far from the middle-class milieu of "Julia." Its popularity led to such follow-up series as "That's My Mama" (1974–75), about a family living in Washington, D.C., "Good Times" (1974–79), "The Jeffersons" (1975–85), "What's Happening!" (1976–79), and "What's Happening Now" (1985–88). In all of these, the usual white family comedy patterns were reversed by a mostly black cast, with white characters appearing as the comic outsiders and buffoons in an Afrocentric universe.

Simultaneously, a number of black police series, based on popular movies, failed to find a television audience, such as "Shaft" (1973–74), "Get Christie Love!" (1974–75), and "Tenafly" (1974–75). Yet black dramatic specials were highlights of the 1970s, such as the television movie, "The Autobiography of Miss Jane Pittman" (1974), with Cicely Tyson, and the miniseries "Roots" (1977) and "Roots: The Next Generations" (1979). Chronicling the entire saga of blacks in the United States, their phenomenal popularity indicated the widespread interest in black history, spanning all races.

By the 1980s, most black shows had disappeared, to be replaced by situation comedies with black children raised by whites, "Diff'rent Strokes" (1978–86) and "Webster" (1983–88). Only one other show, the comedy "Benson" (1979–86), with Robert Guillaume, presented a weekly black lead. The title character in "Benson" had an unlikely odyssey, guiding his incompetent white superiors and rising from butler to lieutenant governor—at a time when the nation was beginning to elect several blacks to this position. The popularity of a one-man show on the Home Box Office cable channel in 1983, "Bill Cosby: Himself," prepared the way for the reemergence of Bill Cosby on a weekly series. "The Cosby Show" premiered in 1984, and lasted through 1992, presenting an idealized image of black professional family life. For the first time, control was in the hands of a black producer, since Cosby shared the functions of star and executive producer.

"The Cosby Show" spawned the spin-off "A Different World" (1987–). Initially a vehicle for Lisa Bonet, it was quickly overhauled to star Jasmine Guy, with Debbie Allen as producer. With the success of such programming, along with the popular daily talk shows "Oprah!" (1986–) and "The Arsenio Hall Show" (1989–), black television series proliferated. The major networks offered comedies like "Family Matters" (1989–), the comedy-drama "Frank's Place" (1987), and such action series as "In the Heat of the Night" (1988–), starring Howard E. Rollins opposite Carroll O'Connor and inspired by the 1967 movie of the same title. The new Fox network followed with such series as "True Colors" (1990–), Keenan Ivory Wayans's "In Living Color" (1990–), and many others. The volume *Three Decades of Television: A Catalog of Television Programs Acquired by the Library of Congress, 1949–1979* (Washington: Library of Congress, 1989; PN1992.9.L3 1989) covers the Library's television holdings acquired through 1979, but in the intervening years the collection has grown enormously. The Library of Congress receives at least scattered episodes of most recent television series for copyright deposit, so as black television series continue to proliferate, the Library's collection of these shows will become even richer.

Although documentation of black history can be found in the visual records made of many events of the twentieth century, special reports and documentaries that appeared on television during the civil rights era focus particularly on African-American history and culture. The Library's collections contain "Segregation Northern Style" (CBS, 1964), "After Civil Rights— Black Power" (ABC, 1967), and programs in the CBS series "Of Black America" (1968) such as "The Black Soldier," "The Heritage of Slavery," "In Search of a Past," and "Portrait of a Deaf City." "Four Portraits in Black" (CBS, 1974) and "Watts: Riot or Revolt?" (CBS, 1965) are among other CBS News productions in the collections. "The Harlem Temper" (CBS, 1963) includes an interview with Malcolm X, and "Black Power, White Backlash" (1966) presents interviews with Stokely Carmichael and Martin Luther King, Jr. Roy Wilkins of the NAACP appeared on "Face the Nation" in 1964, and many other black leaders have appeared on "Meet the Press" over the years. Perhaps the most comprehensive retrospective series on civil rights is "Eyes on the Prize" (PBS, 1987) and its sequel (1990).

The civil rights movement changed the face of America—on the screen and in daily life. The collections of the Library of Congress enrich the nation's historical legacy by their comprehensive documention of the changes wrought by the movement for Americans. Many other materials—in addition to the ones specifically mentioned in this guide—document the changing face of America in the postwar era, and as the Library's collections continue to grow, so too will the possibilities for research and understanding.

INDEX

Page numbers in **boldface type** refer to illustrations.

ISBN 0-16-042076-8

☆ U.S. GOVERNMENT PRINTING OFFICE: 1994—359-631